PETER MIDDLETON AND TIM WOODS

LITERATURES OF MEMORY
History, time and space in postwar writing

MANCHESTER UNIVERSITY PRESS

MANCHESTER AND NEW YORK

distributed exclusively in the USA by St. Martin's Press

Published by Manchester University Press
Oxford Road, Manchester M13 9NR, UK
and Room 400, 175 Fifth Avenue, New York, NY 10010, USA
http://www.manchesteruniversitypress.co.uk

Distributed exclusively in the USA by
St. Martin's Press, Inc., 175 Fifth Avenue, New York,
NY 10010, USA

Distributed exclusively in Canada by
UBC Press, University of British Columbia, 2029 West Mall,
Vancouver, BC, Canada V6T 1Z2

British Library Cataloguing-in-Publication Data
A catalogue record for this book is available from the British Library

Library of Congress Cataloging in-Publication Data
Literatures of memory: History, time and space in postwar writing/Middleton, Peter, 1950-
    Tim Woods 1963–.
        p. cm.
    Includes bibliographical references and index.
    ISBN 0-7190-5949-6 (hardback) — ISBN 0-7190-5950-X (pbk.)
    1. English literature—20th century—History and criticism.
    2. Literature and history—Great Britain—History—20th century.
    3. Literature and history—United States—History and criticism.
    4. American literature—20th century—History and criticism.
    5. World War, 1939–1945—Literature and the war. 6. World War,
    1939–1945—Influence. 7. Space and time in literature. 8. History in
    literature. 9. Memory in literature. 10. War in literature. I. Woods,
    Tim. II. Title.

    PR478.H57 M53 2000
    820.9'358 -- dc21   00–020185

ISBN 0 7190 5949 6 *hardback*
     0 7190 5950 X *paperback*

First published 2000

07 06 05 04 03 02 01 00   10 9 8 7 6 5 4 3 2 1

Typeset by Action Publishing Technology Ltd, Gloucester
Printed in Great Britain
by Biddles Ltd, Guildford and King's Lynn

Contents

Acknowledgements

A collaborative project is never an easy undertaking, especially when stretched between Southampton on the south coast and Aberystwyth in west Wales. Consequently, we have both become familiar with all the routes between these towns – road, rail, telephone and computer. The interdisciplinary scope of the project made additional demands and, as a result, many people have aided us in its development. We would like to thank those friends, colleagues, academics and writers with whom we have discussed these ideas over several years. Our special thanks go to the following people for their help and encouragement in preparing drafts of the book, especially for reading various versions of the book: Brian Cheyette; Steven Connor; Brean Hammond; Ken Hirschkop; Nicola Marsh; Peter Nicholls; Trudi Tate; and several anonymous readers for the press. The authors would also like to thank Matthew Frost at Manchester University Press for his perceptive advice and support for the project in its different stages.

Peter Middleton would like to thank Bob Perelman and Clair Wills, for reading drafts of the poetry section; Stephen Clarke, David Herd, Nicola King and Tony Lopez, for the opportunity to try out ideas on the relations between poetry, time, memory and elegy at conferences and seminar series; all colleagues in the Department of English at the University of Southampton for their support and encouragement – the Department of English continues to sustain an intellectual environment in which research can flourish despite the enormous pressures everyone has been under. A grant from the Leverhulme Trust helped start the research on poetry of which the work in this book is only a part. Two periods of sabbatical leave from the Department of English made it possible to continue the work, which would otherwise have taken even longer. Kate, Harriet and George were remarkably understanding about the long hours demanded by the book, and the permanent presence of a computer even on holidays as the book neared completion, and listened to my developing ideas with care – I owe them special thanks.

Tim Woods would like to thank Andrew Hadfield and David

Rabey for reading drafts of the city and drama sections, and Peter Barry for discussions about contemporary representations of urban space. He would also like to thank his colleagues in the Department of English for providing intellectual and collegial support and encouragement during the completion of this project; and to thank the Department of English and the University of Wales, Aberystwyth, for granting him a sabbatical during which to write parts of this book. Finally, I would like to express my special appreciation to Helena Grice, and to my mother and late father, Judi and Geoff Woods, for their interest in and patience with this book, especially when it meant travelling across the country for the two authors to meet and discuss the project. An earlier version of parts of Chapters 2 and 3 appeared as 'Mending the skin of memory: ethics and history in contemporary narratives', *Rethinking History*, 2:3 (December, 1998), pp. 339–48.

We acknowledge permission from the University of California Press to reprint Robert Creeley's, 'I Keep to Myself Such Measures', published in *Collected Poems of Robert Creeley*, 1945-1975, copyright © 1983 The Regents of the University of California.

Textual memory: an introduction

Historical literature – by which we mean drama and poetry about the past, as well as the historical novel – not only reveals shared understandings of pivotal moments, historical figures and the everyday life of earlier times, it also outlines more general beliefs about the past and its relation to the present. In this study of contemporary British and American historical literature we will trace these internal structures of historicism through their myriad representations as ideas, fantasies and affects of memory, time and space. Contemporary historical literature has become an extremely active sphere of argument about history and the rediscovery of its elided potentialities, as well as an often highly conflicted struggle over what should be remembered and what forgotten. Its use of textual resources ranging from the ubiquitous street fashions of popular genres to one-off avant-garde investigations of language, subjectivity, desire and the conditions of textuality itself – as writing, publication, commerce, material form, performance, reception, object of critique and intertexts – presents an opportunity to study the conditions of representation of the past within contemporary Western culture. Instead of asking only how a specific history – the Second World War or colonial India – is popularly imagined, we will also be exploring the framing axioms at work in the presentation of the past in general. What, we shall ask, are the cultural poetics of history revealed in postwar literature? Memory, both individual and social, plays such a large part in this cultural poetics that the framing axioms of literary historicism are commonly represented by the texts themselves as forms of memory. We have, therefore, entitled this study *Literatures of Memory*, to describe the intersection between this self-understanding of contemporary literature when it looks backward and a prevalent politics of history in public culture which also relies on memory as the mediator between present and past.

The importance of questions about the past in literature – what it is, where it is and how we can imagine it – is borne out by the intensity of public literary debates centred upon the politics, ethics and epistemology of historical literature. The contemporary novel is criticised for a postmodern lack of historical accuracy or praised for its questioning of received narratives of national identity. Realist fictions by writers outside the dominant social formations are celebrated for their bold attempts to provide new histories of peoples whose religion, nationality, gender, sexuality, ethnicity, class and poverty denied them the opportunity to present their stories in the publicly accessible forms of literature. Toni Morrison won a Nobel Prize for historical novels that place the African-American experience of slavery and its aftermath firmly on view in a public culture which had long resisted its acknowledgement. Her most famous novel, *Beloved*, is a public form of reluctant anamnesis; it is 'about something that the characters don't want to remember, I don't want to remember, black people don't want to remember, white people don't want to remember'.[1] She not only writes about the suppressed histories of African-Americans – *The Bluest Eye* also begins with a textual memory of the Second World War in its opening sentence (as did an early draft of the first sentence of *Sula* according to Morrison), in order to signal the importance of tying this memory of the 'traumatic displacement this most wasteful capitalist war had on black people in particular' with the history of slavery.[2] The discourse of trauma and displacement recurs repeatedly in the recent literature of history, as does Morrison's sense of the emotional and cognitive resistances to remembering.

One of the most influential contemporary avant-garde poets, Charles Bernstein, who is associated with the poetic avant-garde now widely known as Language Writing,[3] echoes Morrison's sense of reluctance to remember slavery in his own comments about the Second World War: 'We never discussed the Second World War much when I was growing up. I don't feel much like discussing it now'.[4] He attributes this to a general numbness which writers are only now fully acknowledging: 'the psychological effects of the Second War are still largely repressed and ... we are just beginning to come out of the shock enough to try to make sense of the experience.' Bernstein's admission of the importance of the war for the textual memory of literary practice is especially striking because 'Language Writing's' desire 'to make language opaque so that writing becomes more and more conscious of itself as world generating, object generating' led to a use of 'diminished referentiality' and disjunctive syntax which appeared to put almost any recognisable representation of the past into question.[5] This is probably why he draws attention to a highly significant feature of the new historical literature: 'much of the innovative poetry of these soon-to-be-fifty years following the war register the twined events of Extermination in the West and Holocaust in the East in ways that have not been accounted for'.[6] The context for Bernstein's remarks is contemporary poetry and the Second World War, but his comments could apply to many other new literary genres and histories – the history in much contemporary literature has not yet been recognised by literary studies. There are several reasons for this. Changing experiences of the past are hard to articulate in easily communicable abstract terms; even the precisions of academic research based on empirical investigation and conceptual analysis necessarily lag behind. The textual memory of literature (and other arts) relies on both pre-articulate forms of material – performance, imagery, sound and affects – and non-semiotic cognitive practices (music being the most obvious), as well as the freedoms of its less structured institutional forms to register such changes early and even, in some cases, to initiate them. A second reason is central to Paul Ricoeur's theory of history and narrative:

> It is not when the novel has a direct historical or sociological role, combined with its aesthetic role, that it poses the most interesting problem with respect to its verisimilitude. The true mimesis of action is to be found in the works of art least concerned with reflecting their epoch ... The quasi-past of the narrative voice is then entirely different from the past of historical consciousness.[7]

The historical consciousness of the professional historian or archivist differs from the desire at work in historical literature to elicit the unfulfilled potentialities of the past inspired by the changing relations to the past in everyday life. This is especially the case for social fantasies of the past – fantasies of hiding from it, losing it, redeeming it, even revisiting it – and for radical politics, which also discerns unfinished business in the past, as well as its horror, but treats the past as an ethical demand to which it must bear witness in its actions. Historical literature moves between these poles of fantasy and intervention.

Finally, as Bernstein and Ricoeur imply, existing critical recognition of history in literature has understandably been somewhat narrow – mostly confined to realist historical fiction. This is why the enormously influential periodising concept of postmodernism remains both useful and inadequate. Its rethinking of modernism, its rejection of foundationalism and its questioning of totalising forms of history is crucial for the recognition of these new literatures; its epochal periodising and its coercive generality sometimes obscure the diversity of contemporary genres and their literary histories, as well as their different practices of memory, time and space.

Although the most prominent historical literature remains the novel, in quieter, less prominent ways other genres continue to invent new modes of writing history. Poets as different as the American Language Writer, Susan Howe, and the Irish writer of autobiographical quatrains, Eavan Boland, consider poetry as a form of historical writing.

Howe says, 'it would be hard to think of poetry apart from history';[8] Boland that 'if a poet does not tell the truth about time, his or her work will not survive it'.[9] Similar beliefs can be found across all modes and genres of contemporary writing. The potential reflexivity of literary textuality makes possible subtle, original and, above all, timely and perceptive insights into the changing conditions of social memory and the uses of history. Reflexivity may need some definition here, since it was for a time almost synonymous with a threat to all forms of belief and argument based on the allegedly far-reaching implications of the para-doxes of self-reference.[10] We use it here with a more restrained meaning to describe not a literary mode of self-consciousness but the myriad ways in which literary texts mediate referentiality through artifice and artifice through reference. Reflexivity does not mean a text that consumes itself or a vanishing regression of mirrored discursivity, so much as the capac-ity of highly rhetorical modes which elicit highly attentive readings, to consider the terms of their constitution which may range from language and subjectivity to history and the material structures of the universe. Robert Siegle argues that reflexivity is close to historicism: 'Both historicity and reflexivity destabilize the absolutism of their contraries, however, reflexivity by undoing the philosophical underpinnings of representational poetics, historicity by clarifying the status of philosophi-cal "truth" as a function of a socio-economic matrix rather than an ahistorical absolute of logic or metaphysics'.[11] He considers reflexivity to be one reason why literature can be an active political force.

As is evident from the tenor of the comments by Toni Morrison and Charles Bernstein, and the feminist concerns of Howe and Boland, the new historical writing is often strongly political. Howard Brenton describes the ambitions of the plays written by him and his contempo-raries in the 1970s in strongly activist terms: 'these plays are big, in cast, staging, theme, and publicly declared ambition (they *do* want to change the world, influence opinion, enter fights over political issues) ... they are epic in that they are many scened, full of stories, ironic and argu-mentative, and deliberately written as "history plays for now".'[12] Epic scope emulates the scale of the political world with the ambitious polit-ical aim of intervening within it. The agit-prop theatre of the 1970s in Britain was unusual only in the degree to which it attempted to imbri-cate the special public space of the stage with the wider stage of public spheres; many contemporary works of literature are historical medita-tions which challenge dominant beliefs about the intersections of time, space and history.

When Morrison talks about the suppressed history of African-Americans, she uses a discourse of memory that is widely shared. Contemporary writers rely increasingly on scenes of recollection, witness and anamnesis to represent historicism in action – memory is assumed to be the making of history. Memory's importance makes it increasingly a theme for reflection as well, as it is in Paul Auster's *The Invention of Solitude*, which investigates the relationship between memory, text and subjectivity: 'Memory. Therefore, not simply as the resurrection of one's private past, but an immersion in the past of others, which is to say: history – which one both participates in and is a witness to, is a part of and apart from'.[13] Auster's exceptional ability to track the earliest signs of emergent cultural beliefs points him towards the hope that individual memory will unlock social memory, a hope shared by much contemporary writing, and also underlines the ambitious textualities in process when historical literature thematises memory.

We have entitled this study of history in contemporary literature *Literatures of Memory* because memory is widely portrayed as the superhighway to the past. Yet textual memory sounds periphrastic. Don't we already know that memory is textual; writing surely makes the social memory of history possible? Without the mnemotechnics of written records, so the argument goes, a society is dependent primarily on the unreliable workings of oral memory and, therefore, limited by the cognitive capacities of the individual. With the technology of writing, a vastly extended social memory becomes possible, enabling a society to extend its control over large areas of space and time, and to ensure its posterity by transmitting records of its achievements to descendants on whom its future integrity depends. Paul Connerton summarises this view well: 'what has been fixed in writing enters into a sphere of publicly accessible meanings in which everyone who can subsequently read that writing has potentially a share in its meanings'.[14] That writing can fix in the fashion that Connerton suggests is highly questionable. Nevertheless, reading itself is a practice of memory, because texts are forms of prosthetic social memory by which readers increase and correct their own limited cognitive strengths and participate in a public memorial space. Textual memory also looks forward. It not only empowers societies to manage territories and plan for the future, it also contains a promise that this can be a democratic process. Some ethnographers and historians go even further, and claim that, in the words of Walter Ong, an authority on the relations between oralcy and literacy, the development of 'writing has transformed human consciousness', by facilitating the growth of analytic abilities made possible by writing's support for the careful elaboration of argument through back-scanning, revision and the discipline of composing for a multiform absent audience.[15] Writing, according to Jack Goody (the anthropologist of the early history of language), 'presents us with an instrument capable of transforming our intellectual operations from the

inside.'[16] Not only is the text a form of memory, memories are themselves textual – the periphrasis appears to work in both directions. Ong
and Goody think of these changes in the workings of individual memory
as part of a long revolution of writing and reading that has slowly altered
deep mental habits. Poststructuralists, by contrast, have argued that it is
not so much the novelty of writing itself, as its capacity to manifest more
openly than ever before the conditions that language itself imposes on
thought, which reveals the textuality of memory. In Jacques Derrida's
words, writing actually 'founds memory'; it is not, as it deceptively
appears, simply a 'supplement' to it.[17]

Why then use the term 'textual memory', if the adjective is virtu-
ally redundant and could apply to all texts, not just literary ones? By
making explicit what is now often assumed we indicate that the relations
between texts, literariness and memory are not as compressible into a
single term as is often tacitly imagined. An initial answer to the sceptic
would be that, as Paul Connerton, Deborah Battaglia and other sociologists and ethnographers have convincingly shown, there is plenty of
evidence of other *non-textual* practices of memory, which rely on habit,
bodily practices and performance, both in Western and other cultures,
and these play a part in literary texts too. The behavioural memories of
performance obviously play a large part in drama, but so too do the little
understood corporeal memories of verbal sound (as they also do in poetry
– poetry readings exploit this) and kinesthetic memories of performed or
imagined actions. Memory is, therefore, at work in texts in ways that are
not what is usually encompassed by the description 'textual', and the
term 'textual memory' usefully reminds us of this distinction.

Although we believe this dimension of textuality is important and
undervalued, our main concern here is the workings of textuality of
memory in literary texts. This is primarily why we use the term – its
conjunction of text and memory underlines both their interdependence
and their differences. The difficulty with the dominant theories of textual
memory which conflate texts and memory is that they obscure the different forms of memory at work in different genres and authors, because
they move too quickly beyond the level of the text to what they believe
is a more fundamental, atomic structure which determines the textual
condition. If writing is the elementary particle physics of memory, then
it is not going to matter much to the analysis whether we are talking
about a short autobiographical lyric, a popular novel or an agit-prop play.
It is a fallacy of much scientific and sociological reasoning to assume that
entities can always be broken down into combinations of smaller, more
fundamental elements and structures. In a study of this contemporary
striving for taxonomic simplicity and scientific order, the philosopher
John Dupré makes a powerful counter-case for what he calls a 'promis-

cuous realism'.[18] Instead of assuming that everything in the universe – rocks, birds, rituals, texts and atoms – can be reduced to the outcome of systems of simpler, theoretically more foundational entities – the equivalent of fundamental particles – we would do better to recognise that science has shown only that such reductions are possible in highly specific cases. It may not be possible to explain every feature of a complex system like society by analysing human physiology. The value of this line of reasoning for the study of memory and contemporary literature is that it suggests that it might be better to direct attention to what is irreducible in diversity rather than search for single-source explanations, and so helps us notice the complexity and dissimilarity of different practices and theories of memory and history in contemporary writing. Instead of assuming that one form of writing is fundamental and builds up into all those different forms which we shall encounter, and, therefore, treating each genre as a product of one irreducible constituent, we can investigate the seeming heterogeneity more closely. The conjunction of text and memory in the concept of textual memory signals a complexity that the conflation of memory with texts or texts with memory too readily obscures.

In this study of history in contemporary literature, we therefore focus on specific texts and the genres that structure them, because these are the key sites of literariness; genre is where literary production is not reducible to algorithms of language and cannot be dissolved into wider historical matrices. Our contention is that literary genre is a technic of social memory – textual memory is at work in the invention of new genres and the transformation of old. To say that both writing and the social relations of labour and identity are mediated in literary practice through this technic is not to deny the significance of either language or history, as is sometimes supposed. Genre is too often treated as a formalism, as if it were no more than a form of prosody that could be copied out of a manual. It is better thought of as a code of practice constantly under negotiation between texts and their readers, listeners, publishers, academics and reviewers, which advises them how they are expected to respond to the text. Genre is a projected biography of a text's circulation. It is this temporal extension out into the long history of the interactions of the text which takes it beyond formalism and makes it possible for genre to inscribe a specific technics of memory. As the sociologists, Scott Lash and John Urry, explain: 'There is no single, decontextualised memory separate from the range of contexts and commemorations, pragmatics and rhetorics, in which people have been and are engaging.'[19] Textual memory can, therefore, be as diverse as the inventions arising in different cultural practices of textuality and recall across time and space.

Genre's frequent use as a pejorative term to indicate restricted compositional autonomy and derivative invention can also mislead us when discussing highly distinctive, original or avant-garde texts. Even the most innovative writing presupposes many generic reading and distribution practices. Equally, the most production-line generic text may sometimes test the limits of genre and reformulate them tentatively, because genre is remade by every instance of its use. Like language, it exists only as it is practiced, and its codes are no more than partially articulated recognitions of its more sedimented forms.

History and memory have become major preoccupations within literary studies over the past two decades, and this not only helps clarify the investments at work in postwar historical literature, especially the investigation of 'its own historically relative construction of history', it also offers the opportunity to locate the growing commitment to historicism in literary studies within the wider culture.[20] Historicism, 'new' and old, postcolonial and feminist, is widely felt to be the 'the latest way forward for literary theory'[21] despite the apparent contradictions between historical relativism and the abstract atemporality of some theory. In cases where the dominant collective sense of the past is manifestly deficient in its recognition of other social groups, this is already acknowledged. Certain novels by black, feminist and working-class writers, for example, have offered such vividly realised narratives of hitherto suppressed pasts that they have helped create whole areas of literary study. This literature manifestly adds to historical knowledge, and directs attention to other cognate literary texts whose situation in history may have been less accessible.

Contemporary historical studies has meanwhile become deeply concerned with the troubling persistence of modes of thought that have traditionally been the preserve of the arts and literary study: narrative, imagination and memory. 'Is it not possible', asks Hayden White in the final sentence of an essay on narrative in history, 'that the question of narrative in any discussion of historical theory is always finally about the function of imagination in the production of a specifically human truth?'[22] Imagination and narrative are also troubling for literary and cultural studies, not least because of their long genealogy and the older meanings therefore attached to them, and so, despite their potential for rapprochement, memory is the field in which there is currently the greatest convergence between the two disciplines. The rapidly growing interest among historians in how trauma, 'notably including the deferred recognition of the significance of traumatic series of events', and sites of memory have played a key role in the collective construction of pasts and their management by professional custodians, has a counterpart in the interest among literary and cultural theorists in memory as an important link between theory (notably psychoanalysis and theories of identity) and history.[23]

Our starting point for the research in this book was the widespread conviction among literary and cultural critics and these historians, that the past has been killed, destroyed, lost or at best thinned out so much that it no longer seems relevant. Eras and epistèmes have disappeared and been replaced by new uncharted textualities. Consequently, they argue, we need to do new memory work urgently, 'to cast lifelines to the past and counteract our culture's undisputed tendency toward amnesia under the sign of immediate profit and short-term politics'.[24] We shall argue that their literary contemporaries also ask questions about the past, but usually suggest more complex images of the displaced or traumatic relation to the past. Some literary texts claim that the past is not where we expected to find it because of changes in the common experience of space and time, and such insights could help us better understand the consequences of science and technology for our current theories of postmodernity. Others show that what looks like historical amnesia may be misrecognition of new technologies of memory which seem like white noise to those expecting memory to play by traditional scales. New genres of writing about the past have developed phenomenologies of spacetime that are not yet fully recognised and legitimised by either theory or the institutions of public history. Narrative, memory, performance and the production and circulation of texts are all implicated in the new spacetimes and history, therefore, takes many forms in contemporary literature, some of them far from obvious. We argue that some of the most original investigations of historicity are taking place in literary practices that are especially aware of the changing conditions of life in space and time, and yet do not advertise themselves as historical literatures.

The new historical literature of the past decades is part of the historical turn in literary studies and the turn to memory in historical studies. We show that historical literature articulates several issues that can contribute to the current debate: the necessity for approaching representation of the past as a complex ethical problem; the need to recognise that memory is practised according to hegemonic paradigms which are deeply imbued with aesthetic and temporal features, notably the 'delayed coding' of the past; the complexity of the temporal and spatial locatability of the past; and the still unmapped cultural variousness of the narrativity of the past. Neither a purely materialist nor a wholly discursive approach is sufficient because both entail too many presuppositions about memory, time and space to adequately recognise their diverse participation in social and cultural production.

This book is organised into two sections: Part I discusses concepts of history and the past in postwar literature from the perspectives of post-modernism, theories of memory and the changing dimensionalities of space and time. This forms a prelude to the more detailed Part II, in which case-studies of collective and individual memory, and space and time, are presented through the study of genres in which these dimensions of the past have been subjected to intensive representation – political theatre, the autobiographical lyric, science fiction and the city novel.

Part I begins with the idea that the past has mutated and possibly even died on us. There is surprisingly widespread agreement that the past has altered and, at the very least, lost its epistemological primacy, becoming a rewritable text according to the authority and power of those doing the rewriting. Sociological research does not entirely support these claims. We show that history as an everyday activity is extremely popular, although it is often confined to familial and intimate concerns rather than the broader narratives of public history. Academic history is perceived to be as distant from the ordinary interest in the past as are cultural texts about history. Nevertheless, historical movies and novels are enormously popular, and we show that their success depends on the way in which they address this widespread interest in history-making by offering themselves as models for an understanding of the past. A crucial question is how these cultural texts work with the popular interest in pasts that intersect with both public and personal histories. We, therefore, go on to discuss the fear of the past in works from the opposite ends of the cultural spectrum – Steven Spielberg's *Jurassic Park* and Toni Morrison's *Beloved* – to argue that what distinguishes the novel is not only its recognition of historical complexity but the strenuous commitment it makes to training the reader in a cultural anamnesis as a prelude to becoming a better historian.

This leads us to the theories of postmodernism and their attempts to explain the ambivalence towards history. Historical fiction has traditionally allowed people to construe history as a medium for dispassionate and objective truth. Many postmodern theories of history recoil against this apparently naive approach and have taught us to explore and investigate the investments by groups or ideologies in specific formations of power. This emphasis on the need to recognise diversity applies to the concept of postmodernism itself, which is not a unitary concept. Frequently accused of an inability to enter into alliances with historical studies or ethics, postmodernism's entrapment in 'mere' textuality, it is argued, removes literature from the materiality that underlines moral choice and historical praxis – a withdrawal into 'textuality'. This may be true of some extreme forms, but the opposite is more often true: postmodernism has frequently offered critiques of political and economic domination which may not always be explicit about historicity but nevertheless inscribe it within their investigations of the extent and stability of power. As we probed the frequent debates about history and representations of time and space in postmodernity, it became clear to us that we needed to look more closely at the 'ethics of history', and the increasing calls for justice and responsibility in representing the past. In so doing, we found ourselves (like Paul Auster) inextricably led back to the social function of memory.

By reconsidering recent debates about memory it is possible to see that both psychoanalysis and postmodernism assume that memory is a ground of identity. Despite many differences among theorists about the significance of this (whether identity is always provisional and fragmented or can sometimes achieve at least temporary stability), these concepts of memory rely on questionable models of memory. Recent research into both cognitive and social memory reveal other possibilities which this chapter explores with the help of Pat Barker's *Regeneration Trilogy*. These new models of memory suggest that we need to recognise both the impact of new scientific theories of space and time on the popular imagination, and the politics of the dominant theories of catharsis and recovery through the unveiling of traumatic memory. Memory is widely evaluated according to its achievement of a realism measured in terms of its locational verisimilitude: time and space are necessary for a memory to be current. Even the Holocaust, which is considered by many to have been a war against memory that left it with a possibly irrevocable aporia, has also been treated as a problem of spatio-temporal indeterminacy. The Holocaust has slowly re-entered cultural memory during the past decades, and has sometimes been understood to confirm that all memory works through trauma. We trace the roots of this belief that all memory is generated by traumas of varying force, to the incomplete studies of memory found in Freud, and in strategic revisions of his concepts of repression and belatedness or *Nachträglichkeit*.

Chapter 4 discusses the significance of changing experiences of space and time for the imagination of the past in relation to Margaret Atwood's *Cat's Eye*. This narrative of contemporary confession treats time as a necessary component of memory. Social and cultural theorists agree that the cumulative effects of modernisation, war, globalism, technology and the synchronisations of labour, trade and everyday life which have made them possible, have made this a century deeply preoccupied with time, but they disagree about almost everything else. As Barbara Adam and Peter Osborne have mapped out, there is enormous disagreement about how to conceptualise social time, and both thinkers caution against believing that time is one kind of natural or social construction.

We take the view that Carol Greenhouse's argument that public discourses of time are ways of thinking about social agency in the broadest terms is the most helpful approach to understanding the investments at work when questions of time are raised. She shows us that temporalities are not ideologically neutral. Like Adam and Osborne, she draws our attention to the complex temporal logics that operate when the past is located in time. We differ from Osborne and Greenhouse to the extent that we also argue that scientific time has had a massive influence on the construction of the past: it has destabilised the belief that personal time is firmly grounded in cosmic time; and it has put all its great authority behind the detemporalisation of the world. Through a reading of a typically influential popular science book, Stephen Hawking's *A Brief History of Time,* we show how its primary methodology of knowledge is presented as a detemporalisation of the material world into laws, invariant structures, formulae and observer-independent events. We then discuss the production and representation of space – it is increasingly recognised that the temporalisation of history since the eighteenth century, so evident in our culture's preoccupation with periodisation, has obscured the spatiality active within the different modes of social history and its production. Michael Ondaatje's novel *The English Patient* is read as an argument about the importance of space as the scene of history during the Second World War.

The second part of the book comprises close textual study of work taken from loosely defined sub-genres of the four main areas of contemporary literature: drama; poetry; popular fiction; and the novel. We feel it is important to make these comparisons across the main literary modes in order to understand both the extent of historical literature and the importance of the interrelation between genre and historicism. We could have selected from other well-recognised sub-genres (such as: historical plays written for the commercial theatre, Peter Schaeffer's *Amadeus* for example, the family elegy, historical mysteries, or novels about the classical world) or from more localised, avant-garde or radical writing. Those we have chosen not only reflect areas of expertise, they also seem to us among the most influential forms of contemporary literature and the most revealing of contemporary cultural beliefs.

Part II begins by examining the way British theatre of the 1970s meshed with debates about historical education by staging a new genre of polemical historical drama using the stage as an icon of public space. Literary institutions are historical practices that work with the collective processes of composition, production, circulation and reception, whose infrastructure is itself historicised. Technological, political and economic changes have created far more complex spatio-temporal infrastructures for these institutions than ever before affecting every level of the text.

Our second case-study looks at changes in the construction of collective memory through a study of the implications of the autobiographical turn in contemporary poetry. The belief that identity depends upon the possession of communicable personal memories has become a fundamental part of contemporary poetics, and has provoked some avant-garde writers to examine the workings of this textual memory. We conclude the book with case-studies of the thematic treatment of time and space in science fiction and in novels of the city. Science fiction narratives of the 1950s and early 1960s were preoccupied with plots about the future. Futurity is represented as a field of vast, traversible spatial and temporal distances in which a conflict between the time of science and the time of history can be resolved by redeeming, or at least confronting, the losses of the past. Our final chapter explores space, especially urban space – the theme of many recent novels about the city. These novels map history in the spatial productions of the urban environment which aligns them with the 'New Geographers', while also adding a further dimension to their study of the phenomenology of space by the narrative tracking of previously unrecorded interaction between imagined and built environments.

This book can be read in several ways. The four studies of drama, poetry, popular fiction and the novel could be read individually or in a different order; together they offer a broad spectrum of the major literary genres of the period, as well as more detailed demonstration of the claims we make in Chapters 3 and 4. These two chapters introduce the arguments and evidence for a reconfiguration of the past as both memory and location in time and space. Chapters 1 and 2 outline the contemporary cultural and literary situation of history and the past, respectively.

These studies are provisional contributions to a cultural poetics of contemporary British and American literature. Cultural poetics has already proven broad enough to encompass the self-described historicisms of both Stephen Greenblatt and Fredric Jameson, and more recent studies of culture and cultural difference across time and geography have found an appeal to aesthetics and poetics useful to describe methods of historical analysis that depend not only on the reflexivity of critical theory, but also on strategies for rethinking the relations between texts and their historical moments. As we use the term here, the emphasis on 'poetics' is intended to maintain a tension between the idea of ordering principles on the one hand, and the idea of innovation on the other. It is a recognition that theory does not have a monopoly on new concepts, insights, readings and interventions. Some literary practices are also capable of this work. Cultural poetics recognises the importance of investigating the duality of cultural determinism and innovation which has too often been collapsed into a monolithic resolution that either dissolves the text into its historical determinants or sets aside an autonomous zone of artistic free play. A resolution of this duality has proven hard to articulate in the face of existing modes of cultural analysis which rely largely on causal and determinist models of explanation. Exploring the pluralism of practices of memory and spacetimes helps make clear how both rigid determinisms and transcendent artistic autonomy create decidedly limited, two-dimensional pictures of contemporary literary practices. It also points to possibilities for reformulating determinism and invention by opening out both concepts, giving them time and space to display their interrelations and complexities. Textual memory depends as much on these processes as on the mechanisms of retention, anamnesis and trauma.

The stress on cognitive innovation in cultural poetics also brings with it an ethical initiative. Throughout this book we have tried to acknowledge the ethics and intentionality of literary writing, and espe-cially those occasions when it makes a self-conscious intervention within public spheres that are internally policed as zones of legitimate intellec-tual and cultural enquiry, whose demarcated boundaries often strictly exclude imaginative work or work that does not conform to certain formal or thematic criteria from receptive attention. Treating literary practice as ethical does not, however, mean assuming that self-conscious-ness is a sovereign agency which transcends discourse and history.[25] To do so would be to lift subjectivity out of the spacetime in which we locate its practice. Ethics is notoriously contentious in both philosophical and non-philosophical discourses. We do not attempt to provide an account of ethics and literature, although we should say that we are not just using the word as a shorthand for essential human values. Rather, we tend to use this word as a sign of commitment to and responsibility for justice, often as a means of empowering hitherto underprivileged, silenced or marginalised voices. Following Geoffrey Harpham's presump-tion in *Getting It Right*, we regard ethics as a 'factor of "imperativity" immanent in, but not confined to, the practices of language, analysis, narrative, and creation. Whatever else these may or may not have in common, they share an investment in ethics.'[26] It is the conjunction of history and literary languages that we shall follow up here.[27]

While aiming to represent accurately the broad range of postwar British and American literatures of the past and to make some comparisons with cinema, this book is, therefore, necessarily selective. The familiarity of certain films makes them wonderful examples of contemporary political, aesthetic, psychoanalytic and narrative preoccupations as Slavoj Žižek and others have found before us, and also acts as a reminder of the capital and labour investments demanded by almost all cultural texts (even the contemporary poet whose tools are no more than a pencil and a sheet of recycled paper requires a complex infrastructure of communications and printing to make the work available). Although we believe our analyses could extend into cinema we do not attempt that here. We are also constrained to some extent by existing knowledge and divisions of the material. Long-out-of-print novels, regional writing, specialist avant-garde texts, certain kinds of performance, to name only a few, would also repay investigation, but we have decided to concentrate on readily available texts (most readers will still encounter some less familiar texts) which have helped form existing consensuses about contemporary literature and its relation to history. The use of widely debated work enables us to be more reflexive about the cultural poetics of textual memory's unfolding history of reception; it is not just a strategy to save us from the demands of extended exposition of unfamiliar texts and contexts, useful as this has been. We are both keenly aware that many fine contemporary novels, poems and plays go largely unread because the academic spotlight falls elsewhere. Here, however, we can only mention such work in general terms. Our first concern is to demonstrate the continuing pertinence of new literary work for the aims and ambitions of a developing, politically aware cultural theory and history. This finally is one of our main hopes for the book: to encourage readers to bring these literary texts further into dialogue with theory and politics. Doing so might sharpen our historicist tools and contribute to both the historical understanding and working through of the legacies of modern terror in order to ensure that our future politics are more responsive to otherness, more democratic, and above all, more egalitarian.

Notes

1 Toni Morrison, 'The pain of being black', *Time*, 22 May, 1989, p. 120; cited in Mae G. Henderson, 'Toni Morrison's *Beloved*: re-membering the body as historical text', in Hortense Spillers (ed.), *Comparative American Identities* (London: Routledge, 1991), pp. 62–86, 83.

2 Toni Morrison, 'Unspeakable things unspoken: the Afro-American presence in American literature', *Michigan Quarterly Review*, 28/1 (Winter 1989), 1–34, 26.

3 For examples of Language Writing and discussions of its scope and poetics, see Paul Hoover (ed.), *Postmodern American Poetry: A Norton Anthology* (New York: W. W. Norton, 1994); Douglas Messerli, (ed.), *From the Other Side of the Century: A New American Poetry 1960–1990* (Los Angeles: Sun and Moon Press, 1994); and Ron Silliman (ed.), *In the American Tree* (Orono, ME: National Poetry Foundation, 1986).

4 Charles Bernstein, 'The Second War and postmodern memory', *A Poetics* (Cambridge, MA: Harvard University Press, 1992), pp. 193–217, 197.

5 Charles Bernstein, 'Thought's measure', *Content's Dream: Essays 1975–1984* (Los Angeles: Sun and Moon Press, 1986), pp. 61–88, 71.

6 Bernstein, *A Poetics* (1992), p. 197.

7 Paul Ricoeur, *Time and Narrative, Volume 3*, trans. Kathleen Blaney and David Pellauer (Chicago: University of Chicago Press, [1985] 1988), p. 191.

8 Edward Foster, 'An interview with Susan Howe', *Talisman: A Journal of Contemporary Poetry and Poetics*, 4 (Spring 1990), 14–38, 17.

9 Eavan Boland, *Object Lessons: The Life of the Woman and the Poet in Our Time* (Manchester: Carcanet, 1995), p. 153.

10 See, for example, Hilary Lawson, *Reflexivity: The Postmodern Predicament* (London: Hutchinson, 1985), pp. 10–11.

11 Robert Siegle, *The Politics of Reflexivity: Narrative and the Constitutive Poetics of Culture* (Baltimore: Johns Hopkins University Press, 1986), p. 246.

12 Malcolm Hay and Philip Roberts, 'Interview: Howard Brenton', *Performing Arts Journal*, 3/3 (1979), 138; cited in Richard Boon, *Brenton: The Playwright* (London: Methuen, 1991), p. 118.

13 Paul Auster, *The Invention of Solitude* (London: Faber, 1988), p. 139.

14 Paul Connerton, *How Societies Remember* (Cambridge: Cambridge University Press, 1989), p. 96.

15 Walter J. Ong, *Orality and Literacy: The Technologizing of the Word* (London: Methuen, 1982), p. 79.

16 Jack Goody, *The Interface Between the Written and the Oral* (Cambridge: Cambridge University Press, 1987), p. 255.

17 Jacques Derrida, 'Freud and the scene of writing', *Writing and Difference*, trans. Alan Bass (London: Routledge and Kegan Paul, 1978), p. 228.

18 John Dupré, *The Disorder of Things: Metaphysical Foundations of the Disunity of Science* (Cambridge, MA: Harvard University Press, 1993), p. 7.

19 Scott Lash and John Urry, *Economies of Signs and Space* (London: Sage, 1994), p. 240.

20 Steven Connor, *The English Novel in History 1950–1995* (London: Routledge, 1996), p. 143.

21 Paul Hamilton, *Historicism* (London: Routledge, 1996), p. 2.

22 Hayden White, *The Content of the Form: Narrative Discourse and Historical Representation* (Baltimore: Johns Hopkins University Press, 1987), p. 57.

23 Dominick LaCapra, *History and Memory after Auschwitz* (Ithaca and London: Cornell University Press, 1998), p. 8.

24 Andreas Huyssen, *Twilight Memories: Marking Time in a Culture of Amnesia* (New York: Routledge, 1995), p. 254.

25 Despite the local brilliance of Wayne C. Booth's and Martha Nussbaum's interpretations of character, motivation and scene in fiction and their admirable advocacy of literature as a contributor to ethical theory, they fudge the dialogue between ethics and textuality, which remains elusive. The best recent accounts are to be found in Robert Eaglestone, *Ethical Criticism: Reading After Levinas* (Edinburgh: Edinburgh University Press, 1997), and Adam Zachary Newton, *Narrative Ethics* (Cambridge, MA: Harvard University Press, 1995). Both Eaglestone and Newton argue that Emmanuel Levinas's linguistic turn in his ethics of otherness offers the best way to acknowledge the place of language in the relations between reading, representation, language and the ethical.

26 Geoffrey Harpham, *Getting It Right: Language, Literature, and Ethics* (Chicago: University of Chicago Press, 1992), p. 5.

27 For a discussion of these issues see, Tim Woods, 'The good of history: ethics, poststructuralism and the representation of the past', *Rethinking History*, 2:3 (Autumn 1998), pp. 339–48.

Part I

CHAPTER I

Postmodernism and the death of the past

Throughout *Charlotte Gray* (1998), Sebastian Faulks's historical novel about the Second World War, the protagonist Charlotte Gray, who was born near the end of the First World War, believes that her self-identity has been damaged by a shadowy incident of paternal sexual abuse when she was seven: 'I opened my arms to him as a child would, and when he let me go something terrible had happened. Everything was changed.'[1] Doctors and psychologists had been unable to help alleviate the conse-quent depression – a recurrent disabling 'storm of black panic and half-demented malfunction' (p. 77). At the end of the novel, on a visit to her parents in Scotland after a dangerous mission to help the nascent resistance in France, she discovers that she has been the victim not of sexual abuse but of a false memory syndrome of her own making. She and her father confront her shadowy memories of sexual violence together, and realise that the image of abuse was a 'screen across some-thing worse' (p. 484) – the memories of the First World War that he had imposed on her in a violent emotional outburst one day when they were alone together. Suddenly, he had been unable to contain his guilt any longer at permitting the murder of German prisoners and ordering his own men to certain death, and 'asked a child to bear the weight of those unspeakable things, a weight that drove men mad' (p. 483). Her child's mind could certainly not handle them. It did what any post-Freudian would do and repressed them, creating the intolerable symptoms of depression, which popularised versions of psychoanalysis tell us will result from the failure to work through the memories and to undertake the work of mourning. This new knowledge brings Charlotte immediate release, and she returns to London with a sense of inner peace now that 'as a grown woman she had re-established contact with her childhood self, and there was now a continuous line through her life' (p. 486). The proper workings of memory have established her own history.

The author insists on the accuracy of what he calls the 'historical background' in a note at the end of the novel, but this central plot belongs firmly to the last decade of the twentieth century. Gray's suffering and recovery are examples of the commonplace idea of repression, and her mistaken self-diagnosis exemplifies the recent wave of accusations of sexual abuse which provoked the counter-claim that they were largely the result of false memories induced by manipulative therapy. What is not commonplace is her particular solution to the psychological condition of melancholia, because the novel shows its readers that it was the loss of the past, the repression not only of her father's individual emotional pain and individual memories, but also the collective memories of the horror of the First World War which he carried that warped her mind. 'You told me about it. The millions of dead' (p. 483), she tells her father. Unless the past is remembered, no matter how terrible, it will provoke depression in those who repress that knowledge, and the novel itself, therefore, strives to historicise its material fully by meticulously rendering the details of dress, appearance and analysis of the wider social changes, so that neither will the past be lost nor its fear destroy the psychic equanimity of the future. In doing so, it displays the preoccupation with the risk of epistemological failure which the commentator on postmodernism, Linda Hutcheon, locates at the centre of postmodern discourses: 'in both fiction and history writing today, our confidence in empiricist and positivist epistemologies has been shaken – shaken, but perhaps not yet destroyed'.[2] Unlike the 'historiographic metafiction' which Hutcheon describes, this novel enacts such anxiety largely at the level of plot. We are frequently reminded, for example, that Charlotte Gray's life depends on the historical accuracy with which she is dressed as a young French woman should be, and is compelled to dress in 'coarse stockings, apparently to be held up with the provided pair of garters' before she leaves for the parachute run to France.[3]

Although the novel could not be said to 'problematize the entire question of historical knowledge',[4] both because its questioning of history is occasional and because it uses an unquestioned transparent realism, it is nevertheless troubled by the impossibility of fully historicising the enormity of these events, especially the systematic deportation and murder of Jews. It shifts at least momentarily into the metafictional reflexivity of a postmodern mode when it attempts to narrate the arrival at the gas chamber of the two Jewish children whose worsening situation has been traced throughout the novel, and whom Gray tries and fails to rescue: 'There was another room, another door, with bolts and rubber seals, over whose threshold the two boys, among many others, went through icy air, and disappeared'.[5] They disappear because they die, and also because they cease to be present for the realist perspective of the novel, which requires people and events to appear in the field of view of the narrative's centre of consciousness, once there is no possible human location in which such a centre could survive and witness their death (a gas chamber annihilates the human life necessary for perspective to be possible). The novel itself refuses to let this problem thwart it – realist narration is assumed to be the necessary act of remembrance. Memory is a means of overcoming the limitations of the human condition as it is understood in contemporary culture, by making the past appear once again in the present, despite its temporal, and possibly spatial, distance. This is why the novel as a whole ends with a startlingly parallel sentence describing Gray and her lover, Peter Gregory, with whom she has been reunited at last, as they enter a church for a friend's wedding: 'They crossed into the cold interior of the church, heavy with the scent of cut flowers and the murmuring of the organ, into the soft air, and disappeared' (p. 496). The alignment of the lovers, who have only disappeared from the point of view of someone outside the church, with the murdered Jewish boys through this parallelism of syntax and vocabulary, forces the reader to reflect on the limitations of realism, and the ethical imperative to remember the 'historical background' of the Second World War. Will they, and the entire past about which we have been reading, also disappear, and will this be a kind of murder of the past or a repression leading to collective melancholy?

The use of anamnesis as a main vector of the plot imitates other successful literary novels like *Regeneration* (Pat Barker), *Cat's Eye* (Margaret Atwood) and most notably *Beloved* (Toni Morrison), which all organise their narratives in terms of the demands of a memory compelled to unravel the psychological effects of a traumatic past which lies beyond the temporal horizon of the narrative itself, in a place and time that resists representation. *Charlotte Gray* seems formulaic alongside *Regeneration* or *Beloved*, and is too ready to allow a character the implausibly abstract hindsight necessary to write that the Underground in France is engaged in a 'fight for influence and possession of history' (p. 492), yet all these novels are centrally preoccupied with this fight and the risk that crucial areas of the past have been lost. Recent discussion of historical fiction has tended to see this struggle in epistemological terms, because even 'historiographical metafictions, like both historical fiction and narrative history', as Hutcheon says, 'cannot avoid dealing with the problem of the status of their "facts" and of the nature of their evidence, their documents'.[6] Postmodern historical fiction is unconvinced that there is a single unitary truth of the past waiting to be recovered, and is more interested in who has or had the power to compose 'truths' about it, whereas historical realist fiction tends to assume that the literary narrative has a special power to present the past in a language of the present and give direct access to the thoughts, speech and events of that other time without distorting their significance. But the fear of losing the past, and the means to recover it in Faulks's novel, as in the novels by Barker, Atwood and

Morrison, point in another direction than concerns about the truth of the events. These novels and many other current works of historical literature show a concern with the relation of the past to the present, with where the past is and how it persists in our lives, and how it can be experienced or resisted. The concealed horrors of war, of childhood and of slavery need to be articulated though a history presented as actions, thoughts and feelings happening in a specific place and time for the rememberer with whose position the witnessing reader is encouraged to identify, so that the pasts which were suppressed, repressed or never given access to the basic means of publicity can be made available at last to a public culture. This is why *Charlotte Gray* is willing to risk historical anachronism by making an obviously contemporary model of anamnesis so central to its narratives. Contemporary experiences and beliefs about the ontology of the past appear to make this kind of memorial project a necessity, because otherwise the spatial and temporal conditions attributed to the past may allow it to disappear. Such novels respond to a persistent and widespread contemporary concern that the past is increasingly under threat.

History and postmodernity

Despite the popularity of such historical novels, as well as historical movies, television costume dramas, biographies, heritage sites and museums, many experts believe that the past has changed for the worse in late modernity. The problem is that 'the past is a foreign country' to the twentieth century, according to the historian David Lowenthal, who used this resonant opening phrase from L. P. Hartley's novel, *The Go-Between* (1953), as the title for his own study of the means by which the past persists into the present. This change in the nature of the past from proximity and familiarity to distance and estrangement began in the eighteenth century, but the growing intensity of late twentieth-century efforts to recover and conserve the past make the alienness of the past more salient than ever today. This is especially the case when it appears that the cultural difference of the past revealed by research far outstrips the development of popular methods capable of articulating the otherness that has been discovered. Paradoxically, the result is an impoverishment of collective historical understanding. Lowenthal does not think the movies, books and heritage parks have caused this decline, any more than he thinks that historiography is the sole author of the foreignness of the past. Like other historians, sociologists and cultural theorists he recognises that the rapid development of capitalism and its accompanying transformations of social space and temporality have so thoroughly altered the landscape of late modernity that its continuity with the past is massively disrupted, yet he does not absolve these heterogeneous cultural texts of blame either. They too have failed to keep up with the changing past:

> Specialists learn more than ever about our central biblical and classical traditions, but most people now lack an informed appreciation of them. Our precursors identified with a unitary antiquity whose fragmented vestiges became models for their own creations. Our own more numerous and exotic pasts, prized as vestiges, are divested of the iconographic meanings they once embodied. It is no longer the presence of the past that speaks to us, but its pastness. Now a foreign country with a booming tourist trade, the past has undergone the usual consequences of popularity. The more it is appreciated for its own sake, the less real or relevant it becomes. No longer revered or feared, the past is swallowed up by the ever-expanding present; we enlarge our sense of the contemporary at the expense of realizing its connection with the past. 'We are flooded with disposable memoranda from us to ourselves', as Boorstin puts it, but 'we are tragically inept at receiving messages from our ancestors'.[7]

Popular and literary culture have failed to invent new signifiers of the past, encouraged armchair tourism of its foreign worlds, and ignored the ethical demands of history. One inference from this current state of crass cultural hegemony of the present over the past is that historical literature must be in decline. If only such cultural practices were doing their job, the possible meanings of the past, the work the past offers to those willing to take the trouble to investigate the challenge of its otherness, and the ethical tasks of assessing complicity with history's disasters, would all be more actively underway. Novels like *Charlotte Gray* are right to suspect that the late twentieth-century public has forgotten the past or replaced it with shadowy and misleading monstrosities.

The Past is a Foreign Country is an immensely wide-ranging study of the myriad forms of the historical sense, and it moves far beyond this one metaphor of its title, which is used primarily because of its likely familiarity with readers. Nevertheless, we want to examine its logic a little more closely because it points up the beginnings of an answer to both the question of whether the past has changed and the question of whether cultural texts really have failed to respond. We might begin to consider the latter by noting that the image of the foreign land does come from a historical novel, 'a subtly told story of 1900, filled with a 1950s consciousness', as one critic describes it.[8] Historical literature must be of some help if it can provide an image which a historian can take seriously. More important, however, is the implicit logic of the image of the past as Lowenthal deploys it, because it evokes a discourse of distance, power, fear and otherness which can be construed as loss. It compares the temporal distance of the past from the late twentieth century, to the spatial distance of some foreign nation from the centre of contemporary civilisation, and this gives the past a place-like ontology, capable of spatio-temporal location and measurement, whose absence from the present is measurable as both distance and a form of cultural difference dependent on nation and identity. Ontologising the past through nation and identity implies that people's current conceptions of the past have emerged from twentieth-century politics and history dominated by world wars fought to decide questions of power over foreign countries, by the genocide of those who were foreign and different, and deeply shaped by the economic imperialism enabled by foreignness. In Lowenthal's analysis of the contemporary relation to the past through this image, two opposed forms of external intervention in this topography of cultural difference are at work: first, a scholarly conservation which isolates the location from contamination by modern preconceptions so successfully that it is pushed beyond easy reach of the current representational capacity of cultural texts; and, secondly, a leisure industry which prevents the possibility of being altered by the knowledge or experience of the past by wrapping strangeness in the prophylactic of entertainment, and treating its material cultures as no more than souvenirs of the visit. What is needed, according to Lowenthal's argument, is greater economic equity between nations so that tourism is not simply one-way from rich to poor or centre to periphery, and research is not aimed defensively at keeping things as they were – changes which would be tantamount to accepting that both past and present are mutable under certain conditions. Then the past would not be in decline even if it were changing. 'History can never bring about the death of the past ... but a past known to be altered and alterable sheds at least some of its enchantment, sacred or malign', and requires everyone to recognise the 'artifice no less than the truth of our heritage'.[9] The narrative of progress from magic to science inscribed in this conclusion depends somewhat surprisingly on the additional power of artifice, and although this is a constructivism whose interdependence on the arts is not explored, it is the arts and their cultural texts which investigate the conditions of such artifice most thoroughly.

It is our contention that contemporary literature actively explores the ramifications of such artifice and is, therefore, reflexively historical, not just in realist historical fiction, but far beyond the field of the realist historical novel's explicit accounts of the past, in literary works not usually thought of as historical. Treating the past as a foreign country too readily reproduces the traumatic relations of recent history, unless the underlying ideologies of space, time and memory are investigated textually and thematically. The belief in a pervasive historical ignorance arises from looking in the wrong places for historical awareness and historical literatures. Lowenthal's recourse to an historical novel and to a generalised concept of artifice shows that we must not underestimate the importance of textual memory within literary practice, while his more general conclusions about the changing past suggest that we should begin by looking in a little more detail at what historians and theorists understand by the alterability of the past.

The Marxist historian, Eric Hobsbawm, begins the final volume of his magisterial history of modernity, *Age of Extremes*, with a gloomy justification for his efforts based on the dangers of a disappearing past:

> The destruction of the past, or rather of the social mechanisms that link one's contemporary experience to that of earlier generations, is one of the most characteristic and eerie phenomena of the late twentieth century. Most young men and women at the century's end grow up in a sort of permanent present lacking any organic relation to the public past of the times they live in.[10]

The 'destruction' of the past. This is a strange and threatening image whose rhetorical force derives from its Orwellian evocation of recent totalitarian attempts to conceal the regime's atrocities, and eradicate any possibility that memories of alternative politics and resistance might resurface. These precedents create the fear that the loss of history will somehow make possible similar or even worse future social catastrophes, a possibility that is implied by the metaphorical image and yet concealed by it. Hobsbawm's hasty correction – it is not the past but the means by which the past remains active in the present which is at risk – moves to a more defensible position, which is just as well. After all, what does it mean to talk of the 'destruction of the past', especially given the way that the past already appears to be built on the destruction of the present, as it moves away irretrievably into an absent time and space where only a hypothetical time machine could reach it? The past would appear immune to all change because it is a space and time that no longer exists, and existence would seem to be necessary for change to be possible at all. Commonsense would seem to say that although history, memory and the institutions which maintain continuity and manage transformations of the past certainly alter, the past itself is altogether beyond alteration, so that what's done is done and however much our knowledge of a specific past might change, it is only our constructions that alter. Nevertheless, there is a persistent anxiety evident among contemporary critics who have sounded the alarm about ignorance of the past, that the past may have some such vulnerability.

The American historian, Michael Kammen, who shares Hobsbawm's pessimism about the contemporary world's ignorance of its history, and deplores the nostalgic tourism of the past offered by advertising and the film industry, is careful to attribute this diminished ability to refer to the past to the weakening of social memory.[11] Such 'indiscriminate amnesia' is due to many factors, particularly the rapid pace of building and rebuilding which destroys the physical traces of history so quickly that collective memory is impaired. He thinks the efforts of popular culture to improve the situation are worsening it with its exploitation of nostalgia. The successful 'entrepreneurial mode of selective memory' employed by Walt Disney and others in postwar America, masks the past with simulacra that make it even harder for people to understand their history or worse. It is such developments in America that made the cultural critic Jean Baudrillard question whether history was over. 'What miracle would make history true again?' he asks. 'What miracle would allow us to go back in time so that we may prepare ourselves for its disappearance?'[12] Disneyland is merely a highly salient version of the culture of simulation which has made the past disappear, and encouraged fantasies of time travel as the best solution of which this culture can dream.[13]

Although most commentators do not share Baudrillard's ambivalent mixture of celebration and pessimism about the possibility of public knowledge, or his belief that our society has relocated itself into a zone of virtuality, the idea that the 'past has been modified', as the Marxist critic Fredric Jameson phrases it, does resonate widely; Jameson himself is willing to endorse Baudrillard's analysis to the extent that he can employ it to accuse late capitalism of ensuring its continuance through the manipulation of cultural texts which occlude history:

> The new spatial logic of the simulacrum can now be expected to have a momentous effect on what used to be called historical time. The past is thereby itself modified: what was once, in the historical novel as Lukács defines it, the organic genealogy of the bourgeois collective project – what is still, for the redemptive historiography of an E. P. Thompson or of American 'oral history', for the resurrection of the dead of anonymous and silenced generations, the retrospective dimension indispensable to any vital reorientation of our collective future – has meanwhile itself become a vast collection of images, a multitudinous photographic simulacrum.[14]

Instead of experiencing this as a loss whose tragedy provokes grief and mourning, this new culture produces the celebratory mood of post-modernism for which the past is a style book from which we can borrow and reassemble new histories at whim, with no sense of any ethical, let alone political, demand on us. 'The past as "referent" finds itself gradually bracketed, and then effaced altogether, leaving us with nothing but texts'.[15] Sometimes Jameson slips into the same despair as Hobsbawm, however, and will say simply that 'in the postmodern, then, the past has disappeared (along with the well-known "sense of the past" or historicity and collective memory)'.[16] Or he will appear to admit that the past is still there, but has become merely boring, needing the inventive spice of 'fantastic genealogies, alternate histories' for those who indulge in 'an in-group hobby or adoptive tourism'[17] of history, as if the artifices of historical literature were generally to be deplored. Yet Jameson also holds out the possibility that this is neither ideological manipulation, nor artistic bad faith towards the past. Sometimes he appears to believe that postmodernism is a realism which doesn't recognise its own realism, because the complexity of the world in which we live has outstripped our means of representation, and the new cultural practices of postmodernism are at least trying the best they can with their limited representational means:

> It may now be suggested that this alarming disjunction point between the body and its built environment – which is to the initial bewilderment of the older modernism as the velocities of spacecraft to those of the auto-mobile can itself stand as the symbol and analogon of that even sharper dilemma which is the incapacity of our minds, at least at present, to map the great global multinational and decentred communicational network in which we find ourselves caught as individual subjects.[18]

Perhaps the 'mutation in built space' which Jameson detects in the post-modern architectures of a Frank Gehry or a John Portman, and the 'breakdown of temporality' of a poem by Bob Perelman, are specific modes of an emergent historicism which is hard to read because the past embedded in the new science-fictional 'spacecraft' world of the 'global multinational and decentred communicational network', is different to the past of earlier socio-economic formations. Maybe the past has changed, and the new genres of architecture and poetry are trying to trace its modifications. For a historian expecting to find the past in more traditional locations it might seem, however, as if the past had disap-peared altogether from the social memory evident in such cultural practices.

Both Hobsbawm and Jameson use Marxist theory, for which a consciousness of history is a precondition of transformative social action, so it might be argued that their pessimism is the other side of Francis Fukuyama's conservative celebration of the end of Communist rule as 'the end of history', since the scope for socialist politics appears to have so diminished in the West. A shift to the right in politics would be accompanied by a diminished sense of historical responsibility, a loss of historical consciousness. Another theorist of postmodernity, Andreas Huyssen, in an essay on the German artist Anselm Kiefer, argues that Kiefer's work gains its power because of the degree to which it acknowl-edges and then works through the implications of such a political desire for historical amnesia in postwar Germany: 'While much of Kiefer's mythic painting seems energized by a longing to transcend the terrors of recent German history, the point, driven home relentlessly by subject matter and aesthetic execution, is that this longing will not, cannot be fulfilled.'[19] Not all cultural historians view these changes with gloom. Many contemporary cultural critics would be sceptical about attributing such significance to changes in the ordinary awareness of the past, and would probably agree with Michel Foucault's argument that the kind of history whose loss is lamented by these historians is likely to be the retrospective imposition of a consoling, but false, temporal continuity on heterogeneous events and discourses in order to maintain the sovereignty of the subject position from which the past is surveyed. What has gone is not the past but an invented cause for current effects, which would give an illusion of being in control of history.

Foucault's poststructuralist mode of cultural history based on the study of how institutions, knowledge and their fields of study emerged from discursive practices, depended on a sweeping disavowal of existing historical studies and its implicit ideas about time. His critique of contemporary historicism begins with the assumption that a monolithic sense of the past has come to dominate modern thought. 'Since it is the mode of being of all that is given us in experience, History has become the unavoidable element in our thought'.[20] To be modern is to think of history with an oceanic metaphor, as 'the depths from which all beings emerge into their precarious, glittering existence' because only such vast uncharted spaces could contain the debris of what is 'possibly the most cluttered area of our memory'.[21] When we think of a person, an event or even an abstraction, what we do is experience it as something that has a past, a present and a future, and the past is a receding network of causes which have determined its present state, just as the collision of many contingencies in the present will shape what happens to it in the future. These networks are, according to Foucault, commonly treated as if they were unbroken continuities (even if the links might be sometimes hard to discover) flowing towards the present and on into the future and encourage us to ignore the radical disjunctures that result from the conflictual character of history. History is actually 'violent, bloody and lethal', not a cosy idyll. [22] 'The history which bears and determines us has the form of a war rather than that of a language: relations of power, not relations of meaning. History has no "meaning"'.[23] The scare quotes are meant to indicate that this is the kind of meaning which is meaning for a subject, the sort of meaning that news interviewers ask for from people involved in national events when they might ask, 'what does this new legislation mean for you?'. Foucault is not thinking of the ordinary question asked by an historian – what did a particular action 'mean' and what does it indicate to the backward gaze of analysis about its specific context? His critique is aimed at a mode of historical thought which covertly maintains the authority of conscious reason, for if history is a continuous, evolutionary process then the subject which surveys it is not only the point on which the entire past converges, the subject is also its fruition; its power and autonomy are secured by this teleological narrative of history. 'Continuous history is the indispensable correlative of the founding function of the subject: the guarantee that everything that has eluded him may be restored to him; the certainty that time will disperse nothing without restoring it in a reconstituted unity; the promise that one day the subject – in the form of historical consciousness – will once again be able to appropriate, to bring back under his sway, all those things that are kept at a distance by difference, and find in them what might be called his abode'.[24] Instead of such linear connections, the new historian should be alert to the 'epistèmic breaks', the discontinuities between different eras and their discourses. As so often in Foucault, the targets of his critique are not always evident. He could be talking as much about everyday belief as pointing to the influence of Heidegger or Sartre on contemporary thought, and he is certainly not dismissing the work of all contemporary historians.

Behind the dazzling rhetoric is a familiar claim that earlier modes of historicism are no longer adequate, and that the new historian is cut off by her or his specialist knowledge of the foreignness of the past from the misconceptions and comforting illusions which still circulate widely. 'The cry goes up that one is murdering history',[25] complains Foucault a page later, as if he felt he were being held responsible for the disappearance of the past, when all that has happened is that he has contributed to the articulation of a growing recognition that the past is much more complex, different and discontinuous than had previously been recognised. So we can see that he too acquiesces in the belief that the past has been 'modified', and one version of it is disappearing (not quickly enough for Foucault), although he insists that this does not mean the loss of all historical understanding so much as a transformation of it. The new historian of discursive formations should put her or his own subject position at risk, and not expect to remain safely aboard a history whose continuity can never be broken. It is a compelling image, and one which resonates with much contemporary historical writing which also argues that working through textual memory is a necessary self-endangerment. This argument that the way in which people experience identity, both individually and collectively, is deeply bound up with what they imagine history to be, points in quite another direction than heroic exceptionalism, however; it directs us towards the everyday understanding of what it means to be a historian for oneself. Maybe Lowenthal's image of the two opposed reactions to the foreignness of the past indicates a need for the two forms of historicism to engage in a dialogue, rather than for the scholars to treat populist examples of historical cultural texts as symptoms of an ethical failure of historical awareness.

Everyday practices of history

Two American historians, Roy Rosenzweig and David Thelen, recently became sceptical of the idea that most people were so ignorant of the past that a collective sense of history was in danger of disappearing altogether, and decided to test it by empirical sociological investigation. On what evidence could Lynne Cheney, chair of the National Endowment for the Humanities in the USA, confidently begin a pamphlet called *American Memory* by saying that 'a refusal to remember ... is a primary characteristic of our nation' (ellipses as original).[26] After carrying out extensive sociological interviews of a cross-section of the population, they conclude that far from having disappeared, the past in America at least, is pervasive, 'a natural part of everyday life'.[27] Most Americans do have an interest in history and the majority of these engage in some form of history-making of their own, and even more significantly, given the alleged 'disappearance of the past', these historians discovered that '*the past* was the term that best invited people to talk about family, race, and nation' (emphasis in original),[28] although it was 'the familial and intimate past, along with intimate uses of other pasts'.[29] Not all the findings were encouraging to historians though. Despite this ubiquitous interest in history, most Americans, whatever their status or ethnic background, 'feel unconnected to the past in history classrooms because they don't recognize themselves in the version of the past presented there'.[30] This is partly why they talk about the past and not about history – history is tainted by bad experiences of the classroom. The discovery that contemporary Americans care most for a personal past might encourage a more cynical interpretation of the historical interests of contemporary Americans than the historians offer, one which would support Foucault's claim that the dominant mode of modern historical consciousness is narcissistic. Aren't these people looking for just that security of self-consciousness in history that Foucault deplores for its distortions of the otherness and distance of the past? There is plenty of evidence that this does sometimes happen (the autobiographical turn in contemporary prose and poetry manifests this at times when familial history becomes the only basis for claims to authenticity), yet even in such cases, the Foucauldian notion of a cosy retreat of the ego is challenged by other narratives internal to the work. The detailed renditions of specific interviews carried out for the survey of attitudes to history mostly point away from narcissism. These interviewees were usually working with history as an active part

of wider projects which include those recognisable to ,
ans: 'millions of Americans regularly document, pre
narrate, discuss, and study the past'.[31]

The amateur historians are trying to find intimate, p(
pasts within the public 'official' histories of their time, but th
mean they are looking for mere confirmation of their own sove
subjects. Even calling them amateur can be misleading because
not measure their skill and knowledge against those of profession , and
they are as committed to what they do as any academic. They know they
are putting their identities, emotions and self-representations at risk in
doing so, because they do not see history as a process of self-legitimation
so much as a means for self-transformation. 'In these interviews, the most
powerful meanings of the past come out of the dialogue between the past
and the present, out of the ways the past can be used to answer pressing
current-day questions about relationships, identity, immortality, and
agency'.[32] The people who were interviewed wanted to 'personalize the
public past',[33] in order to locate themselves and their intimate histories
within a larger social field.

> Though some of them spoke about the futility of war or man's inhu-
> manity to man, a much larger group – almost half of those who cited
> World War II – reflected on the war in more personal terms. A 71-year-
> old Philadelphia woman said she learned self-reliance from the war: 'My
> husband was in that. It was a lot of heartache with both of us being
> young and him being away in his early twenties. I learned how to be
> independent and how to take care of myself.' What they didn't talk
> about was the narrative most familiar to us from high school history
> books and popular culture: the war as a story of victory over fascism or
> as a key moment in a patriotic narrative of the nation-state.[34]

This could be read as a version of Jean François Lyotard's theory that
postmodernism has resulted in the abandonment of what he calls the
'grand narratives' of history in favour of 'local knowledges', as if ordinary
Americans were already postmodernists without knowing it. What we
might want to ask in response to this woman's reply to her questioners,
is whether her silence about the patriotic narratives is due to their taken-
for-granted presence as background knowledge which she assumes is
shared with her interlocutors or whether her silence is a form of resistance.

Resistance to such narratives was certainly evident in those groups
which had been victimised by genocide and slavery. The authors noticed
that their African-American and Oglala Sioux interviewees were much
more aware of the prevalence of the overarching narratives of the nation
than the whites to whom they spoke, and that this awareness took the
form of critique. These people were also much readier to locate their

...1 history in relation to public events and figures – African-Americans chose Martin Luther King Jr as the person from the past who had most influenced them much more often than a family figure, quite unlike the white interviewees.[35] One of the interview team who spoke to the Sioux noticed that 'their everyday life becomes the past, the past becomes their everyday life',[36] and significant moments like Wounded Knee remain active landmarks in the present. This is one of the few moments in the study where we can identify a difference in relations to the past that could account for the idea of a loss of the past that was not formulated in terms of indifference to, or ignorance of, the past. To live the past as part of the present in everyday life might be construed as a burden of unfinished suffering and grief or a rich experience of sustained meaning, emotion and connection with the achievements of one's predecessors, and with their contribution to the making of oneself and one's world. The interviewers' use of the verb 'becomes', instead of the copula, suggests that these people actively strive to create this relation rather than simply finding it a given condition. Yet the limitations of such empirical investigation do not allow us to resolve such questions, and we would have to consider contemporary novels, such as Maxine Hong Kingston's *China Men*, Toni Morrison's *Beloved*, or Louise Erdrich's novels, where the implications of such collectively lived retrospection are followed through.

Rosenzweig and Thelen conclude that the past has not been murdered by theorists, teachers or politicians; it is 'very much alive', and only seems to have disappeared to those who fail to recognise that the past 'has many mansions'.[37] This rhetorical equation of heaven ('In my father's house are many mansions' (*John* 14:2)) and the past is indicative of a tendency in their report to treat the past as precisely that condition of all existence which Foucault asks us to question. It results in the avoidance of any discussion of whether these popular pasts are equally valuable, as well as the avoidance of all judgements of epistemology and method. To some extent this is strategic. The authors want to challenge the complacency of historians who believe that only a war on historical ignorance will maintain their discipline, and they do not believe that their findings render academic history irrelevant, but rather that they give grounds for believing that it is academic history which has been ignorant of the changing role and significance of history in contemporary culture. It therefore urgently needs to develop new methods of teaching history and to raise questions about both the uses to which historical knowledge is put and the investments of power in historical enquiry.

When asked when they most felt 'connected to the past', these respondents chose occasions like family gatherings and visits to museums or historical sites, and felt least connected to the past both in the history classroom and when reading books or watching movies and television about the past.[38] Rosenzweig and Thelen's findings that literature and cinema which depicted the past were regarded with the same lesser enthusiasm as the academic study of history, inverts a common perception among cultural critics that literature and film are popular in a way that history and theory could never be. Instead, their results appear to show that literature, film and academic history are perceived in similar ways, that is, as lacking in relevance and intensity, because they hinder as much or more than they give access to – the past. James Cameron, the script-writer and director of the most expensive and profitable movie ever made, *Titanic*, was clearly aware of this popular sentiment when he concluded his preface to a newly-edited version of the US Senate hearings from 1912 on the sinking of the ship, by saying: 'While remaining respectful of the work of the good and thorough historians who have gone before us, each of us must function as his or her own historian, skeptical of everything'.[39] The movie's success among older viewers less likely to be drawn in by the romantic plot, would depend on appealing to the active historian, who, in Linda Hutcheon's words, would 'seriously question who determined and created that truth' of history, and so the movie, therefore, had to engage with any initial disbelief that a fictional historical film could assist their activities.[40]

The American historian of working-class popular culture, George Lipsitz, observes that 'the desire to connect to history, the impulse to pose present problems in historical terms, and the assertion of a temporal and social reality beyond one's own immediate experience pervade popular culture in significant ways.'[41] He shows that popular culture has not lost the past whatever its limitations and flaws. 'Within the interstices of popular culture, a rich collective counter-memory carries on the tasks of historical thinking in new and significant ways'.[42] Angus Calder makes a similar point in the preface to his wonderful study of the home front in the Second World War, *The People's War*:

> No doubt I shall be accused of wilful 'debunking'. But I have not tried to explode received ideas merely for the sake of the bang. Nor can I claim much credit for uncovering falsehoods long concealed. If a mythical version of the war still holds sway in school textbooks and television documentaries, every person who lived through those years knows that those parts of the myth which concern his or her own activities are false.[43]

Calder's recognition of the co-existence of different knowledges and practices of history inspired a generation of British writers. Several of the playwrights we discuss later in the book were fascinated by the possibility of a theatrical bang offered by Calder's history, and by the potential release of political energy to be generated by confronting myth and counter-memory in a public space, as in plays like Howard Brenton's *The Churchill Play*.

The makers of movies like *Titanic*, political playwrights and writers of genre fiction, all know that their work must offer ample room for their audiences to become historians. In his ground-breaking study of the significance of popular history-making, *Theatres of Memory*, Samuel agrees with Rosenzweig and Thelen when he argues that in Britain 'history as a mass activity – or at any rate a pastime – has possibly never had more followers than it does today, when the spectacle of the past excites the kind of attention which earlier epochs attached to the new'.[44] He goes even further by arguing that images and ideas of the past are as much a part of the material of history as people, actions, events and objects, because history 'is a social form of knowledge',[45] so that to understand our history it is necessary to consider all the practices whereby people are and have been busy constructing their history, however mythic or distorted the results might appear to be from an academic standpoint. Only by being aware of the significance of these myriad, popular practices ranging from the visual media of television, photographs and comics to the construction of mock Georgian houses and historical theme parks can the historian comprehend the complexity of the past. This argument suggests that the urban novels, autobiographical lyrics and other generic literatures which we discuss later, are history in process and, therefore, that the resistance to them found by Rosenzweig and Thelen is a sign of struggles over the control of representation and interpretation rather than simply a desire for the immediacy of contact made possible by museums, historical sites and family interactions. Samuel's work amply demonstrates that history is a social knowledge situated within local networks of class, gender, sexuality, ethnicity and race, and there are no distinguishable boundaries between research, cultural texts and popular history-making, which are in practice interdependent. Cultural texts are produced for an audience already in possession of a social knowledge of the past that extends across this range, and these texts must negotiate a passage through their prevailing forms and beliefs.

The need for cultural texts to engage with the resistances and desires of an audience actively in search of pasts, can be found everywhere in their themes, forms and prefatory comment. Even Eric Hobsbawm, who offers his synoptic history of the twentieth century as a scholarly example of the knowledge that is needed for renewal, provides a brief model of reception by offering a personal note on his own relation to the past at the beginning of his volume. He feels secure in his own sense of having been a part of the history he writes, and believes that the growing historical amnesia evident among the young is due to their lack of what he and his generation – whose lives span the twentieth century – took for granted. People like him were actors, observers or at least 'people whose views of the century have been formed by what we have come to see as its crucial events'. He puts it even more forcefully a few lines earlier: 'We are part of this century. It is part of us'.[46] You cannot lose a past which has become part of your identity. Yet Hobsbawm does not base this claim to unbreakable ties with the past on a career at the centres of power, but on his location in space and time at critical junctures. He can associate his own life with momentous historical events like Hitler becoming Chancellor, simply by being an educated Jewish teenager living in Berlin, where he actually saw the newspaper headline announcing Hitler's triumph as he walked home on a winter afternoon: 'I can see it still, as in a dream'.[47] We should observe, however, that this inwardness with the ominous day was not the result of direct observation (he didn't actually witness Hitler taking over the office), but mediated through its report in the newspaper. This is a textual memory. His unself-conscious admission that it now seems a dream implies that history, memory and text have become deeply entwined. One reason the event now seems like a dream must be because his response to it has been overlaid by the knowledge and feelings acquired during his own long career as a historian, enabling him to assimilate such recollections with a sophisticated hindsight which has created a strong sense of participation in a history whose retrospective power is concealed by the dream-like aura of a frequently handled memory. The dream indicates the obscure workings of the zone of connection between the individual and the public history within which texts, fantasies, literature and academic research operate, the zone where the people interviewed by the historians want a direct relation to the past as a guide to the present and future.

Although Hobsbawm claims to have been present as history happened, his account is already textualised. What looks like common ignorance of history may be the result of historicising activities whose textuality is not so easily recognised as the screaming headline – activities which professionals do not register as epistemologically sound knowledge, for reasons which are likely to include the mediation of textual rhetorics and cultural styles that appear anti-historical. Historicism in literary rhetoric may be hard to see.

Anticipated trajectories within the various modes of circulation of contemporary cultural texts – the heterogeneous, active reception and re-inscription they receive in everyday life – will be inscribed in the generic strategies they employ to handle fears of losing the past and accompanying low expectations of historical power in ready-made cultural texts, creating distinctive literary forms of textual memory. Of genres in which such proleptic structures of reception are especially evident, the autobiography is the most familiar, and one which, as Laura Marcus notes in her study of the genre, most insistently raises issues of authenticity.[48] William James said movingly that subjective histories are 'portions of the universe that may be irretrievably lost'.[49] The feared loss of a past represented by the closure of a paper mill in the town of Piedmont, West Virginia where he grew up, prompted Henry Louis Gates Jr (one of the foremost academic scholars of African-American literature) to write a genial, personal memoir of his home town that culminates in a vivid portrait of the 'last colored mill picnic', before the white and coloured annual workforce picnics were amalgamated. The result is a text which is explicit about this difficult issue of the relevance of the historical text to those outside its immediate context, although it does not fully resolve the challenge. It shows us how literary texts might be significant forms of contemporary historicism, in which shifting senses of the pastness of the past – its location and the mechanisms whereby it is maintained and transmitted – are explored in ways that are not available in other discursive modes.

Near the end of the narrative, Gates cites the opening and conclusion of his personal statement in his application to Yale: '"My grandfather was colored, my father was a Negro, and I am black … As always, whitey now sits in judgement of me, preparing to cast my fate. It is your decision either to let me blow with the wind as a non-entity or to encourage the development of self. Allow me to prove myself". I wince at the rhetoric today, but they let me in.'[50] The three names for racial difference are a striking instance of the historical archive at work in our vocabularies. This final sentence manages a complex manœuvre in time and attention, designating this document of the past as a rhetoric in order to encourage the reader to read its textuality closely, and disowning pride by admitting to the emotional response it now creates in him, the embarrassment of it, all the while allowing in another temporal dimension than the opposition of then and now, the future of that past which is nevertheless still a past. The reader is made a historian of this past document and allowed to identify with the author's own historical emotion, all of which will help circumvent the indifference that any writer fears the reader will show to a history distant from his or her own.

The last segregated mill picnic is worth detailed rendition because it is an occasion whose communitarian spirit is paradigmatic of what has been lost, and only by enumerating these tangible and circumstantial details can the scale of this lost and irrecoverable past even be indicated. The last sentence of the book manages a tension between past and present through the use of a reported speech which is almost, but not quite, direct speech: 'Yeah, even the Yankees had colored players now,

Mr. Ozzie mumbled to Daddy, as they packed up Nemo's black cast-iron vat, hoping against hope to boil that corn another day'.[51] An era is ended with this small action of closing the corn boiler. A long 'now' stretches forward from this moment when no more corn will be boiled at coloured-only picnics because they have been integrated to the moment of the writing and reading itself. The tone of regret, puzzling to a reader who assumes that integration brought about an unmitigated improvement in the quality of life, carries over to the entire enterprise of representing this vanished way of life in the public space of a published narrative which can only be a very limited conservation of its diverse and densely textured collective memory. The mood of the book is consistently buoyant, however, because the emotions attached to painful experiences, such as his fatness as a child or his lack of social success, as well as the more generalised experiences of discrimination, are overlaid by the later emotions of a recollection that is trying to value what has been lost, and it is this loss that creates an unusual sense of readership. How can this text avoid being just another of those books that actually reinforces the sense of disconnection from the past for the ordinary reader? Gates's answer seems at first sight extreme. He simply limits his audience to his children, for whom family memory is likely to be of great interest. Instead of appealing to the historian in everyone, or just to his own academic community, or invoking the realist fantasy of a narrational time machine, he frames his narrative with a personal address which enacts the familial connectedness to the past for which Rosenzweig and Thelen found most Americans wished. A preface explains to his children that the autobiography is written for them: 'I have written to you because a world into which I was born, a world that nurtured and sustained me, has mysteriously disappeared'.[52] This preface could have been written in the third person, explaining that the book was written for his children while addressing a general reader, but this would have tacitly admitted that the book was also intended for the general reader, and might have seemed no more than a mere literary device to ward off accusations of egotism. In fact, by addressing his children in this manner, Gates represents the past, exemplified by his memory of this collective event, as a parent of the present, represented by his children, who in turn embody the future. The general reader who does read this widely available text is, therefore, encouraged to read it as both a family history and as an exemplary model of a particular relation to the past, while attributing any failure of historical intensity to the text's segregation from the general reader. In doing so, it also enacts that underlying theme, the lasting effects of racial segregation on the formation of the self.

The fears that the past will be lost if it is not recorded and transmitted to future generations merge with the fear that no one will be listening because the potential audience has lost its historical sense. The evidence suggests that the central problem is one of reception within specific social contexts with which the cultural text needs to negotiate if it is to command a hearing. Most cultural texts have neither the enormous marketing resources of a Hollywood blockbuster nor do they wish to confine their imagined audience to their immediate family circle. Are they therefore doomed to be consumed by a disappointed, inattentive audience wishing for more direct connection with history or is the process more complex than this? The statistical link between academic history and cultural texts points to one answer to this. Just as academic research aims not simply to confirm existing thought but to extend it by providing new evidence, ideas and theories, so too does even the most formulaic cultural text. Some part of the resistance to these texts by the people interviewed is likely to be due to the work these texts demand from their audience, as they articulate in new ways and sometimes challenge the existing images of the past held by the reader. At the same time, these cultural texts need to be extremely aware of the audience's fantasies, ideologies, beliefs and information about the past if they are to achieve a hearing. We should, therefore, be looking in these cultural texts to find evidence of their strategies for active dialogue between text and reader over what form the past takes and what constitute its salient features.

Fear of the past

So far we have discussed the loss of the past as if it were a fact verifiable by empirical research and justifiable by logical argument. We have said almost nothing about fantasy; yet fantasies about the past, both of the kind that make costume dramas, such as the recent television adaptations of novels by Charles Dickens and Jane Austen, so successful, and the darker ones evident in Sylvia Plath's famous poem 'Daddy', play a central role in textual memory. The fear of losing the past often takes the form of a paradoxical fantasy that the past is too dangerous for the self and deserves to be lost; a point familiar from the psychoanalytic theory of repression, but relevant far beyond the field of the individual psyche. Many people tacitly believe that the past deserves to be lost. The 'slaughterbench of history' is a story of suffering which has the power to undermine present motivation and deter plans for the future. The past is, in other words, not just a cognitive domain, but also deeply interfused with emotional investments ranging from the milder forms of nostalgia and regret, to the unbearable intensities of longing, grief and rage which demand that the past be discarded or even destroyed. The popularity of therapies of anamnesis, and their accompanying theories of traumatic memory, suggests that many pasts are knowingly lost because they are no longer tolerable.

Recent fiction has shown a strong interest in the fantasies of memory made by such intolerable pasts on phenomenologies and narratives of lives lived in their shadow. In her fictional autobiography of a Holocaust survivor and poet, Jakob Beer, Anne Michaels tries to anatomise the workings of such abjections of memory by likening the crushing impact of Holocaust history on those who come after, to the work of Jewish prisoners who take on the duty of remembering those whom their Nazi captors compel them to bury. It is less the horror of the corpses than the scale of the memorial burden, first felt somatically, that becomes insupportable to consciousness:

> When the prisoners were forced to dig up the mass graves, the dead entered them through their pores and were carried through their bloodstreams to their brains and hearts. And through their blood into another generation. Their arms were into death up to the elbows, but not only into death – into music, into a memory of the way a husband or son leaned over his dinner, a wife's expression as she watched her child in the bath; into beliefs, mathematical formulas, dreams. As they felt another man's and another's blood-soaked hair through their fingers, the diggers begged forgiveness. And those lost lives made molecular passage into their hands. How can one man take on the memories of even one other man, let alone five or ten or a thousand or ten thousand; how can they be sanctified each? He stops thinking.[53]

Variants of this fantasy of a somatic telepathy run through the novel. The poet and his biographer experience memory as a material force – geological and cosmological – rather than composed of tenuous threads of mentality. Not surprisingly, it is only on an island – geologically separated from the mainland of history – that the poet is finally able to write about the war. At the end of the novel, Beer's biographer goes to the Greek island where the poet wrote his famous poems, and realises that the poet only felt safe enough at this point in his life to begin the work of memory: 'you descended into horror slowly, as divers descend, with will and method ... The house did possess the silence that is the wake of a monumental event ... Your poems from those few years with Michaela, poems of a man who feels, for the first time, a future'.[54] The pun on 'wake' is the sign of the grace of this special house which enables him to find creative defences against the fear of being annihilated by the past while beginning to let it enter his own bloodstream. This mnemonic fantasy of material transmission from the bedrock of the past is also a limitation of the novel. Those prisoners on burial detail did not absorb the memories of the dead through merely handling them – if only they had. The mass murder of Jews did destroy large areas of cultural memory which can only be partially reconstructed, and not, unfortunately, by any sort of laying-on of hands or somatic telepathy. This is a consolatory fantasy that actually hides some of the horror even while it finds a striking image for other features of it, in its attempts to acknowledge and hold at bay the terrible power of this threatening past.

Michaels's novel shows that charges of ignorance and indifference to history underestimate the widely perceived dangers of the past. Santayana's maxim that if we fail to understand the past we are doomed to repeat it, much too readily assumes that understanding is a straightforward procedure with an entrance and exit. For many people, it is what Thomas Pynchon described in *The Crying of Lot 49* as the 'exitlessness' of contemporary America that is their experience of looking back to the past – amnesia can appear to be a reasonable option.[55] If the audience wants to lose at least some part of the past, forget and bury its threatening terrors, how can the cultural text approach it without being rejected, and what kinds of insight might the cultural text be able to offer into the consequences of this condition? We can see the power of this fear and the strategies for approaching the past with caution and respect for its persistent power to shape the present as well as its apparent power to thwart or devour attempts to develop away from its problems, in Stephen Spielberg's movie *Jurassic Park* (1993) based on Michael Crichton's novel of the same name (1991). This is a movie which shows that the past in the contemporary text is not always located where convention would place it, nor are the old social mechanisms always the means to recover it.

Dinosaurs have become pervasive images of the past since the Second World War, promulgated by a culture industry willing to invest millions to entertain this fascination with vanished monsters and the fragmentary traces they left behind. 'Big, fierce, and extinct' in Stephen Jay Gould's words, they are therefore 'alluringly scary, but sufficiently safe' because they are after all tucked out of the way in the distant past, and therefore make perfect screen icons for massive commercial exploitation.[56] What Gould does not say is that dinosaurs also have a close association with death, because most people encounter them as gigantic skeletons displayed in the great natural history museums of the world. The fossilised bones override awareness that the see-through monsters are just reconstructions, and we are only rarely reminded openly of just how speculative they really are, as we were when the brontosaurus's tail was suddenly lifted into the air to accord with new knowledge of their anatomy. However much these giant skeletons act as evidence for the scale of prehistoric fauna living on earth, they are also massive reminders of the fate of all living things, and so these oversize creatures carry great symbolic weight. The land artist Robert Smithson was fascinated by dinosaurs, and noted that most of the imagery of these creatures available until the 1960s derived from the illustrations of Charles R. Knight, who also sometimes provided brief, revealing commentaries for his scenes. Smithson cites an example that captures perfectly the significance of these monsters for contemporary culture, where Knight describes the tar pits in which skeletons had been found as a place which elicits horror at the past: 'Peaceful as the place looks now, tragedy, both dark and terrible, long hung about its gloomy depths'.[57] To Smithson, Knight's dinosaurs seem at first to be 'reformulated symbols of total or original Evil', because of the way they are constantly depicted as devouring and anni-hilating everything in their path. Then he looks past this surface to another possibility, saying that 'the word teratoid [monster] like the word dinosaur suggests extraordinary scale, immense regions, and infinite quantity',[58] in order to articulate the marvels of monstrosity (knowing that the usual idiomatic meaning of 'dinosaur' is old-fashioned and slow to change, he wittily likens the 'Art World' to a dinosaur on the grounds that both art world and the imagined saurian past, traffic in the marvel-lous). Could the dinosaurs in Spielberg's film be reflexive images of the power to create marvels of the art world of cinematic representation, as well as images of the apparently infinite power of the past?

The plot of both novel and film is an extrapolation of the thesis that DNA preserved in blood ingested by an insect preserved in amber might make it possible to re-grow dinosaurs. DNA is treated as a very material form of mechanism for maintaining connection with the past as if it were a kind of supermemory, although current science gives little support for this hypothesis, not least because DNA decays fairly rapidly, even under the most favourable preservation conditions, so that by about 100,000 years it is all gone. Recent popular interpretations of genetics that treat DNA as the real player in biological history help lend this signifier of memory a sufficient credibility to work as a plot device. Moreover, this basic premiss that the past endures in tangible germinal form ready to recreate itself carries a symbolic power whose visceral conviction far outweighs scientific probability. The movie was one of the most success-ful of all time thanks to the subliminal power of the temporal fantasy that such acts represent, which Crichton had cleverly identified at work in the contemporary cultural obsession with dinosaurs, as much as the visual thrill of the animatronic predator Tyrannosaurus Rex's predilection for eating people in public. All the reconstructions point to an archaic belief that the past is not gone forever but could re-emerge from even the tiniest vestige of genetic memory and become a monster ready to consume us. The film, therefore, stages the recreation of the past, and shows that it cannot be contained within the limits of representation symbolised by the tourist park where the beasts are supposed to be safely constrained for the visitor to gaze upon. Instead the park's boundaries are breached and the troubleshooters have to go in and defeat the monsters. The dinosaur's scale is such that they dominate the visual field and the sound-track, and their oral ferocity enables them to consume people utterly. The very art of the cinema is shown to be capable of over-whelming our defences when it is in the service of the representation of the immensity of the past.

The only resolution possible is to use daring, courage and the heavy weaponry of our future-oriented technology against the monsters from history and wipe them out. There is no place for them in our world, not even in the supposedly safe haven of an island zoo, because these oral fantasies of being swallowed by the past are too powerful and too 'other' for negotiation to work. Spielberg had earlier combined similar fears about the power of the past to destroy us if allowed to erupt into present-day consciousness, with a more plausible historical narrative in the comic adventure film, *Raiders of the Lost Ark* (1981), set in the late 1930s. In this film, the rediscovered Ark of the Covenant turns out to have a monstrous appetite for consuming evil, somewhat stereotypically repre-sented in this film by scheming Nazis. The Ark is a more complex symbol than the dinosaurs, representing at once the bond with Yahweh, the history of the Jews and the ancient world of the Middle East; it destroys evil people by accelerating time so that whoever is touched by its forces turns suddenly old and then into a skeleton, as if they had been wrenched violently into the deadly past with mortal results. Complex it may be, but it carries such a weight of symbolism that this Tyrannosaurus Ark becomes silly, and unable to sustain its dual nature as a symbol of religious history and a ravening monster without violating the conven-tions of visual representation and the fairly plausible historical narrative. It is not surprising that Spielberg has a comic closure in which this most valuable of all historical artifacts is then boxed in an anonymous crate and last seen stored in a giant US government warehouse. America has annexed even this history and yet in the process has so neutralised it that its pastness has been lost. Or is the Ark waiting to be found once again, and will the whole cycle of myth and violence begin again?

It is hard not to think that the making and release of *Jurassic Park* just before he tackled the most difficult of all modern images of the past in his film *Schindler's List* (1993), was due as much to his sense of the danger of presenting this unbearable history, as to any need to make a box office hit in order to justify the obvious risk accompanying a Holocaust movie. *Schindler's List* dramatises what many survivors have called a war on memory, and has seemed to many postwar thinkers to be capable of consuming all attempts to represent and understand it. It was

perhaps not surprising that the head of Walt Disney studic
Spielberg's film about the Holocaust, by apparently uncoi
ing to *Jurassic Park*: 'At a moment in time, it is going to r
the dark side, and do it in a way in which, whenever t
monster is lurking somewhere, this movie is going to
again'.[59] Quite what he meant by pressing it down is no
willingness to accept Spielberg's cinematic treatment of the past as a
monster is evident. Spielberg himself appears to have seen his task in
Schindler's List as the overcoming of viewers' resistance to the depiction
of this history as a problem of technique: 'I didn't say I'm going to use a
lot of handheld camera. I simply tried to pull the events closer to the
audience by reducing the artifice'.[60] *Jurassic Park* is a crude narrative, and
not what is ordinarily meant by an historical novel (or movie), although
it dramatises the fear that the past might devour the present with great
emotional power. What is missing, of course, is any insight into what
constitutes those fears, and therefore how the fearful might begin to
work through their fantasies towards greater understanding, rather than
trying to annihilate a symbol of the terror.

The belief that the past has disappeared is the obverse of the fear
that the successfully repressed past will return as a terrifying present; the
dead past is the antithesis of the fantasy that memory will project itself
forward into reality and ontologise itself. Both the fear of loss and the
fear that it is not lost enough are structures of fantasy which offer ideological energy to everyone trying to locate a past for the future of their
bewildering present. One novel which shows remarkable insight into
these problems of how to challenge the teratoid past, a novel with affinities to *Charlotte Gray*, is Toni Morrison's *Beloved*, which has become one
of the most lionised of all contemporary novels, not least for the way it
acknowledges this fear of being swallowed up by the horrors of the
past.[61] Unlike the movie or even Faulks's novel, it manages the
extremely difficult task of working through the fears and resistances of
the reader towards the traumas of history, by showing the reader stage by
stage how to recover a traumatic history through increasingly demanding
modes of attention to the after-effects and responsibilities of its suffering.

As most readers will know, it tells the story of the recovery of
memory and confrontation with an impossibly painful past by an escaped
slave, Sethe, who had murdered her own daughter to prevent their
owner from recapturing her and the child and taking them back to servi-
tude. The traumatic events of the slave farm are shown in long retrospect
from a time many years after the murder, and the novel is consequently
cast in the tense of a concern with memory and loss, both given eerily
tangible form as the apparently resurrected daughter, Beloved, who
appears one day from nowhere and moves into Sethe's house. She grad-

lly consumes all the life from her mother, who literally wastes away as the spectral daughter fattens, and only disappears again when Sethe attempts to kill another white man whom she believes has come to take Beloved away. The past is shown as a daughter returned from the dead demanding impossible emotional reparations, because Morrison portrays the traumas of slavery as damage to the psychological foundations of the everyday sense of the past, especially as this manifests itself in a pathological tie between mother and child. Incarnating history in tangible form as Beloved means that within the conventions of fiction it can be gendered, given rudimentary self-consciousness ('she had two dreams: exploding and being swallowed'), and form relations with others.

Morrison's embodiment of the past creates plot improbabilities that are not absurd in the manner of the Ark that consumes people, but still pose problems of representation. Beloved is both a flesh-and-blood person and a ghost, an instability which threatens the novel's important claim to historical verisimilitude in its treatment of slavery. The revenant daughter's apparent ability to starve the woman she claims is her mother, as if sucking all the nourishment from her, has an almost vampiric action that the narrative does not fully explain. Embodiment of the unbearable past of the middle passage, slavery and violence, as a person, almost overwhelms the woman who bears this symbolic burden, even given the generic borrowings from the contemporary horror novel, and threatens that generic collapse and narrative turbulence that we saw in Spielberg's *Raiders of the Lost Ark*. Morrison's novel contains this disturbance in part by enacting a training in the development of a historical understanding for the reader, who is also drawn into collusion about the mystery of Beloved's origins. Believing that the girl is the ghost of the murdered child is to collude in an avoidance of historical work that the novel wishes to demonstrate, but this demonstration will only work if the reader does first enter into this magical view of the past. Only by believing that the past could rear up and return like the dinosaurs out of DNA, can the reader become a historian of the atrocities and lasting effects of slavery, but only by giving up this belief in magic afterwards can this past begin to become a resource for the present.

The novel places anamnesis, or what its central character calls in her pre-Freudian discourse, 'rememory', at the heart of the narrative, and most accounts of the novel see little difficulty in translating the work of memory into the psychoanalytic world of its future. This is certainly a novel that owes much to the culture of traumatic memory, yet its relation to the reader depends on a wider field of hermeneutic action than this unacknowledged futurisation of the novel recognises. Morrison's novel is didactic in its treatment of the problem of the simultaneous fear of loss and resurrection of the past, in a manner that is only more thorough and more firmly based in hermeneutic theory, than most of its counterparts. It shares a belief expressed by E. L. Doctorow, in the need to articulate lost histories in order to make a radical politics possible:

> Well, first of all, history as written by historians is clearly insufficient. And the historians are the first to express skepticism over the 'objectivity' of the discipline. A lot of people discovered after World War II and in the fifties that much of what was taken by the younger generation as history was highly interpreted history. ... And it turned out that there were not only individuals but whole peoples whom we had simply written out of our history – black people, Chinese people, Indians. At the same time, there is so little a country this size has in the way of cohesive, identifying marks that we can all refer to and recognize each other from. It turns out that history, as insufficient and poorly accommodated as it may be, is one of the few things we have in common here. I happen to think that there's enormous pressure on us all to become as faceless and peculiarly indistinct and compliant as possible. In that case, you see, the need to find color or definition becomes very, very strong. For all of us to read about what happened to us fifty or a hundred years ago suddenly becomes an act of community.[62]

Morrison is less confident that such a reading will just happen. *Beloved* shows that she believes the cultural text has to train its audience in historical understanding to some extent in order to work with the resistances we have already seen. In the case of *Beloved*, which is concerned with a passage of American history that collective memory finds extremely difficult and national history often ignores, this need to work with the reader is even more pronounced.

Morrison's text, therefore, offers its unfolding memory as a history of a past that cannot simply be narrated in an objective mode without omitting all that is most significant to understanding its power over the present. The question that the text wants the reader to ask, is how to read to remember this textual memory of a passage of American history which still shapes contemporary culture and politics. Sethe's long and difficult experience of recovering the memories of her husband and her own murderousness towards her baby, is meant to exemplify for the reader their own necessary orientation towards the past as a trial of the subjectivity of the present. One way that Morrison does this is to offer different forms of relationship as examples of different attitudes to the past. The most salient of these is the nearly fatal absorption by the past represented by the seemingly reincarnated baby, Beloved, whose danger lies in the way she seems to so fully embody the past that Sethe does not need to undergo the rigors of understanding it. '"Thank God I don't have to rememory or say a thing", thinks Sethe, "because you know it. All".'[63] The novel shows that the past cannot be taken for granted in this way. Neither the amnesia which has dominated the house for years and driven away Sethe's boys, nor this assumption that the past is so well embodied and present to the world that it does not need to be made conscious and articulate will suffice. Immediately after thinking that Beloved knows the past, Sethe's interior monologue begins to remember the past anyway, as if safe in the assumption that to do so is merely to immerse herself further in Beloved's encompassing memorial subjectivity, rather than to begin the difficult work of a talking cure with a person who may bear the transference but remains apart from it. Such passages place the reader in an impossible position, not sure whether these words are spoken or thought, not sure whether they place the reader in the position of Beloved attending to Sethe, and not sure what kind of anamnesic process this might be. Only by experiencing these uncertainties will the reader be ready to recognise the need for other forms of historical knowledge than such comforting immersion. How can something as intangible as a different stance towards knowledge of the past be rendered in a novel? The novel's answer is to show them as forms of relationship.

We can see what this entails by comparing the incremental stages of historical awareness with those proposed by the German philosopher Hans Georg Gadamer, in his major work on hermeneutics, *Truth and Method*.[64] His aim is to 'understand what the human sciences truly are',[65] but in order to do this he has to show how important it is to grasp the importance of historical understanding for the human sciences (which would include literary and cultural studies). Although he articulates the problem as 'a state of constant overstimulation of our historical consciousness',[66] this ambiguous adjective 'overstimulation' could be describing the contradictory affects of loss and fear that we have been tracing in recent debates about history. His answer is to think of history not as objective knowledge independent of individual perspective, but as a form of interaction. History, he argues, can be likened to different degrees of reflexivity and intersubjectivity active in ordinary relationships. Although he congregates them into three different intellectual positions that might actually co-exist, he describes them with a definite sense of incremental progression that is extremely illuminating for a reading of historical fiction that attempts to transform the reader's awareness.

One evasive way of reading Morrison's novel, especially for a white reader, would be to treat it as information about an alien race in a past also wholly alien to her or himself because it is now over and done with, and because, as people say, 'we have moved on'. The novel offers a damning judgement of such resistance to complicity and interdependence on this earlier world. Such a view assumes that the past of slavery and reconstruction can be fully comprehended objectively through the intellect, with the aim of tracing out and understanding its local features, its morality, science and general culture. The novel implies that doing so may actually reproduce the internal ethic of slavery, which also depended on a disjuncture between the respective histories of white and coloured peoples. According to Gadamer, the most rudimentary historical method merely tries to understand the past, in the same way that a person might try to cognize what is typical of another person in order to predict their behaviour, as if they had no more emotional or moral claim on us than does an object of scientific study. One of Sethe's more unbearable memories unfolds as she ruminates on the past with Beloved, and she recalls how deeply shocked she was when she overheard the slaveowner they called Schoolteacher teaching his boys about slavery, and using Sethe as an example: 'I told you to put her human characteristics on the left; her animal ones on the right'.[67] The slaveowner's attitude corresponds to what Gadamer calls a denial of 'the continuing action of tradition, in which he himself has his historical reality'.[68] This might seem surprising since the slaveowners constantly invoked tradition to support their right to enslave Africans. Tradition has a special meaning for Gadamer, however, and he does not intend it to mean a conservative ensemble of habits, beliefs, hierarchies and authority which comprise an ideology that supports the status quo (although some of his critics are sceptical that tradition can ever be much more than a form of historical inertia). In this discussion, Gadamer is talking about what Paul Ricoeur suggests we might better think of as 'traditionality', the idea of a past that is neither finished with nor simply an extension of the present, but rather 'a process of mediation' based on a continuing re-interpretation of the past which acknowledges its effects on the present.[69] Schoolteacher's assessment of Sethe's use of the hacksaw on her own daughter acknowledges no connection between his past and hers. The killing of the baby was 'all testimony to the results of a little so-called freedom imposed on people who needed every care and guidance in the world to keep them from the cannibal life they preferred'.[70]

A second way of reading the book would seem at first to be the best way of approaching the past. This would not be tourism or scientific detachment, but the attempt to live there and live as its inhabitants do, to read with as much identification and imaginative immersion as possible. Gadamer likens such an historicism to a relationship in which each person tries to 'understand the other better than the other understands himself'. This sounds attractive until Gadamer points out that the consequence is likely to be a deadly struggle for mutual recognition of the kind that Hegel outlined in his master/slave dialectic in *The Phenomenology of*

Spirit, about which Gadamer wrily comments that at least there is a 'genuine dialectical relationship' between master and slave. The would-be historian who tries to step wholly outside her or his own spacetime, and comprehend the uniqueness of a past world with complete objectivity, lacks even this stunted dialectic because she or he behaves like a person whose relation to the other is entirely self-centred, not submitting themselves to any of the demands of the relationship, whatever their good intentions. 'A person who reflects himself out of the mutuality of such a relation changes this relationship and destroys its moral bond. A person who reflects himself out of a living relationship to tradition destroys the true meaning of this tradition in exactly the same way'.[71] This might be a description of the slavery practised by the 'good' slave-owners, the Garners, who preceded Schoolteacher. Mrs Garner talks to Sethe like a friend, yet treats Sethe's desire to marry a fellow farm slave, Halle, as an absurd desire for a slave. Sethe's own treatment of the daughter she killed to protect her from a future of slavery, is also a denial of mutuality which helps destroy the moral bond preventing murder. Beloved's treatment of her adoptive mother is the most powerful version of this understanding of the past. Throughout the novel it is repeatedly stressed that Sethe finds a perfect understanding in the revenant daughter, who provides the occasion for much of the novel's narrative of life at Sweet Home, especially the recovery of the memories of what exactly went wrong with the planned escape, and this perfect understanding gives Beloved extraordinary power over Sethe, as if Beloved were re-enacting this dominant, liberal historicism. By doing 'blindly what the other desires', and telling the stories that Beloved desperately wants to hear, because they affirm her identification with the past, as Sethe does, she actually perpetuates her own subservience. Gadamer aptly says: 'we call such a person a slave'.[72]

What then is the reader supposed to do with the past, how learn about it, remember it, articulate it, and yet avoid becoming simply its master or its slave? The novel struggles with this and barely manages to represent what Gadamer calls the third, hermeneutic mode of historical understanding, which he describes as being like a relationship of mutuality, in which the self listens to the other with an openness that is ready to respond with change, and expects the other to do likewise. The reader is expected to be affected by the past, letting the past be active in the present, while not giving up as Sethe does, at least for a while, her or his own present-day boundaries to simply merge with the past. Plot is the main vehicle for demonstrating this third relation to the past. When Sethe's daughter Denver goes off at the end of the novel to find work, she does so with a new sense of self, of 'having a self to look out for and preserve',[73] and is only able to gain work from the white patrons who have allowed Sethe to live in their house, by telling the story of Sethe and Beloved to the Bodwin's servant, Janey Wagon. Denver's action tells the reader that this past must be taken into the present and future. The consequences of Denver's action eventually lead to Beloved's expulsion. As a result of her plea for help, the community learns about the desperate situation and Ella takes charge, deciding to chase out the dangerous 'something-or-other' that is draining the life out of Sethe, because she 'didn't like the idea of past errors taking possession of the present'. There has been enough anamnesis. The convergence of Denver's new white employer, Mr Bodwin, and the African-American women on the house, Sethe's belief that Schoolteacher is coming for her again and her attempt to kill him, the rescue and the cathartic expulsion of Beloved who disappears now that Sethe's rage is directed outwards at the white world, all try to project a new way of thinking of the past. Yet this remains hard to articulate in the novel, and there is only a brief explicit glimpse of this mode of living with the past evident when we are shown Sethe listening to her lover and fellow survivor of the slave farm, Paul D, tell her: 'Sethe ... me and you, we got more yesterday than anybody. We need some kind of tomorrow ... You your best thing, Sethe'.[74] By saying that they have both 'got more yesterday than anybody', and also that she is her own 'best thing', he articulates the insight that she can be affected by her past, know it and yet allow it sufficient distance so that her present and future maintain some autonomy too. This new relationship to self and past will also be embodied in their relationship if she is willing, and this new relationship will help exemplify a sustaining relation to the past of slavery. As a different model of the relation to the past, this poignant moment projects the possibility of a transformation from enslavement by traumatic memory into a hermeneutic freedom of knowledge.

Morrison's novel subtly shows the self-conscious anguish that different relations to the past and its joys and horrors embody in practice. Gadamer's rhetorically anodyne appeal to the past as 'tradition' is given a necessary terror in the words of Sethe's mother-in-law: 'not a house in the country ain't packed to its rafters with some dead Negro's grief'.[75] The novel also struggles with the limits of the genre of realist, historical fiction, which creates problems of representation for this narrative of historical education. Realism demands that events are witnessable, that subjective experience is narratable as free indirect discourse and nameable emotions, and that complex social processes can be represented by specific individuals and incidents. Since the novel is committed to the belief that freedom from the past requires a hermeneutic historicism, and that such responsiveness and fusion of the horizons of past and present can only be achieved through transference and a narrative which works through repression and forgetting, it has to stage the process as an actual interaction. Beloved is a convenient interlocutor to whom Sethe can explain her past and undergo the talking cure, but this creates a problem that the novel is honest enough to allow to show up as a disturbance of realism caused by the presence of a revenant. Once a reader wonders whether talking to a liminal figure like Beloved could really be sufficient to transform Sethe, and asks what kind of complicity the narrative standpoint is offering (since it is written as if Beloved were an actual, responsive adult who is also the dead baby), the novel reaches its limits. The final question the novel asks of its readers is why the depiction of the past of slavery, and the possibility of recovery from its hold over the memory and temporal situation of its survivors, requires the distortion of realism that brings in a gothic character like Beloved. Is it realism, or the theory of therapeutic memory, or simply the trauma of slavery itself that exceeds representation?

These problems are not confined to Morrison's novel. We shall argue that they help account for the dispersal of historiographic writing into literary genres other than the historical novel, and into areas of fiction that are not usually considered historical.

In this chapter we have seen in the work of novelists, historians and cultural theorists that there is a widespread sense that the past has changed, but considerable disagreement as to whether it has mutated, become foreign, dangerous, been murdered or lost all its power and become a treasury of souvenirs, a heritage park and a spectacle for the time travel of modern knowledge. We are left with a number of questions. Is this the result of the expansion of historical scholarship, the use of nostalgia and tradition by the leisure industries who commodify the past? Is it the result of rapid social and economic change which sweeps away the structures of social memory? Is it due to a loss of belief in public and national narratives of the past accompanying the growth of cultures of autobiography? Is it the result of a failure of history and cultural texts to mediate between the interests in history promoted by institutions and the intimate concerns with the past of the mass of people interested in everyday investigations of the past that intersects with them? Is there a structure of fantasy and desire at work in which the past threatens to engulf the adult self with its regressive longings or guilts at primal crimes? How much are these changes simply a part of all historical process whereby each generation lives in a world precipitated from the labours of earlier ones and is, therefore, different even in relatively static societies? What, in other words, is distinctive about these changes in the past other than an alteration of the furniture and style? Recent research and debate in literary and cultural studies has considered these questions primarily through theories of postmodernism or theories of trauma. We shall discuss these later in Chapters two and three. We shall argue that these discussions need to be placed alongside another set of discussions which have been taking place elsewhere – in anthropology, geography, philosophy and sociology – about the nature of time and space in twentieth-century thought and society. The temporality and spaces of postmodernism and memory derive from a dialectic of scientific and social developments whose implications are still emerging.

Notes

1 Sebastian Faulks, Charlotte Gray (London: Vintage, 1999), p. 333.
2 Linda Hutcheon, The Politics of Postmodernism (London: Routledge, 1989), p. 55.
3 Faulks, Charlotte Gray, p. 153.
4 Hutcheon, The Politics of Postmodernism, p. 54.
5 Faulks, Charlotte Gray, p. 460.
6 Hutcheon, The Politics of Postmodernism, p. 70.
7 David Lowenthal, The Past is a Foreign Country (Cambridge: Cambridge University Press, 1985), p. xvii; Daniel Boorstin, 'The enlarged contemporary', The Listener, 11 December 1975, pp. 786–9, 787.
8 Neil McEwan, Perspective in British Historical Fiction Today (Wolfeboro, NH: Longwood Academic, 1987), p. 9.
9 Lowenthal, The Past is a Foreign Country, p. 412.
10 Eric Hobsbawm, Age of Extremes: The Short Twentieth Century 1914–1991 (London: Michael Joseph, 1994), p. 3.
11 Michael Kammen, Mystic Chords of Memory: The Transformation of Tradition in American Culture (New York: Alfred A. Knopf, 1991), p. 534.
12 Jean Baudrillard, Selected Writings, ed. Mark Poster (Cambridge: Polity Press, 1988), p. 191.
13 Jean Baudrillard, Simulations, trans. Paul Foss et al. (New York: Semiotexte, 1983), pp. 19–26.
14 Fredric Jameson, Postmodernism, or, The Cultural Logic of Late Capitalism (London: Verso, 1991), p. 18.
15 Ibid., p. 18.
16 Ibid., p. 309.
17 ibid., p. 361.
18 Ibid., p. 44.
19 Andreas Huyssen, 'Anselm Kiefer: The terror of history, the temptation of myth', Twilight Memories: Marking Time in a Culture of Amnesia (New York: Routledge, 1995), p. 211.
20 Michel Foucault, The Order of Things: An Archaeology of the Human Sciences (London: Tavistock, [1966] 1970), p. 219.
21 Ibid., p. 219.
22 Michel Foucault, 'Truth and Power', in Michel Foucault, Power/Knowledge: Selected Interviews and Other Writings 1972–1977, ed. Colin Gordon (New York: Pantheon Books, 1980), p. 115.
23 Ibid., p. 114.
24 Michel Foucault, The Archaeology of Knowledge (London: Tavistock, 1972), p. 12.
25 Ibid., p. 14.
26 Roy Rosenzweig and David Thelen, The Presence of the Past: Popular Uses of History in American Life (New York: Columbia University Press, 1998), p. 9.
27 Ibid.
28 Ibid., p. 6.

29 Ibid., p. 12.

30 Ibid.

31 Ibid., p. 24.

32 Ibid., p. 178.

33 Ibid., p. 115.

34 Ibid., p. 116

35 Ibid., p. 153.

36 Ibid., p. 167.

37 Ibid., p. 180.

38 Ibid., p. 20.

39 James Cameron, Preface to Tom Kuntz (ed.), *The Titanic Disaster Hearings: The Official Transcripts of the 1912 Senate Investigation* (New York: Pocket Books, 1998), p. xiv.

40 Linda Hutcheon, 'The pasttime of past time: Fiction, history, historiographic metafiction', in Michael J. Hoffman and Patrick D. Murphy (eds), *Essentials of the Theory of Fiction*, 2nd edn (London: Leicester University Press, 1996), pp. 474–95, 485.

41 George Lipsitz, *Time Passages: Collective Memory and American Popular Culture* (Minneapolis: University of Minnesota Press, 1990), p. 36.

42 Ibid., p. 231.

43 Angus Calder, *The People's War: Britain 1939–1945* (London: Panther, [1969] 1971), p. 17. In practice, the facts and the myths are almost impossible to disentangle. His dry comment that 'to judge from certain versions of the blitz, it was a mean and pusillanimous Londoner indeed who did not emerge from the debris with a wisecrack on his lips' (p. 217), and the many different memories of life underground during the bombing, ranging from the young Bernard Kops's anarchic fascination with weighing machines and the mysteries of the tunnels, to Richie Calder's recollection of an underground shelter at Stepney where an optician, Mickey Davis, had set up a democratic committee to run it, are indicative of the tensions in the material.

44 Raphael Samuel, *Theatres of Memory: Volume I: Past and Present in Contemporary Culture* (London: Verso, 1994), p. 25.

45 Ibid., p. 8.

46 Hobsbawm, *Age of Extremes*, pp. 3–4.

47 Ibid., p. 4.

48 Laura Marcus, *Auto/biographical Discourses: Criticism, Theory, Practice* (Manchester: Manchester University Press, 1994), p. 261 *passim*.

49 William James, 'Postscript', in *The Varieties of Religious Experience: A Study in Human Nature*, ed. Martin E. Marty (London: Penguin, 1982), p. 526.

50 Henry Louis Gates Jr, *Colored People* (New York: Alfred Knopf, 1994), p. 201.

51 Ibid., p. 216.

52 Ibid., p. xi.

53 Anne Michaels, *Fugitive Pieces* (London: Bloomsbury, [1996] 1998), p. 52.

54 Ibid., pp. 266–7.

55 Thomas Pynchon, *The Crying of Lot 49* (London: Picador, 1979).

56 Stephen Jay Gould, 'Dinomania', in *Dinosaur in a Haystack* (London: Penguin, 1997), p. 223.

57 Robert Smithson, 'A museum of language in the vicinity of art' (1968), in *The Writings of Robert Smithson*, ed. Nancy Holt (New York: New York University Press, 1979), p. 72.

58 Ibid., p. 73.

59 Jeffrey Kalzenberg, cited in Stephen Schiff, 'Seriously Spielberg', *The New Yorker*, 21 March, 1994, collected in Thomas Fensch (ed.), *Oskar Schindler and his List* (Forest Dale, VT: Paul S. Eriksson, 1995), p. 146.

60 David Ansen, 'Spielberg's obsession', in Fensch, *Oskar Schindler*, p. 58.

61 Toni Morrison, *Beloved* (London: Picador, 1988).

62 E. L. Doctorow, in Richard Trenner (ed.), *E. L. Doctorow: Essays and Conversations* (Princeton: Ontario Review Press, 1983), pp. 58–9.

63 Morrison, *Beloved*, p. 191.

64 Hans-Georg Gadamer, *Truth and Method* (1965; London: Sheed and Ward, 1979).

65 Ibid., p. xiii.

66 Ibid., p. xiv.

67 Morrison, *Beloved*, p. 193.

68 Gadamer, *Truth and Method*, p. 322.

69 Paul Ricoeur, *Time and Narrative*, trans. Kathleen Blamey and David Pellauer (Chicago: University of Chicago Press, 1988), p. 220. Ricoeur contrasts two visions of the past: finished and inaccessible, or still active within the present. 'Uncrossable distance or annulled distance, this seems to be the dilemma. But traditionality designates the dialectic between remoteness and distanciation, and makes time, in Gadamer's words, "the supportive ground of the process in which the present is rooted"' (Gadamer, *Truth and Method*, p. 264).

70 Morrison, *Beloved*, p. 151.

71 Gadamer, *Truth and Method*, p. 324.

72 Ibid.

73 Morrison, *Beloved*, p. 252.

74 Ibid., p. 273.

75 Ibid., p. 5.

CHAPTER 2

The ethics of historical fiction

In the first chapter we asked what contribution literature had made to the ordinary understanding of history in everyday life since the Second World War. How had it responded to the widespread sense that contemporary Western culture is liable to historical amnesia or a paralysing fear of the return of the past? Was literature partly the cause of the problem, providing substitute fantasies of the past and offering easy access to it, or was literature actually attempting to renegotiate the terms of social memory in some way? Novelists committed to the rewriting of history have been keenly aware of the resistance to what they do. Morrison's *Beloved* ends with a single phrase repeated twice – 'It was not a story to pass on' – and then altered a third time – 'This is not a story to pass on' – as if the injunction were still active. Her own novel is a refusal to heed this commonsense wisdom of the African-American community; she not only transmits this memory, she gives it textual form. The entire structure and style of the book demonstrate the difficulty of constructing this textual memory in the face of the desire to 'disremember' the past by *actively* forgetting it, and the uncertainty about both how to locate the past and then how to reach it. She has to work through new models of memory, and rethink the location of the past in time and space, because the late twentieth century now experiences the past differently – time, space and memory have all changed.

Most of the texts we have discussed so far have been historical novels. Despite the revival of interest in historical drama in the 1960s and 1970s in Britain, and the persistent interest in history among some modernist and postmodernist poets, historical fiction has dominated the field of historical literature. The novel is still popularly believed to be the best textual means of re-enacting the past; its full use of the capacity of narrative to show the effects of time on identity and consciousness enables the reader to inhabit a past world and understand the thoughts, feelings and actions of those who lived in a completely different environment. For some writers and readers, realism has become too conservative to be adequate to political aspirations. For much of the postwar period, narrative has appeared as a compromised literary form because of its collaboration with a realism that concealed the degree to which its solidities were social constructions, and coercively presented history as a continuum uniting all peoples and events in its development from past to present.

Postmodernism has presented itself as both critique and solution to these limitations. More a theory of the past than the present or future, postmodernity, contrary to modernity's conception of the past as a 'single history', now replaces such 'grand narratives' with 'local knowledges', and calls into doubt the ineluctable progress of 'reason'. The association of reason with 'rationalisation' and with the progress of humanity has lost much of its persuasiveness after Auschwitz and Hiroshima, and prompted a new turn to the many lost 'archipelagos' of the past. Postmodernity represents itself as the leading resistance to the hegemonic history that buried these narratives under a false coherence. Its continuing importance lies partly in this loud cultural advertisement for diversity and incommensurability. The contexts and totemic meanings from which our collective consciousness of the past emerges are no longer the result of singular, homogeneous narratives, and they arise at sites that are far from unified: they are conflictual spaces and symbolic ruptures in society; textual memories are polyvalent and polysemic practices that draw upon the resources of many different cultural myths for a plurality of ideological and political purposes.

In this chapter we shall look more closely at theories and practices of modern historical fiction to see how its realism represents the past, before considering the challenge of postmodernism. Despite its preoccupation with history and the changing temporality of the past, it has been unable to rethink fully the changes in time, space and memory which have made the past vanish or turn dangerous. The impact of science on social time and the politics and poetics of memory, have eluded its antifoundationalism. We shall argue that it is not directly postmodern theories of history and the past which prove most useful for understanding the history in contemporary literature, but the postmodernist renewal of an ethics of history. Postmodernist theory has been slow to recognise the significance of research into memory, time and space in other disciplines; ethics rather than new epistemologies and ontologies are its greatest contribution to our enquiry.

Both Sebastian Faulks's novel, *Charlotte Gray*, and Toni Morrison's *Beloved*, demonstrate the tensions which beset the genre of historical fiction. Although such historical novels are usually categorised as literary, they also enjoy large popular audiences and display an authorial willingness to write for the reader without specialist knowledge of the past leading to a complicated relation between the use of folk knowledge of the past and the research of professional historians. As we saw in Chapter I, even ordinary readers mistrust the novelisation of fact, although it is the use of invention which helps these novels gain large readerships. The novels have to look both ways at once, claiming to present truths about the past and working hard to ensure the appearance of verisimilitude, while borrowing ahistorical, generic elements from the romance or the ghost story. Even postmodern historical fiction remains beholden to these contradictory conditions. One reason for their persistence is the conceptual framework applied to historical fiction which has its roots in a philosophical tradition that can be traced back to Hegel and has recently been given a brilliant recapitulatory synthesis in Paul Ricoeur's *Time and Narrative*. Narrative is believed by this tradition to be the foundation of textual memory. The problem, as we shall see, is the relation between narrative and different literary genres. Narrative is often conflated with fiction, instead of being followed out into the many different literary forms it can take. This has sometimes led to the neglect of other literary genres which have picked up narrative signals from hitherto suppressed or non-textual pasts and begun mapping them out in modes that can look very different from the conventional historical novel, however metafictional. But this is to look ahead. For now we will concentrate on one of the most brilliant of these new metafictional histories and its challenge to the critical orthodoxies surrounding historical fiction.

Postmodernism and historical fiction

The largest compound in Amritsar is called Jallianwala Bagh. ... On April 13th, many thousands of Indians are crowding through this alleyway. 'It is a peaceful protest,' someone tells Doctor Aziz. Swept along by the crowds, he arrives at the mouth of the alley. ... Brigadier R. E. Dyer arrives at the entrance to the alleyway, followed by fifty crack troops. He is Martial Law Commander of Amritsar. ... As Brigadier Dyer issues a command the sneeze hits my grandfather full in the face. 'Yaaaaakh-*thoooo*!' he sneezes and falls forward, losing his balance ... There is a noise like teeth chattering in winter and someone falls on him. Red stuff stains his shirt. There are screams now and sobs and the strange chattering continues. More and more people seem to have stumbled and fallen on top of my grandfather. ... Brigadier Dyer's fifty men put down their machine-guns and go away. They have fired a total of one thousand six hundred and fifty rounds into the unarmed crowd. Of these, one thousand five hundred and sixteen have found their mark, killing or wounding some person (our ellipses).[1]

This is an account of the infamous 1919 Amritsar Massacre, in the Punjab, India, when General Dyer killed 380 of Mahatma Ghandi's followers, taken from Salman Rushdie's prize-winning novel, *Midnight's Children* (1980). It is told from the immediate perspective of Dr Aadam Aziz, the grandfather of the novel's protagonist, Saleem Sinai. The novel also narrates a number of other significant events from the history of India in the twentieth century, notably the rift between Hindus and Moslems leading to Partition in 1947 to form India and Pakistan, and the troubles in Kashmir province. These features might make it seem to be an historical novel of the kind described by Avrom Fleishman, who argues in his influential study, *The English Historical Novel* (1971), that there is broad agreement about the distinguishing features of the historical novel: it is set at least two generations in the past; includes actual historical events and figures; and tries to convey 'the feeling of how it was to be alive in another age' through the perspective of specific participants.[2] Dyer's presence in the same sentence with the big sneeze seems to make at least this section of Rushdie's novel qualify on all these counts, even though it is by common consent an archetypal example of postmodernist culture, and postmodernism is widely believed to be antipathetic to both history and realism. The paradox diminishes, however, when we consider the manner in which Fleishman goes on to summarise what is best in historical fiction:

> The historical novelist writes trans-temporally: he is rooted in the history of his own time and yet can conceive another. In ranging back into history he discovers not merely his own origins but his historicity, his existence as a historical being. What makes a historical novel historical is the active presence of a concept of history as a shaping force – acting not only upon the characters in the novel but on the author and readers outside it. In the course of reading, we find that the protagonists of such novels confront not only the forces of history of their own time, but its impact on life in any time. The universal conception of the individual's career as fate becomes symbolized not by the gods but by history.[3]

Everything about this passage now reads like a summary of what postmodernist thought has opposed: universal human values and essences; a reified and teleological history; and an endorsement of the unifying power of consciousness. Most self-avowed postmodernist commentators dismiss empirical history and its claims to realism and truth, pointing to the ideological investments in the construction of the past that undermine claims to neutrality, the persistent assumption of teleological continuities that ultimately justify the position of the historian and the ideology behind her or him, and to the textuality of the past that subordinates historical knowledge to the textual condition and makes objectivity a positivist illusion. A postmodernist, historical novel appears to be a paradox, unless we either jettison the postmodernist critique of history, or discard historical accuracy as an impossibility – an oppressive ideological fiction designed to legitimate existing power by concealing the artifice of certitude. Or is there another way of maintaining the historicity of the historical novel without the unwanted model of history and consciousness, as some critics have argued? Is it possible to disengage Fleishman's self-evident characteristics of historical fiction from these other universalist models of history and consciousness?

Historical fiction has never attracted much critical interest. This is probably due to several factors: its suspect popularity; what Dean Rehberger calls its 'utility' as a source of historical knowledge for the ordinary reader[4]; and its epistemological hybridity.[5] This is a type of novel which cannot claim the artistic autonomy of most literary genres, because readers expect a considerable degree of verisimilitude and historical accuracy, which makes it dependent on an external knowledge of the past. It is, therefore, always required to subordinate imagination, the play of the signifier, unity or textuality, to the final authority of historical realism. It is also, as most of its critics point out, hard to categorise because it is not primarily defined by its form or method of presentation. Its content or referentiality is what marks it out. This lack of critical interest means that contemporary discussion of the historical novel still takes place in the long shadow of Georg Lukács's classic study of nineteenth-century realism, *The Historical Novel* (1937). Lukács maintained that the greatest writers, like Balzac, Tolstoy and Scott, are those who can bring the complexities of society into a totality in the novel, thus combating the alienation and fragmentation so endemic to capitalist society. Only this 'historical realism' can bring together the most historically significant and progressive perspectives, linking the individual to the social whole, thus laying bare the society's inner structure and dynamic. According to Lukács, it is the unique property of the realist novel that it alone can flesh out such skeletal forces:

> The historical novel therefore has to *demonstrate* by *artistic* means that historical circumstances and characters existed in precisely such and such a way. . . . a total historical picture depends upon a rich and graded interaction between different levels of response to any major disturbance of life. It must disclose artistically the *connexion* between the spontaneous reaction of the masses and the historical consciousness of the leading personalities.
>
> Such connexions are of decisive importance for the understanding of history. . . .
>
> The great historical figure, as a minor character, is able to live himself out to the full as a human being, to display freely all his splendid and petty human qualities. However, his place in the action is such that he can only act and express himself in situations of historical importance.

He achieves here a many-sided and full expression of his personality, but only in so far as it is linked with the big events of history (our ellipses).[6]

Historical realism in novels has, therefore, been regarded as the pre-eminent mode of history in literature. When critics have demurred from the definitions offered by Lukács and Fleishman, it has usually been in the cause of an extension of the genre to include historical novels about contemporary life (Rushdie's novel would be one of these in its later pages), or novels in which there are no actual historical personages at all. David Cowart says in *History and the Contemporary Novel* (1989): 'I myself prefer to define historical fiction simply and broadly as fiction in which the past figures with some prominence'.[7] This undemanding definition allows him to include a chapter on literary science fiction, arguing as we do later in this book, that it can be considered to be a form of historical fiction. His general assumption that some science fiction 'novelists address themselves to those broader events in the human aggregate that constitute history' when they 'imagine the way it will be', is persuasive, as is his statement that 'in fictions of this type, the future recapitulates the past or satirically mirrors the present'.[8] The problem, as we shall argue later, is that science fiction novels cannot be read in isolation from the entire genre and its reception history without losing sight of much of what is significant about its handling of the future. Neither can we simply say that historical literature includes the past, as if we knew what that was already, and what readers expect. For similar reasons, another critic attempting to produce some broad guidelines for what constitutes histor-ical fiction, Joseph W. Turner, suggests that we should think of three degrees of emphasis in historical fiction: 'those that invent a past, those that disguise a documented past, and those that re-create a documented past'.[9] These distinctions will not be entirely clear cut in practice – a single novel may employ all three techniques – neither will they be fully inherent in the texts themselves. It will be readers who draw these distinctions. He concludes, therefore, that historical fiction is at its best not, as Fleishman believed, when it is an articulation of universal truths in a local historical context, but when it offers a narrative 'which is ulti-mately about itself, about the meaning and making of history, about man's fate to live in history and his attempt to live in awareness of it.'

These under-theorised accounts of historical fiction assume a rela-tion to the recent past which creates a problem when applied to contemporary literature, because they do not reflect upon the disconti-nuities of modern history that have unfixed their own position within it. Cowart was writing when postmodernist theories of history and textual-ity were already becoming current, but like too many commentators he interprets the seeming paradox of the postmodernist historical novel as resulting from the alleged postmodern Midas touch of textuality: all reality has become a merely linguistic effect. He is willing to agree that 'an independent, objectively verifiable historical reality does not exist independently of the language with which one speaks', but then contradicts himself by insisting that 'the most reliable explorer of the past is the one best able to integrate facts into a living imagined reality'.[10] The recourse to the discourse of absolute facts is prompted by an intense ethical anxiety. He bases his resistance on the belief that an historical novelist ought to recognise a moral responsibility towards history, because this is a present that seems more than capable of destroying itself with nuclear weapons (he identifies a prospective temporal category for contemporary historical literature which he calls 'pre-apocalypse'), and we need to understand the past that made this present dilemma possible.[11] Approaching historical literature from the standpoint of ethics as well as epistemology holds out much more hope of recognising the complexities of the genre of realist historical fiction, and in addition, might offer clues as to where other historical practices might be active in non-realist fictions and other non-narrative literary genres. As Edward Soja says: 'It is precisely the critical and potentially emancipatory value of the historical imagination, of people "making history" rather than taking it for granted, that has made it so compulsively appealing.'[12] Non-realist genres often foreground their production as an analogue of such historical facture.

Cowart's study is devoted to the 'contemporary' novel. Terms such as 'contemporary', 'postwar', 'modern', 'postmodern', 'postcolonial' and 'twentieth century' are regularly used to describe 'recent' literature, and for most purposes they can be deployed without too much self-reflexiveness, but when applied to the texts whose relation to time and history is integral to their workings, certain problems emerge. These concepts are themselves theories of the relation of present to past, as well as historically specific to the period of time in which we live. Their implicit assumptions about temporality and pastness act as filters which only allow certain manifestations of the past to be evident. Before we can say more about the significance of postmodernist historical literature, we need to contrast the selective spectra of the different concepts of periodisation.

For the temporal logic of modernity, the 'contemporary' of a critic of ten years ago is no longer contemporary and, therefore, perhaps no longer modern, even though it is recent. Modernity is a temporalising of history by a logic of constant transformation whose implicit claim to have surpassed the traditions of past culture is constantly threatened by its identification of this achievement with the current moment – a moment which is always slipping away into that pre-modernist past, rendering the modernist culture itself pre-modern, and requiring continual novelty to sustain itself. The 'postwar', which seems almost as neutral as the term 'contemporary', also carries with it certain assumptions, as Barbara Adam points out: 'The present post-war period, for example, would cease to be the present only after some major social upheaval, affecting all other relations in such a fundamental way that the present could no longer be defined by the social turning point of World War II but by that new decisive focus'.[13] Postwar literature occurs in the future of a wartime that encompassed extraordinarily destructive human events – worldwide conflict and highly organised genocide – so the term carries with it an assumption that all subsequent literary themes and forms are shadowed by these horrors. The problem is not so much that the actual relation of the literature to the war varies widely in its degree of scarring and acknowledgement, as that the term tacitly assumes a fixed temporal relation with the calendar and thus obscures both other temporalities and, even more importantly, the possibilities of creating new histories and new pasts capable of founding emancipatory social change. It is for these reasons that the terms postcolonial and especially, postmodern, are significant. They foreground the problems of temporal relation much more openly.

In his wide-ranging critique of the concepts of time implicit in theories of the postmodern, Peter Osborne persuasively argues that postmodernism is a new awareness of the self-images of modernity in its cultures of modernism, rather than a new distinct chronological period. The common tendency to treat postmodernism as a chronological period is in part an attempt to evade this regressive temporal logic. The 'post' of 'postmodernism' alludes to the need to understand that modernism is a particular way of totalising history which the postmodern challenges. Postmodernism is really a sign of renewed debate about modernism's conception of time, history and the past, rather than either a new historical phase or a new theoretical perspective. He argues that what is needed is 'the development of new forms of dialectical thought, grounded in the immanent development of the time-consciousness of modernity itself', although he seems at times willing to leave room for poststructuralism as well, as long as it too practices a similar immanence, recognising its position as a Western practice.[14] Yet his conclusion is dismissive of postmodernism: 'To think "our present time in history", ... requires not the confusing novelty of the concept of the postmodern, but a rethinking of the dialectics of modernity as a structure of temporalization (the *historically* new) which inscribes the spatial logic of social differences into a totalization of historical time.'[15]

Novelty is often confusing, but this is no reason to exclude it. To do so might sustain a backward-looking conservatism, which is certainly a risk in literary studies. Osborne values the debates that postmodernism has helped foster, and such debate almost always begins with confusion, uncertainty and puzzlement. His objection is to the conceptual resources of the periodising itself, and with this we agree, but since postmodernism is not just a theory of history, but also a rethinking of what had seemed necessary foundations of reason and the subject as forms of Western privilege (which Osborne allows to be the value of poststructuralism), we believe it remains an important resource for the close study of the workings of literary texts themselves. We would argue that postmodernism remains useful for discussing history in recent literature because of this intersection of debates about the position and power of the present in time and space, with textual investigations of the resources of representation and narrative to re-imagine history. For the category of the postwar in literature, the past is all too easily recreated in all its monstrousness from the tiniest vestige, and the task of writers and readers is to mitigate this impact by recognition and understanding. Postmodernism seems to know that these monsters are also artifice, an animatronics of the signifier. 'Postwar' is an informal, untheorised label of convenience for aggregating works between particular dates under a melancholy threat of war; the postmodern has been an interpretative algorithm capable of inaugurating mourning and emancipation. Although Fredric Jameson, Jean-François Lyotard and other well-known promoters of the idea of the postmodern, have variously identified the new arts in both critical and celebratory terms ranging from a failure of historical consciousness symptomatised by a lack of temporal depth, to an abandonment of all metanarratives of historical development leading to the present, the idea of a renewed sense of the aftershocks and ethical projects of the past is a common theme.

For critics like Cowart, postmodernism appears to be a negative historicism whose anarchic epistemology is in need of the critical theory's compensatory re-historicism, but this assessment of postmodernist practice surely underestimates the ethical historicism of even the most salient and uncompromisingly postmodern works. The most famous of all postmodern fictions, *Gravity's Rainbow* (1973), is a historical novel about the Second World War, even if it is what Brian McHale (in his defining study of the postmodern novel) calls a 'paranoiac secret mode of history' uninterested in simply veracity.[16] Veridical it may not be (how could the banana breakfast or the dream detective, let alone all those astral figures, be 'real'?), but it is, in Ricoeur's words, 'moved by the desire to do justice to the past'.[17] A similar intention is evident in many other literary works which have been taken to represent postmodernist fiction.

McHale tries to explain the wildly inventive historicism that prompted the hostile critiques of postmodern fiction as the result of a new cultural imperative to call 'official history' into question, because understanding of the past has lost confidence in official versions, and the hegemonic institutions of public record have lost much of their legitimacy. We are all, he claims, no longer confident that 'the historical record reliably captured the experience of the human beings who really suffered and enacted history'.[18] The recent Norton anthology of *Postmodern American Poetry* (1994) lends support to this description of postmodernism, by opening with a poem by one of the first twentieth-century writers to use the term 'postmodern'. 'In Cold Hell, In Thicket' (1953) written by Charles Olson, is an account of a visit to the battlefield of Gettysburg, which likens the experience of visiting this place nearly one hundred years after it last saw battle to the condition of everyone faced with the destruction and ethical betrayals of the past, from the Holocaust back beyond the genocidal advent of Europeans in the Americas. The poem uses the war memorial that the battlefield has become to ask what possible relation to the histories and memorials of such destruction is possible today, and concludes that everything about history, time and space requires reassessment, when 'even forever wavers'.[19] The task of the postmodern historical novel would be to read between the wavering lines of history.

The new mistrust of official history that McHale believes can help explain the postmodern turn, was already there in modernist writing. What is new, is that this mistrust has itself undergone a postmodern turn into a more active reflection on the aesthetic and ethical consequences for the work of art, and this is especially evident in the art that first helped make postmodernism visible. Many of the most entrenched prejudices and principles of postmodernist cultural theory emerged from the highly visible urban architecture of postmodernism which seemed to many to signal not a new sense of the continuing force of past traditions but a failure of the historical sense. The problem of locating the past, of representing it with fidelity, of doing justice to the debts we still owe it are instructive for the reading of texts, because the public impact of these issues has meant that the debate moves beyond epistemological objections to the playfulness of postmodernist history to questions about the economics, politics and ethics of attempts to represent the past in social space. Reservations like Cowart's about the epistemological distortions of postmodernist historicising are magnified in the reception of postmodern buildings. Charles Newman, for example, stigmatised it as architectural tourism of history and a 'gesture of historical pathos without content; the restoration of historical images with no co-ordinates'.[20] Architectural postmodernism certainly might appear to encourage this conclusion with its willingness to mingle styles from Egypt, Greece and popular culture into postmodern façades for shopping centres. Almost any recent shopping centre will give you a taste of the ancient world and a few knowing references to the icons in the museum of cultural capital, behind the video monitors, potted plants and security guards in its air-conditioned environment. Is the historicist collage of architectural postmodernism and its verbal counterparts really just an attempt to market 'pastness' in the way some chain stores now offer replicas of the jewellery of earlier ages alongside scarves with Celtic or renaissance patterns and tapes of early music? Or are these references to earlier styles attempts to rethink 'pastness' itself? These are questions which have not yet been properly addressed by literary studies, which remains preoccupied with the epistemological issues.

Much postmodernist architecture is no more than the current equivalent of Egyptian frontages on large brick cinemas, and is driven solely by the advertiser's search for eye-catching novelty. Not all the building is insubstantial, however. One defence of the best of the new architecture has been to argue that postmodernist art emerged from a renewed historical awareness among modernists who did not want to return to a pre-modern style. As Neil Levine puts it: 'during the high moment of modernism in the first half of this century, most of the forms and organizational patterns of traditional architecture had in fact been jettisoned in the hope of arriving at something unforeseen, a new architecture that would be specifically appropriate to the machine age'.[21] Levine shows that in the postwar era, leading modernist architects struggled hard to reintroduce some historicising elements into their work. Their work points to the development of postmodernist forms. Louis Kahn's Salk Meeting House, for example, links contemporary and Roman elements together in a manner he described as 'wrapping ruins around buildings'.[22] The story of how the design for this building came about shows that the pastiche is a result of a certain tension between the site and its situation in both recent and long cultural histories. A junior architect working on the project traced a portion of Hadrian's villa on to what Kahn was calling 'an unmeasurable site' (a phrase which resonates with Smithson's idea of the past represented by the 'extraordinary scale, immense regions and infinite quantity' of the dinosaur world) as if the site were an unlocatable spacetime that therefore eluded representation.[23] At first Kahn did not recognise the source of the construction drawing with which his assistant had presented him, and simply accepted it as a promising interim solution. Soon afterwards he began to solve the problem of the unmeasurable site by constructing outer walls, or 'ruins', that were distinct from the inner surfaces, and controlled light and glare. Levine argues that the idea of the ruin as a model of the past allowed the architect to make a self-conscious and, therefore, partial investment in it and to find a means of representing the distance between present and past as material space. We might add that it seems to have been the inability to measure this distance that made the site and the problem of location that it symbolised impossible to work with earlier. Kahn's story offers a way of thinking of postmodern historicising collage as something more than the result of treating the past as a foreign country for the tourist to enjoy – it reveals a desire to find other signifying measures of the past than chronology. The use of ruins in a contemporary structure like James Stirling's Staätsgalerie in Stuttgart, which has several blocks of stone lying casually in a heap on the grass, as if they had only just fallen out of the wall, can be read not as a playful dismissal of the determinations of history and class, but as a playful investigation of their workings as a spatial environment.

The best of architectural postmodernism suggests that we should look more closely at the arguments about veridicality and imagination in postmodernist historical fiction. In the most influential of these critiques, Brian McHale's, *Postmodernist Fiction*, the report in *Midnight's Children* that the historical figure Sanjay Gandhi cloned himself repeatedly, is used as an example of this willingness to blend fact and fiction. Earlier historical fiction confined its inventions to what he calls the 'dark areas' of history, those passages of time in an historical figure's life for which the historical record cannot account, or those inner thought processes which are not recorded.[24] Even then, the fiction worked hard not to be anachronistic or to set up potential contradictions. Fleishman cites the historical novelist Mary Renault explaining that for her it would have been inconceivable to invent something like the Sanjay cloning, let alone take the liberties Pynchon does in *Gravity's Rainbow*:

> Often of course I must have done through ignorance what would horrify me if I could revisit the past ... But one can at least desire the truth; and it is inconceivable to me how anyone can decide deliberately to betray it; to alter some fact which was central to the life of a real human being, however long it is since he ceased to live, in order to make a smoother story, or to exploit him as propaganda for some cause (ellipses in Fleishman).[25]

For her, verisimilitude based on accepted historical knowledge is the only way to sustain an ethics of history. Some postmodern novelists and their readers clearly believe that a moral responsibility to the past need not entail uniform and unremitting accuracy of this kind. Neither Rushdie nor presumably most of his readers feel that any betrayal has happened in his novel, because the ideology of the Sanjay Youth Volunteers is captured so effectively by imagining them as bearing his own face. McHale's explanation for the changing attitude to historical fidelity is, as we discussed above, that the sense of the past itself has changed and most readers no longer trust official histories to be reliable, since they recognise the degree to which all knowledge of the past is a construction. The postmodern novelist answers that sense of dislocation and loss we discussed in Chapter I by wrapping ruins of earlier textualities around the narrative. But is McHale's explanation sufficient? Maybe unremitting historical precision no longer works, but does this mean that all responsibility to history can be abandoned?

Saleem, the narrator of *Midnight's Children* is plagued by this problem. He sometimes sounds like a self-justifying postmodernist trying to find meaning in history, and afraid that this will inevitably lead to a distortion of the past as he rewrites the whole of the recent history of India in order to place himself in a central role. This also entails the persistent construction of analogues, parallels and patterns between apparently diverse material that he justifies as a necessary resistance to the pervasive force of chance. What Saleem comes to believe is that the 'forces of history are not controlled by destiny or regulative mechanisms, but respond to haphazard conflicts. They do not manifest the successive forms of a primordial intention and their attraction is not that of a conclusion, for they always appear through the singular randomness of events.'[26] He is compelled to recognise the ethics of historicism as a continuing process of negotiation and reflection and, therefore, produces a history which he imagines is the result of his personal actions within Indian society. This is a history which is closely tied to the personal, a history/knowledge derived from an invented perspective: the Midnight Children are being slowly wiped out by a government that perceives them to be a threat to its own power: 'Let me state this quite unequivocally: it is my firm conviction that the hidden purpose of the Indo-Pakistani war of 1965 was nothing more nor less than the elimination of my benighted family from the face of the earth'.[27] The absurdity of this only highlights the need to find some better way of narrating recent history.

In a rare attempt to reconcile historical fact and postmodern textuality, the cultural historian Linda Hutcheon argues that historical fiction like Rushdie's unceasingly negotiates between contingency and possibility. She recognises that there is an uneasy balance involved in achieving this, which she articulates in terms of intelligibility rather than accuracy: 'Postmodern texts paradoxically point to the opaque nature of their representational strategies and at the same time to their complicity with the notion of the transparency of representation'.[28] She makes clear that in her view postmodern fiction is intricately tied to representations of history: the real issue for her is how and for whom those representations work. Public history may be a legitimation narrative for the state and those in power, but if we cannot junk all existing historical knowledge, how does the writer decide which is valuable? How can we decide what are useful ruins? Hutcheon's answer underestimates the incommensurability of the contending opposites of history and textuality in most current theories of fiction. We contend that many writers make their distinctions on the basis of their understanding of the mechanisms by which the past is known, especially memory, and the ontology of time and space on which the locatability of the past rests, just as Louis Kahn allegedly did.

The Sanjay effect relies on a distinction that helps clarify how this works. A postmodern historical novel cannot abandon its modernist heritage altogether and remain historical, so McHale identifies an 'onto-logical boundary' between the historical actuality in a historical novel (like the existence of Sanjay) and the fictional invention (the cloning). In earlier historical realist fiction the boundary was crossed silently and unobtrusively (in Bainbridge's historical novel of the sinking of the *Titanic*, *Every Man for Himself* (1996), the fictional Morgan unobtrusively goes from an actual gangway on the *Titanic* into an actual cabin with fictional additions, where he witnesses wholly fictional sex),[29] whereas postmodern novels cross it with shocking effect (as Billy Pilgrim is jerked from one time to another in Kurt Vonnegut's *Slaughterhouse Five* (1969)). Postmodernist fiction, according to McHale, places its characters and events in ontologically different worlds and sometimes in several. Although history and historical fiction are not his primary concern, he draws our attention to the potential significance of the ontology of the world of the historical novel, especially its temporal and spatial frame. The open display of ontology in postmodernist fiction raises what one critic calls 'the literary problem of how to represent time and space' in a world for which these are no longer fixed, unchanging foundations.[30]

Saleem's narration charts the collapse of his belief that any narrative will ever be capable of representing the strange reversals of history. Even randomness is unreliable: 'Unless, of course, there's no such thing as chance; ... "If they can change time just like that, what's real any more? I ask you? What's true?"'.[31] History can only be narrated as a self-avowed fantasy: the narratives of postmodernist fiction like *Midnight's Children* and others such as *Gravity's Rainbow* offer DIY grand narratives because the culture provides nothing credible by way of history for narrators like Saleem or observers like Tyrone Slothrop, who feel compelled to provide their own however bizarre. They feel driven to the conviction that the history of our century can only be told through 'outlandish' points of view – the history of India being too unimaginable to be represented except as a secret magic conspiracy of Midnight's Children; the experi-ence of twentieth-century monopoly capitalism being so crazy that it can only be told as a fantastic allegory of conspiracy during the end of the Second World War. Or perhaps the problem is the historical novel itself. Is it up to the job of what Jameson calls, in a sonorous phrase, the neces-sary 'aesthetic of cognitive mapping'?[32] 'Cognitive mapping' is a reorientation of our experience of time and space in an era when the opportunity to place ourselves into a definable timespace location (*viz.* a place with a unique, individual identity) is systematically challenged by the culture of global capitalism (think how it replicates the same chain stores, fast-food outlets, theme pubs and shopping malls across the land). Even the collision of discourses in this formulation of Jameson's seems part of this: the use of judgement that is not determined by rules; the cognitivism of the psychology of consciousness which treats mental activity as logical, replicable operations; and the construction of symbolic models or maps of geographies. It is hard to imagine an actual practice that would correspond to all this. The aesthetic and the cognitive are usually thought of as opposing practices of individual selves, while mapping is a procedure that is necessarily collective because it is communicative. This difficulty makes Jameson's point. We should look for engagements with history not only in realism but also in other radical literary forms, and these are likely to be signalled by a concern with the ethics of historicism more than by an emulation of the objectivity of specialist historians. As Andreas Huyssen says, 'the clarion call to objective truth will simply not do'.[33]

This is something very clearly recognised by the philosopher Paul Ricoeur, whose systematic critique of the linguistic turn in French philosophy that led to structuralism and poststructuralism, drew him to write an extended study of time and history in fiction. His third volume of *Time and Narrative* (1988) remains the central contemporary study of historical fiction, despite its scarcity of textual examples or close readings of literary texts. He argues that not even historical writing by professional historians can provide a discourse which corresponds truthfully to what it narrates; it owes a debt not only to the past but also depends upon a complex relation to the traces of the past for its discourse and value. Like Hutcheon he recognises the need to move past the sterile opposition of fact and fantasy, and resists tilting the balance to either the 'verbal force invested in our redescriptions' or to the 'incitations to redescription that arise from the past itself'.[34] What is needed, and he admits the extreme difficulty of articulating it, is a means of describing 'the role of the imaginary in intending the world as it actually was'.[35] Any historical writing has to 'stand for' a past that is absent, and this is more than representation but less than direct metonymy. Fiction is capable of 'provoking an illusion of presence, but one controlled by critical distance'.[36] In a particularly memorable phrase he defends the right, indeed the crucial importance, of literary witnesses of unique catastrophes like the Holocaust: 'fiction gives eyes to the horrified narrator'[37] by its achievement of a '"pastlike" note',[38] or 'quasi-past', rather than by accuracy in itself. The scare quotes and the adjective that has proven so useful to scientists and politicans when confronted by entities – quasi-stellar objects or quasi-nongovernmental bodies – which defy categorisation within the existing framework and are not significant enough to inaugrate its overhaul either, indicate just how difficult it is to find abstract terms for what some literary writing achieves. One implication of Ricoeur's argument is that postmodernist fiction is a continuation of modernism and realism by other means. It is doing nothing new except, like Saleem, calling attention to the complex mimesis at work in historical fiction, and thereby to the wider changes at work in our relations to the past. All historical fiction will reveal the unfulfilled possibilities of the past, and use the complex temporalities of tensed narration to explore otherwise hard to articulate temporal experiences orthogonal to linear time.

Despite the extraordinary range and subtlety of Ricoeur's survey of the entire field of time and literature, he makes two assumptions based on traditional assumptions about time and narrative that should be questioned. One is his assumption that physical time can be adequately represented by Aristotelian ideas of movement. In Chapter 4 we shall question this. His other assumption is that only fictional narrative is able to reconcile subjective time and the time of physics or cosmology; not even Heideggerian phenomenology can do it. Narratives can show what it is like to sustain a sense of identity through time, because narrative is necessary to maintain continuity, and without it the identity of a person would seem just smoke and mirrors hiding an amorphous swirl of material constituents, situations and behaviours constantly altering over time, an instability which would make the idea of an identity based on absolute self-sameness untenable. Narrative also provides a means of presenting a coherent identity to others, and in addition, allows the subject the possibility of self-transformation through renarrativisation. Narrative, therefore, has a prospective character as it reshapes the past and offers routes into the future. Narratives are not merely calendrical stories, because as hypothetical worlds they enjoy a freedom from the inhibiting constraints of cosmological veracity that allows them to explore the 'resources of phenomenological time' as well. The relationships of everyday life are lived within times of expectation, memory and repetition that characterise our relationships with others. Intersubjectivity is, therefore, inherently temporal, a claim which he argues goes beyond Heidegger's limited concept of sociality. The freedom to investigate the experience of intersubjectivity in time helps complicate the already complex and changing relations between literature and history.

The problem, quite simply, is the equation of narrative with a specific form of fiction which, although possibly not intended by Ricoeur, is not countered either. He allows narrative to remain potentially a capacious literary mode, but his derivation of the arguments about narrative hark back to a more restrictive interpretation which continues to have great influence. To see why, we need to ask why fictional narrative is usually considered to be the only literary means of presenting our lives in spacetime, and trace the answer back to its sources in Lukács and Hegel.

Peter Brooks is a useful guide here, because his critical study of modern fiction, *Reading for the Plot* (1984), makes explicit assumptions which are usually taken for granted by this tradition of narrative theory. Narrative is the primary means by which Western culture represents the existential experience of time – the sense of 'time-boundedness' – and it does this through the often undervalued construction of plot.[39] A plot is a logical 'syntax of meanings that are temporally unfolded'; its literary structure creates a reading experience which combines retrospective reflection on a sequence of completed actions with the experience of their moment by moment unfolding. The temporal performance embodied in a plot, however fictional, can recreate the current understanding of what it means to live in history. The scale of fiction is crucial to this. The small scale of poems makes them too readily apprehensible to be able to sustain a compelling enactment of the changes, anticipations and recollections which together weave our experience of time:

> Lyric poetry, we feel, strives toward an ideal simultaneity of meaning, encouraging us to read backward as well as forward (through rhyme and repetition, for instance), to grasp the whole in one visual and auditory image; and expository argument, while it can have a narrative, generally seeks to suppress its force in favor of an atemporal structure of understanding; whereas narrative stories depend on meanings delayed, partially filled-in, stretched out.[40]

This passage makes very clear how Brooks actually thinks a text engenders temporality in its reader: the duration of the act of reading is mimetic of the time internal to the world that this reading depicts. The more time used to read, the more distance within the thought processes it requires and, therefore, the more energy to amplify the temporal themes of plot and narrative. Not surprisingly, therefore, he considers that short poems will ordinarily lack suspense. Thought will be too big and powerful for these small poems and will simply take them over entirely without experiencing any deficit in its administrative cognition of these small linguistic enterprises. Novels by contrast are organisations too large for thought to manage within a single moment of consciousness, and so their narratives exercise sovereignty over the subject, folding cognition into their imagined spacetimes of history, judgement and prediction as if they were nations providing epic temporal and spatial horizons for their subjects. There is something immediately unconvincing about this argument. Scale conceals a distinction between initial and repeat readings, because sufficient rereading of all but the most lengthy and complex novels would eventually fill in those meanings and eliminate the distance that would help signify temporal process. Enough rereading would create the ideal simultaneity that he discerns in the reading of poems. Would this mean that the novel would then cease to do the task of enacting existential time? Brooks's unconvincing explanation of the pre-eminence of novelistic representations of time leaves out the social relations of reading from its calculations because they would blur or eliminate the distinction. Why then strive to maintain it? Why not accept that other literary forms might also be able to create an understanding of what it means to live in history at a particular moment? Couldn't other literary forms successfully convey 'time-boundedness'?

Ricoeur and Brooks are working with an inherited distinction between lyric and epic for which scale, like self-reflexivity, is a rationalisation that has come to serve cultural interests. The distinction between poetry and novel (which says little about the position of drama) is one whose investments can be traced back to one of its most influential formulations, Hegel's *Aesthetics*. Although little read outside Continental Philosophy, these lectures on the arts have indirectly influenced most modern theorists of textuality and narrative because of their extraordinary scope and their intimate connection with his theory of the dialectic. Hegel confines lyric poetry to the inner life of the poet, whereas the epic narrative is capable of an historical sweep: 'over and above the encompassing national life on which the action is based, both inner life and outer reality have their place, and thus here is spread out before us all the detail of what can be regarded as the poetry of human existence'.[41] Such comprehensiveness demands a level of collective self-consciousness that only arises over time, and so the epic 'necessarily arises later than the life and the spirit which is naively at home in its immediate poetic existence'.[42] An epic is, therefore, always historical in the sense that it looks back to the past, because it is a belated account of the events which helped form the culture out of which it emerges as the articulation of the culture's self-image. This might make the epic seem no more than an act of historical reconstruction, a kind of belated historical poetry, no different and perhaps less significant than other modes of history writing, because if the events to be recounted occurred in a moderately distant past, much of their significance will have disappeared from the collective memory leaving only memorials and whatever histories such early societies might have bequeathed to their successors. Hegel's answer is a not wholly convincing claim that individual poets overcome this by the force of their recall:

In spite of this separation in time, a close connection must nevertheless still be left between the poet and his material. The poet must still be wholly absorbed in these old circumstances, ways of looking at things, and faith, and all he needs to do is to bring a poetic consciousness and artistic portrayal to his subject which is in fact the real basis of his actual life.[43]

The epic poet is not living in modernity since there is no temporal break with the past, no modernising abandonment of the traditions of those earlier epic times as mere 'superstition, and an empty decoration provided by poetic machinery'.[44] This is one reason why we should treat the later distinction between narrative fiction and other genres with a certain scepticism. In Hegel's exposition, the epic lacks modernism's temporal logic and, therefore, to treat the novel as a replacement for the epic, as Lukács did, is to overlook the way in which the novelist is estranged from the past by the very modernist form of the genre. Although many contemporary writers appear to have believed that the answer would be to jettison modernist form in order to maintain continuity with some desired past, this will not work either because the dialectic is at work whatever the author imagines. An anti-modernist work as Theodor Adorno argued repeatedly, is simply one that fails to engage with history at all, because the past and its histories are already constructed through this logic of modernity. To change that would require change in the entire social order.

What is the truly modern literary form? Surprisingly, Hegel gave the lyric poem the role of modernist representation because he thought it transcended history. The lyric poem seems an unpromising representative of modernity as its ambit shrinks down from the amplitude of the social to the fragmented self of a poet, where it must find a mood or object that can represent like a snapshot in words the momentarily unified subjectivity of the poet: 'he must identify *himself* with this particularization of himself as with himself, so that in it he feels and envisages *himself*. In this way alone does he become a self-bounded subjective entirety and express only what issues from this determinate situation and stands in connection with it' (emphasis in original).[45] Now we can see that the lyric poem is modern because it is the textual memory of self-consciousness, a crucial stage in human development. The specular relation with self makes possible not only full consciousness but also, ultimately, society as well. Epic narrative would lack authenticity in the modern world, whereas lyric poetry can still represent our temporal condition by means of its unremitting care for the introspective detail of the poet's own emotional universe. He makes the distinction using the categories of space and time in a manner that has been copied ever since:

The sort of mood and whole mode of treatment has to be announced in the metre. For the outpouring of lyric stands to time, as an external element of communication, in a much closer relation than epic narrative does. The latter places real phenomena in the past and juxtaposes them or interweaves them in rather a spatial extension, whereas lyric portrays the momentary emergence of feelings and ideas in the temporal succession of their origin and development and therefore has to give proper artistic shape to varied kinds of temporal movement.[46]

Hegel has little to say about the novel, and unfortunately does not say much more about these different temporalities or about the significance of spatiality in literature. However, by saying that lyric poetry has to be formally inventive in order to represent 'varied kinds of temporal movement', Hegel opened up the possibility of a formalist avant-garde, for his speculation implies that there might be a range of old and new temporal movements, or temporalities, which existing textual structures may be insufficient to perform. New forms may have to be invented in order to remain fully answerable to the temporal conditions of history. This in turn raises questions about the unrealised temporal movements themselves. What are they, what is their history, and how can lyric poetry or any literary genre represent them if it is not itself a practice of history? Could these new forms also represent emergent spatial phenomenologies? In whatever way these questions are answered, it seems likely that such new literary forms are going to be difficult to recognise, since if a temporality has hitherto gone unrecognised, this is probably in part because current modes of symbolisation are not up to the job, and possibly also because dominant discourses of time have suppressed them.

This praise for the modernity of lyric was double-edged – it depended on the reluctant admission that no plausible version of the historicising epic now existed. What was needed was a replacement, and the critical tradition eventually anointed the novel in this role. Lukács was able to insert the later nineteenth-century realist novel into this mode of argument about literary form by identifying the novel as the successor to epic, and the only modern literary mode capable of representing history. His pre-Marxist work, *Theory of the Novel*, effectively reproduces Hegel's assessment of poetry as further support for this move: 'In lyric poetry, only the great moment exists ... At the lyrical moment the purest interiority of the soul, set apart from duration without choice, lifted above the obscurely-determined multiplicity of things, solidifies into substance ... sudden flashes of the substance become like lost original manuscripts suddenly made legible'.[47] Lyric time is outside ordinary duration and, therefore, able to manifest the inwardness of the self which presumably transcends the time of the material world. Such achievements are analogous to the recovery of the past through lost documents, because these pure individual revelations act like recovered collective memories. Hegel's persisting influence on the categorisation of narrative and lyric as modes of temporal inscription can be felt even among those poststructuralists who have done most to break with traditional methodologies. This is why when Michel Foucault ends *The Archaeology of Knowledge* by having an anonymous voice speak for his new theory by saying, 'discourse is not life: its time is not your time; in it you will not be reconciled to death', he is still arguing with Hegel, and with those who would treat writing, especially poetry, as if its time were that of the interior self, a time outside history that is yet somehow able to memorialise the fleeting, contingent moment.[48]

Postmodern history and ethics

The postmodern fascination with the past is, in a resonant phrase, an attempt, 'however fragile and fraught with contradiction, to cast lifelines to the past'.[49] The most important aspect of postmodernism for the study of history in contemporary literature is, therefore, not simply its admittedly confused recognition of the temporal logics of modernism, but the path it opens towards rethinking the ethics of historical representation. Huyssen's concern with the need to face the dangers of historicism is shared by some contemporary writers, who not only acknowledge the importance of trying to democratise history by recognising alterity and difference while reconceiving subjectivity and personal agency, but who also turn explicitly to ethics. They have begun to discern a new function for literature in the construction of an ethically usable past. Yet the extent to which literature and history perform a healing act for subjectivity raises a number of complex questions. What 'good' is there in history? Does literature have any ethical task in representing the past? Can one represent the past unethically? Would such a representation be the author's responsibility? If recent literature is treated as a practice of cultural memory it would seem to some critics necessarily a site of ethical relations: 'Remembering comprises contextually situated assertions of continuity on the part of the subjects and claims about the significance of past experience. Such tacit assertions and claims, based as much on cumulative wisdom and moral vision as an individual interest, form a kind of moral practice.'[50] The implication of memory and its vicissitudes in the ethics of history is an issue of great importance for historical literature as we shall see in the next section. But how do we conceptualise the moral practice itself apart from the use of memory?

The work of the French philosopher Emmanuel Levinas proves helpful here, because he starts by challenging not just existing concepts of time and space, but the very foundation on which they rest – being.

He argues that most ethical philosophies have operated within an impossible constraint: the world's existence, or 'being', and our human existence or 'being' within it, are taken for granted, and philosophical attention begins with the problems of the relation between the two (Descartes called his work 'first philosophy'). Ethics has to find its place in an already constructed field that conceals the degree to which the 'other' is the impetus for ethical action – the subject is actually responsible for the 'other'. Even to talk about the 'other' is difficult for us because we tend to think immediately of a material entity or its representation, a being, a person. Levinas himself began by thinking of the other as representable by the face, and then felt compelled to transform his arguments into a poststructuralist mode after critiques of this assumption that the face could elude essentialism. In his later work, notably *Otherwise Than Being*, the 'other' is a pre-linguistic alterity, a 'trace' that cannot be recuperated through a more 'faithful' representation. This trace practices a double signification: the other always manifests itself within a cultural and linguistic context, but instead of being absorbed by this situation, the 'other' dislocates the context in which it occurs and divests itself from the forms in which it appears. In Levinas's later terminology, this process is the 'Saying' of the 'Said',[51] terms which indicate how closely this ethics is thought of in terms of dialogue and the temporalities of utterance. Ethical life from a Levinasian perspective is being wholly indebted to the 'other' which persistently interrupts, upsets and displaces the apparent seamlessness of existence. Although he wrote a small amount of literary criticism, he never pursued the implications of this for the writing and reading of literary texts. He interprets Paul Celan's belief in an 'absolute poem that does not exist' as active desire in the poetry for 'the defection of all dimensions', but the implications for both form and history are not pursued.[52] Moreover, as Robert Eaglestone shows in his trenchant and persuasive account of how Levinas might provide the basis for an ethical criticism capable of fully acknowledging textuality (unlike Wayne Booth and Martha Nussbaum in Eaglestone's view), Levinas tends to treat history as the field of violence, war and resistance to ethics.[53] Eaglestone argues that a Levinasian literary criticism would 'make its interpretation continual interruption', and it would acknowledge that it always 'risks being said, and covering up the saying, in the very moment of exposing the saying'.[54] It is beyond the scope of his book to offer extended examples of how this would work. We do suggest, however, that it is the conjunction of this emphasis on the saying as the ground out of which an ethics can be formulated, and the 'defection of all dimension' – the challenge to foundational spacetime – that points us in the direction of a possible ethics of historical fiction.

How can the writing and reading of literary texts perform this recognition of a saying that precedes being? Levinas's ethical philosophy became a central issue for French poststructuralist thought because his displacement of the sovereign subject meant that most ethical discourse was no longer valid within its terms. Working with an opportunistically eclectic mix of ideas from psychoanalysis, the Prague School, structuralism and the growing influence of figures like Levinas on her generation of theorists, Julia Kristeva attempted to find precise connections between formal literary structures and both psychic and cultural processes on the other. An ethics of writing can be adequate only if it recognises the way subjectivity and its life of meaning are constantly tested in the reading of literary language. She argued, therefore, that a new concept of practice was needed as the main site of an 'ethical history':

> Practice, ... positing and dissolving meaning and the unity of the subject, therefore encompasses the ethical. The text, in its signifying disposition and its signification, is a practice assuming all positivity in order to negativize it and thereby make visible the *process* underlying it. It can thus be considered, precisely, as that which carries out the ethical imperative.[55]

The 'ethical imperative' is thus to make visible the processes underlying the production and dissolution of meaning and identity, the processes that constitute the subject itself. She associates this with a modernist mistrust of explicit moralising: 'the univocal enunciation of such a message would itself represent a suppression of the ethical function as we understand it ... the text fulfils its ethical function only when it pluralizes, pulverizes, "musicates" these truths, which is to say, on the condition that it develop them to the point of laughter'.[56] Ethical literary texts raise questions of identity, meaning and truth without supplying answers; they disclose corporeal aspects of the unconscious. Kristeva's perspectives on the ethical function of art and practice have some important practical consequences for historical literature, as a commentator on her work explains: 'if we accept her notion that anything univocally stated is inherently anti-ethical, because univocality involves suppression rather than expression of the ethical function, then monolithic statements of any sort are to be avoided, including those which claim to state moral truths'.[57] This would appear to make the case for anti-realist historical literature so strongly that it might disallow realist narrative altogether. Only avant-garde writing would achieve an ethics of history. A less black and white approach to the diversity of historical literatures could, however, emphasise the implicit emphasis not on radical onslaughts on reified literary forms but on experimental, tentative, questioning literary strategies that depend as much on active work by audiences as on anti-realist techniques. Kristeva herself emphasises the degree to which this is a textual *via negativa*: 'The ethical cannot be stated, instead it is practiced

to the point of loss, and the text is one of the most accomplished examples of such a practice'.[58]

In a poem entitled 'Wonders of Obligation', the British poet, Roy
Fisher, whose poem 'City' is one of the most important longer poems of
the postwar period, writes about his personal intersection with the history
of Birmingham since the Second World War, and gestures to this responsibility of the present to the past. He offers an everyday action as an
image of a literary ethics of history:

> The things we make up out of language
> turn into common property.
> To feel responsible
> I put my poor footprint back in.[59]

In the image of placing one's foot in the 'tracks of history', putting
oneself in the 'trace' of history, Fisher's poems suggests that history
produces a moral obligation to repeatedly retell history. Indeed, retelling
history immediately raises a social obligation and responsibility for others.
Out of this 'obligation' also stems wonder at the past, a sense that the
hidden past can produce awe, rather than mere dismissal. Fisher's history
of Birmingham becomes a representation which is as much an ethical
duty as a satisfying addition to knowledge made possible by the retrieval
of lost memories. History is not represented here as simply an archaeology (*pace* Seamus Heaney's poems about the preservative actions of peat
bogs), in which history becomes a preserver/conserver of the past in
'sedimented layers'; history is a daily flowering of opportunities in the
present. Rather than something passively recorded, literature offers
history as a permanent reactivation of the past in a critique of the present,
and at the level of content offers a textual anamnesis for the hitherto
ignored, unacknowledged or repressed pasts marginalised by the dominant histories – feminist narratives, ethnic narratives, non-heterosexual
narratives. Literature can also act ethically by altering its form to put the
'other' first, and in this way dominant aesthetic and cultural forms are
reconfigured in order to make room for narrative modes and cultural
forms which stand for the other, manifested as different 'ways of telling'.
Lost, defeated, or unknown pasts emerge through forms of the 'other'
which have been suppressed.

This locates an ethics of history in the reflexive, performative
writing of the past. By putting one's foot back into the track of history,
one's present position is reorientated by the direction of that track, not to
mention shaped by the track. If history is an 'impression' in the mind of
generations, then it is a case of filling out that 'impression' – ex-pressing
it. History is as much the form of the narratives we tell, as the events

that are related: 'The moral function of history is to compel us to confront what we – and all around us – wish to leave behind. Societies must provide cultural forms and occasions for remembering the past'.[60] As Kristeva makes clear, the 'ethical imperative' is a constantly negative procedure, a persistent unfixing of positionality and identity; an ethical text is a 'laying bare' of the signifier, a text that opens up the processes of its own production to scrutiny by the reader. Resistance is broached by the text's push against its own linguistic boundaries.

Writing about the massacre at Amritsar seemed to require an impossible combination of writerly virtues, historical accuracy and ethically effective imaginative invention. The distance between epistemology and ontology, or historical knowledge and literary fiction could be negotiated only by some kind of moral practice, although a morality of tradition or universalising precepts is insufficient for the textual conditions of late modernity. Levinas and Kristeva both draw attention to the performative practice of writing, its unceasing reflexive reconstructions of meaning and subjectivity, which can be activated by new genres and new deconstructions of realism. What we have found is that writers and cultural historians believe that the changes of the late modern past require new attentions to its construction as memory, and its situatedness in time and space. As Huyssen says: 'Both personal and social memory today are affected by an emerging new structure of temporality generated by the quickening pace of material life on the one hand and by the acceleration of media images and information on the other. Speed destroys space, and it erases temporal distance'.[61] Maybe just as computers constantly demand faster memory, writers will have to write faster texts, but what would they look like and how would we read them? The next two chapters investigate what it would mean to answer this question, and ask whether space has been destroyed and time erased, or whether they too have been relocated.

Notes

1 Salman Rushdie, *Midnight's Children* (London: Picador, 1981), pp. 35–6.
2 Avrom Fleishman, *The English Historical Novel: Walter Scott to Virginia Woolf* (Baltimore: Johns Hopkins University Press, 1971), p. 4.
3 Ibid., p. 15.
4 Dean Rehberger, 'Vulgar fiction, impure history: the neglect of historical fiction', *Journal of American Culture*, 18/4 (1995), 59–65, 60.
5 'The genre is unashamedly a hybrid: it contemplates the universal but does not depart from the rich factuality of history in order to reach that elevation'. See Fleishman, *The English Historical Novel*, p. 8.
6 Georg Lukács, *The Historical Novel* (London: Penguin, [1937] 1981), pp. 45–7.
7 David Cowart, *History and the Contemporary Novel* (Carbondale and Edwardsville: Southern Illinois University Press, 1989), p. 6.

8 Ibid., pp. 76–7.

9 Joseph W. Turner, 'The kinds of historical fiction: an essay in definition and methodology', *Genre*, XII (1979), 333–55, 335.

10 Cowart, *History and the Contemporary Novel* (1989), p. 28.

11 Ibid., pp. 28–9.

12 Edward Soja, *Postmodern Geographies* (London: Verso, 1989), p. 130.

13 Barbara Adam, *Time and Social Theory* (Cambridge: Polity Press, 1990), p. 39.

14 Peter Osborne, *The Politics of Time: Modernity and Avant-Garde* (London: Verso, 1995), p. 18.

15 Ibid., p. 198.

16 Brian McHale, *Postmodernist Fiction* (London: Methuen, 1987), p. 91.

17 Paul Ricoeur, *Time and Narrative*, trans. Kathleen Blamey and David Pellauer (Chicago: University of Chicago Press, 1988), p. 153.

18 McHale, *Postmodernist Fiction*, p. 96.

19 Charles Olson, 'In cold hell, in thicket', in Paul Hoover (ed.), *Postmodern American Poetry* (New York: W. W. Norton, 1994), pp. 3–8, 7.

20 Charles Newman, *The Post Modern Aura: The Act of Fiction in an Age of Inflation* (Evanston: University of Illinois, 1985), p. 182; cited in William J. R. Curtis, *Modern Architecture Since 1900*, 3rd edn (London: Phaidon, 1996), p. 621.

21 Neil Levine, 'Robert Venturi and "The return of historicism"', in Christopher Mead (ed.), *The Architecture of Robert Venturi* (Albuquerque: University of New Mexico Press, 1989), p. 50.

22 Ibid., p. 55.

23 Daniel S. Friedman, 'Salk Institute for Biological Studies', in David B. Brownlee and David G. De Long, (eds), *Louis Kahn: In the Realm of Architecture* (New York: Rizzoli, 1991), p. 335.

24 McHale, *Postmodernist Fiction*, p. 87.

25 Mary Renault, 'Notes on *The King Must Die*', in Thomas McCormack (ed.), *Afterwords: Novelists on their Novels* (New York: Harper and Row, 1969), pp. 84–6.

26 Michel Foucault, *Language, Counter-Memory, Practice* (Ithaca: Cornell University Press, 1980), p. 154.

27 Rushdie, *Midnight's Children*, p. 338.

28 Linda Hutcheon, *The Politics of Postmodernism* (London: Routledge, 1989), p. 18.

29 Beryl Bainbridge, *Every Man For Himself* (London: Abacus, [1996] 1997), pp. 140–1.

30 Amy J. Elias, 'Defining spatial history in postmodernist historical novels', in Theo D'haen and Hans Bertens (eds), *Narrative Turns and Minor Genres in Postmodernism* (Amsterdam: Rodopi, 1995), p. 109.

31 Rushdie, *Midnight's Children*, pp. 78–9.

32 Fredric Jameson, 'Postmodernism, or the cultural logic of late capitalism', *New Left Review*, 146 (July–August, 1984), 89.

33 Andreas Huyssen, *Twilight Memory* (London: Routledge, 1995), p. 254.

34 Ricoeur, *Time and Narrative*, p. 154.

35 Ibid., p. 181.

36 Ibid., p. 188.

37 Ibid.

38 Ibid., p. 191.

39 Peter Brooks, *Reading for the Plot: Design and Invention in Narrative* (Cambridge, MA: Harvard University Press, 1984), pp. 20–1.

40 Ibid., pp. 20–1.

41 G. W. F. Hegel, *Aesthetics: Lectures on Fine Art*, Vol. II, trans. T. M. Knox

(Oxford: Oxford University Press, 1975), p. 1078.

42 Ibid., p. 1046.

43 Ibid., p. 1047.

44 Ibid.

45 Ibid., p. 1133.

46 ibid., p. 1136.

47 Georg Lukács, *The Theory of the Novel* (London: Merlin Press, 1978), p. 63.

48 Michel Foucault, *The Archaeology of Knowledge*, trans. A. M. Sheridan Smith (London: Tavistock, 1972), p. 211.

49 Huyssen, *Twilight Memory*, pp. 253–4.

50 Michael Lambek, 'The past imperfect: remembering as moral practice', in Paul Antze and Michael Lambek (eds), *Tense Past: Cultural Essays in Trauma and Memory* (London: Routledge, 1996), p. 248.

51 See Emmanuel Levinas, *Otherwise Than Being: or, Beyond Essence*, trans. Alphonso Lingis (The Hague: Martinus Nijhoff, 1981), which explores the manner in which the 'transcendent' Saying interweaves with the 'immanent' Said, thereby manifesting the ethical.

52 Emmanuel Levinas, *Proper Names*, trans. Michael B. Smith (Stanford, CA: Stanford University Press, 1996), p. 46.

53 Robert Eaglestone, *Ethical Criticism: Reading After Levinas* (Edinburgh: Edinburgh University Press, 1997), p. 140.

54 Ibid., p. 177.

55 Julia Kristeva, *Revolution in Poetic Language* (New York: Columbia University Press, 1984), p. 233.

56 Ibid., p. 233.

57 Jean Graybeal, 'Kristeva's delphic oracle: "practice encompasses the ethical"', in Kelly Oliver (ed.), *Ethics, Politics, and Difference in Julia Kristeva's Writing* (New York and London: Routledge, 1993), p. 38.

58 Kristeva, *Revolution in Poetic Language*, p. 234.

59 Roy Fisher, 'Wonders of obligation', in *Poems 1955–1987* (Oxford: Oxford University Press, 1988), p. 156.

60 Laurence J. Kirmayer, 'Landscapes of memory: trauma, narrative, and dissociation', in Paul Antze and Michael Lambek (eds), *Tense Past*, p. 193.

61 Huyssen, *Twilight Memory*, p. 253.

CHAPTER 3

Memory's realism

Postmodernism is haunted by memory: memories of disaster, genocide, war, the Holocaust and the persistent destruction of human possibility by economic and political means; by the unrepresentable excess of these memories; and by the memory of memory itself. Where memory was there is now an unstable discourse divided by temporality, fragmented in space and lost for words. Memory haunts postmodernism as the unnameable outsider who has to be indicated by negative critique: *différance*, *Nachträglichkeit*, mourning, the linguistic unconscious, are all spectral placeholders for what earlier phenomenologies would have interpellated as memory. Even that most properly footnote-conscious academic concept, intertextuality, is sometimes a respectable name for unplaced desires and figures rising from social memory. A fictional treatise on the significance of spectres, Maxine Hong Kingston's brilliant cross-generic history of Chinese immigration to America, *The Woman Warrior*, can help us think about these postmodern liminalities of memory. Her text is inhabited by ghosts – the sitting ghost or the newspaper boy ghost – whose ontology varies enormously as far as the Western reader is concerned from mythic being, to daydream, to ordinary white Westerner. That is the point. From the Chinese standpoint they are all ontologically equal, for when a culture fails to find a place for the new it abjects it into the spectral, while the spectres themselves make things worse by fulfilling the unaccepting culture's fantasies of whiteness, hostility and unboundedness. The usual postmodernist answer would be that memory deserves to fade out of theoretical discourse, because it is a part of the ideology of consciousness and intention which projects a sovereign subject exercising rule over its territories of space and time. It is the old subject and its memories that is now easy to see through.

We shall argue in this chapter and Chapter 4 that this is only part of the story. The insistent temporalisation of memory so evident in the concepts of deferral, retranscription and aftershock, is a measure of the inability of older models of memory to cope with radical changes in social time and space. The dialectic of Enlightenment, colonialism, the

Holocaust and total war, have all contributed to the rejection by post-modernism of history as grand narrative, its critiques of subjectivity, logocentrism and the elision of difference, and consequently, its relegation of memory to liminality. In this we are indebted to Freud's key notion of 'deferred action', or what he called *Nachträglichkeit*, an operation within the formation of certain psychopathological symptoms that appears to disturb temporal and logical linearity. This concept refers to the way the psychical temporality and causality of experiences, impressions and memory traces are revised at a later date to make them dovetail with fresh experiences or with the attainment of a new stage of development. Memory after the disaster or trauma, however, is also different. It is not just that no existing forms of social or individual memory could mourn or represent such negative sublimity. The very spatio-temporal frameworks on which such memory would have been constructed have changed and so have the institutions and sites of memory, to the extent that new modes of memory now mediate history.

Postmodernism is, therefore, also haunted by the new popular culture of memory, which it constantly abjects and readmits to play and pastiche. The past is now widely believed to depend upon memory, personal and social, traumatic and repressed, involuntary and planned. What this does to the past and our relation to it is much less examined than the vicissitudes of subjectivity and memory, depending on the degree of acceptance of different gendered and national identities. Postmodernism wants nothing to do with these ghosts it has seen through, while popular culture thinks they provide the answer to its uneasy sense of having been cut loose from history. Both rely on underlying theories of memory, which like new concepts of space and time, belong to the culture of experts, of medicine and of science. Only in the arts and literature has this new mnemonics of history been fully registered, and criticism is only just beginning to recognise how far-reaching this engagement has been, and how effectively certain writers have managed to develop critiques of the new politics of memory.

Postmodernist criticism has recognised one feature of this new popular interest in the past as memory, in the widespread use of inter-textuality in everything from shopping malls to world music and metafictional novels. Linda Hutcheon, for example, says that 'postmodern intertextuality ... directly confronts the past of literature' in the new postmodern modes of 'historiographic metafiction' – historical novels like *A Maggot*, *Foe*, *No Place on Earth* or *Waterland*. This formulation borrows its verb of confrontation from the agency of social memory, obliquely implying that we could replace 'intertexts' with 'textual memory' in her proposition – 'intertexts can be both historical and aesthetic in their nature and function' – and say 'textual memories can be both historical and aesthetic in their nature and function'.[1] In this chapter we shall argue that some of our most significant novelists and poets have recognised the implications of this interdependence of the historical and the aesthetic, although they have often done so in other forms than the intertext.

Hutcheon's formulation derives in part from the work of Roland Barthes, particularly his extremely influential essay 'From Work to Text'. A discussion of the role of time, space and memory in this theory of reading will show further why we need to look again at the modern sciences of memory and their implications for both everyday beliefs about the past and its manifestation as memory, and at the locations of memory in literary texts. The confusions and lacunae in Barthes's analysis of inter-textuality point to a missing analysis of the workings of social memory in the production of textual meaning.

This intense, elliptical essay tries to convert ordinary assumptions that a piece of writing is a material entity located in time and space, perhaps as a physical object like a book, to the recognition that most writings are processes that extend beyond presence. The old way of conceiving of a piece of writing is 'Newtonian', whereas the new text requires the recognition of 'the relativity of the frames of reference' of Einsteinian physics.[2] Analysis, therefore, might require a new discourse of temporality, although Barthes does not try to supply it. He saves his most powerful rhetoric for the attempt to conjure up the multiplicity, and even mayhem, of the new text, which is only a momentary convergence of a vast background of intertexts ('citations, references, echoes, cultural languages ... antecedent or contemporary').[3] Barthes does not describe this explicitly as an act of memory, but most readers of his essay are irresistibly persuaded that it is. Mary Bittner Wiseman, for example, explains the concept in just such terms: 'the textual network is complex and open in that, for example, one member of a paradigm to which a given sign belongs itself belongs to other paradigms, and the sign's *recalling* the one member opens the way to that member's recalling members of the other paradigms to which it belongs, and so on endlessly' (our italics).[4] 'Members' and 'recall': these textual elements seem remarkably like people who belong to the same organisation, yet they are supposedly signs even though able to remember one another autonomously without the intervention of any individual intention. For Barthes, it is the new reader summoned up by this new text who provides the space for such activities, a space that he surrealistically and charmingly likens to a leisurely stroll, over which he rhapsodises in the manner of a sentimental Impressionist painter, or a pastoral Situationist on a *dérive*, a walk through a landscape in which distinct moments in specific places create a 'multiple, irreducible' and heterogeneous series of perspectives. This powerful conceit deflects attention from the question of whether all these traces of the past are present in the landscape of the text, or require more than attentive perception, perhaps memory or a knowledge of history, to be recognised. Surely this walk-reader must also be a rememberer, because the sights and sounds of the stroll will inevitably be enmeshed with moment-by-moment memories as well as perceptions? Walking provides a spatio-temporal opportunity for the unfolding of events, as if reading were analogous to the continual renewal of the world itself in Bergsonian terms, as it constantly emerges out of the past into the present and then sinks into oblivion. The relation of this text to its intertexts is, therefore, treated as an instance of the way traces of the past emerge in the present as textual echoes, determinations and directions which issue in what he calls this 'semelfactive' (belonging only to one instant of time) text. This seemingly neutral term of relation, this 'inter' of 'intertextuality' is actually encompassing many different forms of activity, that might well also be called 'cross-textuality', 'chronotextuality', or 'mnemotextuality'. These are potentially radically different modes of intertextuality, and they are also made more diverse by their possibly differing relations to history and the aesthetic. They all rely somehow on memory.

Barthes's silence about memory in this text is symptomatic of the difficulty of finding a theory of memory that acknowledges the significance of textuality as anything more than a recording system. It also reflects a tendency to assume that memory is a natural function, however complex its vicissitudes, dreams, neuroses and other creations might be. This at first sight is a picture that theories of memory would confirm, not least because their seeming incompatibility helps mask an underlying assumption. There are two main fields of research into memory: psychoanalysis and cognitive psychology. Psychoanalysis has entirely made the running in literary and cultural theory, which is one reason why memory has been both prominent and under-theorised – Freud's primary concern was not the mechanism of memory but its vicissitudes. Cognitive psychology has always treated memory as a central feature of mental activity, but only recently has it recognised that some forms of memory could never be investigated under ordinary laboratory conditions, because they depend on unique personal histories. Literary theory has, mistakenly in our view, treated cognitive psychology with indifference or contempt probably based on both ignorance and misunderstanding of its aims and achievements. We do not want to replace psychoanalysis with another form of psychology, however, on the grounds that the new one is somehow more scientific, more accurate, or simply new to our field. Our argument is that cognitive psychology, as much as psychoanalysis, is based on the extensive observation of individual and social practices of memory and, therefore, provides a useful source of material on the recent history of memory for the study of contemporary literary texts. In addition, like psychoanalysis, it helps form the unexamined background knowledge by which our cultures explain memory to themselves. Neither theory has been very effective at considering its own reflexive relation to social knowledge. How much are these theories of memory actually the outcome of observations of people acting under the belief that memory works in a certain manner, and how much do they provide directive theorising for everyday acts of recollection? Literary texts have been particularly effective at tracing the consequences of living out the belief in, say, traumatic memory, or memory as a vivid spatio-temporal re-enactment of the past. We shall, therefore, discuss in some detail the models of memory at work in both cognitive psychology and psychoanalysis which have been taken up by writers. It is not that writers have always been assiduous readers of the theoretical literature (although some, like Pat Barker, have clearly ventured some way into its obscured history) so much as that these theories have now become part of the ideology of history.

Feedback is at work in maintaining these practices of memory. Now the dominant models of individual memory help shape the self-understanding of social memory too and sometimes direct the memories themselves. Although some cultural theorists have argued that concepts of individual memory, especially from psychoanalysis, can be extended to social groups, historians and sociologists have largely focused on the social relations and institutions by which individual memories are managed. Since Maurice Halbwachs's work on collective memory was published posthumously (he died in Buchenwald) in 1952,[5] historians and social theorists have recognised the importance of what has variously been called collective memory, social memory and cultural memory. They have shown that this memory is not just a passive or unconscious accumulation by a social group, or a kind of shared weather; it requires organised activity, conscious reflection and sustained social interaction. As Patrick Geary insists: 'All memory, whether "individual", "collective", or "historical", is memory *for* something, and this political (in a broad sense) purpose cannot be ignored'.[6] Geary's studies of medieval memory, like those of Mary Carruthers, M. T. Clanchy and James Fentress and Chris Wickham, have not only added much to our knowledge of that period, but also thrown light on the workings of memory today. Mary Carruthers shows in great detail that the medieval book was 'a support for the various activities of *memoria*' rather than a material form of memory itself, and that most readers memorised as much as they could for themselves.[7] She finds something very similar to Lyotard's dual temporality of postmodern memory at work. There is no primacy of text or originating memory: 'In this way, reading a book extends the process whereby one memory engages another in a continuing dialogue ... not a "hermeneutical circle" (which implies mere solipsism) but more like a "hermeneutical dialogue" between two memories'.[8] The text is not a record of memory but a participant in the workings of memory as the time of a discourse.

All societies invest their energies in the creation and destruction of history through many different kinds of oral, written and material memory. For these thinkers, social memory is a deliberately open-ended term. It could refer to the role of the book in medieval culture, the significance of First World War memorials, shared oral history of a strike or armed resistance to outside rule, the custodianship of documents, as well as textual memory. A few commentators have questioned whether social memory exists at all, since memory is always an internal individual practice, but such arguments appear to work with a reductive concept of sociality. Others, like Paul Connerton, think that all theories of memory over-emphasise the role of texts, and argue that non-inscriptional memory is as important as writing even today. Bodily practices ranging from habit to ritual behaviours help sustain a society's continuity with the past and retain an awareness of what and where it has been. We use the term 'social memory' extensively in this chapter and elsewhere in the book because of its acknowledgement that memory is at least assisted if not shaped by collective practices (some of which are cultural or textual), and because it is not associated with any one model of psychology. Social memory allows for the possibility that even individual memory is shaped by metanarratives of both temporality and the necessary conditions for social relations with the past.

Metamemory in Pat Barker's *Regeneration*

Siegfried Sassoon's arrival at Craiglockhart hospital presents the psychiatrist W. H. Rivers with a special difficulty in Pat Barker's novel *Regeneration* (1991).[9] The problem is Sassoon's poetry. He may have published an open letter against the war and narrowly missed a court-martial through the machinations of his friend Robert Graves, who has managed to have him certified as a war neurotic, and more difficult still, he may actually be suffering from war neurosis, since he was having hallucinations of corpses in the street before he arrived at the hospital, but it is the power which poetry gives to the poet to take control of his own history that leaves Rivers uncertain of his position as a psychiatrist when confronted with the officer-poet. Poetry makes Rivers feel 'inadequate' (p. 189), partly because he feels he lacks understanding of the aesthetic practices at work in poetry and the hermeneutic skills they demand, and partly because he thinks of poetry as a form of memory. Since 'Rivers's treatment sometimes consisted simply of encouraging the patient to abandon his hopeless attempt to forget, and advising him instead to spend some part of every day remembering' (p. 26), a new and radical style of treatment he has adapted from psychoanalysis, he feels more helpless than usual in the face of someone who writes poetry about the war. If writing poetry is a form of self-analysis, then poems are themselves complex aesthetic forms of anamnesis. 'Writing the poems had obviously been therapeutic, but then Rivers suspected that writing the Declaration might have been therapeutic too. He thought that Sassoon's poetry and his protest sprang from a single source, and each could be linked to his recovery from that terrible period of nightmares and hallucinations' (p. 26). This concept of poetry is not just Rivers's own defence against a competing knowledge. Sassoon himself appears to share Rivers's idea that poetry is memory and can be a means of handling trauma. During a conversation with Wilfred Owen, in which Sassoon offers advice about the writing of poetry to the younger and less experienced poet, Sassoon advises him to try reworking one of his poems, and then hesitates. 'It's not too traumatic, is it? That memory' (p. 124).

At work are several significant assumptions: poetry, and perhaps all literary texts including *Regeneration* itself are forms of textual memory; all memory is ultimately memory of trauma because its aftershocks easily dominate the psyche; self-consciousness is denied access to severe memories of trauma by a mysterious mechanism of repression; and certain literary texts can help undo the repression of trauma, because they are already internal to it. Most memories are slight enough to leave little or no impact on the psyche, or traumas of pleasure which disturb the self with recurrent and possibly painful nostalgia or desire rather than the more extreme 'shell-shock' damage to control of body and mind.

Not only do the poets write about memory, they become friends by exchanging highly personal memories, and as they do, another central assumption about memory becomes apparent. The two men are strangers when they first meet in the novel, and, although they share an interest in poetry, their differences keep them distant from one another until Owen takes the plunge and shares a specific and intense memory with his new acquaintance:

> Sometimes when you're alone, in the trenches, I mean, at night you get the sense of something *ancient*. As if the trenches had always been there. You know one trench we held, it had skulls in the side. You looked back along and ... Like mushrooms. And do you know, it was actually *easier* to believe they were men from Marlborough's army than to to to think they'd been alive two years ago. It's as if all other wars had somehow

> ... distilled themselves into this war, and that makes it something you ... almost can't challenge. (ellipses in original, p. 83)

Sassoon replies with his own memory of temporal displacement: 'I was going up with the rations one night and I saw the limbers against the skyline, and the flares going up. What you see every night. Only I seemed to be seeing it from the future' (p. 84). A bond is formed and subsequently they meet to discuss their poetry and poetics in detail, with the result that Owen becomes a poet of war rather than a poet for whom poetry is a 'refuge' from war.

Their autobiographical memories are redolent of the sights and sounds of a particular moment, made special by the experience of relativistic spatio-temporal distortions. These distantiations of spacetime borrow from certain familiar textual strategies – the backward gaze of the historical novel, and the allegorisation inherent in the metonymies of realism – and the effect is that the realist memories undergo a postmodern turn. The logic of the plot makes this turn a result of the special perception of the writer. Confronted with the carnage, the horror, the endless ethical violations of the war, these writers find that the ordinary realism of memory is no longer adequate and must re-imagine the spacetime of the past.

Realist personal memories have recently become a significant area of psychological research. The cognitive psychologist David B. Pillemer has studied autobiographical, or 'personal event memory', through both interviews and laboratory research, and shown that it has a crucial role in everyday interaction. 'When a speaker makes a point by sharing a personal memory rather than by stating a general belief or feeling, this specialized form of communication signals emotionality and intimacy', and this encourages listeners to respond empathically, as happens with Owen and Sassoon.[10] Sharing memories is effective, not only because listeners can more easily link them to their own experience the more vivid they are, but because most people believe that vivid memories of this kind are signs of strong emotions. It is for this reason they are also likely to be treated as accurate recollections. Several studies have shown, for example, that jurors are more likely to believe witnesses who tell autobiographical stories with vivid details, especially detail which is not directly relevant to the point of the story, like the fact that Sassoon was carrying rations when he had his disorienting vision.[11] This expectation that recounted memories replete with circumstantial detail are likely to be veridical means that, as another psychologist, Daniel L. Schacter, explains: 'if an imagined or fantasized event does contain a wealth of details about the context and setting of an event, we will be inclined to believe that it is a real memory'.[12] Whether or not memory universally works like this, these psychologists establish the strength of the contemporary Western belief that memory is fundamentally realist.

The imagined world of an historical novel like *Regeneration* contains just such a wealth of what Pillemer calls the 'idiosyncratic peripheral details of personal circumstances', which it uses to emulate the signs of believable memory. It convinces us of its fidelity to what probably happened by its narrative bric-a-brac, as much as the historical accuracy of its costume, idiom, objects and landscapes. The net curtain that billows out behind Rivers when he first talks to Sassoon, or the 'half shrug, half flounce' that Billy Prior makes just before Rivers hypnotises him to recover the repressed memory which rendered him mute for a time, are incidental to what is happening but reassure us of its tangibility, its reality. Such novelistic display is widely admired. But there are other ways in which the realist modality also emulates what is ordinarily expected of memory. The curtain and the flounce belong to one consciousness (in these cases Rivers's), like almost all the observed detail in the novel, and this concurs with the consistent everyday belief about autobiographical memory that, as Brewer puts it, 'the remembered episode was personally experienced by the individual in that individual's past'.[13]

Detail is only one feature of the standard model of memory. Not only does personal event memory supposedly always carry this sense that it happened to a particular person, it has two characteristic forms of occurrence. Freud observed that two perspectival modes of autobiographical memory seemed to be at work in his patient's memories, and the earliest were those in which the patient was an observer of the early self: 'In the majority of significant and in other respects unimpeachable childhood scenes the subject sees himself in the recollection as a child, with the knowledge that this child is himself; he sees this child, however, as an observer from outside the scene would see him'.[14] A field memory occurs when the rememberer witnesses the scene of a memory from the standpoint in which it was lived, whereas in an observer memory the memory shows oneself within the scene which is then witnessed as a whole.[15] Subsequent psychological research has confirmed that field and observer memory can coexist (although there is considerable disagreement about whether a field memory is just a later revision of an observer memory), and realist fiction makes extensive use of this duality, presenting events in the third person as if they were observer memories for various characters, and using the first person for field memories. *Regeneration* consistently uses the third person and free indirect discourse to create the sense of closely rendered observer memories: Rivers might himself actually be remembering the arrival of Sassoon in that scene with the curtain, or Sassoon recalling his work on Owen's poem 'An Anthem for Doomed Youth'. This doesn't always work quite so neatly, of course

– the first meeting of the poets is awkward partly because the narrator's point of view shifts uncomfortably from one man to the other and then later to a virtual point where their two minds meet: 'They'd gone further than either of them had intended'[16] is an observation that could only be made by either an omniscient narrator or as a result of a shared consciousness. Such transgressions of the illusion are rare, and only occur for reasons like this when the novel needs an economical means of indicating the meeting of minds.

These various analogues between realist historical fiction and ordinary recollective memory all depend on one central parallelism between fictional realism and recollective memory. Autobiographical memory, according to all the current researchers, 'typically appears to be a "reliving" of the individual's phenomenal experience during that earlier moment'[17] and it takes place in a specific place and time. Autobiographical memory is articulated through re-enactment in tangible locations of space and time. This locational specificity was one of the main characteristics noted by the pioneer of recent memory studies, Endel Tulving. His own term for such memory, 'episodic memory', was adopted to distinguish it from the forms of memory then typically researched in behaviourist or cognitive psychology, based on retention of information in laboratory-controlled conditions. He wrote in his key paper on memory: 'There is something special about the subjective experience of explicitly remembering past incidents that separates it from other uses of memory ... In order to be experienced as a memory, the retrieved information must be recollected in the context of a particular time and place and with some reference to oneself as a participant in the episode'.[18] Such memory is 'characterized by a distinctive, unique awareness of reexperiencing here and now something that happened before, at another time and place'[19] which he ventures to say has a science-fictional quality to it, because it is 'mental time travel'.[20] This is almost exactly what a novel like *Regeneration* offers: a reliving of the past as if the reader had discovered a memory of these events and was now able to relive them by reading the text, convinced of their general veracity because they fulfil ordinary expectations of what constitutes proper autobiographical memories. The past is understood to be a place located in a time accessible to the re-enactment of memory. A novel like *Regeneration* effectively asserts that the past is a memory of time and space, conditioned by the mechanisms of identity formation and the repression of trauma to whose vicissitudes memory is subject.

This commitment to realism is in tension with its thematic treatment of theories and therapies of memory. Tulving argues that the subjective conviction that memory is simply a system of retrieving impressions of the past is a poor basis for theorising a mechanism of memory retrieval. He is insistent that a specific occurrence of memory 'derives its "contents", its informational ingredients, not only from the engram [trace] in episodic memory but also from the retrieval cue as interpreted by the semantic system and the general cognitive environment in which retrieval occurs'.[21] In the novel, the 'general cognitive environment' might extend outwards to both the new techniques of anamnesis and catharsis applied by Rivers, and in another direction, to the late twentieth-century preoccupation with recovered memory. We could read the distortions of spacetime in the poets' shared memories as signifiers of a loss of confidence in this shared environment, not least in its spatial and temporal stability.

The novel's brilliance lies in its treatment of the genealogy of modern beliefs about identity, memory and history in the *ad hoc* military psychology used to try and deal with the physical, moral and spiritual destruction of the First World War. It shows in great detail how Paul Fussell's belief that 'anxiety without end, without purpose, without reward, and without meaning is woven into the fabric of contemporary life', is justified by the experience of soldiers trying to work through the war histories which have riven their sense of identity.[22] The novel is also intensely aware of the myriad late twentieth-century debates about the troubles of memory, especially the arguments about repression and recovered memory, and the history of mnemic research. The stories of Rivers, Sassoon, Wilfred Owen and the fictional characters Prior and Burns, are interwoven with a background debate about the efficacy of different methods of working with traumatic memory and its repression, ranging from aversion therapy to golf. Prior gradually comes to terms with his memories of the front by talking about them, while another, Burns, has been so tormented by his unwanted memories that they have produced 'a complete disintegration of personality'.[23]

Some features of memory must be based in a shared physiology but we don't really know to what extent the findings of the research psychologists about memory depend on the body, or on the historical constitution of the person in Western culture. This is not to say that we can then discount their findings. They represent, as fully as is available, a reliable account of how contemporary memory works, and the consonance with realist fiction shows that novelists and readers share the sense that this is, indeed, how memory works. It is more fruitful to argue as the psychiatrist, Laurence J. Kirmayer does, that we would do well to direct more attention to the degree to which the workings of both individual and social memory rely on such collectively-shared expectations about how memory works and what it can provide. He suggests in particular that we should look for 'meta-memory' at work in the structuring of autobiographical memory:

the distinctive qualities of trauma narratives can also be understood as differences in the culturally constructed *landscape of memory*, the metaphoric terrain that shapes the distance and effort to remember affectively charged and socially defined events that may initially be vague, impressionistic, or simply absent from memory. Landscapes of memory are given shape by the personal and social significance of specific memories but also draw from *meta-memory* – implicit models of memory which influence what can be recalled and cited as veridical. Narratives of trauma may be understood then as cultural constructions of personal and historical memory.[24]

Meta-memory is likely to be as embedded in theoretical speculation as in everyday usage, and so we need to approach all theories of memory with a certain caution, whether they come from psychoanalysis or cognitive psychology. There is no one theory that can act as a reliable measure for literary practice, which itself is as active in investigating the connections between memory and history as the cultural theorists or the psychoanalysts.

Identity and trauma

Barker's novel is committed to realism largely because it affords a powerful means of presenting two specific models of memory that have come to dominate recent thought about identity and the after-effects of historical catastrophes: the idea that our identities are formed by memory; and the idea that memories can be repressed and then shape the personality from within. Both depend on the realism that we have been discussing, the idea that the past is relivable in the form of vivid images and conversations located in time and space. Postmodernism's preoccupation with spacetime resembles the sharing of memories by Owen and Sassoon in this, that it is a haunting by forms of memory that are not yet fully articulated. These are all background expectancies, the embedded taken-for-granted knowledge necessary to participate in contemporary Western culture. None of these models is ordinarily very explicit, and when stated baldly, might not command direct assent. They tend to be most effective when inscribed in other discourses and concepts, as is especially evident with the first of these models, the belief that our integrity and authenticity as people depends upon the possession of a coherent and communicable *curriculum vitae* of genuine memories.

The 'disintegration of personality' that Rivers notices in the shell-shocked Burns, results from the destruction of his memory. It is now widely believed that memory is the foundation of personal identity, and that anything that damages it will threaten the self, a belief that has become of central importance to the hegemonic mode of poetry, the autobiographic lyric, discussed in Chapter 6. The idea that memories are an inalienable foundation of identity underlies claims that a writer who presented plagiarised images of a childhood during the Holocaust as authentically his own was 'a memory thief' as the title of one article calls him. This case is particularly interesting because he is accused of claiming that intertextuality is authentic individual recollection; he has treated textual memories as if they were personal memories. It is now widely believed that the Swiss writer Binjamin Wilkomirski, the author of *Fragments: Memories of a Childhood, 1939–1948*, stole the images and experiences in his memoir from the archives.[25] Wilkomirski says near the opening of his short book, that his 'early childhood memories are planted, first and foremost, in exact snapshots of my photographic memory and in the feelings imprinted in them, and the physical sensations.'[26] The idea that memory is like a photograph ought to have given some readers pause for reflection, since as Kirmayer says, the most basic folk concept of memory treats it as a series of 'snapshots', captured at the time of initial experience through a process of recording which we can then harbour throughout our lives, recalling them when we need them, like opening a photo album.[27] This is one of the latest reinventions of a persistent Western model of memory as what David Farrell Krell calls the 'incising of a figure on the waxy surface of the mind or soul'.[28] Kirmayer tries to capture what is wrong with this idea with another image evocative of the modern urban environment: 'Memory is anything but a photographic record of experience; it is a roadway full of potholes, badly in need of repair, worked on day and night by revisionist crews'.[29] Wilkomirski qualifies his own statement about the photographic memories of childhood with a similar image, as if trying to use both the fragmentariness of his narrative as credible evidence of the wear and tear on his memories, and wanting to acknowledge the theorists' cautions about the reconstructive practices of memory. His memories, he says, are more rubble than album.[30] He ends the book with the briefest explanation for it, which nevertheless concurs with much contemporary psychotherapy: 'I wrote these fragments of memory to explore both myself and my earliest childhood; it may also have been an attempt to set myself free'.[31] The real self is the self of memory, not the identity that was 'imposed' on him by the authorities at the end of the war, the one represented by the document he was then given about his birth. 'The truth of a life' resides in memories, however hard to recover. Yet according to Gourevitch, instead of forming an identity, they are simply a costume he has worn over his own real identity, 'decking himself out in second-hand memories, borrowed memories, and outright stolen memories'.[32] Even the more sympathetic investigator of his case, Elena Lappin, thinks that he rewrote his identity.[33] Both Wilkomirski and Gourevitch appear to agree, however, that identity depends upon the possession of true memories, and the language of theft shows how much memories have taken on the status of possessions which confer special status on their owner, 'property that includes inviolable, sacred memories belonging to their rightful owners'.[34] The possibility that all memories might be more like clothes than skin is not considered.

The language of possessions and theft paradoxically demonstrates that memories are not simply indissociable elements of the individual self, however much like a house or cherished mementoes they might help sustain a core sense of self. Memory can only sustain identity because it is communicable, and this textual transmissability opens it to the effects of textuality. Such cases as these plagiarisms are still relatively rare, although there does seem to be a rising incidence of cases of both writers and war veterans inventing pasts for themselves to give their narratives added value. The usual effect of this linguistic intersubjectivity of memory is the narrativisation of memory.

The idea that personal identity depends upon the ability to tell a coherent narrative of one's history based on personal memory seems such a modern idea that it is worth reminding ourselves that it had a long history before psychology took hold of it, as Ian Hacking shows.[35] John Locke, for example, argued that 'personal identity' subsists in the 'identity of consciousness' and then immediately raised the problem of amnesia, because such continuity of identity seemed to him to be dependent on memory. His conclusion is still resonant because it shows how important the proper working of memory will seem to be if we base identity on it, and how disruptive amnesia might be:

> Suppose I wholly lose the memory of some parts of my life beyond a possibility of retrieving them, so that perhaps I shall never be conscious of them again: yet am I not the same person that did those actions, had those thoughts, that I once was conscious of, though I have forgot them? To which I answer ... if it be possible for the same man to have distinct incommunicable consciousness at different times, it is past doubt the same man would at different times make different persons.[36]

Daniel Schacter's contemporary account of the importance of memory retains much of this force: 'Extensively rehearsed and elaborated memories come to form the core of our life stories – narratives of self that help us define and understand our identity and our place in the world'.[37] What differentiates the modern view from Locke, or even the nineteenth-century idea, is that we are much more concerned to hang on to the continuity of identity, even if it means that the memorial narrative of identity is more like clothing than body. Schacter, for example, is careful to say that such signs of identity are 'extensively rehearsed', and Pillemer insists that the significance of these memories lies in the way they are 'psychologically real entities', rather than what he calls their 'truth value'. Yet the paradox remains. Like a bodystocking, the identity narrative must seem to be skin. This leads some psychologists to blame the incommunicability of early states of mind: not on the expectations we now place on the power of memory to sustain the self, but on the failures of space and time at the moment when a memory was conceived. Craig Barclay has studied Holocaust survivors who have not had the opportunity to work through their memories to the point where they have been rehearsed enough to be readily communicable. He argues that the conditions under which they lived (the imposed ignorance of their location, fate, and the reasons for their treatment), as well as the emotional shocks, mean that 'their narratives do not often have well-formed temporal-spatial, causal-conditional, and evaluative elements that would tend to increase memory accuracy'.[38] As a result their autobiographical narratives are 'incoherent and difficult to understand', and by implication they lack a strong sense of identity. These people were undoubtedly painfully disoriented by their savage treatment (as the fictional Owen and Sassoon are), but this somewhat literal explanation is made to do too much work and avoids confronting difficult questions about the equation of memories locatable by standardised forms of space and time, directly with self-identity. What is missing is a sense of the necessary mediation of social memory and especially its textual forms.

This is the work that the trauma theory of memory is often called upon to do. Memory's role in the maintenance of identity has, as we saw in Locke's speculations, long been recognised as vulnerable to loss. The psychoanalytic discovery that memories could be deliberately lost because they represented unwanted desires, therefore, opened up a complex field of investigation into the formation of the personality, and provided help for First World War psychiatrists faced with soldiers whose minds could no longer cope with grief and violation. There was a need for some mechanism for overcoming this resistance, and Barker provides an example of the textbook method in the scene where Billy Prior is hypnotised by Rivers and then undergoes a rapid cathartic recovery from the repressed memory which had directly inhibited Prior's ability to form his own narrative identity by making him mute. This diagnosed neurasthenic had arrived at Craiglockhart unable to speak, and even when he has recovered from his mutism he still has no memory of anything that happened after his first six months in France. Prior sees Rivers for a series of unsuccessful sessions of psychotherapy, hampered apparently by Prior's belief that, as he says, 'I don't think talking *helps*' (emphasis in original).[39] Eventually he explains why to Rivers: 'I mean *you're* more or less saying: things are real, you've got to face them, but how *can* I face them when I don't know what they are?' (emphasis in original).[40] Talking will not overcome the amnesia caused by his repression of the war trauma. The historical Rivers, like the fictional character, was generally opposed to the use of hypnosis, because he feared that it could increase the patient's dissociative state (he actually believed that the kinds of neurosis suffered by the ordinary soldier produced very similar symptoms to hypnotic suggestion[41]). It was not in itself the discovery of a shocking memory that mattered, or the discharge of the affects associated with it (the reliving of its emotional impact), but the work of communicating it in a coherent narrative form which would heal the patient. Anne Whitehead, in an important article on Barker's novel, explains that Rivers believed that the pathology arose not from a terrible shock itself, but the subsequent attempt at protective amnesia (Whitehead identifies this as a 'present conflict' rather than a pathology based in a past aetiology). Despite these fears, however, Rivers agrees to hypnotise Prior when he comes back that same evening and the method appears to work – the narrative plunges us abruptly into Prior's unfolding observer memory, a richly detailed autobiographical memory full of convincing peripheral detail, like the creak of chicken wire as he leans toward the table in the dugout. For several pages the reader is treated to a highly articulate, richly, if uncomfortably, sensuous, unfolding recollection, moving spontaneously and yet in a well co-ordinated trajectory through a specific location in space and time to its shocking climax in which he is left holding an eye. The artifice of this is concealed behind the implicit claim that this is indeed how recovered memories should appear. When the memory ends, white space on the page indicates that the narrative is now back in the 'real time' of Rivers's office: 'Rivers watched the play of emotions on Prior's face as he fitted the recovered memory into his past'.[42]

Up to this point, the narrative could be a textbook demonstration of Freud and Breuer's account of the aetiology of hysteria. Like Rivers they were concerned with patients who had lost sections of memory: 'these memories, unlike other memories of their past lives, are not at the patient's disposal. On the contrary, *these experiences are completely absent from the patients' memory when they are in a normal psychical state, or are present only in a highly summary form*' (italics in original).[43] Even to these enthusiasts for hypnosis, it seemed almost too good to be true: 'For we found, to our great surprise at first, that *each individual hysterical symptom immediately and permanently disappeared when we had succeeded in bringing clearly to light the memory of the event by which it was provoked and in arousing its accompanying affect, and when the patient had described that event in the greatest possible detail and had put the affect into words*' (italics in original).[44] It was too good to be true, and so it proves in Barker's novel also, for as Whitehead notes, Prior's reaction complicates things. To River's surprise, Prior says sharply, 'is that all?' and then says dismissively, 'it was nothing'. The ensuing argument makes plain that Prior may merely be expressing surprise that this one particular atrocity out of so many he has witnessed should have done him in, but there is also a hint that any healing will be temporary. Subsequent events, especially in the second volume of the trilogy, *The Eye in the Door* (1993), where he develops a second personality and blanks out for periods of time, bear out his suspicion that the therapy has not worked.

Regeneration as a whole offers a sceptical context for Rivers's theory of recovered memory for two reasons. One problem is conveyed by Prior's remark, 'is that all' – the events of the war exceed the capacity of utterance on which Freud and Breuer relied, and which Rivers takes for granted. The past is not so neatly packaged into recoverable traumatic memories that can be separated out from the vast background of the past. A second reason for the novel's scepticism is only implicit in the indistinguishable forms of narration for hypnosis and actuality. How can special force be claimed of hypnosis if its manifestation is so similar to ordinary recollection and narrative? Does this mean all narrative is hypnotic and potentially therapeutic or, as we think the novel implies, does it mean that hypnosis is more likely to be nothing more than an intensification of ordinary memory at work?

Belief in the power of hypnosis or direct questioning to elicit or 'recover' repressed memories and free the patient of the damaging effects on their identity of the trauma, has been widespread during the past two decades. A traumatic incident overwhelms the capacity of the mind to process the emotions and thoughts it produces, with the result that the entire event is repressed and, therefore, out of reach of the conscious mind. Therapy, especially when it carefully directs the patient to the areas of difficulty, can provide the necessary leverage through the act of supportive witness offered by the therapist to recover the memory. This memory returns whole, as a vivid, accurate composition of narrative and image, ready to be slotted back into the hole it left in the otherwise complete tapestry of memory. This is a model which has been widely used by both the 'barefoot' psychoanalytic movements and professional therapists and counsellors. Even hypnosis has been widely used, and given rise to one of the strangest features of the contemporary politics of memory – alien abduction narratives which imbricate science fiction and trauma theory. The psychologist John E. Mack, who uses hypnosis to study experiences of alien abduction among Americans, reports that his subjects are not always convinced by what they recall (one abductee, Scott, who 'recalled that since early childhood he experienced himself as having "two personalities" ... and now believes that the doubting and denying of his alien experience has been a destructive process in his life' sounds quite like Prior), but doesn't see this as indicative of any problems with his method.[45] No warning bells seem to sound when a woman who has been recovering memories of alien spaceships says, 'I still don't remember it like a real memory, as in I remember I went to work yesterday'.[46] Lacking the affect and detail of realist memory to start with, these memories have to be worked up into narratives, which Mack's book does very well.

Alien abduction narratives are a reminder that avowedly imaginary literatures like science fiction can provide such powerful generic cognitive structures that they eventually cross over into other areas of experience. They are now the exotic end of a wide spectrum of recovered memory discourses active today. According to a hostile critic of these developments, Frederick C. Crews, the diagnosis of repressed memories of sexual abuse grew to 'epidemic frequency' during the past twenty years, and an estimated 50,000 therapists were ready to help their clients recover these events.[47] Perhaps because she was aware of these 'memory wars', Barker clearly began to have further doubts about recovered memory. In *The Eye in the Door*, when Billy Prior once again presses Rivers to use hypnosis to help him understand the recurrence of his war neurosis (which he experiences as 'missing time', a symptom widely invoked by the alien abductees), Rivers replies with an answer that might have come from a recent summary of false memory syndrome: 'You see, one of the things people who believe in ... the extensive use of hypnosis claim – well, they don't even claim it, they assume it – is that memories recovered in that way are genuine memories. But they're very often not. They can be fantasies, or they can be responses to suggestions from the therapist'.[48] The difficulty is still represented as the problem of separating the true from the false, however, rather than a problem with the underlying assumption about identity, and this has been the emphasis of those who defend current therapies that recover memories. This preoccupation with accuracy may represent an unfulfilled wish to come to terms with the difficulty of locating the past in contemporary history.

This is strongly suggested by the terms in which some proponents of the trauma theory and recovered memory write about its value. Alongside his own essays, Crews includes letters and other responses to the essays that form the book, and these repeatedly insist that he is missing the crux of the issue. Sexual abuse of children is widespread (around 1 per cent of American women in some estimates); many if not most victims do not base their claims to abuse purely on recovered memories but have enduring memories of trouble since childhood; Crews and other opponents of this therapy simplify the concept of repression in order to dismiss it as unproven. This is therefore also a political debate. As Linda Alcoff and Laura Gray said in a careful article in *Signs* (1993), the aim of what they call 'survivor discourse' has been to bear witness in public to the effects of men's power, in order to educate people about the problems, influence opinion, and demonstrate that this is a social not a private concern.[49] Although they obviously find some validity in the model of repressed memory, and mention the possibility that partial amnesia follows abuse, they rely most on a Foucauldian analysis of discourse and power, and shy away from argument about specific psychic mechanisms. For them, the problem with psychoanalysis is its own turning away from the moral and political significance of adult stories of childhood sexual abuse by categorising them generically as seduction fantasies. The narratives need to be read as history, while recognising the hermeneutic demands of their textual memory. Characteristically, they are not very interested in examining specific mechanisms of memory. History is what matters. This caution is also evident in Schacter's useful summary of the implications of the memory wars for psychological research. Like other temperate commentators on the whole phenomenon, he believes the real problem is that the elicitation of misleading memories by dubious therapeutic methods has led to the doubting of genuine cases of sexual and other abuse. Repression is dubious science. There is little evidence that a major emotional or physical shock to a person usually creates amnesia, except in the immediate aftermath when the brain does not function well. Neither is there any credible scientific evidence for the reliability of recovered memories of sexual abuse, and much counter-evidence that 'freely imagining an event, and then exploring it and talking about it as if it were real, is a potentially powerful means of creating the kind of subjective feeling that accompanies an authentic memory'.[50] Why then is the meta-memory of trauma so compelling, so that, as LaCapra puts it, there is often an 'indiscriminate conflation of all history with trauma'?[51] Could the intensively detailed imagination at work in realist fiction anticipate such effects on the social memory too?

The problem with hypnosis for its critics is that it is so realistic that the hypnotised subject cannot tell what is fiction and what is fact, and often neither can its practitioners and, therefore, hypnosis is much like reading a powerful realist novel. Barker can warn that 'fact and fiction are so interwoven in this book that it may help the reader to know what is historical and what is not', but no similar measure of epistemological reliability is likely to be available to those involved in recovering memories of alien surgery or long-ago satanic rituals. Even Barker can only do so much without writing another book entirely, and does not answer the question that we might ask here. In what, exactly, does her help consist? The very offer implies that fictional realism might induce false social memory syndrome. Does this mean that fictional realism itself might be too much like hypnosis? Mary Renault's horror at the thought of distorting historical truth mentioned in Chapter 2 might be due to a belief in the power of fiction as much as in the debt owed to the past. Judgements on the significance of historical truth, either realist or postmodernist, may divert attention too quickly from the possibilities which such affinities between hypnosis, or suggestion and realism have suggested to writers. Mikkel Borch-Jacobsen has persuasively shown that hypnosis remained important to Freud throughout his career, long after his abandonment of it as therapy, both because it was evidence of the activity of the unconscious as powerful as the dream, and because it represented the basic 'emotional tie' with others. The transference was supposed to have taken the place of hypnosis, but it enacted certain features of hypnosis, especially the giving up of one's ego to the subjectivity of the hypnotist. Transferential passions 'mean that the purely autobiographical narrative of the patient tended to transform itself yet again into a current relationship, one that was acted out (not to say mimed).'[52] 'Mimed' because the patient falls in love with the analyst, analysis and its theory and tries to imitate and enact them in her or his own life. In doing so, the patient is close to allowing the 'radical *forgetting of the other*' (italics in original) which takes place in hypnosis, to occur in the analytic situation. It is not only the other that disappears. The transference is also a forgetting of past and future, because only the emotions experienced in the present are active, and the representations or memories which stir them are hidden. Realist fiction is, therefore, both specially placed to reflect on the workings of the transference as a re-enactment of childhood patterns of attachment and repulsion, and potentially too complicit to provide sufficient critical distance for understanding. The result is a dilemma for realist historical fiction, and one reason why other new literary genres ranging from postmodernist metafiction to entirely new modes of writing, have emerged over the past half century.

The affinities between psychoanalysis and narrative fiction depend on much more than just powerful identification. The trauma theory of identity depends upon a temporal structure, delayed affect and retranscription of memory in ways which are very close to the structure of narrative. This is especially striking in the case of the fate of the repression hypothesis in psychoanalysis, and its postmodern appropriations in the concept of *Nachträglichkeit*. The repression hypothesis retains its considerable power because it is so readily aligned with the idea that those areas of the collective past whose history has been suppressed have suffered this as the result of social mechanisms comparable to the work of repression, requiring a critical method similar to analytic anamnesis to undertake the moral work of recovery. In its simpler form, as we have seen, it has become the most influential of all current metamemory strategies for representing social memory. Although this popular concept of repression was not what Freud meant by repression once he abandoned his early theories, his work has given authority to the repression hypothesis in its widely disseminated forms, because of both the continuing currency of his early statements about trauma, and the indistinctness of his general theories of memory. This, too, is why much of Jacques Lacan's most innovative theory was directed towards rethinking time and memory in Freud's legacy.

The problem is that Freud had little to say about memory as such, even though it permeates his theorising. A full theory of memory ceased to be a primary interest after the 'Project' of 1895. It is characteristic of the neglect which he sanctioned, that one historian of psychoanalysis, Reuben Fine, devotes just three out of over six hundred pages in his history to Freud's conception of memory, and Laplanche and Pontalis in their psychoanalytic dictionary entry for memory say at once that the concept of the 'memory-trace' was 'never fully expounded'.[53] There is a paradox here, of course. It was the observation of amnesias, refusals to recollect, the reconstruction of memories and, above all, the patients' obsession with specific memory images and narratives that prompted Freud to develop his theories. It is not surprising that Lacan's summary of psychoanalysis in his Rome address (1953) says 'what we teach the subject to recognise is his unconscious in his history'. Lacan speaks as if the task of analysis is for analyst and analysand to compose a historical narrative together: 'it is certainly this assumption of his history by the subject, in so far as it is constituted by the speech addressed to the other, that constitutes the ground of the new method that Freud called psychoanalysis'.[54] When Freud explains why there can be unconscious ideas but not unconscious emotions in his essay, 'The Unconscious' (1915), he takes for granted that the unconscious is a store of memories: 'ideas are cathexes – basically of memory-traces – while affects and emotions correspond to processes of discharge, the final manifestations of which are perceived as feelings'.[55] This is one of Freud's most fundamental principles. Emotions are never remembered; they can only be enacted in the present moment when prompted by the emergence of representations of past experience to consciousness.

Earlier in the essay, he refers to the enormous quantity of 'latent memories' each of us possesses, and which have to be kept unconscious if they are not to overload the consciousness. These 'latent' memories really belong to a different theoretical paradigm – they are simply elements of the ordinary memory system which enables us to locate ourselves in the world from day to day. Freud rarely talks about this ordinary memory despite its centrality in everyday life. When he does, he is usually preoccupied with this idea of an almost ungovernable quantity of memories. In 'A Note on the Mystic Writing Pad', he pointed out that writing systems like ink and paper or a slate, could be compared with different models of memory, although our minds seem to solve the technical problems better than any known writing system. A sheet of paper, like the mind, can only hold so much experience without becoming overloaded and incoherent; the slate manages the problem by erasure or forgetting, but this is a permanent loss. The mystic writing pad solves the problem of storage by creating two systems, the wax paper above and the impressionable wax below, with a layer of celluloid on top and the separation of the sheets from the wax erases the writing, which nevertheless remains as a permanent faint impression below. Similarly, the conscious and the unconscious maintain a continual dialectic of proximity and distance. What interests Freud above all, is the curious way in which memory comes and goes in everyday thought. Repression is just a striking example of something basic to the workings of the mind. In *The Ego and the Id* (1923) for example, Freud describes the 'word-presentations' of the pre-conscious, which are capable of becoming conscious, as 'residues of memories; they were at one time perceptions, and like all mnemic residues they can become conscious again'.[56] Freud thinks of memory in terms of repression, and this is why affects are neither remembered nor unconscious.

Laplanche and Pontalis conclude that repression is a 'universal mental process' and 'lies at the root of the constitution of the unconscious as a domain separate from the rest of the psyche'.[57] To talk about repression is to talk about the entire system of memory for reasons that Malcolm Bowie neatly summarises: 'For Lacan, as for Freud, it made much more sense to suppose that a single set of rules governed all mental events and that the pathogenic ones were a lens through which the structure of subjectivity could be viewed'.[58] This is very evident in Freud's most explicit account of repression, 'Repression' (1915), which argues that instincts manifest themselves as ideas, and it is the ideas that are repressed because of the strong cathexes of affect attached to them, not the instincts or the emotions themselves. Repression is not conceptualised as the suppression of a memory of a traumatic event, but rather as a means of controlling the 'psychical (ideational) representative of the instinct' which might well have been implicated in a particular traumatic incident. These provoking ideas are repressed in order to avoid the painful emotions they awaken when they appear in consciousness: 'the essence of repression lies simply in turning something away, and keeping it at a distance, from the conscious'.[59] Repression works night and day and, therefore, requires 'a persistent expenditure of force'.[60]

Such ideas have been widely popularised in a simplified form, and have helped to create the metamemory terrain of trauma on which the memory wars have been fought, and the sketchiness of the memory theory made this appropriation easier than it ought to have been. It also encouraged revisionists to give prominence to undeveloped ideas in Freud's work. Lacan rescued Freud's German term *Nachträglichkeit* from the neglect of translators in order to alert psychoanalysts and cultural critics to another more radical temporality at work in the theory of repression, one which runs counter to ideas of stored memories and originating traumatic events. He realised that Freud thought the 'afterwardsness', or retroaction of neuroses linked to early memories, required a rethinking of the causality and temporality of memory. The Wolf Man received an impression of his parents' copulation at a very early age but only later, as a result of his sexual development, was he able to feel the affect. A later scene makes possible the memory of an earlier one, and Freud was very willing to acknowledge that the past was being rewritten in the process. For him, the significance of the 'observer' memories of early childhood lay in the evidence that this silent restaging of the earlier scene showed that a working through of the memory had taken place. 'Whenever in a memory the subject himself appears in this way as an object among other objects, this contrast between the acting and recollecting ego may be taken as evidence that the original impression has been worked over'.[61] The appearance of an observer memory is proof that the initial state of the memory has been reworked, because Freud assumes that memories must start out as field memories. Third-person accounts are renarrativisations of the past. These memories resist ordinary temporal explanations because ordinary linear time does not seem to elapse between the moments, and the previously unacknowledged happening only becomes an *event* at some later point of intense emotional upsurge. As Peter Nicholls points out, '*Nachträglichkeit* calls into question traditional notions of causality – the second event is presented now as the "cause" of the first'.[62]

The concept of *Nachträglichkeit* makes explicit why the concept of trauma is so pervasive in our culture. Trauma is assumed to be capable of standing for a non-linear temporal relation to the past, because the force of the initiating event cancels the intervening time as its memory residues remain in the timeless unconscious and, therefore, overleap the intervening continuum of contingent events. This is why trauma is such a seductive idea despite its risks. The trouble is, as the recent history of recovered memory accusations, alien abductions and the development of a 'wound culture' shows, the cost of using trauma to gain access to a malleable past is very high in personal and social terms, as well as conceptual clarity.

In several recent articles, Mark Seltzer has shown that we need to be careful about treating contemporary culture's relation to trauma as a constructive paradigm for universal emulation. He proposes that we think of a 'pathological public sphere' to account for the apparently pervasive fascination in our culture with violence and the display of wounds. 'One discovers again and again the excitations in the opening of private and bodily and psychic interiors; the exhibition and witnessing, the endlessly reproducible display of wounded bodies and wounded minds in public'.[63] He raises doubts about the continued use of the theory that adult violence is the future of childhood trauma as a 'mimetic identification intensified to the point of reproduction'.[64] Seltzer here detects a theory of sociality based on mimetic identification, whereby trauma is a moment when people experience mergers of the self and other, either directly or vicariously through the pathological public sphere. The provision of an individualised explanation of social violence neglects to investigate the nature of trauma itself. Psychoanalytic theory of trauma depends on the axiom that psychic trauma is endogenous because the psychic domain is treated as autonomous, although trauma itself must have some relation with the external world and it, therefore, troubles the assumption of psychic autonomy, as well as being closely associated with the experience of an uncertainty about whether representations are produced from outside or within. The trauma 'is the product, not of an event itself, but of how the subject repeats or represents it to himself'.[65] Seltzer cites an article in *Newsweek* that demonstrated the popular belief that representation of violence is violent, which used *Jurassic Park* as an example: 'These beasts look state-of-the-art real. And they *eat* people'. The magazine is an instance of a fear that we discussed in Chapter 1, that 'one might be devoured by representations'.[66] Our explanation of this fear factors in the past as part of the terror. It is not just representation and violence that make these representations seem dangerous, but the residue of history transmogrified into a devouring beast returned to consume the present and its hopes for the future that is at work. Seltzer's brilliant insights into contemporary culture demonstrate just how deeply collective historical trauma must have worked itself into all our cultural practices and the theories we use to comprehend them, and cautions us against using these models of metamemory as if they were unchallengeable dogma, rather than cultural landscapes of spacetime.

Trauma is not only a short-cut to sociality, it is also a short-cut to a renewed relation to the past. This dimension of the recovered memory model is closely tied to the Freudian discourse of energetics and storage as discursivity, to a degree which becomes evident in a radical rereading of Freud by Jacques Derrida, who obliquely brings out the degree to which the entire later Freudian project is a challenge to linear time. Most therapists and many cultural theorists have wanted the power of this non-chronological relation to the past, but not been able to have it without the pathologisation of intimacy and public life. It is worth pausing, therefore, on the important poststructuralist essay where Derrida offered this unusual interpretation of Freud, in order to see where he finds the temporal possibilities in Freud. The essay also shows how the relative neglect of wider problems of memory in poststructuralist cultural theory has been sustained by this translation of memory into a textual epiphenomenon.

Derrida's extended essay on Freud's short discussion of the child's 'Mystic pad' justifies its interpretative licence by calling the Freudian topology of memory an 'unbelievable mythology' and, therefore, treating it as a demonstration of metaphoricity.[67] Derrida's key move is to introduce twentieth-century models of time into the argument in order to develop a more adequate theory of memory. Although Freud said categorically that 'the processes of the system *Ucs.* are *timeless*; i.e. they are not ordered temporally, are not altered by the passage of time; they have no reference to time at all',[68] Derrida argues that we should now interpret this to mean that these processes do not act within linear or calendrical time. They may well, however, manifest other forms of temporality and, therefore, are not in the absolute sense, timeless. This enables him to attribute a proto-grammatological theory to Freud: 'he [i.e. Freud] will link a discontinuist conception of time, as the periodicity and spacing of writing, to a whole chain of hypotheses which stretch from the *Letters to Fliess* to *Beyond the Pleasure Principle*, and which, once again, are constructed, consolidated, confirmed, and solidified in the Mystic Pad'.[69] We can see why *Nachträglichkeit* could become an important concept. It would link memory with temporal discontinuity because it elides time as one continuous causal chain, without resorting to such a radical rereading of Freud. The difficulty with accepting Derrida's interpretation, however, is that it underestimates the technics of memory, with the result that, as one commentator expresses it in a related context, 'Derrida's thinking of time can appear formalist'.[70] Although Derrida locates memory entirely in the discursive apparatus by arguing that memory is created by the relation between, on the one hand, machines for externalising memory, like the Mystic Pad, and on the other, the psyche, through their mutual dependency on writing, this inflation of the idea of textual memory loses sight of memory altogether. Memory turns into writing: 'writing is the stage of history and the play of the world'.[71] Memory is necessarily textual memory, not because of the material role of texts in the maintenance of cultural memory but because of the inherent temporality of writing. Derrida's essay demonstrates that there is an insistent pressure to find models of memory that respond to new modes of social times.

The reasoning behind this has been most fully explored with the application of the concept of *Nachträglichkeit* to social memory and history. Nicholls argues that it plays an important part in an aspect of postmodern thought that is sometimes overlooked in summaries – its intensive reconfiguring of the temporality of history. He cites Lyotard's account of post-Holocaust memory in *Heidegger and 'the Jews'* where history becomes 'a collision of two temporalities'[72] and requires, in Lyotard's words, 'an aesthetics of shock' because the past invades us without warning. Left to its own devices, narrative misrepresents the relation with the past:

> This chronologization of a time that is not chronological, this retrieval of a time (the first blow) that is lost because it has not had place and time in the psychic apparatus, that has not been noticed there, fulfills exactly the presumed function that Freud attributes to it in *Jenseits*. Narrative organization is constitutive of diachronic time, and the time that it constitutes has the effect of 'neutralizing' an 'initial' violence, of representing a presence without representation, of staging the obscene, of dissociating the past from the present, and of staging a recollection that must be a reappropriation of the improper, achronological affect.[73]

Realism we might say, if this didn't risk sounding flippant, needs trauma to overcome its inscription of linear time. We can see these tensions at work in Barker's novel. The achronological memories that Owen and Sassoon exchange are not able to find a place in the narrative frame of the novel itself, and remain at odds with the realist time.

The novel can only find a place for these other relations to the past by remaining absent from the battle front and observing it all through the temporal vicissitudes of traumatic memory at the psychiatric hospital. Rivers's departure from the hospital is as much a conclusion as Sassoon's return to the trench warfare he had publically condemned at the start of the novel. Lyotard is wrong to suggest that realism always enforces linear time, however. In Chapter 7 we discuss the use of the future in science fiction as a way of avoiding the neutralisations of diachronic time that realist fiction seems to entail. The future is the location where the first blow, our history, is belatedly manifest in the fantasy projections of our traumatic pasts into a world which will be the outcome of our own, making this gleaming futurity a narrative strategy of *Nachträglichkeit*.

Social memory

The historian Jacques Le Goff calls for contemporary 'specialists in memory ... to make of the struggle for the democratization of social memory one of the primary imperatives of their scientific objectivity'.[74]

Democratisation could mean no more than responsible popularisation, but it might also point us towards the ethical relation to the past which we discussed in Chapter 2, and from there towards a political activity of remembering, reconstructing and textualising the past. Le Goff talks only of objectivity. Why not look to a democratisation that can engage in the emotional working through of memory as well as the reflexive aesthetics of fantasy? We cited earlier Barker's avowed wish to help the reader understand the relations between objectivity and imagination in her novel. We might conjecture that she hopes that the reader of this novel, which attempts to demonstrate why we must not forget the horror of the First World War, will go on to learn more about the history in order to more firmly establish an ethical relation between the present and this past. The novel will, if it has worked, have taken us inside the horror, and horror, according to Ricoeur, is a measure of the uniqueness of a terrible historical event that fiction has a special power to depict. No conventional analytic means can ever be quite effective at conveying this uniqueness because such methods depend upon 'a work of explanation that connects things together'. This locates causes, calendrical relations, patterns, similarities, data and locations, but in doing so it has to diminish the absoluteness of the actual phenomeno-logical experience, which in such cases is orthogonal to any sense of temporal or causal progression: 'Individuation by means of the horrible, to which we are particularly attentive, would be blind feeling, regardless of how elevated or how profound it might be, without the quasi-intu-itiveness of fiction. Fiction gives eyes to the horrified narrator. Eyes to see and to weep.'[75] Once having seen what happened and begun to mourn, the reader will be able to go on to work through the implications in the social memory. Anne Whitehead reports that the biographer Miranda Seymour, who was writing a biography of Robert Graves, found Barker's account of Rivers and his influence on the lives of the poets, 'more compelling' than the existing historical record: 'the power of the fictional narrative to transform and reconfigure the past is clearly in evidence here'.[76]

This process of reconfiguration is, therefore, not simply a judicial sifting of the documentary record in the full light of reason which requires only the assistance of expository discourse. If the facts were already revealed in the archive, the careful biographer would have been able to see this possibility without help. Reading the material was not enough; a change of relation to the past was also required. It was the historical novel which helped make this possible through its special work with memory. The case of the biographer makes clear that this is a process which takes place on a boundary between individual understand-ing and a social memory that is not simply already fully manifest in the textual archive. One way to explain this transformation of the past is offered by Dominick LaCapra in his cautiously psychoanalytic account of fictions of the Holocaust.

Unlike many theorists, he believes that psychoanalytic theory can be extended to social memory. Many of the key concepts are based not on hypotheses about endopsychic processes but on extensive observation of the intersubjective encounter between analyst and patient during the analytic session, especially as it develops within the transference. Rivers may be treated as a father figure by Prior, but the significance of these exchanges extends much further. Their sessions are a synecdoche of wider social processes; for example, medical ethics encountering the masculine doctrines of the army. Therefore, LaCapra believes that many psychoanalytic concepts describe the dynamics of the network of emotional ties and other intersubjective bonds which sustain sociality: 'these concepts refer to processes that always involve modes of interaction, mutual reinforcement, conflict, censorship, orientation toward others, and so forth, and their relative individual or collective status should not be prejudged'.[77] Freud certainly gives opportunity for thinking of some forms of memory in this way. In his essay, 'Remembering, Repeating, and Working-Through' (1915), he talks as if memories circulated outward between analyst and patient to form part of their mutual dialogue. He locates the 'awakening of the memories' in the 'intermediate region', or intersubjective space, of the transference, the location of the 'arduous task' of the 'working-through of the resistances'.[78]

'Acting-out' and 'working-through' (Freud's later revision of 'working-over'), are the concepts which LaCapra believes best fit the demands of explaining the role of literary texts in mediating between personal and collective memory of the Holocaust, and he devotes most of his discussion to them. Working-through is an unsurprising choice for talking about the ethics of a textualised relation to the past, since it describes the hard emotional work of discharging emotion cathected to repressed and damaging memories, and then rethinking one's relation to the past that they represent. Freud's description of mourning in 'Mourning and Melancholia' remains the best summary of what is involved in this effort: 'each single one of the memories and expectations in which the libido is bound to the object is brought up and hyper-cathected, and detachment of the libido is accomplished in respect of it'.[79] Acting-out is usually thought of as a bad thing, a repetition of a neurotic obsession and, therefore, incidental to the work of transforming memory's paralysing force. It is a name for incorporation (the object is split off from the ego which refuses to recognise its otherness), and corresponds to what Freud called melancholia, while working-through corresponds to introjection (the object is accessible and yet clearly differentiated from the ego), and emerges from the process of mourning.[80] Despite the pejorative use of the popular term 'acting-out', it is not so easily distinguished from 'working-through' as is commonly supposed because incorporation overlaps with introjection. In Freud's exposition, the moment when the memory is 'brought up' will still belong to the zone of incorporation, and will appear to happen in an unmediated manner to the subject. LaCapra recognises this in his own attempt to describe it, which could be a description of the workings of a realist historical novel like Barker's: 'In acting-out one has a mimetic relation to the past which is regenerated or relived as if it were fully present rather than represented in memory and inscription'.[81] He treats 'acting-out' as a first step in the process of mourning, because the mimetic re-enactment of the past at least makes conscious what needs reconfiguration and, therefore, can help in the 'mitigation of trauma'. What is needed to make acting-out more than egocentric depression and unreflective self-display is the co-presence of the second stage of working-through.

The pairing of the concepts makes it possible to think of literary texts as practices of social memory. Lawrence Langer, for example, makes a distinction between story and plot in Holocaust testimony which shows how we might translate this conjunction into narratological terms: story is the chronological narrative, while plot is the 'memory's confrontation with details embedded in moments of trauma'.[82] Plot is, therefore, similar to the bringing up of memories prior to working through them, but it depends on this wider structure, which also requires the local intensities of plot to prevent it from evading the demands of unique anguish. This implies two differing types of representation of the past embedded within the same narrative: one which seeks transcendence; and one which enmeshes the witness in the events of the past. By extension, both novel and autobiographical memory can be considered as a stage on the way to 'critical judgement' and the recognition that what is acted out is not a past reliving itself but a product of textual memory. Barker's reader acts out the story of Sassoon, Rivers and Prior, and then is able to move on to mourn the First World War in constructive ways that look to the future as well as the past (the fictional Wilfred Owen's hallucination that the First World War somehow imbricated all wars within its symbolic remit, and the fictional Sassoon's glimpse of the future's perspective on the war, are both reminders that this war will present a moral task to the future).

The memory practices of acting-out and working-through do not necessarily require narrative forms, however, and this is even more true of their wider, more collective counterparts. Indeed, social memory is not sustained by texts alone even in the late twentieth century. Paul Connerton argues that the well-publicised differences between psychoanalysis and cognitive psychology distract attention from a third form of social memory, because social theorists have allowed their intense hermeneutic interest in these 'inscribing practices' to obscure the significance of equally important 'incorporating practices' which co-exist alongside them.[83] Corporeal memory comprises bodily habits, postures and behaviours by which a group transmits 'values and categories which it is most anxious to conserve' because it knows 'how well the past can be kept in mind by a habitual memory sedimented in the body'.[84] Although he argues strongly that bodily memories are effective not only insofar as they are signifiers within a semiotic system, but also as non-cognitive practice, he does allow for an interplay of both inscription and incorporational memory.

We can see this at work in the testimony of Charlotte Delbo, a survivor of Auschwitz, who has written extensively about the traumatic problems and personal consequences of remembering and forgetting the Holocaust, especially about the way in which memory can toughen and harden the further one gets away from the events:

> The skin covering the memory of Auschwitz is tough. Sometimes, however, it bursts, and gives back its contents. In a dream, the will is powerless. And in these dreams, there I see myself again, *me*, yes *me*, just as I know I was: scarcely able to stand ... pierced with cold, filthy, gaunt, and the pain is unbearable, so exactly the pain I suffered there, that I feel it again physically, I feel it again through my whole body, which becomes a block of pain, and I feel death seizing me, I feel myself die. Fortunately, in my anguish, I cry out. The cry awakens me, and I emerge from the nightmare, exhausted. It takes days for everything to return to normal, for memory to be 'refilled' and for the skin of memory to mend itself. I become myself again, the one you know, who can speak to you of Auschwitz without showing any sign of distress or emotion.[85]

Delbo characterises the way a buried memory can erupt unexpectedly, bursting through the skin of one's self-consciousness like an 'alien', traumatising the self to such a degree that one feels dead in a discourse similar to that of Lyotard's *Nachträglich* history. Her reflections on this are motivated by the moral question of how a survivor can speak for and remember the dead. Writing about her experiences in Auschwitz – part narrative, part documentary – is her attempt to mend the skin of memory; reconstructing history, permitting anamnesis, giving space for the repetitive emergence of an uncontrollable 'other', and forming tentative narratives are her attempt to find and transmit a therapeutic practice.

Connerton's primary instance of public corporeal memory is not the skin but performance and, although he passes over its aesthetic potential, the poetics of performance point to possible literary practices of corporeal memory. An obvious example would be the way in which sound in poetry carries a non-semiotic significance for poets[86] and singers, as Roland Barthes acknowledged when he somewhat romanticised the Russian cantor, saying that their entire culture played forth from their lips: 'something which is directly the cantor's body, brought to your ears in one and the same movement from deep down in the cavities, the muscles, the membranes, the cartilages, and from deep down in the Slavonic language, as though a single skin lined the inner flesh of the performer and the music he sings'.[87] Sound as a means of working with social memory is one of the least explored features of both drama and poetry in performance, and why we might look beyond the mnemic technologies of verbal patterning which make poetry in oral cultures, as Pierre Bourdieu expresses it: 'the preservation technique par excellence'.[88] The sounding of words in performance is a central feature of theatre, alongside the physical presence of the actor's bodies producing visual images and articulations of physical space and kinesthetic representations of states of being, within the intersubjective matrix of the designated public space of the theatre. Since Connerton's principal metaphor for the dynamic of corporeal social memory is performance, we might look to drama to see it at work in a reflexive mode. At this point a further possibility presents itself. The use of the term 'acting' in acting-out is based on the strong mimetic identifications at work in this psychic process, and its frequently bold physical gestures. Drama would be exceptionally well placed, therefore, for a certain kind of metacorporeal social memory to work through its emotional investments, repressions and interpretations. In Chapter 5 we, therefore, look at the workings of the textual memory in historical theatre of the 1970s, and show just how the past can be inscribed and incorporated in historical literature other than as narrative.

One final example of a culture without writing, where performance and art take its place, offers a final corrective to an inevitable emphasis on the recovery of memory rather than the forgetting of the past. The island of Sabarl, three hundred miles from New Guinea, is still reliant on art today for its sense of continuity with the past according to the anthropologist, Deborah Battaglia, who studied its culture in the 1970s. Even spoken language is not considered important for memory by these islanders who rely primarily upon 'concrete, witnessable images', such as objects, places and particularly funeral rites to generate their collective sense of history.[89] These special feasts (the 'segaiya') to memorialise the dead, are theatrical rituals that help create a 'new, edited image of the person' that can then become an active part of their collective life in the present and future. Like Connerton, she believes that to consider such performance a text can be misleading because it is effective only as 'an ephemeral "text enacted", forever under revision' and cannot act as a measure of one's knowledge[90] – there is no final edition of the deceased. The idea that the task is not so much to remember the past as to rework it for the future, is helpful for considering what happens in historical literature. Historical literature's imaginative inventions 'edit' the past not out of mere unprofessional playful disregard for historical truth nor out of an aesthetic impulse to shape the material into coherent forms, but from a more socially responsive wish to edit the social memory for the future.

The historian Patrick Geary cites the words of a Bavarian monk writing in the eleventh century about the aims of the historian, which remain pertinent to the analysis of literary texts today: 'Not only is it proper for the new things to change the old ones, but even, if the old ones are disordered, they should be entirely thrown away, or if, however, they conform to the proper order of things but are of little use, they should be buried with reverence'.[91] This sounds remarkably like the modernist attitude to earlier literary modes.

Burying the past with reverence is the really striking description though. It finds a telling counterpart in what has recently happened in South Africa. The Truth and Reconciliation Commission, established in South Africa in 1995, aimed to help the nation along the path to national unity after the crippling years of apartheid. Anxious about watching history not just repeating itself, but taking tragedy and turning it into farce, many people have been very sceptical about the value of this national exhumation of racial trauma in order to rebury its otherwise haunting reminders properly. Archbishop Desmond Tutu, the man charged with heading the Truth Commission, forthrightly maintained in an interview that nations do suffer psychic trauma as much as individuals, saying that the Truth Commission's aim is 'to assist in the healing of a traumatised, divided, wounded, polarised people'. In response to the further question 'So how important is it that the Commission addresses these scars?', he continued:

> Absolutely crucial. You see there are some people who have tried to be very facile and say let bygones be bygones: they want us to have a national amnesia. And you have to keep saying to those people that to pretend that nothing happened, to not acknowledge that something horrendous did happen to them, is to victimise the victims yet again. But even more important, experience worldwide shows that if you do not deal with a dark past such as ours, effectively look the beast in the eye, that beast is not going to lie down quietly; it is going, as sure as anything, to come back and haunt you horrendously. We are saying we need to deal with this past as quickly as possible – acknowledge that we have a disgraceful past – then close the door on it and concentrate on the present and future.[92]

The past has to be 'dealt with' and then reburied with a form of closure that will keep it from disturbing the future. Implicit in the Truth Commission's procedures is the notion that testifying to one's own past guilt is both necessary and the most difficult thing to achieve. It gives a particular meaning to Levinas's claim that ethics comes before history and makes it possible. This is a notion of the possibility of history which is not a turning backward but a looking forward to new possibilities.

We reach the conclusion here that some historical literature aims to redo what recovered memory and the trauma model tried to undo, except that this re-inscription of history, this editing of the social body, is aimed not at caging the beast of the past but at transforming it (the metaphor strains here). In Chapter 5 we show that this is one reason for the slapstick historicism of the British historical theatre of the 1970s, and in Chapter 6 we suggest that personal memories are often deployed in contemporary poetry with the aim of editing a history represented by intimate memories. But historical literature can also play the ruthless editor and simply cut the past. So much contemporary historical literature is fundamentally irreverent as it buries the past, whether Churchill in *The Churchill Play*, or Sanjay in *Midnight's Children* – yet irreverence is not ignorance or indifference; it can be a working-through capable of ridding the present of former orders of power that might hold back social transformation towards a more egalitarian society.

Notes

1 'Intertexts can be both historical and aesthetic in their nature and function'. See Linda Hutcheon, *The Politics of Postmodernism* (London: Routledge, 1989), p. 67.
2 Roland Barthes, 'From work to text', trans. Stephen Heath, *Image–Music–Text* (London: Fontana, 1977), p. 156.
3 Ibid., p. 160.
4 Mary Bittner Wiseman, *The Ecstasies of Roland Barthes* (London: Routledge, 1989), p. 97.
5 Maurice Halbwachs, *On Collective Memory*, trans. and ed. Lewis A. Coser (Chicago: University of Chicago Press, [1941 and 1952] 1992).
6 Patrick J. Geary, *Phantoms of Remembrance: Memory and Oblivion at the End of the First Millennium* (Princeton: Princeton University Press), p. 12.
7 Mary J. Carruthers, *The Book of Memory: A Study of Memory in Medieval Culture* (Cambridge: Cambridge University Press, 1990), p. 215.
8 Ibid., p. 169.
9 Pat Barker, *Regeneration* (London: Penguin, 1992).
10 David B. Pillemer, *Momentous Events, Vivid Memories* (Cambridge, MA: Harvard University Press, 1998), p. 149.
11 See the general discussion in William F. Brewer, 'What is recollective memory?', in David C. Rubin, *Remembering Our Past: Studies in Autobiographical Memory* (Cambridge: Cambridge University Press, 1996), pp. 19–66, 44.
12 Daniel L. Schacter, *Searching for Memory: The Brain, the Mind, and the Past* (New

York: Basic Books, 1996), p. 116.

13 Brewer, 'What is recollective memory?', p. 61.

14 Sigmund Freud, 'Screen memories', *Standard Edition of the Complete Psychological Works of Sigmund Freud*, 24 vols, trans. and ed. James Strachey, with Anna Freud, assisted by Alix Strachey and Alan Tyson (London: Hogarth Press/Institute for Psychoanalysis, 1953–73), Vol. III, p. 321.

15 Schacter, *Searching for Memory*, p. 22.

16 Barker, *Regeneration*, p. 84.

17 Brewer, 'What is recollective memory?', pp. 19–66, 61.

18 Cited in Schacter, *Searching for Memory*, p. 17.

19 Cited in Pillemer, *Momentous Events*, p. 49.

20 Cited in Schacter, *Searching for Memory*, p. 22.

21 Endel Tulving, *Elements of Episodic Memory* (Oxford: Clarendon Press, 1983), p. 180.

22 Paul Fussell, *The Great War and Modern Memory* (Oxford: Oxford University Press, 1975), p. 320.

23 Barker, *Regeneration*, p. 184.

24 Laurence J. Kirmayer, 'Landscapes of memory: trauma, narrative, and dissociation', in Paul Antze and Michael Lambek (eds), *Tense Past: Cultural Essays in Trauma and Memory* (New York and London: Routledge, 1996), p. 175.

25 See Philip Gourevitch, 'The memory thief', *The New Yorker*, 14 June (1999), pp. 48–68, 67.

26 Binjamin Wilkomirski, *Fragments: Memories of a Childhood, 1939–1948*, trans. Carol Brown Janeway (London: Picador, [1995] 1997), p. 4.

27 Kirmayer, 'Landscapes of Memory', p. 176.

28 David Farrell Krell, *Of Memory, Reminiscence, and Writing: On the Verge* (Bloomington: Indiana University Press, 1990), p. 3.

29 Kirmayer, 'Landscapes of Memory', p. 176.

30 Wilkomirski, *Fragments*, p. 4.

31 Ibid., p. 155.

32 Gourevitch, 'The memory thief', p. 68.

33 Elena Lappin, 'The man with two heads', *Granta*, 66 (1999), 7–65, 58.

34 Michael Lambek, 'The past imperfect: remembering as moral practice', in Paul Antze and Michael Lambek (eds), *Tense Past*, pp. 235–54, 245.

35 Ian Hacking, *Rewriting the Soul: Multiple Personality and the Sciences of Memory* (Princeton: Princeton University Press, 1995), p. 198.

36 John Locke, *An Essay Concerning Human Understanding*, ed. Roger Woolhouse (Harmondsworth: Penguin, 1997), p. 308.

37 Schacter, *Searching for Memory*, p. 299.

38 Craig R. Barclay, 'Autobiographical remembering: narrative constraints on objectified selves', in Rubin (ed.), *Remembering our Past*, pp. 95–125, 121.

39 Barker, *Regeneration*, p. 51.

40 Ibid.

41 W. H. Rivers, *Instinct and the Unconscious: A Contribution to a Biological Theory of the Psycho-Neuroses*, 2nd edn (Cambridge: Cambridge University Press, 1922), p. 221.

42 Barker, *Regeneration*, p. 104.

43 Freud, 'Screen Memories', p. 60.

44 Ibid., p. 57.

45 John E. Mack, *Abduction: Human Encounters with Aliens*, revised edn (New York: Ballantine, 1994), p. 83.

46 Ibid., p. 142.
47 Frederick C. Crews, *The Memory Wars: Freud's Legacy in Dispute* (London: Granta, 1997), p. 159.
48 Pat Barker, *The Eye in the Door* (Harmondsworth: Penguin, 1993), p. 135.
49 Linda Alcoff and Laura Gray, 'Survivor Discourse: Transgression or Recuperation,' *Signs* 18:2, 1993, pp. 260–90.
50 Schacter, *Searching for Memory*, p. 272.
51 Dominick LaCapra, *History and Memory after Auschwitz* (Ithaca: Cornell University Press, 1998), p. 46.
52 Mikkel Borch-Jacobsen, *The Emotional Tie: Psychoanalysis, Mimesis and Affect* (Stanford: Stanford University Press, 1992), p. 51.
53 Reuben Fine, *The History of Psychoanalysis*, 2nd edn (New York: Continuum, 1990), pp. 352–4; J. Laplanche and J.-B. Pontalis, *The Language of Psychoanalysis*, trans. Donald Nicholson-Smith (London: Hogarth Press, 1983), p. 247.
54 Jacques Lacan, *Ecrits: A Selection*, trans. Alan Sheridan (London: Tavistock, 1977), p. 48.
55 Freud, *Standard Edition*, Vol. II, p. 181.
56 Ibid., p. 358.
57 Laplanche and Pontalis, *The Language of Psychoanalysis*, p. 390.
58 Malcom Bowie, *Lacan* (London: Fontana, 1991), p. 180.
59 Freud, 'Repression', *Standard Edition*, p. 147.
60 Ibid., p. 151.
61 Freud, 'Screen memories', *Standard Edition*, Vol. III, p. 321.
62 Peter Nicholls, 'The belated postmodern: history, phantoms and Toni Morrison', in Sue Vice (ed.), *Psychoanalytic Criticism: A Reader* (Cambridge: Polity Press, 1996), pp. 50–74, 54.
63 Mark Seltzer, 'Wound culture; trauma in the pathological public sphere', *October* 80 (1997), pp. 3–26, 3.
64 Ibid., p. 8.
65 Ibid., p. 11.
66 Ibid., p. 13.
67 Jacques Derrida, 'Freud and the scene of writing', *Writing and Difference*, trans. Alan Bass (London: Routledge & Kegan Paul, 1978).
68 Freud, *Standard Edition*, Vol. II, p. 191.
69 Derrida, *Writing and Difference*, p. 225.
70 Richard Beardsworth, *Derrida and the Political* (London: Routledge, 1996), p. 155. Beardsworth argues that although Derrida does acknowledge that 'access to the experience of time is only possible through technics', he does not resolve a seeming tension between its originary status and the originary status he accords to the 'promise' of a 'democracy to come'.
71 Derrida, *Writing and Difference*, p. 228.
72 Nicholls, 'The belated postmodern', p. 56.
73 Jean-François Lyotard, *Heidegger and 'the Jews'*, trans. Andreas Michel and Mark S. Roberts (Minneapolis: University of Minnesota, 1990), p. 16.
74 Jacques Le Goff, *History and Memory*, trans. Steven Rendall and Elizabeth Claman (New York: Columbia University Press, [1977] 1992), p. 99.
75 Paul Ricoeur, *Time and Narrative*, trans. Kathleen Blamey and David Pellauer (Chicago: University of Chicago Press, 1988), pp. 187–8.
76 Anne Whitehead, 'Open to suggestion: hypnosis and history in Pat Barker's *Regeneration*', *Modern Fiction Studies* 44:3 (1988), pp. 674–94, p. 691.
77 LaCapra, *History and Memory after Auschwitz*, p. 43.

78 Freud, 'Remembering, repeating and working-through', *Standard Edition*, Vol. XII, p. 154–5.

79 Freud, 'Mourning and Melancholia', *Standard Edition*, Vol. II, p. 253.

80 'Identification is seen as the most primary form of emotional attachment, whereby the subject seeks to modify itself to resemble the object; incorporation is compared to ingestion and, unlike identification, requires a subject/object differentiation in order to carry out assimilation; introjection maintains the object's otherness even while internalized so that relations may be carried on with it intrapsychically'. Elizabeth Mayes, 'The fantasy of internalization in the theoretical imaginary', *Representations*, 62 (1998), 100–10, 105.

81 LaCapra, *History and Memory after Auschwitz*, p. 45.

82 Lawrence Langer, *Holocaust Testimonies: The Ruins of Memory* (New Haven and London: Yale University Press, 1994), p. 174.

83 Paul Connerton, *How Societies Remember* (Cambridge: Cambridge University Press), pp. 72–3.

84 Ibid., p. 102.

85 Charlotte Delbo, *La mémoire et les jours* (Paris: Berg International, 1985), pp. 13–14, cited in Langer, *Holocaust Testimonies*, pp. 6–7.

86 See Peter Middleton, 'The contemporary poetry reading', in Charles Bernstein (ed.), *Close Listening: Poetry and the Performed Word* (New York: Oxford University Press, 1998), pp. 262–99.

87 Roland Barthes, 'The grain of the voice', Image–Music–Text, p. 181.

88 Pierre Bourdieu, *Outline of a Theory of Practice*, trans. Richard Nice (Cambridge: Cambridge University Press, 1977), p. 187.

89 Debbora Battaglia, *On the Bones of the Serpent* (Chicago: Chicago University Press, 1990).

90 Ibid., p. 10.

91 Geary, *Phantoms of Remembrance*, p. 8.

92 Desmond Tutu, 'Interview: healing a nation', *Index on Censorship*, 25/5 (1996), pp. 39–43.

CHAPTER 4

Practising spacetime

When Owen and Sassoon break the ice between them, they do so by exchanging memories whose temporality is anachronistic, as if these are the most intimate of all the memories which acknowledge the new temporalities of the twentieth century. Owen finds other pasts superimposed on the present, as if the present had regressed into the past under the severe pressure of the war's disorienting placeless violence, lacking sufficient support from whatever it is that maintains a subject's firm position in the present. Sassoon finds himself looking over the novelist's shoulder with a backward gaze from the future, as if he were another Billy Pilgrim, the soldier who travels back and forth throughout his lifetime in unpredictable temporal swoops and forays in Kurt Vonnegut's novel *Slaughterhouse Five* (1969). Anachronism becomes a necessary measure of the working-through and ethical relation to history. The world of Craiglockhart has no discourse for this retemporalisation of memory, although scientists were even then busy creating new theories of spacetime in which time would be as traversable as space, and philosophers were busy challenging the belief that time is a linear continuity of moments and their datable locations. The exchange of memories is one of the many points at which Barker's subtle realism indicates its limits to the reader with an implicit question: how can such pasts be relocated in space and time? In this chapter we shall begin with a novel which does try to articulate the other times and space of modern memory by resituating the temporal discourse of the new physics into personal and social memory. It is an attempt whose contradictions help point out the often extreme tensions between scientific time and social time in the late twentieth century, and the curious effects of this anachronisation of social time on the pastness of the past.

The relativistic physics of memory: Margaret Atwood's *Cat's Eye*

Margaret Atwood's novel *Cat's Eye* (1988) emerged directly out of the debates about recovered memory of the past three decades, which we discussed in Chapter 3.[1] Its plot is centred entirely upon the workings of memory and childhood trauma: Elaine Risley, a painter now about fifty, revisits Toronto, the city where she grew up, for a retrospective of her work and gradually recovers the memory of a traumatic period of her childhood the memories of which she has hitherto repressed, and also traces out its far-reaching consequences for her character, actions and art between then and now. Although this is the story of trauma, repression and recovered memory, it differs in one important aspect from the prevalent narratives: it was not sexual abuse by an adult (or Satanic agents or alien vivisectionists), but bullying by her girl friends when she was nine that left lasting psychological scars. Otherwise the pattern of repression and recovery follows the standard model. At the end of the novel, she experiences a recollective epiphany on the same bridge across a ravine where she nearly drowned as a nine-year-old child, after her friends lured her on to the dangerous ice on the stream by tauntingly throwing her hat down on the ice below. Atwood even manages to incorporate a brilliant example of *Nachträglichkeit*. Elaine had been inspired to save herself as she fell through the ice by listening to the encouraging words of a shadowy Virgin Mary figure on the bridge above, but at the very end of the novel the reader realises that this figure is the adult Elaine placing herself on the bridge, and not only re-imagining the earlier event but also talking to her earlier self. A retranscription of the earlier memory has occurred so that the seemingly accurate, because so detailed, account of the incident earlier in the novel, was already filtered through the later consciousness of the narrator's temporal dislocation – except that memory has no consciousness of this time-loop.

The careful plotting of two time lines – the present of Toronto and the past of her earlier life in the suburbs before she moved away – is constructed from everyday experience and emotions, with the exception of one intrusive incident that might have been borrowed from a thriller. Her older brother, Stephen, who has become a physicist well-known for his research on spacetime, is killed by terrorists in a plane hijacking, an event which although narrated competently enough, is wholly at odds with the texture of everyday life elsewhere in the novel; it clearly belongs in another genre. It evokes in the reader the sense that an inconvenient character is being killed off. Why? To answer this, we need to look at his role in the novel both as child and man. As a boy he was Elaine's only sibling, and had a large influence on her early identity because the family lived a nomadic and isolated life while their biologist father worked out in the field. The young Elaine had no clear sense of the cultural differences between childhood femininity and masculinity, which is one reason why she is later so easily victimised by her girl friends. Nevertheless, this uncertainty of early childhood gender identity provides only an occasional opportunity for commentary on masculine and feminine styles. It is as a man that Stephen gains his real significance, because he can then plausibly be a source of knowledge about time for his sister, providing the plot justification for the discourse of time which pervades the novel. Mostly this transfer of the discourse is only implied, but we do once see Elaine attend a public lecture of his: '"When we gaze at the night sky", he says, "we are looking at fragments of the past"' (p. 331). The meeting after the lecture is not entirely successful, because Elaine's attempts at intimacy based on an exchange of memories mostly fall flat. He may be able to see the past in the sky but he has trouble seeing it on the ground. After some prompting, he admits that he does remember burying a jar of marbles, including cat's eyes, in the ground under the bridge, and this is why in plot terms he has to die. If he had lived, even if he were far away, Elaine could ring him up and ask him about their past, possibly obviating the need to undergo the psychic pain of recovering memory. This risk to the plausibility of the conclusion has to be eliminated – the character has to die. When he does, his loss conveniently kills off their parents with grief soon after, so that Elaine can undergo the painful recovery of memory and the healing of trauma with no check on its accuracy or supplement from intersubjective memory.

Why does the novel need this discourse of time so badly the author is willing to risk the implausible thriller scene, if its principal preoccupation is memory and the effects of trauma? Why does the reconstruction of the psychological effects of the bullying elicit such phrases as 'time is missing' (p. 201), and why does she describe her experiments with fainting and opting out of awareness as 'stepping sideways, out of your own body, out of time' (p. 171)? One answer would be that because personal memory (and possibly some forms of social memory also) is, in the words of the psychologist Endel Tulving cited earlier, 'mental time travel', time is integral to its effects. Personal event memories are located in time, which raises the question of what we know about time and its workings. Psychology, however, is not the most obvious field to look for a theory of time (didn't Freud after all say that the unconscious is timeless, and even an eminent cognitive psychologist can still say confidently that memories 'do not contain any direct representation of time'[2]), so another more authoritative discourse is needed.

Elaine makes an observation about her paintings as they stand displayed in her exhibition, which looks beyond psychology. She says, looking at the paintings of her mother – an opportunity for a psychoanalytic judgement if ever there was one – that these particular paintings simply highlight a general feature of her art, because they, 'like everything else, are drenched in time'.[3] This idea has a substantial modernist genealogy: Kafka, for example, also saw paintings drenched in time – he is reported to have responded to Picasso by saying that 'art is a mirror, which goes "fast", like a watch – sometimes'.[4] He probably meant that the familiar idea that art is a mirror held up to the world had been given a new twist by the futurist aspirations of avant-garde painters, but his image of a variable rate of time also acknowledges just how much the arts were affected by the new times of science and philosophy. A modernist art is a time art, because if modern works of art are going to be adequately responsive to the conditions of modernity then they must, as Theodor Adorno expresses it, seek to 'lose themselves in time so as not to become its prey'.[5] Previous historical periods had other means available to elude time's effects. Within the earlier Christian world of western Europe, eternity was the salvation of time, and the world of duration and suffering was simply a stage on the path towards the eternal city of God where the soul would no longer be prey to time. In a more secular, scientific age this eternity has been ceded to other forms of authority, to the state and to science, but has the effect of giving new force to the belief that the everyday, irreversible time of becoming is the fundamental truth of the modern condition. The passage of time as *durée* or 'duration', in the endless passing away and renewal of time in every moment, which Henri Bergson made into the cornerstone of his widely influential philosophy, becomes so pressing that art sometimes responds by embracing it rather than attempting to find transcendent moments, truths and meanings beyond history. Bergson invited such artistic strategies because he located innovation in time itself: *durée* 'means invention, the creation of forms, the continual elaboration of the absolutely new'.[6] The invention of the cinema provided him with an analogy for the failure of the mind to grasp this fully. 'The cinematographic character of our knowledge' means that thought can work only with a series of static images of what is really a fluid, ever-changing world including ourselves, and is the experiential basis of the misleading idea of the point instant of time produced by physics.[7]

Atwood's novel tries to demonstrate just how much even the most intimate experiences of the past have been affected by the new discourses of time developed by modern science. Adorno observed that modernist art had registered the changes in everyday experience resulting from massive economic and political transformation because it was able to track them deep into subjective life:

> The substantive element of artistic production draws its power from the fact that the most advanced procedures of material production and orga-
> nization are not limited to the sphere in which they originate. In a
> manner scarcely analyzed yet by sociology, they radiate out into areas of
> life far removed from them, deep into the zones of subjective experi-
> ence, which does not notice this and guards the sanctity of its reserves.[8]

This adverse judgement on sociology is, as we shall see, no longer true. Adam, Giddens, Greenhouse, Kosellek, Lefebvre and others have extensively investigated the effects on the everyday experience of temporality and space, although some of the radiation from reorganised production still remains largely untheorised, and almost unacknowledged outside the arts. Yet the impact of scientific time remains unclear despite general acknowledgement of its importance and the visibility of its achievements and destructions. One might well, therefore, look directly to modern physics which has, after all, like Stephen, had much to say about time. Perhaps the theoretical vision that enables the physicist to see fragments of the past out in the cosmos, can be turned back onto the mundane world of social history too. The novel certainly thinks this is possible and, therefore, uses a quotation from another Stephen, the physicist of time, Stephen Hawking, as one of its two epigraphs: 'Why do we remember the past, and not the future?'[9] We must not forget also that the novel kills its physicist. Is it also saying that the time of physics fails those who would rely on it for insight into personal, social and textual memory? Is Stephen's death an allegory of the incapacity of scientific theories of time to negotiate the earthbound, global politics of time? Atwood's novel has nothing more to say about this possibility which haunts the text, and the death of temporal physics is simply set aside for Elaine's culminating revelations of recovered memory.

Ambivalence towards physics is figured awkwardly in these undeveloped speculations about the politics of time. It is helpful, therefore, before we look at what Atwood's favourite physicist, Stephen Hawking (who makes no claims to address political issues at all), offers to the public as a picture of cosmological time, to consider a novel in which a theoretical physicist solves political problems with his new theories of time. Ursula Le Guin's novel, *The Dispossessed* (1974) (its echo of Dostoevsky is indicative of her ambitions as a writer), also looks to a physicist for answers, but its physicist lives in the future and this imaginative freedom enables the novel to resolve some of the most difficult problems of reconciling social and scientific time within a political framework.[10] Le Guin gives the physicist centre stage in her story because he eventually solves the problem of coevalness in this future universe of interplanetary conflict. The narrative proposes that one solution to the danger of recurrent conflict would be the discovery of a means of instantaneous communication across the barriers of distance that delay ordinary transmission of messages to the creeping pace of the speed of light and allow mistrust and hostility to flourish in the resultant intervals. Her physicist hero develops a new 'coherent theory of Simultaneity' (p. 99), because he believes that the common understanding of time as a road from past to future fails to recognise that 'the past and the future were made part of the present by memory and intention, there was, in human terms, no road, nowhere to go' (p. 157). The value of this new technology, according to a diplomat from Earth, is that it could make possible a new form of interplanetary society, a 'league' of the populated planets, and the diplomat becomes so excited when he grasps this that he adds: 'It's as if you had invented human speech. We can talk – at last we can talk together' (p. 285). What separates the superpowers is not as it appears, different ideologies, represented allegorically in the novel by spatial distance, but different histories, represented by the incommensurability of different spacetimes. This is why Shevek, 'the chronosophist' as he is called, believes that proper understanding of time would be a liberation from the monad of the self: 'Outside the locked room is the landscape of time, in which the spirit may, with luck and courage, construct the fragile, makeshift, improbable roads and cities of fidelity: a landscape inhabitable by human beings' (p. 277). These improbable routes and cities may be the best way to reconfigure history, to free us from the hold of linear time and the fixity of a past, both of which obstruct the development of new routes into the future. A new theory of time might just be the basis for radical social change, and chronosophism a useful image for the form of resolution required by the Cold War. Its implausibility when stated so baldly, suggests that reconciling modern history with the new science of time will require more than a purely technological answer.

Science and social time

Why do we remember the past and not the future? Stephen Hawking's answer to this in his immensely successful popular science book, *A Brief History of Time* (1988), is that the conditions of the universe require the three different types of time – cosmological time, thermodynamic time and psychological time – to all point in the same direction. But the way he answers the question underlines the degree to which modern physics has upset ordinary conceptions of time, and has elicited literary and philosophical attempts to understand the consequences for everyday life in time. Hawking's mathematical analyses of the history of the universe suggest that it began as a point in spacetime, expanded to the stage in which we now live and will continue to do so, until one day it begins to collapse back into its original form. What happens then? Hawking disarmingly admits that he has changed his mind about this: 'At first, I believed that disorder would decrease when the universe collapsed ... This would mean that the contracting phase would be the time reverse of the expanding phase. People in the contracting phase would live their lives backwards: they would die before they are born and get younger as the universe contracted'.[11] Even now he still has doubts about the ordinary perception of time. Physics and mathematics appear to allow for temporal reversibility, a seeming asymmetry between physics and experience which has persisted for centuries, since 'the laws of science do not distinguish between the forward and backward directions of time'.[12] At points of maximum theoretical speculation, his text seems to blame not science but literature for these strange possibilities, especially what he evidently thinks of as the epistemological promiscuity of a science fiction answerable only to the pragmatics of satisfying narrative outcomes, and not to the complex process of scientific legitimation by experimenters, theorists and mathematicians:

> It is greatly to be hoped that some version of the censorship hypothesis holds because close to naked singularities it may be possible to travel into the past. While this would be fine for writers of science fiction, it would mean that no-one's life would ever be safe: someone might go into the past and kill your father or mother before you were conceived![13]

The censorship hypothesis is the assumption that in the actual universe there are no solutions to the equations of general relativity in which time is reversed (except possibly in the initial or final conditions), but the text manages to make it sound as if textuality is what needs censorship. A similar textual pressure point occurs in a passage outlining Richard Feynman's theory of quantum gravity, when Hawking explains that a particular calculation of 'particle histories' has to be done in 'imaginary time'. In case his readers might mistakenly think this had something to do with either fantasy or textual imagination, he defensively explains that 'imaginary time may sound like science fiction but it is in fact a well-defined mathematical concept'.[14] The question, of course, the one which was implicit in Atwood's use of the epigraph, is whether this has any social meaning beyond mathematics.

Speculations about memory and the future are less significant as autonomous ideas than as signs of other more pervasive assumptions about time which Hawking derives from modern scientific method. Nowhere is this more evident than in his treatment of scientific discovery. The vision of a future in which we do remember the future and not the past was previously offered with full scientific authority, and would then have appeared to be a prediction about everyday experience. At one point in recent history, reputable scientists were promulgating the fact that at some distant point in the future, time would reverse itself and we would be able to remember the future. Now that the scientific hypothesis has passed its date stamp, we can look forward to a future in which we always remember the past, because it turns out that the physical nature of the universe ensures this. However, the change of cosmological time is more disturbing than the idea of precognitive images of the future. What is to stop physicists making more discoveries and mathematicians more equations, which once again alter the relation of memory to time and space? Hawking is unruffled by this, and talks elsewhere in the book about calculating not just the history of the universe but a sum of all possible histories, so that all eventualities are covered. By this means we would have not one past, or even a many-sided complex past always under revision, but an infinite set of pasts whose probability could be mapped by the new mathematics. Earlier twentieth-century visions of this, as we shall see in Chapter 7, inspired science fiction writers like Isaac Asimov to envision a future in which history could be controlled by science and mathematics.

Hawking, writing in the standard discourse of modern physics (suitably simplified for ordinary readers), can talk of a set of histories of the world, and at the same time of a change in the scientific view of time and the past, because he works with the two forms of time we mentioned earlier, duration and eternity. His narrative methodology, typical of modern science, actually detemporalises history as it proceeds, as this typical sentence shows: 'Up to the beginning of this century people believed in an absolute time'.[15] This presents scientific knowledge as the relation between two different kinds of time: the time of physical nature the knowledge of which emerges through a series of discoveries which form a narrative sequence organised by questions about the universe; and time that has its origins in Greek thought. These questions are apparently answered at an accelerating rate in the postwar period: 'Recent breakthroughs in physics, made possible in part by fantastic new technologies, suggest answers to some of these longstanding questions'. It is important to the continuing welfare of the scientific project that only some questions have been answered, while other questions whose antiquity attests to their cultural importance still remain to guarantee a future for this science: 'Before 1915, space and time were thought of as a fixed arena in which events took place, but which was not affected by what happened in it'.[16] Now this old conception of the time–space continuum has been, and continues to be, transformed by astronomy and physics:

> Further encouragement for the existence of black holes came in 1967 with the discovery by a research student at Cambridge, Jocelyn Bell, of objects in the sky that were emitting regular pulses of radio waves. At first Bell and her supervisor, Antony Hewish, thought they might have made contact with an alien civilization in the galaxy! ... In the end, however, they and everyone else came to the less romantic conclusion that these objects, which were given the name pulsars, were in fact rotating neutron stars that were emitting pulses of radio waves because of a complicated interaction between their magnetic fields and

surrounding matter. This was bad news for writers of space westerns.[17]

In fact, further material for speculation was good news. Black holes became as common as gulches in westerns, and the science-fiction writer, Larry Niven, christened a collection of stories *Neutron Star* (1968).[18] For the scientist, however, these facts are not only not scientific fictions, they are not subject to the historicising effects of narrative. What is discovered is something that is part of the known system of material processes existing independently of time and history. Although they don't exist for us until they are discovered, that doesn't mean they did not exist at all before scientists noticed them; and once they have been discovered, however much our knowledge of them might change, the fact of their existence and process remains the same.

This two-timing of knowledge is basic to the structure of Hawking's book. The time of history, discovery, subjective reasoning and the social relations of scientists affected by wars, nationality, institutions and the media of communication, is constantly signalled to the reader through dates and other markers. This time is constantly surpassing the shortcomings of the past in its future-oriented passage of development, prediction and results, while the other, ahistorical, time or detemporalised existence, has no rhetorical displays to indicate its importance, and is simply presented implicitly as an assumed condition of the known, law-governed material processes discovered within the first sort of time. This time is the determining, fundamental one, as Pierre Bourdieu has observed in his critique of the 'detemporalising' effect of scientific method.[19] It produces a division between the eternity of physical law and the history of material activity. At one point, Hawking's account employs a grammatical elision that marks the extent to which such narratives display a nervousness about the ontological status of these discoveries that is only partially contained by tropes from the discourse of explorers venturing into unknown lands. Instead of saying 'further encouragement for believing in the existence of black holes', or 'further encouragement for accepting the theory of black holes', he simply writes 'further encouragement for the existence of black holes', as if the scientific finding actually encouraged the black hole to exist, the way novels might be said to encourage their characters to exist. His version reads better than the more precise paraphrases but it also subliminally scales up the claims made for such discoveries by missing out the cumbersome and limiting mediation of subjectively conceived models, beliefs, hypotheses and theories. Science can encourage black holes to exist, but once they do exist they are on their own, because Hawking's science is not responsible for their creation, only their discovery. This dualist temporality creates a ghostly future for itself, a world of new scientific laws, materials, forces which have not yet been discovered, yet must already exist just out of sight of our present scientific methods that holds out the possibility of a reconciliation of the world of science and the world of the failing body in time. There is nothing unusual about Hawking's deployment of these two temporalities. This is the standard scientific world picture, and it has been enormously influential.

Hawking's book inadvertently demonstrates what has been so disturbing about modern physics of time and space – its claim to authoritative control over the imagination of social time and its relation to the past. This hegemony would not have been so significant if not for the widespread perception that modern or relativistic physics has somehow detemporalised experience. The new relativistic universe of spacetime promulgated by Einstein's theory of relativity replaced the space which was a neutral container of matter assumed by Descartes and earlier physics, and the Newtonian time which could move forwards or backwards at a uniform rate, with a pliable four-dimensional medium whose characteristics could alter with location and perspective. It was not conceived as a theory of experience, yet from the start its treatment of space and time as if they were somehow the same, and its strange speculations about the possibility of time itself behaving like a watch that could go faster or slower, led people to wonder about the implications for our lived experience of space and time. Physicists were often happy to oblige. When challenged once about the validity of the new theory, Einstein himself said that 'what is seen as commonplace changes over time'.[20] By implication the past itself would have to give way, but how? Einstein himself always remained cautious and late in his life was still saying that 'the mathematical difficulties of a comparison with experience are prohibitive for the time being'.[21] From the beginning others were less restrained. One of the earliest and most influential attempts to explain the wider implications of relativistic physics was written by Hermann Weyl, in a book called *Space-Time-Matter* first published in German in 1918, and translated into English in 1922.[22] It is not nearly as reader-friendly as Hawking's book, but before plunging into complex equations, it does offer a brief non-mathematical outline of the phenomenology of time and space: 'Since the human mind first wakened from slumber, and was allowed to give itself free rein, it has never ceased to feel the profoundly mysterious nature of time-consciousness, of the progression of the world in time – of Becoming. It is one of those ultimate metaphysical problems which philosophy has striven to elucidate and unravel at every stage of its history'.[23] The implication is that now these metaphysical problems will be dispelled by the new physics, since what we ordinarily experience as space and time are only human forms of perception that 'have no place in the world constructed by mathematical physics'.[24] Relativistic mathematics appears to demonstrate both that time and space are simply interchangeable dimensions, and that our lived experience of existing between a past and a future is merely an existential misrepresentation of the underlying reality in which time might be said to be as static as space.

This is strong stuff. It means that not only memory, but also history and almost all forms of textual memory are simply wrong. Some early twentieth-century thinkers feared that time as a historical dimension had been abolished by the theory of relativity, and the universe had become one vast synchronic space. Weyl confirmed such anxieties in a later work: 'All that is happening is the successively experienced perception by a subject who is travelling "along the world-line of its body". But no temporality can be attributed to the physical world, to the perceptual object; nothing happens in it; it simply is'.[25] The theory of relativity seemed to ascribe temporal difference entirely to perspective, which could be understood as a merely subjective limitation added to the mathematically formulable objective reality of a spacetime which already contained the future alongside the present and the past. Kurt Vonnegut's amusing spoof on the popular image of the time of the new physics in *Slaughterhouse Five*[26] shows how disturbing this idea has been. It also implicates the new physics in the failures of social memory, a connection that remains only a barely glimpsed possibility in Atwood's precise delineation of a single personal memory.

Billy Pilgrim, an American prisoner of war who survived the Dresden fire-bombing during the Second World War, becomes a time traveller after being kidnapped by aliens from Tralfamadore for their zoo. The novel cuts back and forth throughout his life, each time prefacing the temporal transfer (which is otherwise a common feature of modern fictional narratives) with some such phrase as 'he traveled in time' (p. 52). Billy tries to explain his existence as a subject travelling rapidly along his own world-line but people think he is crazy. An opening chapter – apparently written in the author's own voice – explains that he had hitherto been unable to write about the bombing of Dresden (through which he himself lived) because the finality of the 'massacre' makes it impossible to say anything 'intelligent'; instead he has written the self-consciously clumsy fiction about Billy Pilgrim, who 'came unstuck in time' during the raid. He calls it a failure because it is so inadequate to the unique horror of the fire-bombing, but can only measure this failure by showing the reader that the advanced scientific discourse of spacetime which ought to be the best means of writing about the new experiences of the century, appears absurd and renders its possessor mad in the eyes of the ordinary world. Pilgrim is a Siegfried Sassoon for whom the backward gaze is a permanent, if ever-changing, way of life.[27]

Vonnegut's parody of relativity can be read as no more than a dismissal of the relevance of science to the crises of modernity, but it suggests another reading as well. Perhaps modern memory's sometimes uncontrollable *Nachträglichkeit* does result from changes to the locatability of the past resulting from the new temporalities of science. Relativistic physics, of the kind that Hawking expounds, turns time into a spatial dimension, so that in theory at least it is possible to move backwards and forwards in it just as we can cross space. The arrow of time becomes only one possibility among many, making the past's stability waver. Alongside this potential reversibility and homogenising of time into a fourth dimension, another reshaping of time is also at work – the detemporalisation of scientific method – complicating the relation between scientific and social time, and making it harder to trace the relations between different temporalities.

Scientific method controls access to the source of time, the timelessness of physical law and its invariances; history is then the progressive revelation of this eternity. The combined force of physical theory and stance towards temporality has had radical behind-the-scenes implications for everyday life.

One reason Hawking is interested in the attempt to explain to the ordinary reader what current science has discovered, is that his own bodily condition makes him acutely aware of the distance between phenomenological and cosmological time. Much of the force of his book derives from its explicit references to the disarticulation between the cognitive realm of mathematics and the material world it aspires to represent, especially when represented by the contrast between the author's own bodily weakness and his brilliant mathematical reasoning. Although this contrast is mostly implicit in the biographical knowledge that readers bring to the book, it is made occasionally explicit in modest references to the writer's disabling illness. Going to bed is a slow and difficult physical process, we are told, which can be alleviated by working out theoretical problems like the boundary conditions of black holes. His own physical suffering projects an allegory of the division between the two modes of temporality: the untrue, subjective perception; and the panoptic explanatory theory. While it would be an exaggeration to say that the scientific model offers both to heal the traumas of modernity, and might be somehow complicit with them, recent reflections on the history of anthropology and its attempts to apply the detemporalising method of the natural sciences to the study of cultures, does suggest that scientific method has been a debilitating radiation working as deeply as Adorno's 'advanced procedures of material production and organization' on the culture of everyday life.

This was happening not just in remote corners of the world, but in

America in the twentieth century. The great anthropologist of Native America, A. L. Kroeber, the father of the novelist Ursula Le Guin, speaks of the Arapaho in his monograph published between 1902 and 1907 as if they inhabited a timeless realm, not the first decade of a century in which they would soon be driving cars and riding in airplanes: 'A brother and sister must not speak to each other more than is necessary. A sister is supposed to sit at some distance from her brother'.[28] But as his remark that 'there are no fixed rules as to inheritance' indicates, this timelessness is really the primordiality of a set of rules of which their actual time-bound behaviour is an instance. Time belongs to the world of the anthropologist theorising this other culture and, therefore, as in Hawking's account, it is not difficult to see the tensions of the dual time structure at work. The proof of the timeless structure is sometimes a specific event which has been narrated to the anthropologist on a partic-ular occasion: 'Supernatural power of whatever kind is believed among the Arapaho to be usually acquired at a time of fasting and isolation ... A man does not necessarily have supernatural experiences only once in his life ... A man fasted on a hill for four days crying. The fourth morning, at sunrise, he saw a badger. ... To the badger belong all medicines that grow on the ground'.[29] The present tense is used to describe their ritual behaviour, because the present tense is also the tense of propositional truths that will legitimate science independently of a relation to social time. The relation between the two kinds of time is also a relation between two cultures: the indigenous culture of the Arapaho; and the alien culture of Western science that has emigrated to this culture and is here represented by the generalising anthropologist. Johannes Fabian argues that such an emulation of the 'naturalized-spatialized time' of physics serves to establish social and political distance between the cultures; it 'is made for the purpose of distancing those who are observed from the Time of the observer'.[30] This detem-poralising perspective which searches for local cultural laws also hinders communication – it refuses to allow the scientific observer to recognise that she or he might be coeval with the culture under study. The result is a lack of intercultural contact, because 'for human communication to occur, coevalness has to be created. Communication is, ultimately, about creating shared Time'.[31] This was also the conclusion of *The Dispossessed*, and it is possible to read the novel as a renegotiation of the legacy of her father's anthropological perspective.

Modern philosophers, including Henri Bergson, Edmund Husserl, Alfred North Whitehead, G. H. Mead and, most famously, Martin Heidegger all attempted to challenge the scientific model of time with varying degrees of success. They argued that time cannot be cut up into infinitely small instants; time is not a linear continuum but an ever-emerging passage from one state of affairs to another; the present has thickness enough to contain a recent past and an imminent future; time is inherent in being. The influence of both these philosophical theories and the scientific models they challenged on everyday life and the experience of the past is hard to measure and, therefore, some cultural historians and social theorists are sceptical about whether the new physics, or science in general, has had much influence on culture. Stephen Kern's account of the early twentieth-century's response to the new theories of time doubts that the new mathematical theory had much influence despite all the other developments in the technologies of time-management. He shows how the adoption of World Standard Time provoked a backlash which led to the kinds of affirmation of existential, private time but believes that it was only the present that really changed, notably from the thickening of the sense of simultaneity. The future was imagined as no more than a 'reconstruction of past experience projected ahead in time', and the past 'was not qualitatively different from older notions'.[32] So few people understood Einstein's theory, Kern argues, that its social impact was negligible in the first decades of the century. Carol Greenhouse, an ethnographer, makes a similar but more sweeping claim about the significance of scientific views of time in her study of social time.[33] Her opening paragraph announces that she is not concerned with the time of physicists, because however 'real' it might be it has had no influence on ideas of social time. She is also dismissive of the philosophers who make claims about the essence of temporal experience which can be readily disproved by cross-cultural comparisons. Mortality may be essential to the Western conception of time but it plays little part in other cultures studied by ethnographers.[34] She, like Kern, would look to the changing structure of social life to explain the impact of new temporal discourses on the cultural imagination.

Making time for diversity

The sociologist Anthony Giddens provides some of the strongest arguments for the belief that the past has altered as a result of changes in the experience of time, but he too observes changes that have arisen from changes in social organisation rather than changes in cosmology. For modern societies, 'reflexive self-regulation is manifested as history' – a history which is the self-aware maintenance of sociality in all its forms, in a modernity that has achieved a wholly new organisation of space and time.[35] Twentieth-century Western societies have extended their power enormously to manage institutions across great spatial and temporal distances. One of the main driving forces today, for example, is information technology, which 'is a fundamental phenomenon permitting time-space distanciation and a thread that ties together the various sorts of allocative and authoritative resources in reproduced structures of domination'.[36] This occurs as what he calls 'disembedding': 'by disembedding, I mean the "lifting out" of social relations from local contexts of interaction and their restructuring across indefinite spans of timespace'.[37] Lived experience is increasingly detached from specific places and locations, and increasingly distinguished from one another as well. In earlier societies most social practices depended on close temporal and spatial proximity. Today, social relations and the consequent institutional practices are dependent upon organisational structures that far exceed relations of physical proximity, and achieve a dynamic interrelation of local and global activities that was never before achieved. The vast galactic distances in Le Guin's novel function allegorically as signs of the existential distances that result from processes like the 'time-space compression' which David Harvey discerns as the underlying cause of the 'speed' of late capitalism. He, too, believes that these 'processes so revolutionize the objective qualities of space and time that we are forced to alter, sometimes in quite radical ways, how we represent the world to ourselves'.[38]

But we don't need to choose between science and society as the causes of changes in the representation of the past as these theorists assume. One reason is implicit in Greenhouse's argument that time is always projected by a politics of representation. Although she dismisses the entire issue of the physical or metaphysical nature of time, she does not, therefore, negate the possibility that science and philosophy have major indirect influences through the influence of discourses of time. In her view it is representations of time and discourses of temporality that influence politics and social life, because 'time and space are ways of regarding social relationships'.[39] We should not look directly to theories of the essence of spacetime to understand the character of social time, because time and space are always mediated through signs and representations, and she identifies three main social forms that time discourse takes as 'agency, narrative, and space'.[40] Her original contribution to studies of social time is to focus on agency, and argue that 'time's many forms are cultural propositions about the nature and distribution of agency across social space'.[41] Agency is aggregated into the social order through the powers of literacy, law and mortality but only because it begins in individuals, which means that 'the distribution of agency and its inevitable singularization and alienation imply some force outside society, a temporality outside time, as it were'.[42] Postmodernity, for example, can therefore be viewed from two directions. From the safer upper reaches of the social system it brings play, indeterminacy and fracture, but in the poorer and least politically influential sections of society, it arises from 'denials of the ways in which the state's self-legitimations are challenged in public and private, specifically insofar as states must claim to monopolise the agency of their citizens'.[43] William Gibson's *Neuromancer* (discussed in more detail in Chapter 8) finds powerful images of this in the contrast between the ungoverned and, therefore, dangerous enterprise zone of Night City – 'a deranged experiment in social Darwinism' – and the virtual reality of informational space controlled by the giant corporations – the 'zaibatsus' – where the 'multinationals that shaped the course of human history, had transcended old barriers'.[44]

Agency may seem too abstract a term for use in the discussion of literary texts, or too compromised by its association with the idea of a subject to be able to control its own agency, but Greenhouse does not use it in this manner. It derives from Giddens's sociological theory. Agency is not measured in terms of intention or self-consciousness – like power, it refers to the capability that persons have of doing things. He uses the term to distinguish it from other concepts like power or will, although it partakes of both, because he does not want to attribute agency entirely to society and its institutions as he argues Foucault does, or to individuals as humanism usually did. Greenhouse adds a sensitivity to discursivity to the concept of agency. Time emerges from the representation and distribution of agency rather than the ideas of an autonomous subject who pre-exists discourse and representation.

Nevertheless, it helps to think of agency as practice because then we can shift the argument away from arguing simply about whether the new physics directly shapes the tacit knowledge and existential narratives of everyday life, to a wider view of how the West has worked both with and against these new times. A few isolated examples of writers and ethnographers who have located tangible examples of agency as practice will show what this implies. The American poet, Charles Olson, whose teaching and example inspired an entire generation of postwar American poets, offered the idea that to be human is 'to practice space and time', drawing on philosophers who had tried to find philosophical responses to the new physics, notably Alfred North Whitehead and Martin Heidegger, as well as his own idiosyncratic interpretation of the new physics, as the basis for this arresting epigram in his lectures at Black Mountain in 1956.[45] The question is then how and in what forms is it practiced. Olson never provided an explicit account of this, preferring to work it out in the unparaphrasable forms of his poetry.[46]

A contemporary anthropologist of Australia and Melanesia, Nancy Munn, who has worked extensively on the anthropology of time, offers a particularly helpful version of what might be entailed in such a practice, based on the lives of the island-bound people of Gawa in the Pacific. Although they are remote from relativistic physics or even modern science, she believes that their lives, especially their relations with other islands, show that time and space are intermingled because both arise from their own practice. Time is, she says:

> a symbolic process continually being produced in everyday practices. People are 'in' a sociocultural time of multiple dimensions (sequencing, timing, past-present-future relations, etc.) that they are forming in their 'projects'. In any given instance, particular temporal dimensions may be the foci of attention or only tacitly known. Either way, these dimensions are lived or apprehended concretely via the various meaningful connectivities among persons, objects, and space continually being made in and through the everyday world.[47]

It is a spacetime, rather than a space in time, because time and space are not lived distinctly. The process of making a time is much more than simply imposing the information from a clock or a calendar onto a spatio-temporally amorphous phenomenology. To live in time, whether a time based on Western divisions of the day and year, or the activities of bodies and environments, is not just to have an abstract concept of one's time, but to attend to such reference points 'as part of a project that engages the past and future in the present'.[48] She calls human activity 'projects' in order to emphasise that spacetime is an integral part of what it means to have purposes, intentions and to act. For the Gawans, value is measured in terms of 'an act's relative capacity to extend or expand ... inter-subjective spacetime'.[49] This means that spacetime depends upon the activities of the members of the island community, and 'a given type of act or practice forms a spatiotemporal process, a particular mode of spacetime'.[50] The Kula exchange of precious shell ornaments between different islands in this region of the Pacific, is one of the ways these people extend their liveable spacetime to their own benefit. These shell ornaments sometimes have names and histories, and confer great prestige upon their temporary possessors, who constantly negotiate to own and exchange such shells: 'the travels of kula shells create an emergent space-time of their own that transcends that of specific, immediate transactions'.[51] Gift exchange of these objects actually creates and sustains part of the world in which they live. Does the circulation of literary texts work similarly?

The social theorist Barbara Adam provides the terms in which this question might be answered, by showing how remarkably incommensurable current theories of time are. She investigates their differences, and then points to the multi-dimensional temporality which a global theory of time would have to explain. 'It is not either winter or December, or hibernation time for the tortoise, or one o'clock, or time for Christmas dinner. It is planetary time, biological time, clock and calendar time,

natural and social time all at once'.[52] The heterogeneity of time is manifested in a myriad ways. It occurs as 'timing, tempo, and temporality' (by
which she means the way we all live in extended cultural moments); it
can be 'measure, sense, boundary, resource and commodity'; through
'entropy, ageing, and growth' it has an irreversible direction; and
'through its rhythmicity life becomes predictable'.[53] She goes even
further than Greenhouse and Munn, arguing that not only is time not a
fourth quasi-spatial dimension, or a misleading subjective projection onto
an atemporal materiality; time would be better imagined as actually in
things.[54] Unlike Greenhouse, she also recognises the pervasive significance of scientific theory: 'Physical time forms a deeply sedimented
aspect of our everyday working knowledge. Newtonian physics pervades
our daily lives through both our technologies and the way physics is
taught at school: not as a way of understanding but as being the fundamental reality. We live and practice thermodynamics each time we put
the kettle on'.[55] Spacetime is practised whenever we drive a car, use the
telephone, save a computer file, read a book or watch World Cup football. The temporal lag between advanced scientific theory and the
background knowledges of everyday life which Adam calls the difference
between the old Newtonian mechanics and the new relativistic and
quantum mechanics, is not just a delay which social theory must overcome, as she persuasively suggests. It is important to recognise that there
is not one scientific theory of time current in the popular imaginary, to
say nothing of mathematics and current scientific theorising. The mathematical time of Einstein's general theory of relativity, the time of
evolution and the irreversibility of the thermodynamic theory of entropy,
have all shaped our lives. When we analyse time in social life, we need
to recognise that 'order, organization, control, power, resource,
commodity, concept, measure, horizon, external frame, and internal age
are not available choices that may be abstracted for study on an either/or
basis. They are all simultaneously implied in any one aspect' of time.[56]

Modern experience can find no one inclusive theory of time, but
neither can it ignore the influence of competing temporalities. It is this
explosion of hypotheses, and a still growing recognition of the diversity
of times in different cultures and within the everyday experience of
Western culture, which has most altered the past. They present what the
philosopher John Dupré, whom we mentioned in the Introduction, calls
a 'promiscuous realism'.[57] Perhaps time and space are also names for such
heterogeneity. Instead of assuming that some one form of space or time
is fundamental, and builds up into all the different forms which we shall
encounter and, therefore, treating each kind of scientific, social,
phenomenological and theoretical space as products of one irreducible
constituent, we can investigate the seeming heterogeneity more closely.

Critiques of the postmodern condition in terms of space-time compression also lack this recognition, and tend to work with unexamined traditional images of space and time. They are not always reflexive enough about what is at stake in such discourses. As Greenhouse says, discourses of time are always discourses of social agency, or in our terms, representations of the practice of space and time – subjectivity, narrative and agency, are all likely to be implicated in any attempt to represent the time of textual memory.

Bergson thought time was the source of creativity. What we have seen is that the creativity of time is a social practice and not simply inherent in an abstract time of the universe. Time's unceasing novelty is not just the result of continual transformation; it is also the result of the unmapped diversity of incommensurable temporalities which are endlessly worked into new forms. Time is practised in writing in many modalities: as the deferral of meaning; in narrative as the phenomenology of existential time; and as the analepses of intertextuality and the prolepses of reception in all its heterogeneity. Writing can sometimes catch a glint of these other shifting temporalities in its reflexive moments, which always exceed its capacity to find stable forms of narrative, image, appearance, rhythm, sound and rhetorics to explore the condition of living in time.

Throughout this discussion, space has remained a shadowy but omnipresent partner with time; sometimes transforming time into a more complex manifold – spacetime – sometimes providing a venue for moments and memories. The unveiling of Elaine Risley's memory may be explained in temporal discourse, but it relies throughout on different forms of space. Looking into a cat's eye marble, walking the city of Toronto and reading its cityscape as a material memory of her childhood, locating different memories in rooms, streets and the awful bridge are only some of the many productions of personal and social space for memory. As Georges Perec (whose novel *W* is one of the most poignant renditions of the destruction of memory and narrative by the Holocaust) said, 'To live is to pass from one space to another, while doing your very best not to bump yourself'.[58] It is now time to look at the effect the bumps and discontinuities of space have had in the making of contemporary pasts.

The spatialisation of history

Count Ladislaus de Almásy, the man who has been mistakenly identified as English in Michael Ondaatje's novel *The English Patient* (1992), yearns for space free of the influence of modern states, as he lies dying in a ruined villa in Italy cared for by a young Canadian nurse. He thought he had found it in the North African desert, because he believed it 'could not be claimed or owned'; there he could shed his national identity like clothing.[59] His mapping, his documentation of the cave drawings, and his search for the fabled oasis of Zerzura, a place which makes such a faint impression on the voids of the desert that it disappears for hundreds of years at a time (p. 141), all enable him to immerse himself in the illusion of spatial freedom. He even uses the spatial language of the cartographer to explain how he fell in love with a married woman: 'He said later it was propinquity. Propinquity in the desert' (p. 150). Now, ironically, he has achieved statelessness at the cost of mortal wounds – his face is destroyed and 'all identification consumed in a fire' (p. 48). His burned body is a sign that the free space of the desert was an illusion, that it cannot resist the desire of nations to create places, identities and property, and then fight over them. The war destroys space as a place of freedom, as is evident when Kip, the Sikh bomb-disposal expert, is working on an Esau bomb buried halfway into the ground. Kip has to work barefoot because the mud might seize his boots and break his ankles when he is lifted clear, but even so the mud begins to catch him: 'there was so little space between him and the bomb he could feel the change in temperature already' (pp. 210–11). The loss of space extends to his sense of location, and he cannot remember what town he is in, and what is worse, wherever he goes places have lost their prospects. Now all places look futureless, because they seem ready to explode: 'He was unable to look at a room or a field without seeing the possibilities of weapons there' (p. 75). The war similarly destroys the nurse, Hana's, sense of place: 'Where was and what was Toronto anymore in her mind' she thinks, as she is constantly surrounded by the wounded and dying in the makeshift hospitals of the Allied advance through Italy. The only place with any stability in the novel is the Villa San Girolamo, where the nurse, the patient, the sapper and a self-appointed minder, Caravaggio, another Canadian, are all temporarily marooned by the war. It is made of fragments of former histories, of religion, culture, politics – one day Hana finds Caravaggio 'near the headless statue of a count' (p. 34). Her attempt to replace two missing stairs by nailing books from the library to the floor represents the damage done to this past embedded in the fabric of the building, which nevertheless remains as a token possibility of a world beyond the war in the past and future.

The preoccupation with space centres on the count's belief that space is more fundamental than culture and its warring nation states – a belief strongly challenged by the pessimistic plot of the narrative. All the main characters have national identities which place them on the margins of the conflict between the great powers, and all of them struggle for recognition of their difference. There appears to be no place for a marriage of India and Canada in the characters of Hana and Kip; the desert's neutrality is destroyed, and an Englishness symbolic of the power of the state to eliminate diversity is imposed on the count. Instead, the novel shows how much the imagined neutrality of space, like that of time, has consistently underwritten hegemonic Western perspectives. *The English Patient* is also very much of its time with its interest in place, space and their history, because these have increasingly become themes for research. Its affinity with this work is most evident in the way in which the temporalisation of history has lost all linearity. Fragments of individual and social memory, history, and material traces of the past appear in every form from flashback to formal narrative. Only the places manage to hold time and history to any coherence, and as the novel investigates these practices of space and temporality it makes an implicit claim that it is only by finding ways to represent these that one can locate otherwise inaccessible aspects of the history of the Second World War. Only by understanding space more thoroughly can some aspects of the past be even recognised, let alone understood.

Space has always puzzled philosophers and scientists because it seems to be a contradictory entity, at once particular, concrete and physical, and yet neither material, nor, worse still, perceptible. Many attempts have been devised in the past to give space some kind of material, yet imperceptible, structure. Some thinkers even wondered if it makes sense to attribute any reality to space at all. What would change if everything in the universe became suddenly twice as big, if everything were suddenly an inflated version of itself? Leibniz argued that nothing would alter because all the internal relations would remain the same and, therefore, it is the relations between things which matter not the spatial container. Leibniz's clever argument took for granted that Euclidean geometry was the inherent framework for the universe, but in the twentieth century this is no longer possible because of the effects of new geometries, and consequent uncertainties about whether we can even know what the underlying spatial structure of the universe might be.[60]

As far back as the 1950s, Charles Olson liked to say that we lived in a postmodern age as a result of such developments. He could call D. H. Lawrence 'post-modern' because the postmodern era had begun half a century earlier, around 1870, when the mathematicians Nikolai Lobachevski and Georg Friedrich Riemann developed the first non-Euclidean geometries.[61] Like many other twentieth-century thinkers, he realised that the seemingly abstract theories of these mathematicians helped bring about a profound shift in our relations with the world. Hitherto it had been possible to believe that our minds might one day fully comprehend the universe because, although much of it might be beyond our current powers of reason, the remarkably powerful logic of the geometry formalised by the Alexandrian mathematician, Euclid, demonstrated that it was possible for us to know exactly what at least one aspect of the world was truly like. Geometry was a form of symbolic reasoning that matched the spatial relations of the real world so perfectly that it appeared to be a direct manifestation of that world in our thought. Geometrical knowledge of space proved that we were at home in the world, and so by inference, space was the location of our consciousness of being in the world. The arrival of new geometries whose validity as systems of reasoning about space could not be faulted, and yet differed from the familiar Euclidean model (notably on the question of the character of parallel lines), meant that the mathematics of space was not a direct line to the real world.[62] An epistemological alienation swept aside the old *lares* of geometry, rendering the mind homeless in the world, and its consequences have continued to be felt throughout the twentieth century. Leibniz's proof that space was irrelevant to our knowledge of things became untenable. Replace Euclidean space with one of the new non-Euclidean spaces and the doubling of everything in the universe certainly changes the relations between things. Imagine, for example, what happens if you enlarge a triangle made up of those straight-line great circles inscribed on the surface of a sphere. As it grows larger, the angles at the vertices grow larger too. Space cannot be assumed to be a neutral background, and yet its nature has paradoxically become less certain as a result of these developments in mathematics.

Space has recently become a distinct field of investigation for contemporary cultural analysts, whose methodologies sometimes verge upon the unnerving abandonment of historical process, or at least its temporal form, diachrony. Cultural geographers such as Edward Soja, David Harvey, Doreen Massey and Derek Gregory have been instrumental in arguing for a new emphasis on the study of space. Although Soja is not one to ignore the efficacy of historical approaches to the study of society, he contends that theorists such as Foucault and Lefebvre have shown us that 'space more than time hides things from us, that the demystification of spatiality and its veiled instrumentality of power is the key to making practical, political, and theoretical sense of the contemporary era'.[63] The desert in Ondaatje's novel is revealed to be hiding not mysterious oases but the realities of European power politics. Soja is concerned that we re-examine the ways in which social practices exist in space, although he does recognise the danger of preserving an ahistorical discourse; but like the other new geographers, he construes spaces as providing the opportunity for continually experiencing processes which occur through time. Time is experienced in and through the experiencing of space. When the influential geographer Kevin Lynch produced his book *What Time is This Place?* (1972), he was conscious of the way in which people are disturbed by the way places change time and how each place is situated within multiple temporal and spatial contexts. Contemporary cultural geography initiates a spacing of time, fictional representations of which will be discussed later in this book in relation to urban space and the city.

These critical interventions were responding to the inert, inflexible spatial imaginary that provided the backdrop for the activisms of dialectical materialism and more generally for the high-energy causalities of historical process. Treating space as if it were theatrical flats hid the social mechanisms which produced not only space but also time and memory. Henri Lefebvre, who pioneered this new field, argues that although space has become increasingly important to twentieth-century social thinkers, most of them continue to treat it as if it were an independent container for human practices, as their rhetoric makes plain:

> We are forever hearing about the space of this and/or the space of that: about literary space, ideological spaces, the space of the dream, psychoanalytic topologies, and so on and so forth. Conspicuous by its absence from supposedly fundamental epistemological studies is not only the idea of 'man' but also that of space – the fact that 'space' is mentioned on every page notwithstanding. Thus Michel Foucault can calmly assert that 'knowledge [savoir] is also the space in which the subject may take up a position and speak of the objects with which he deals in his discourse'. Foucault never explains what space it is that he is referring to, nor how it bridges the gap between the theoretical (epistemological) realm and the practical one, between mental and social, between the space of the philosophers and the space of the people who deal with material things.[64]

What makes Ondaatje's novel so effective, despite its nostalgia for a prewar unfallen world of free travel, is its insistence on the materiality and historicity of space; space is always produced by social relations however much objectified in the structure.

As Edward Soja has observed, Lefebvre's intervention has acted as a significant corrective to the traditional materialist Marxist narratives of history, by countering with a new injunction to always spatialise when you historicise.[65] This means that, in Hayden White's words, 'in Lefebvre's view ... The fundamental subject matter of history is space ... the secret of history's meaning'.[66] Lefebvre's pioneering investigations of the history and politics of space reverse the usually implicit relations between objects and space, and both historicise space and spatialise history. In an ambitious programme for future research, he calls for new methods for social and cultural research. Its importance requires extensive quotation:

> 4. an approach which would analyse not things in space but space itself, with a view to uncovering the social relationships embedded in it.

The dominant tendency fragments space and cuts it up into pieces. It enumerates the things, the various objects, that space contains.

. . .

5. The forces of production and technology now permit of intervention at every level of space: local, regional, national, worldwide. Space as a whole, geographical or historical space, is thus modified, but without any concomitant abolition of its underpinnings – those initial 'points', those first foci or nexuses, those 'places' (localities, regions, countries) lying at different levels of a social space in which nature's space has been replaced by a space-qua-product.

. . .

6. What is urgently required here is the clear distinction between an imagined or sought-after 'science of space' on the one hand and real knowledge of the production of space on the other. Such a knowledge, in contrast to the dissection, interpretations and representations of a would-be science of space, may be expected to rediscover *time* (and in the first place the time of production) in and through space.

7. The real knowledge that we hope to attain would have a retrospective as well as a prospective import. Its implications for history, for example, and for our understanding of time, will become apparent if our hypothesis turns out to be correct. It will help us grasp how societies generate their (social) space and time – their representational spaces and their representations of space. It should also allow us, not to foresee the future, but to bring relevant factors to bear on the future in prospect – on the project, in other words, of another space and another time in another (possible or impossible) society.[67]

Much of this analysis recapitulates what we found earlier about time. Space, like time, cannot simply be treated as a continuous manifold of infinitely divisible points and detachable areas. Space is as much a discourse of agency as time, and changes in material production and social organisation (like the 'disembedding' of which Giddens writes) have reached far into subjective life. Scientific models of space form part of the social discourse of space and help produce social space, which in turn is reinscribed in the conceptual landscapes of the theories themselves. We can neither ignore scientific space nor treat it as fundamentally determining of cultural practice. A full understanding of periodisation, especially postmodernism and postcolonialism, will depend upon a better understanding of the way social and economic change alters the production of space in tension with existing regionalisms and localities. Most important of all, by studying both the discourses of space and the spaces of discourse, we can register the changing face of the past because space appears to be the very condition of representation.

The temptation has been to find time only in narrative fiction, while space is found everywhere in literature, but as Soja says, this is a space which conceals historicity and power. The desire for a pure space in which the past can be located, like the Zerzura oasis on a map of history, can lead attention away from other spaces in literary practice, where its workings are evident as disturbances of time, realism and memory. In our discussion of urban fictions we show that cities both produce space and are produced by the space they make available for textual memory to go to work.

Textual memory has been changed by the new theories of space and time, and the new paradigms of memory, because the past has also been altered. It can appear that literature has not risen to meet the challenge if we confine ourselves only to realist historical fiction. What the following chapters show is that there are many sites of history in contemporary writing that remain underexplored, and that the cultural poetics of the genre is especially important for understanding how the past is understood and remembered as a means to creating new political possibilities for the present and future. We begin with historical drama in which the history is prominent but usually a broad-brush history unconcerned with scholarly accuracy. Its manipulation of the conditions of staging and its emulation of the public sphere suggest new ways of thinking of the practice of historicism in literature. From there, we trace the underlying circuits of exchange which have made autobiographical lyric poetry the dominant mode over the past four decades. A memory economy has developed that underwrites the perceived losses of both individual and social memory. We then move to a very different genre of commercial, popular writing in which readers and writers collaborate to speculate about the consequences of technological and social change by treating the future as a representable space. Despite the crudity of much of the writing, its cumulative effect is a complex investigation of the contested temporalities we have discussed in this chapter. In the final chapter we turn to the city in recent fiction as a space which is increasingly a structure of textual memory embedded in the concrete and sociality of urbanism. All four genres are not what is ordinarily thought of as historical literature, and are offered both as instances of the arrival of new scenes of the past as well as signs of changing cultural experiences of the past.

Notes

1 Margaret Atwood, *Cat's Eye* (London: Virago, [1988] 1990), pp. 331–2.
2 William F. Brewer, 'What is recollective memory?', in David C. Rubin (ed.), *Remembering Our Past: Studies in Autobiographical Memory* (Cambridge: Cambridge University Press, 1996), pp. 19–66, 61.
3 Atwood, *Cat's Eye*, p. 151.
4 Gustav Janouch, *Conversations with Kafka* (London: Deutsch, 1971), p. 211.

5 Theodor W. Adorno, *Aesthetic Theory*, trans. Robert Hullot-Kentor (Minneapolis: University of Minnesota Press, 1997), p. 28.

6 Henri Bergson, *Creative Evolution*, trans. Arthur Mitchell (Lanham, MD: University Press of America, [1911] 1983), p. 11.

7 Ibid., pp. 330–4.

8 Adorno, *Aesthetic Theory*, p. 34.

9 Stephen Hawking, *A Brief History of Time: From the Big Bang to Black Holes* (London: Bantam, 1988), p. 160.

10 Ursula K. LeGuin, *The Dispossessed* (London: Granada, 1975).

11 Hawking, *A Brief History of Time*, pp. 166–7.

12 Ibid., p. 169.

13 Ibid., p. 98.

14 Ibid., p. 149.

15 Ibid., p. 159.

16 Ibid., p. 38.

17 Ibid., p. 103.

18 Larry Niven, *Neutron Star* (London: Futura, [1968] 1978).

19 Pierre Bourdieu, *Outline of a Theory of Practice*, trans. Richard Nice (Cambridge: Cambridge University Press, 1977), p. 9.

20 Dennis Brian, *Einstein: A Life* (New York: John Wiley and Sons, 1996), p. 113.

21 Albrecht Fölsing, *Albert Einstein: A Biography*, trans. and abridged Ewald Osers (Harmondsworth: Penguin, 1998), p. 735.

22 Hermann Weyl, *Space-Time-Matter*, trans. Henry L. Brose (London: Methuen, 1922).

23 Ibid., p. 4.

24 Ibid., p. 3.

25 Hans Joas, *G. H. Mead* (New York: Scribner, 1992), p. 169.

26 Kurt Vonnegut, *Slaughterhouse Five* (London: Granada, 1979).

27 For a discussion of *Slaughterhouse Five* within the context of debates about time, history and ethics, see Tim Woods, 'Spectres of History: Ethics and Postmodern Fictions of Temporality', in D. Rainsford and T. Woods (eds), *Critical Ethics: Text, Theory and Responsibility* (Basingstoke: Macmillan, 1999), pp. 105–21.

28 Alfred L. Kroeber, *The Arapaho* (Lincoln: University of Nebraska Press, 1983), p. 11.

29 Ibid., pp. 418–19.

30 Johannes Fabian, *Time and the Other: How Anthropology Makes its Other* (New York: Columbia University Press, 1993), p. 25.

31 Ibid., pp. 30–1.

32 Stephen Kern, *The Culture of Time and Space, 1880–1918* (Cambridge, MA: Harvard University Press, 1983), p. 314.

33 Carol Greenhouse, *A Moment's Notice* (Ithaca: Cornell University Press, 1996).

34 This is a critique of Heidegger, in particular, who assumes that mortality's temporalisation of *Dasein* or individual being is a universal given.

35 Anthony Giddens, *The Constitution of Society: Outline of the Theory of Structuration* (Cambridge: Polity Press, 1984), p. 203.

36 Ibid., p. 262.

37 Anthony Giddens, *The Consequences of Modernity* (Cambridge: Polity Press, 1990), p. 21.

38 David Harvey, *The Condition of Postmodernity: An Enquiry into the Origins of Cultural Change* (Oxford: Blackwell, 1989), p. 240.

39 Greenhouse, *A Moment's Notice*, p. 104.

40 Ibid., p. 147.

41 Ibid., p. 82.

42 Ibid., p. 60.

43 Ibid., p. 234.

44 William Gibson, *Neuromancer* (London: Collins, [1984] 1986), pp. 14, 243.

45 Charles Olson, *The Special View of History*, ed. Ann Charters (Berkeley: Oyez, 1970), p. 28.

46 A fuller account of Olson's interest in time and history can be found in Peter Middleton, 'Olson's History', *Boxkite* 3, forthcoming.

47 Nancy Munn, 'The cultural anthropology of time: a critical essay', *American Review of Anthropology*, 21 (1992), 116.

48 Ibid., p. 104.

49 Ibid., p. 9.

50 Ibid., p. 10.

51 Ibid., p. 58.

52 Barbara Adam, *Time and Social Theory* (Cambridge: Polity Press, 1990), p. 16.

53 Ibid., p. 169.

54 Ibid., p. 38.

55 Ibid., p. 68–9.

56 Ibid., p. 126.

57 John Dupré, *The Disorder of Things: Metaphysical Foundations of the Disunity of Science* (Cambridge, MA: Harvard University Press, 1993), p. 7.

58 Georges Perec, 'Species of spaces', *Species of Spaces and Other Pieces*, ed. and trans. John Sturrock (Harmondsworth: Penguin, 1997), p. 6.

59 Michael Ondaatje, *The English Patient* (London: Picador, [1992] 1993), pp. 138–9.

60 Graham Nerlich, *What Spacetime Explains: Metaphysical Essays on Space and Time* (Cambridge: Cambridge University Press, 1994), p. 55.

61 Charles Olson, *Selected Writings of Charles Olson*, ed. Robert Creeley (New York: New Directions, 1966), p. 44.

62 In Euclidean geometry, if you choose any point on a two-dimensional plane and draw a line that does not pass through this point, then there is only one parallel line that can be drawn through this point. On the surface of a sphere, however, another geometry applies. If a great circle is treated as a straight line then given a point and a line, there is no parallel line to be drawn. On other kinds of surface it is possible to draw an infinite number of parallel lines through a point. Astronomers have tried inconclusively to work out whether the universe obeys one of these geometries, but there is no guarantee that other geometric systems in multiple dimensions might not exist.

63 Edward Soja, *Postmodern Geographies: The Reassertion of Space in Critical Social Theory* (London: Verso, 1989), p. 61.

64 Henri Lefebvre, *The Production of Space*, trans. Donald Nicholson-Smith (Oxford: Blackwell, 1991), pp. 3–4.

65 See, for example, Edward Soja, 'The socio-spatial dialectic', *Annals of the Associaiton of American Geographers*, 70 (1980), 207–25. Lefebvre's theorisations of space and its relation to time also drives Soja's recent book *Thirdspace: Journeys to Los Angeles and Other Real-And-Imagined Places* (Oxford: Basil Blackwell, 1996), which urges readers to maintain a consciousness of the historicity and sociality of space when thinking about the actions of everyday life.

66 Hayden White, review of *The Production of Space*, by Henri Lefebvre, *Design Book Review*, 29–30 (Summer–Fall 1993), 90–3.

67 Lefebvre, *The production of space*, pp. 90–2.

Part II

CHAPTER 5

Staged histories: radical theatre in Britain and America, 1968–88

On 17 June 1976, Sir Keith Joseph, a future Secretary of State for Industry in Margaret Thatcher's government, addressed the International Monetary Conference in San Francisco on the subject of 'Recovery without Inflation'. His speech laid down many of the tenets of monetarism that had become central to the ideology of the British Conservative Party in the 1980s. He finished by quoting approvingly from Adam Smith, the ideological father of monetarist politics:

> The uniform, constant and uninterrupted effort of every man to better his condition, the principle from which public and national, as well as private opulence is originally derived, is frequently powerful enough to maintain the natural progress of things towards improvement, in spite of the extravagance of government and the greatest errors of administration. Like the unknown principle of animal life, it frequently restores health and vigour to the constitution, in spite not only of the disease, but of the absurd prescriptions of the doctor.[1]

At first glance this may appear somewhat peripheral to monetarist politics. Yet what underlies Keith Joseph's ideology here is a belief in history as the triumphant march to the present, a confirmation of what we are, the historical inevitability of the present order of things. A healthy nation is one which allows the 'natural' progression of events and actions to 'flow', as one-time Secretary for Education, Kenneth Baker, notes in his Introduction to *The Faber Book of English History in Verse*: 'This sea of men and women flows through our history, shaping and defining our national character'.[2] It is this notion of history which has long defined Conservative notions of history and national identity, and which the Party increasingly sought to institutionalise during its recent years of political power, involving them in a series of difficult struggles on a variety of differing social fronts.

Ten years after this speech, by the mid-1980s, the challenges to the state which the Left was able to mount had long been systematically eroded. Following their far-reaching restructuring of Britain's economic, social and cultural life, the Conservative government under Margaret

Thatcher finally focused its ideological attention on teaching history in the nation's schools. In fact, the process was put into operation by Sir Keith Joseph's address to the Historical Association in February 1984, when he outlined his sense of history as a continuous evolutionary progress of 'shared values', a 'commonality that defines us as a society'.[3] After putting forward the somewhat idiosyncratic notion that chemistry could be left to the chemists and music to the musicians, he claimed that history was different; far from being a procrustean bed of academic interest, it was deemed to be a national property.

This became undeclared Party policy. Decisions about the teaching of history in the National Curriculum in the early 1990s can be interpreted as a right-wing attempt to claw back the national self-image, a sense of heritage and purpose, that the Left had so openly challenged and sought to appropriate in the 1970s and early 1980s. Successive Conservative Secretaries of State for Education during the 1980s and 1990s battled to implement their educational reforms with the institution of the National Curriculum, around which history became a *cause célèbre* for the arguments of various opposing historians, politicians, educationalists and journalists, as well as the wider public. Margaret Thatcher was at the vanguard of the new proposals for history teaching:

> Perhaps the hardest battle I fought on the national curriculum was about history. Though not an historian myself, I had a very clear − and I had naively imagined uncontroversial − idea of what history was. History is an account of what happened in the past. Learning history, therefore, requires knowledge of events. It is impossible to make sense of such events without absorbing sufficient factual information and without being able to place matters in a clear chronological framework − which means knowing dates. No amount of imaginative sympathy for historical characters or situations can be a substitute for the initially tedious but ultimately rewarding business of memorizing what actually happened. ... In July 1989 the History Working Group produced its interim report. I was appalled. It put the emphasis on interpretation and enquiry as against content and knowledge. There was insufficient weight given to British history. There was not enough emphasis on history as chronological study. I considered the document comprehensively flawed.[4]

Thatcher put her finger on several problems that needed to be addressed concerning the teaching of history, although her characteristically arrogant sense that she was cutting through the Gordian knot of unnecessary academic quandaries, makes her pose too simplistic an opposition between knowledge and sympathy, between 'what actually happened' and 'imaginative sympathy'. While the empathetic approach to history can lead into a quagmire of difficulties, the hard ground of her realist epistemology of history is not nearly as solid as Thatcher purports.

During the passage of the National Curriculum reforms through Parliament in the late 1980s, a Conservative backbench MP, Sir John Stokes, spoke for many in his Party when he said in the House of Commons:

> A knowledge of history is absolutely essential if we are to retain our identity as a nation ... Some people are shy about dwelling too much on our island history for fear of upsetting the immigrants among us. That is a mistaken view. Immigrants, like everyone else, expect us to be true to ourselves and to our history and identity as a nation. ... Children should be made to learn the dates of the great events of past centuries. ... They will thus in due course begin to realise the remarkable continuity of the history of our small island. ... We in Parliament are trustees of posterity and must hand on the torch of our civilisation to succeeding generations. We have contributed a great deal to the civilisation of the world and we should be proud of that. We still have a great deal to give the world and we should rejoice in that. I am happy to say that at present our standing among nations remains high.[5]

For Stokes, history means several things: (1) a method of creating identity (and nations do have identities); (2) a means of being true to a collective self; (3) a record of the creation of civilisation; and (4) above all, a creation of order and continuity. The familiar themes of Tory history are perpetuated here: the ready conflation of conservatism and the country in the rousing elision of the phrase '*our* identity as a *nation*' (our italics); the unproblematic notion of date-learning as the essential foundation of history; the vexed alignment of a singular British history with a multicultural and regional population, who are expected to learn a new identity from it; and most importantly, the key sense of history as a continuous flow of events and people. The purple prose conclusion sinks into the most clichéd and stereotypical right-wing rhetoric of imperial nostalgia concerning British history and the international political standing of the nation.

The debate about the teaching of history raged for many more months. Countering the elitist view of history, Christopher Hill added his voice in the *Guardian* in 1989:

> The most fruitful change in historical attitudes in my time, I think, has been the emergence of 'history from below' – the realisation that ordinary people also have a history, perhaps that they played more part in determining the shape of the historical process, whether for change or for continuity, than we have thought. ... History no longer deals exclusively with kings and their mistresses, prime ministers and wars, statutes and debates in Parliament. ... We must get away from history exclusively from on top. ... If we just go back to national self-glorifi-

cation, to painting the map red, history will be in danger of becoming the plaything of party politics, to be changed with a change of government.[6]

Hill's words were already somewhat late. This was the culmination of a process of redefinition that had been going on since the late 1970s. During this period, the very concept of 'history' itself had become a site of increasing political struggle, over which different power interests battled and sought to impose their meaning. As the Marxist linguistic philosopher Volosinov has argued, every signifier is the product of an addresser to an addressee, and is subsequently to be thought of as a two-sided act, or an 'intersecting of accents'.[7] Since this Janus-faced sign does not belong to any individual (it is always the property of another, possessing other meanings), it becomes a sensitive register of social and political negotiation, and 'this *inner dialectic quality* of the sign comes out fully in the open in times of social crises or revolutionary changes'.[8] Consequently, the ruling hegemony seeks to suppress the 'multi-accentuality' of every sign, desiring to make the sign appear 'monological' and to deny its material properties, stabilising the sign 'in the dialectical flux of the social generative process, so accentuating yesterday's truth as to make it appear today's'.[9] This attempted preservation of an immobile history results in what Guy Debord characterises as 'the society of the spectacle', in which the ruling hegemony of the bourgeoisie imposes an irreversible historical time on society.[10] Consequently, for the radical, 'reasoning about history is inseparably *reasoning about power*'.[11] During the late 1970s and 1980s, the Conservative Party sought to 'uni-accentualise' history by gradually involving itself in debates about the educational value of British history – about what ought to be considered as the content of British history, as much as what ought to be the concept of history *per se* – and using ideological constructions of history to establish a sense of nationhood.

From the retrospective vantage point of the end of the century, the intense effort of various Conservative ministers during the 1980s to circumscribe and delimit the public discussion of history in the spheres of education, cultural practice, politics and social life, appears to be the response to a deeply felt need to protect an ideological lynch-pin of Conservative ideology. It was part of the protection of what J. K. Galbraith has termed the 'constituency of contentment'.[12] The Party was reacting on behalf of a social hegemony to a perceived threat to its security from emergent forms of social and textual memory, which challenged its control over dominant ideological narratives of past political events and political figures, especially within twentieth century history following the end of the Second World War. What was the source of these threats and from where were they emanating?

We will suggest that the emergence of an active radical drama during the 1970s and the early 1980s, that was concerned explicitly with debating various models of history, was one significant site of this ideological disruption. It gained what force it had as part of a larger challenge to conservative social ideologies from the Left (as an agglomeration of various Marxist, feminist and gay/lesbian groups) during the 1970s. Drama constituted an important part of the public sphere where a democratic political space continued. It was a space where a 'moral economy' was tried and tested, where the effects of economic and political ideas on people's lives were put on display. The act of putting this on display was important, because it offered a version of the past for open public discussion and consumption. Drama of this sort fulfilled a need for public debate about the social and national consciousness of the past. Rejecting the inevitability of the slow atomisation of society as a result of the forces unleashed by an increasingly open market capitalism (and the concomitant abolition of any 'moral economy'), this drama offered models of what a society might look like as a burgeoning free market eroded any concept of citizenship as a responsibility for the economic and moral well-being of a heterogeneous community; as well as offering alternative structures as to the ways society could be constructed on intersubjective relationships. It sought to analyse the basis of contemporary and future social power by linking it directly to the versions of the past and the narratives of national identity that constituted popular social history. This drama was, therefore, attempting to initiate and participate in a public debate about how the past is constructed, with the aim of altering present and future social relationships.

Borrowing the terminology of Jürgen Habermas's analysis of the public sphere, one can perceive in this historical drama a specific attempt to prompt a public deliberation through 'ideal role-taking', a process in which observers and participants of the drama would try to understand the situations and perspectives of others by giving them equal weight to their own.[13] This process of 'imaginative empathy' sought to create an orientation toward a broader-ranging social justice than merely a concern with those of one's own group. Remaining closely tied to the specific context of action and experience, and thereby resisting the idealising presuppositions and abstractions of practical discourse, the aim of this mode of dramatic communication, which enables individuals to adopt a more reflective attitude towards their own expressive manifestations to see through the irrational limitations to which they are subject and to clarify their own systematic self-deceptions, might ultimately be construed as a form of social therapy. The dramatists sought to make the performance an aesthetic experience sufficiently authentic to become a rational motive for attempting to alter the paradigms of the past which help sustain existing social structures. They assumed that an audience's wants, needs, feelings, emotions, attitudes and sentiments are not directly shaped by the force of arguments. Rather, our eyes are opened by the values disclosed or discredited in certain exemplary circumstances. Hence, although drama cannot substitute for experience, this historical drama nevertheless sought to act as a transformative power of experience through reflective discussion, to articulate and guide social experience.

Furthermore, drama, as a form of sensual and somatic movement and sound, is able to intimate phenomenologies which are part of history, yet which get forgotten by abstract theories and conceptual models of the past. In a manner akin to Proust's description of the effects of eating the madeleine cake, drama is able to explore how moods, conjunctions, bodies, sounds and smells all form part of the past and often trigger memories of the past otherwise unavailable. Drama affects the public debate in a way that is not merely conceptual; it offers up the sensual and imaginary for public memory and scrutiny as a 'bodily practice'.

This chapter has begun by looking at Conservative accounts and paradigms of history in their efforts to define what ought to be taught in school education during the 1980s. These political arguments will now lead us back a decade to consider just what was proposed by the histori- cal drama of the 1970s. There were many debates about the best form in which to make a critique of the Right – agitprop theatre or naturalist theatre; there were debates about the way society's gender bias was perpetuated by certain political dramas; and there were debates about what was the most appropriate and most effective drama to fund. Different forms of drama offered different forms of history. 'Case- studies' of several very different playwrights will demonstrate the variety of ways in which this historical drama intervened in the public sphere. We conclude with a study of a play by an African-American dramatist written during this period, which helps clarify what was distinctive about the British debates on effective political drama in comparison with the American context.

The rhetoric of privacy and autonomous subjects ushered in by the Conservatives, served to restrict the sphere of legitimate public contesta- tion. Drama during the 1970s and early 1980s was able to make a significant contribution to the debate about what constituted the national historical consciousness. It was a debate about recovery – the recovery of hitherto suppressed histories now made into discursive forms which can enter the public sphere from which their creators' culture was so long excluded. In certain cases, this recovery is more than simply 'political' – it is redemptive because some silences in the historical record elude articulation in functional discourses. Verbalisation depends on many factors – the development of reflective judgement, time and the opportunity to develop concentration for its witness, and the political freedom to utter the words. It was more than an epiphenomenon of the Left's deeper trend towards challenging the Conservative political hegemony of British public life. The real significance of this historical drama of the 1970s and early 1980s was its attempt to do more than just redefine the popular conceptions of the past; it aimed to reassert the importance of what constitutes a 'civil society'.

This historical drama prompted a debate about how aesthetic and textual activity was able to influence or shape a society's political and social structures of memory. In effect, it was an attempt to forge a public sphere of social integration based upon interactive communication rather than unilateral domination. The advent of the Conservative government in 1978 shifted that equation by imagining the public sphere as occupied only by autonomous individuals, thereby making publicity less an occasion for reasoned progressive consensus formation than an opportunity for the manipulation of popular opinion. The consequence was that 'monetarist economy' abolished any 'moral economy'; and nearly twenty years later in the aftermath of the unprecedented massive electoral defeat of the Conservative Party in May 1997, and the untimely death of Diana, Princess of Wales, the ethical and moral bankruptcy of the social sphere induced by the Conservative political hegemony appears to be gradually coming home to roost, as the British nation appears to have manifested a desperate and near-wretched need to demonstrate a missing ethical kernel to its everyday life world.

The gradual control over history went hand-in-hand with the increasing politicisation of the mechanisms of Arts Council funding, as it slowly starved the left-wing fringe theatre of resources. A broadly based symposium on 'Theatre in Thatcher's Britain' held in 1989 at Goldsmith's College, London, which brought together artists, directors and academics recognised the extent to which the Arts Council's new criteria for economic aid for alternative theatre had effectively impeded and prohibited new developments, as well as sending some of the groups to the wall (like Foco Novo). In a retrospective analysis of the effects of the Arts Council on theatre in the 1980s, many have argued that the Arts Council became 'an arm of government'.[14] The debilitating reductions in public funding for the arts, as well as the pressures on theatre groups to procure private capital and to operate more forcefully within the 'free market', marked a recognisable impetus by the Tory government towards the privatisation of the theatre, and this effectively acted as a form of censorship on left-biased theatres and ideas. John McGrath, one of the foremost dramatists of the new history, described how his company, 7:84 Scotland, was 'told that funding from the Arts Council would cease at the end of 1988 unless certain administrative changes were made'.[15] These changes included the replacement of the company's board with business people, a move which McGrath perceived to be a thinly disguised attempt to wrest artistic control over the content of the company's productions away from its left-wing allegiances. It was widely felt that theatrical space, as a non-disciplined, manipulable, non-organised space, had gradually been colonised and regimented in Britain by the imposition of government 'stool pigeons' during the 1970s and early 1980s. McGrath lamented that one of the consequences of this 'privatisation' of the theatre was an imperceptible shift from popular to populist theatre, especially with the Arts Council's anti-new play policy. These interventions were widely perceived as an attack on civil liberties, as dictatorial party control over national education and the cynical and blinkered manipulation of cultural knowledge and consciousness for right-wing political ends (even the Labour Party was supine over the issue of funding for the arts, often evincing an old-fashioned philistinism about what should and should not be funded), but their real target was the everyday relation to the past. The stage of history had changed and, therefore, a new history had to be staged.

Staging history

These varying representations and constructions of history in the British theatre during the two decades following the abolition of the Lord Chancellor's power of censorship in 1968, raise questions that we want to address. What is it that dramatists perceived in history? As history became the site of openly acknowledged ideological struggle, how did drama increasingly intervene in and manipulate the public perception of history during the late 1970s and 1980s? Was it possible for the drama to make statements about history that could not be articulated in other cultural media? Did feminists make different claims about the representation of history? We shall focus on the dramatic use of history in a selection of plays in an attempt to foreground the way in which drama sought to engage questions and issues concerning consciousness of the national past. We also want to explore the way in which these dramatists have sought to shift an essentially individualistic concept of history, to one that would explore the interrelationship between the spheres of public and private experience.

The Conservative seizure of the ideological apparatus was a response to earlier struggles over the public narrations of the past that had intensified after May 1968. When the student riots occurred on the streets of Paris in May 1968, the seismic tremors were felt in London almost immediately, as socialist intellectuals, artists and political activists sought to use similar tactics to undermine British institutions. As the CS gas cleared, some of the major aftershocks were felt in the new directions and transformations that occurred in British theatre, as playwrights seized the opportunity to challenge the central tenets of Tory ideology. They began to explore alternative, suppressed versions of history, histories that could not be considered a linear flow of the past into a progressive present, and to demythologise hegemonic representations of history as the results of heroic individuals' actions. In his rendering of official culture as a tawdry illusion, Howard Brenton has specifically acknowledged the effect of the events of May 1968 (and the work of the Situationist International in particular) on himself and a number of other playwrights.[16] As Alice describes in Brenton's *Magnificence*, the Situationists wanted revolutionary change: 'A violent intervention. A disruption. A spectacle against the spectacle. A firework in the face of the Ruling Class'.[17] Elsewhere in the play, Jed, the anarchist revolutionary, likens the Situationists' political critique to a bottle thrown through a cinema screen revealing the superficial surface of the picture: 'Bomb 'em. Again and again. Right through their silver screen. Disrupt the spectacle. The obscene parade, bring it to a halt! Scatter the dolly girls, let advertisements bleed ... Bomb'em, again and again!' (Sc.vii, 96). In his frantic eagerness for fervent political activity, Jed fails to see the irony of his being so completely saturated by a social structure of spectacle that he thinks it requires a countermanding spectacle to deny the power of the dominant one.

The Situationist International produced a singular critique of the boredom and apathetic indifference which characterised affluent capitalist middle-class society during the 1950s and 1960s. Perceiving commodification extending into every intimate aspect of people's everyday lives, the Situationists argued that in the morass of this world of spectacular consumption, people became mere observers, having lost control over their own lives and environments. The French social analyst and cultural theoretician, Guy Debord, published the Situationists' seminal book entitled *The Society of the Spectacle* (1967), first translated into English in 1970. The Situationists 'characterised modern capitalist society as an organisation of spectacles: a frozen moment of history in which it is impossible to experience real life or actively participate in the construction of the lived world'.[18] For Debord, 'The spectacle, as the present social organization of the paralysis of history and memory, of the abandonment of history built on the foundation of historical time, is the *false consciousness of time*'.[19] On the face of it, Debord's sense of temporality appears to coincide with the Conservative's conception of time, in that they both want flow. However, the Tories' sense of historical flow is actually a disguise for the fixing of the present by a particular national past which they wanted. This dehistoricisation rested on an idea of time as an eternal, irreversible present; it is linear, progressive and places the status quo firmly in the right place. It situates the observer at a distance from history and through enforced contemplation removes any possibility of engagement with history – time is one long stretch of unchanging permanence. It is precisely this illusion that Debord seeks to puncture. His concept of temporal flow is aimed at countering time as a series of disjunct spectacular 'commodities', the saleable units of time like two-week package holidays, 'time-share' apartments and 'free' time, made all the more desirable by being distanced. In its place, Debord's temporal flow reintroduces qualitative differences into a quantified world by resisting the separations and specialisations of a spectacularised world. As Sadie Plant puts it, 'to the immobile surfaces of the spectacular world, [the Situationists] responded with a dynamic conception of dialectical critique, intended to expose the spectacle as a particular moment of the historical time it denies, undermining its claims to universality and revealing it as a partial construct masquerading as a real world'.[20] Masquerade was combated with dramatic interventions, the Situationist International proving itself to be the master of spontaneous theatre in Paris during the riots. As bricoleurs – improvising with what is to hand – they mounted a hard-hitting critique of bourgeois France in the late 1960s. Arguably, 1968 itself was the result of bricolage: an improvised resistance, which so shocked the official Left (the PCF) because it thought that it organised the people. Reacting to the collapse of left-wing political direction, people took action into their own hands in the hope that they could regain control over everyday life. This immediacy and spontaneity was part of the appeal of the Situationist International for British artists, playwrights and cultural critics, who were invigorated by the Situationists' provocative style derived from Dada and Surrealism, as much as their own outspoken cravings for autonomy. Although they condemned the spectacle for its circumscription of reality, they nevertheless believed that this did not exclude the possibility of choosing a better world of relations and experiences beyond its constraints. Indeed, this utopian vision of a transformation of everyday life embedded in its critique of social complacency was another important point of appeal. As Greil Marcus has noted, the Situationists' critique of the blank superficiality of contemporary society also fed into the punk explosion against British authority in the late 1970s, led by figures like Malcolm McLaren.

Yet as the advent of punk suggests, the growth of various music groups, design styles, fringe, agitprop and theatre groups and their powerful political critique, emerged in a political matrix which went beyond the major tremors in Paris. This included the rejection of Labour Party politics by the post-1968 New Left, the abandonment of theatre censorship in 1968, an increase in extra-parliamentary political activism with the growth of movements like CND, and the consolidation of a new feminist political consciousness. The plays that were written for these politically conscious fringe theatre groups were variously propagandist, satirical and activist, and the *modus operandi* of these theatre companies tended to be *ad hoc* performances with minimal staging and token make-up and costume. Aiming to raise public consciousness of political issues, venues were frequently open-air public spaces like streets, public squares, parks and commons and, in some cases, outside factories. Political activists on the Left in the society of the late 1960s, increasingly moved into service- and consumption-oriented industries, feeling that society was most effectively disrupted at these new points of economic organisation. British playwrights like Edgar, Brenton, Hare and Griffiths similarly perceived British politics to have so successfully sewn up the organisation of the working-class at the point of production, that the easiest site to disrupt middle-class ideology was at the point of consumption.

The burgeoning new political drama inaugurated a new form of ideology critique aimed at the consumption of public images of the past. Christopher Bigsby has noted that many of the plays of post-1968:

> were set in the past partly because the true subject of revolution is history. That is, they were inclined to endorse E. H. Carr's conviction that history is a dialogue between the events of the past and progressively emerging future ends ... their efforts did not mean that England was necessarily experiencing a sudden interest in historical drama. Rather, they suggest that history is offered as a clue to the present, that theirs is offered as a drama of praxis.[21]

Bigsby's explanation is somewhat puzzling since it could apply to the drama of any period. Nevertheless, the theatre and history have constantly supplied each other with figures of speech, as dramatic metaphors pervade constructions of history: 'the stage of history'; 'the main protagonist of the political action'; 'the spectacle of history'; or the 'key players'. The verb 'staged' suggests that history is deliberately used for effect, as well as being consciously manipulated and highlighted as an artificial construction. These playwrights were forging a theory of history and culture similar to that of the later New Historicism. Both eschew positivist and metaphysical versions of history and rob them of political innocence by exposing their discrete commitments and collusions in the cultural struggle for power. The drama is perceived of as part of a larger political economy, as a site through which the defining signs of culture circulate, which also accords drama a creative and reciprocal role in the shaping of its time.

At first sight, several of these playwrights seem interested only in the past for its symbolic possibilities, as if it were a more convenient language for representing the present. Timberlake Wertenbaker says in the note to her play *The Grace of Mary Traverse*:

> Although this play is set in the eighteenth century, it is not a historical
> play. All the characters are my own invention and whenever I have used
> historical events such as the Gordon Riots I have taken great freedom
> with reported fact. I found the eighteenth century a valid metaphor, and
> I was concerned to free the people of the play from contemporary
> preconceptions.[22]

History has this special status for a variety of reasons. It has frequently
been used and manipulated by the forces of reaction as a potent weapon
in preserving the social and economic status quo. First, these dramatists
seek to undercut the iconic status of the historic hero, the single 'great
man' who constructs history and society through his great actions.
Instead, history is presented as the outcome of a variety of societal and
collective economic pressures, after which the actions of certain people
are retrospectively selected for special narrative attention. What becomes
significant in these plays is the sense of a communal past which is critical
to everyone's present circumstances and their futures. Secondly, the
paralysis of history as a spectacle is opened up to more analytical depth.
Since it is acknowledged that society is mediated by images, these playwrights use the 'spectacular image' as a means of subverting the
representational basis, the iconic hegemony, of that society. The ability
of drama to confront an audience *en masse* with an alternative history,
makes it an acutely apt medium to challenge people's everyday beliefs
about history and the society based upon that history. Since the social and
political actors are often self-consciously aware of staging history – with
set-piece summits, 'soundbites', camera poses, public appearances –
the theatre can in turn self-consciously subvert this theatrically staged
history.

It has, therefore, become something of a commonplace among critical interpretations and reactions to much of the British drama written in
the late 1960s, 1970s, and early 1980s, to say that it is 'about history' –
Brenton's historical deconstructions, Hare's 'History Plays', Griffiths'
and Edgar's demystifications of socialist politics, not to mention the
various adaptations of Shakespeare's histories like *The Wars of the Roses*
and *The Plantagenets*. But it is less acknowledged that the construction
of history in these playwrights' work varies tremendously – history as
narrative, socialist realist accounts, history as source of resistance, as
source of despair. Furthermore, as feminist playwrights such as Caryl
Churchill's, Timberlake Wertenbaker's and Pam Gems' plays about
repressed social and gender histories and Michelene Wandor's clear
arguments demonstrate,[23] the history is almost exclusively male:
women are treated as unable to initiate historical actions.

Many of the playwrights of the late 1960s and 1970s perceived the key to the problems of contemporary British society in the immediate post-Second World War decades, to lie in histories that were constantly occluded from public debate. Consequently, time and again their plays probe the history of the past fifty years, looking for the causes, reasons and influences of the social structures which had inhibited, retarded and paralysed Britain up to the late 1960s. As we have noted, the events of 1968 are frequently referred to as pivotal in this analysis.[24] John Bull catalogues the ways in which history has been used by these dramatists:

> During the 1970s this radical treatment of history was intended to achieve a number of political aims. These were variously to convince ordinary people that they could be agents of their own destiny; by means of iconoclasm to demythologise bourgeois history; to suggest the reasons why, during the post-war years, socialism had not won the hearts and minds of the British public; to present history in Marxist terms as one of class conflict; and to utilise dramatic form in order to achieve these ends.[25]

This marked a renaissance in British theatre comparable to the proliferation of drama under the reign of the first Elizabeth.[26] Although Bull's description rightly attests to a utilitarian drama of political exhortation, it does not highlight the explicitly 'redemptive' character of many of these plays. Sounding very different from Bull, Howard Brenton has remarked that this theatrical renaissance was fuelled by a utopianism that was searching for a new consciousness about the world, its possibilities and its future: 'My generation shares an idea that the theatre not only describes but actually shows new possibilities, that you can write so forcefully that a possibility of a new way of looking at the world, a new way of living, can actually be found through the theatre. ... It's like a new renaissance feeling – that we may be the predecessors of an extraordinary end to this century. We may well discover – just as the renaissance discovered humanist egocentric thought, or the Middle Ages discovered romantic love – a new way of looking at man and his behaviour. This sounds very ambitious – but why not be ambitious?'[27] Beguiling and egocentric as it is, this view bears witness to the powerful utopian ethic that impelled this drama towards an openness to unimagined possibilities as an incitement to a radical transformation of the present.

'Hammering on the pipes of the tenement': David Hare and Howard Brenton

> I offer this view of history. It is a paradox. The older order, unchecked, will bring forth a new and harsher form of itself. ... And you will learn that where power has rested, there it shall rest. For a thousand years.[28]

Paul Connerton argues that appeals to collective representations of history, especially in the bodily practices of commemorative ceremonies, have always been used to forge the sense of enduring national identity: 'Thus we may say that our experiences of the present largely depend upon our knowledge of the past, and that our images of the past commonly serve to legitimate a present social order'.[29] Among his economy of 'the technologies of memory', Connerton distinguishes the commemorative ceremony as a significant enactment of the past as a ritual performance demonstrating the immutability of the past. Yet, as Connerton points out, this is an illusion, for history is about change not stasis. David Hare is explicit about the dialectic of historical change which infuses his drama: 'Political practice answers to theory and yet modifies it; the party answers to the people and is modified by it. The fight is for political structures which answer people's needs; and people themselves are changed by living out theoretical ideas. It is a story of change and progress'.[30] He goes on to say: '[A playwright] can put people's sufferings in a historical context; and by doing that, he can help to explain their pain. But what I mean by history will not be the mechanised absolving force theorists would like it to be; it will be those strange uneasy factors that make a place here and nowhere else, make a time now and no other time'.[31] Resisting abstract patterns in favour of specificities, this idea of history as irreducible particularity clearly owes something to Theodor Adorno's *Negative Dialectics*, although Adorno would be wary of Hare's implicit dismissal of theory. As far as Hare is concerned, the reasons for history and politics being the principal foci of drama in the early 1970s, lie at least partly in drama's 'unique suitability to illustrating an age in which men's ideals and men's practice bear no relation to each other; ... The theatre is the best way of showing the gap between what is said and what is seen to be done ...'.[32] This 'showing' is drama as ideology critique. Hare is conscious that history is a complex multiple narrative, which cannot be reduced to a single, nationally unifying structure:

> I try to show the English their history. I write tribal pieces, trying to show how people behaved on this island, off this continental shelf, in this century. How this Empire vanished, how these ideals died. Reading Angus Calder's *The People's War* changed a lot of my thinking as a writer; an account of the Second World War through the eyes of ordinary people, it attempts a complete alternative history to the phoney and corrupting history I was taught at school ... if you write about now, just today and nothing else, then you seem to be confronting only stasis, but if you begin to describe the undulations of history, if you write plays that cover passages of time, then you begin to find a sense of movement, of social change, if you like.[33]

Brenton's, Hare's and Griffiths' indebtedness for their alternative accounts of the war to the socialist historian Angus Calder's *The People's War* (1969), has been widely documented. Opening with Churchill's speech proclaiming that 'This is a war of the unknown warriors', Calder's book fastidiously considers the effects of the war on all aspects of civilian life. Partly iconoclastic, partly debunking previous histories of the war, Calder's work explores the lives of the 'unknown warriors' who helped fight the war behind the lines, lives which have not been subsequently commemorated in the form of collected letters, personal memoirs, or other celebrated *livres du jour*. The drama that was inspired by Calder's approach to history is a clear example of a literary genre producing accounts of people's history that are not found elsewhere. Furthermore, as Keith Peacock's excellent book *Radical Stages: Alternative History in Modern British Drama* (1991) makes clear, these dramatists also acknowledge the liberating explanations of British history by E. P. Thompson, Raymond Williams, E. J. Hobsbawm and George Rude. Like Calder, these historians scrutinise not only the roles played by political leaders, but the parts played by ordinary people, and as Peacock states, 'this stood in direct opposition to the individualism of bourgeois history'.[34] Indeed, the ideological focus and historical methodology of these historians' work contested that concept of 'ordinariness', arguing for a more 'collective' and incorporative perspective of the national struggle.

Playwrights such as Brenton, Hare, Edgar, Churchill and Griffiths argue that contemporary Britain needs imaginative reconstructions of the inner logic and the aleatory trajectories, the advances and retreats of society in the past forty years to understand the present position of the country. Such reconstructions help grasp how things might have been different, as well as mourn what did happen, and also perhaps inspire some redemptive hope in the present. In his recent book entitled *Theories and Narratives: Reflections on the Philosophy of History* (1995), Alex Callinicos draws a useful distinction between philosophies of history which he argues are teleological in nature (that historical development is predetermined by its outcome), and theories of history which it is argued are non-teleological (they have a directionality, but not a unique path and sequence of development). Callinicos's thesis is that history needs narrativisation: narratives supplement theories of history in that they 'allow us to recover the contingencies of the historical process, the junctures at which particular choices and chances tipped the balance between significantly different possible outcomes. A theory of history which rejects the idea of inevitability therefore needs narrative historiography to gain insight into the situations in which events decisively took one course rather than another'.[35] Brian Friel's play, *Making History,* self-consciously discusses this characteristic of narrative and history, almost too conveniently allowing playwrights to claim importance for their act of making:

> O'NEILL: But you'll tell the truth?
>
> LOMBARD: If you're asking me will my story be as accurate as possible – of course it will. But are truth and falsity the proper criteria? I don't know. Maybe when the time comes my first responsibility will be to tell the best possible narrative. Isn't that what history is, a kind of story-telling?
>
> O'NEILL: Is it?
>
> LOMBARD: Imposing a pattern on events that were mostly casual and haphazard and shaping them into a narrative that is logical and interesting. Oh, yes, I think so.
>
> O'NEILL: And where does the truth come into all this?
>
> LOMBARD: I'm not sure that 'truth' is a primary ingredient – is that a shocking thing to say? Maybe when the time comes, imagination will be as important as information. But one thing I will promise you: nothing will be put down on paper for years and years. History has to be made – before it is remade.[36]

The 'heresy' of 'truth' not being significant in historical record implies that history is not about exactitude, but about stimulating narrative. Imagination rather than factual accuracy is the crucial requirement for the 'remaking' of history.

David Hare makes such beliefs about history central to all his drama. History is a continuum that is constantly changing, resisting closure; it is multiple, indicating that more than one account of the past can be given. He wants audiences to become conscious of history as enabling rather than disempowering and incapacitating people's contemporary existences. Plays like *Brassneck* (by Hare and Brenton) (1973), *Knuckle* (1973), *Plenty* (1978) and *Destiny* (1978), analyse the conditions under which racism and fascism can organise and proliferate within a purportedly democratic system. They establish the historical legacy of Britain emerging from the Second World War, beginning with British politics after VE Day and charting its consequent development up to the 1970s. In *Brassneck*, a portrayal of three generations of the Bagley family and their unscrupulous economic activities and political machinations, political parties of all colours collaborate in political corruption. The play uses the development of the Bagley family to lament the fact that Britain has never managed to shrug off the individualist, competitive and adversarial social structure of an earlier capitalist ideology. Families are broken apart, communities are merely targets for exploitation, political progress is less about aptitude and ability and more about social niceties like playing golf. Social organisations, like the Masons and local government, are merely instruments with which to further the financial and political advantage of an already small but powerful hegemony: 'The English Social Structure, is a complex and beautiful thing. Interlocking escalators'.[37] The drama is cynical about human behaviour, cartoon-like in its characterisation, and blunt in its critique. *Knuckle* presents a similar picture of an insidious corruption of the country, this time embodied in Curly's gun-running and arms activities, and his cynical, selfish and derisive attitude towards people's sufferings: 'The exploitation of the masses should be conducted as quietly as possible'.[38] Curly envisages Britain in the early 1970s as a country 'aching to be fleeced',[39] whose business classes are all involved in exculpating themselves with an ideology of naturalism:

> PATRICK: I told her stories of life in the City – the casual cruelty of each day; take-over bids, redundancies, men ruined overnight, jobs lost, trusts betrayed, reputations smashed, life in that great trough called the City of London, sploshing about in the cash. And I asked, what I have always asked: how will that ever change?
> CURLEY: Tell me of any society that has not operated in this way.
> PATRICK: Five years after a revolution ...
> CURLEY: The shit rises ...
> PATRICK: The same pattern ...
> CURLEY: The weak go to the wall ...
> PATRICK: Somebody's bound to get hurt ...
> CURLEY: You can't make omelettes ...
> PATRICK: The pursuit of money is a force for progress ...
> CURLEY: It's always been the same ...
> PATRICK: The making of money ...
> CURLEY: The breaking of men.
> PATRICK: The two together. Always. The sound of progress.
> CURLEY: The making of money. The breaking of men.
> (Pause.)
> PATRICK: If I didn't do it ...
> CURLEY: Somebody else would. (*Knuckle*: Sc.15, pp. 81–2)

The litany of trite catch-phrases used to excuse their collusion with the supposed inevitability of exploitative human actions and goals, and the way they already know the answers enough to be able to finish the other's sentences, indicate how saturated they are by capitalism's deterministic theory of history. This bleak (albeit comic and almost jokey) representation of a society that seems to have no internal moral or ethical standards and no mechanism to regulate its activities, goes hand-in-hand with the general critique of the failure of British society to keep in check the sheer greed that leads to the exploitation of the mass of the population. It is drama as something of a blunt instrument; there is a curiously implausible explicitness in most of Curly's lines, almost as if the exploiter is a theorist of his conditions, which tends to betray the uncompromising monovisual political attitude of the dramatist.

This implausibly articulate self-awareness points to the potential limitations of this 'new left' dramatic response to political and economic exploitation. For although it may be recognised that history may be multiple, with more than one history running in parallel, there is no shattering of the basic modern conceptual paradigm of the linearity of history, no 'postmodernist' sense of history as anti-linear. Indeed, one criticism might be that in the more polemical plays about the denial of the working-class history, one merely gets new 'heroes' of history, as those instances where there is merely an inversion of the central protagonist, from the previously famous upper-class male to the contemporary unknown working-class male.

One such case of the mythic heroic individual to have dominated modern British history is Winston Churchill. Haunted by the concept of the 'great man', Churchill was obsessed with his own 'greatness' from an early age. Biographies, too numerous to mention, a commemorative series of postage stamps and his hunched statue brooding in Parliament Square in London, testify to his imprint on the national consciousness of the postwar generation. Synonymous with British 'bulldog' pluckiness and the nation's imperial ambitions, Churchill has often figured in a construction of history in Britain which both treats the national past as a social memory which must be conserved, and as a commodity whose consumption will maintain the well-being of the nation. The emergence of the 'heritage' industry, part of the commodification of history in the 1970s and 1980s, has contributed to this. It avoids critical confrontation with the past and elides the repressions, barbarisms, abuses and coercions by which the nation has been governed and exploited.

Brenton's *The Churchill Play* received its first performance in 1974, and uses the device of a play within the play, arranged by the inmates of the Churchill Camp correction centre at a time in the near future (1984), to produce a series of Brechtian '*verfremdungseffekts*' to demystify various illusions about history. The play's opening is not initially recognisable as the rehearsal of a play about Winston Churchill, so its subsequent revelation reinforces the viewer's perception of a 'staged history'. The dramatic device forces one to confront history as theatre, as well as facing up to the manner in which the structures of history and narrative are intricately bound together. From the very outset, Brenton stresses that history is a set of varying narratives which determine our perspectives on society – with the Welsh soldier regarding Churchill as an enemy of the Welsh miners, and Colonel Ball regarding him as a famous and great British leader. The four branches of the military guarding Churchill's catafalque in Westminster are also representatives of the four nations of Britain, and in each of these spokesmen one sees a different version of British history. History is seen to have fractious national implications which cannot be covered up by some appeal to the greatness of a particular national leader. Initially described by the soldiers as a vampire – part of the 'living dead. All the leaders of the world. Imagine them in the Gents Toilet at the United Nations, sucking each other's necks'[40] – the Churchill character, in a self-conscious theatricalisation of history, describes himself as leaping onto 'history's stage' (Act I). The exaggeratedly tough image, so typical of Brenton's style, makes power appear to be based upon a repressed homoeroticism. The play proceeds to demonstrate that representations of history are also interpretations of social politics: both plays are as much about class politics as they are about the nature of history. The Captain, the Sergeant and the ordinary soldiers all constantly rake over the embers of places where class conflict perpetually flares into flames: the élitism of public school; Ireland; class battles in the mines; etc. For this reason the play seems constrained by its adherence to ideological images; history is represented as a conflict of stereotypes, a series of myths battling with each other:

CHURCHILL: Glasgow lad, aren't you?

MIKE: I may be.

CHURCHILL: A grey, overcast day. The June of 1945. Spoke in the open air. Boys perched in the trees. Men stood in serried ranks on the roofs, round about. Wonderful sight. The beauty of so many faces lit in a flash with welcome and joy. Young women whose beauty charmed the eye, old ladies brought out in chairs, or waved flags from windows. Dazzled me. When I had said my few words they sang 'Will Ye No Come Back Agin'. Glasgow dazzled me.

MIKE: Dazzled you? Glasgow? Old man you don't know the half. Clydebank, my father was born. Thirteenth of March, 1941. Night of the first great German air raid. The people walked out of the town. Out to the moors. Some stayed for weeks, camped out in the open air. And the next night, fourteenth of March, came the second great air raid. Of twelve thousand dwellings, seven only not hit.

CHURCHILL: The lights went out and the bombs came down. Out of the jaws of death.

MIKE: Old man, we don't live in the same world.

CHURCHILL: It's not all ermine robes to wipe your bottom where I come from.

MIKE: Nor is it all cloth caps and waving flags where I come from.

CHURCHILL: We're both of the Island Race. Out of the Celtic mist. The Saxon fen. And bitter, dark green Normandy.

MIKE: I did not understand a word of that. (*The Churchill Play*, p. 163).[41]

Events are Janus-faced for Churchill and Mike; the same city, the same events and the same period, belong to different histories. Both men seek to present the 'real' events, and yet, as Mike says, the two men are talking different languages. Although the play clearly believes that Churchill's high-flown rhetoric blinds him to the world which Mike experiences, as nostalgia and sentiment taint his memory of his years as Prime Minister during the war, even Mike's populist language evokes an ideological rhetoric, the rhetoric of Brenton's ideological allegiances.

History replaces psychology in Brenton's plays. He offers a trajectory of history which refuses to conceptualise the historical process as a sequence whose course is predetermined by its outcome. History's events are contingent rather than part of a fixed series of events governed by a generative principle. For Brenton, the issue is one of explanation and justification – are events pre-ordained, random or intelligible but not inevitable? He rejects the mythicisation of history which seeks to legitimise a natural order of things, by lifting a narrative or character out of history into an intangible and metaphysical realm. He does this because he believes in the possibility of drama effecting political change within a hegemonic social structure, albeit recognising that this effectiveness is patchy, sometimes stunted, always a struggle: 'I dream of a play acting like a bushfire, smouldering into public consciousness. Or like hammering on the pipes being heard all through the tenement'.[42] The extent to which this is no more than a dream can be measured by the evidence in the plays. *The Churchill Play* sets out to consider how historical myths like that of Churchill as the saviour of Britain became established as history. In this respect *The Churchill Play* is a hammering at the pipes, although Brenton's aim is not so much to debunk the man as the myth. As H. Zeifman has noted, Brenton's drama frequently deals with historical figures – Christie, Wesley, Scott of the Antarctic, Violette Szabo and Churchill; and in all cases, Brenton's deconstructions of historical figures are attacks on romanticising ideologies of the past, and mythologised images of war, masculinity and individual nobility.[43] As Brenton himself has acknowledged: 'I'm very interested in people who could be called saints, perverse saints, who try to drive a straight line through very complex situations, and usually become honed down to the point of death.'[44] Yet he resists putting them on the psychoanalyst's couch. Brenton has argued that psychology in plays has a socially debilitating effect, since it becomes too mechanical an explanation for people's actions ('the idea that "this man is a criminal because ..." or "this man is a violent policeman because ..."'),[45] and that it produces a humanism that is wholly conservative. Psychology traps people in phenomena that are deemed 'natural', thus removing their agency and preventing them from effecting changes in their lives. It diverts them from recognising social and human differences in the past so they can question how social ideologies have changed. Analysing states of mind avoids the exploration of the minds of states.

When the play within the play is performed for the visiting Select Committee of Members of Parliament, it is presented as 'The Other Second World War',[46] which, in addition to suggesting that there are different histories of the Second World War, also suggests that the alternative versions are critical to the contemporary class consciousness of the actors/inmates. In this alternative play, Brenton associates Churchill's reminiscences and speeches with 'survival for all that the British Empire has stood for'.[47] Yet at the prompting of Black Dog, the figurative representation of Churchill's depression, this history is parodically rewritten: 'His-tory. Fam-ily. Privil-ege. Duuuuu-ty. His-toreeeee'.[48] Brenton makes Churchill acknowledge the vagaries of his historical significance and that there was no 'manifest destiny' in his life, when he recognises that 'A little shift of history ... and I would be remembered as a minor English impressionist painter'.[49] As always in Brenton, his characters talk in abstractions. One is presented with a Churchill who depicts a childhood that was emotionally repressed, educationally brutalised and psychologically scarred. His memory of his father, Randolph Churchill, 'the man they said would run the English Twentieth Century',[50] is a mixture of 'filthy disease', quintessential Englishness and heroic individualism, with the 'natural right of an English gentleman to rule ... for there was a quality of History about him ... shone about his very features'.[51] This abstraction of history, the cult of the masculine hero and the perpetuation of national greatness and power, is all undercut by Churchill's acknowledgement that he will edit history by censoring his resolve to commit suicide if he contracted syphilis from his father ('Won't read that in the official biography').[52]

The play's debunking of myths is given added emphasis in Act IV, when Churchill's written record of his visit to the site of the Peckham land mine explosion, is shown to warp the actual event by hiding class conflict. In the play, the recollection of this incident engages him in another tangle with Mike's alternative version of events. Churchill is shown to remember the crowd shouting 'We can take it, Guv. Give it 'em back',[53] and is deeply moved by the apparently patriotic, spirited defiance of the general public. Mike, however, declares that this is 'Not like my Uncle Ern told me it',[54] and Ernie affirms 'Yer dead right. That were myth. This is like it was'.[55] In Ernie's account, Churchill is 'the myth. Standing there. Like he'd come down from a cinema screen, out of a film show. Winnie'.[56] The dialogue between Churchill and Ernie is then reported, this time clearly demonstrating the class antagonism buried within it:

> ERNIE: Thought you'd come to see us.
> CHURCHILL: Ah. Ah.
> ERNIE: We can take it.
> CHURCHILL: Ah.
> ERNIE: But we just might give it back to you one day.
> MIKE: We just might give it back to you one day.
> ERNIE: And in his book on war he wrote it down as ... Give it 'em
> back.[57]

The conclusion of the play, as the prisoners make their abortive escape attempt, is also constructed as a class confrontation: there is a certain amount of confusion among the prisoners as to a course of action as they hold their hostages, and it is given the pessimistic description of 'the Third World War'.

Brenton's replacement of psychology by history has a paradoxical result. The play cannot account for the roots of the class confrontation, because it has to invest Churchill with such power that he becomes the source of all conflict as a figure of Tory privilege (as well as disease and corruption). Furthermore, the MPs are represented as paltry characters, straw figures who cannot stand up to the onslaught of class action. This overlooks the fact that the correction camp is the literal institution of parliamentary power, which seeks to 'correct' the behaviour of class opposition rather than negotiate with it. The play is also weak in its analysis of the Left, since it presents one politician as an archetype of the Labour Party, yet fails to analyse how this political complicity occurred, as well as tarring the whole Party with the same brush. These faults undercut the play's analysis of history, and suggest that there is a 'truer' history somewhere else. *The Churchill Play* assumes a kind of class consciousness, even a kind of articulation, that is only possible within the explicit socialist debate of its period. Consequently, Brenton's drama, like Hare's, risks being dominated by a language of protest without analysis. Their attempt to break out of the historicism of the Marxists and Conservatives – those who see history as a march, a progress, a dialectic or any determinate process that would deny any possibility of retrospective reconfiguration – makes them willing to gamble on the power of a one-dimensional, cartoon history to effect emancipatory social change.

Agitprop versus realist history: John McGrath

Despite Bigsby's rather damning dismissal of these new plays as albeit 'aesthetically open', 'ideologically closed. They begin with their conclusions',[58] the new political theatre was far from closed in its own debates about dramatic method, and had its own fervent disagreements and heated ideological debates about the most efficacious and incisive forms and modes of presenting history. During the 1970s, Brenton, Hare, Griffiths and Edgar gradually moved away from agitprop drama towards a socialist realist theatre. This occasioned considerable criticism from those who regard this latter representation of history as complicit with the structures of the capitalist commodification of history. It also prompted defensive words from the playwrights who were not willing to admit the limits of this agitprop theatre. Edgar was one of the most articulate about what he felt to be its shortcomings:

> unlike the bourgeois form of naturalism (which attempts to portray a surface view of human behaviour as accurately as possible), realism is 'selective' and 'strives towards the typical'. The actions of people are presented within a 'total' context: the central character's actions are felt 'as part of the life of the class, society and universe'.
>
> Realism, in other words, does not show people's individual behaviour as being somehow independent of the society in which they live; it relates people's recognisable activities to the history that is going on around them. ...
>
> Faced with the barrage of bourgeois culture, the response of agitprop is precisely to eliminate the surface appearance of the situation it presents, and to portray instead what it regards as the political reality beneath. ...
>
> The move away from pure agitprop towards more complex theatrical forms seems to me satisfactorily explained in terms of a considered response [to the failure of economism in the post-1974 period]. ... agitprop, although a good weapon for confirming workers in their struggles and drawing practical lessons from their experiences (in other words, a form ideal to the subject-matter of economic militancy), is not suited to the tasks of a period of class retreat.[59]

In its rejection of the Brechtian modernism of agitprop, this is pure, unadulterated, one hundred per cent Lukács. John McGrath was not satisfied with this explanation, and countered Edgar's defence of the return to social realist theatrical politics with an impassioned defence of working-class, agitprop theatre on the grounds that political interventions could be made from within the drama in a manner unavailable to productions constrained by the theatre itself. Plays which challenge bourgeois ideology from within the institutions of the theatre are much less effective than agitprop, since 'They become "product" and the process remains the same: they are in constant danger of being appropriated in production by the very ideology they set out to oppose.'[60] Playwrights *need* to try ideology critique. Summing up this controversy, Keith Peacock suggested that 'if therefore Agit-Prop is the theatre of Marxist theory, then Social Realism is the drama of Socialism as morality.'[61] He concludes that 'whereas McGrath referred to history ... for its evidence of working-class resistance to exploitation, Hare and Edgar have focused upon the gradual disintegration of Socialist ideals during the post-war period'.[62]

The *locus classicus* for McGrath's argument in the 1970s, must surely be the tremendously successful production of *The Cheviot, the Stag and the Black, Black Oil*. In an interview, McGrath stated the political principles of his historicism:

> Nearly all our shows have got a rather long historical perspective. It's why naturalism doesn't work in our terms, because naturalism is incapable of making long historical connections, and is usually an examination of relationships between people on a stage internally, looking in. I'm interested in a kind of theatre which makes longer connections, where you can see where you come from, and you can see how it can affect where you go to. It's also Gramscian in that we're interested in a definition of a nation's popular culture.[63]

McGrath opposes epic drama to the naturalism of more mainstream theatre. Self-professedly a play which sought to raise the consciousness of Scottish working people as members of a class with interests in common, the tour of *The Cheviot* in 1973–74 was a graphic illustration of the power of agitprop theatre to re-present people's experiences and history within the context of an easily absorbed performance of political and economic theory, with a summons for pertinent political action as the desired result. As the original programme notes put it:

> The people of the Highlands are intensely aware of the tragedy of their past. They are increasingly aware of the challenge facing them today. Due to the impersonality and remoteness from their lives of the decision-making process, some may have come to see their future as something outside their control, something pre-determined. This play tries to show *why* the tragedies of the past happened: because the forces of capitalism were stronger than the organisation of the people. It tries to show that the future is *not* pre-determined, that there are alternatives, and it is the responsibility of everyone to fight and agitate for the alternative which is going to benefit the people of the Highlands, rather than the multi-national corporations, intent on profit. Passive acceptance now means losing control of the future. Socialism, and the planned exploitation of natural resources for the benefit of all humanity, is the alternative the play calls for.[64]

Cataloguing the barbarous history of the Scottish Clearances in the eighteenth century, the appropriation and 'colonisation' of the Highlands by absentee English landlords in the eighteenth and nineteenth centuries, and the more recent exploitation of the Scottish people and lands during the oil boom in the 1970s, the play seeks to represent people's sufferings in an historical context, not to indulge their personal misery, but to articulate the mechanisms of the political and economic forces which under-pin their experiences. The play is concerned to establish a rapport between the company and the audience and to construct an interrelated dynamic by engaging the whole theatre in popular song and dance from the outset. Deliberately utilising the popular Highland form of the ceilidh as a structural framework, the narrative is interspersed with popular song, dialogue, music, speech and comic sketches. The audience is made to feel that it has a stake in the performance of history that is happening in front of them.

The incorporation of popular culture into the structure and content of the play is part of McGrath's sense that if theatre is going to provide an alternative account of history, then the adoption of the techniques and dynamics of carnival and festival is vital to its success. In fact, despite their differences of opinion with regard to the respective political effica-cies of socialist realism and agitprop theatre, both Edgar and McGrath agreed that the way forward for a politically active theatre was the appro-priation of a Bakhtinian carnivalesque. In his analysis of rites as symbolic representations, Connerton suggests that (after Bakhtin) carnival might be regarded as 'anticipative representations' which act as levers for social liberation:

> Carnival is here seen as an act in which 'the people' organize themselves 'in their own way' as a collectivity in which the individual members become an inseparable part of the human mass, such that 'the people' become aware of their sensual-material bodily unity.[65]

The coalescence of such a collective body allows a symbolic representa-tion of Utopia to be manifested, and McGrath thinks it therefore proffers a useable dramatic mechanism for social liberation:

> The idea of 'carnival', as expressed by Bakhtin, again may need qualifi-cation in terms of history, and of its attitudes towards women, but remains very attractive in the twentieth century. His idea of carnival expressing the 'whole' human being, eating, drinking, defecating and copulating, as well as thinking, praying and wielding power, obscene as well as divine, is something that has meaning when set against the narrowness of the concept of humanity in mass telly-culture. ... As to ... the dispossessed, The Resistance – they are the non-people, the work-shy who have to be kept quiet, orderly and out of the way of the Great Machine. The carnival is above all for them. To form part of an unofficial counter-culture that will enrich lives, raise spirits and prepare the way for the future. Out of the language, the experience, the imag-ination, the needs of the people, a truly popular art.[66]

Along similar lines, Edgar perceives carnival as a challenge to official culture 'in which everything is vertical, complete and hierarchical, with the horizontal, unfinished world of carnival, of which the paradigm is the human body itself, and particularly the lower half of it, with its tumescent protuberances and welcoming hollows, its permanent condition of ingestion and evacuation, the simultaneous site of birth and death.'[67] And like McGrath, Edgar, quoting Bakhtin's words about carnival as a 'space of utopian freedom ... utopian radicalism', perceives the real value of carnival to be its *prefigurative* quality': '... I relate very strongly to the idea that the theatre is not just about what is but about what could be'.[68]

'Prefigurative' is a key term for these playwrights, since it describes the ability of representations of drama to raise consciousnesses about the as yet unrealised future. The prefigurative is a powerful inversion of the resignation to history. As Michel Foucault has constantly urged, analysing the genealogies produced by history compels us to face up to how we intend to produce the future, and the role of these dramatic representations of history could be seen, therefore, to possess what one might term an 'ethics of temporality'. Not only does textual memory hinge upon how one represents the past; but the very representation of time itself becomes a critical issue of political power for human possibilities in the political struggles of everyday social life.

Although not necessarily utopian, *The Cheviot* does work towards a conviction that the future may learn from the history of the exploitation of the Scottish; and especially from a vision in which, as a possibility, the final song puts it, 'The wheel will turn for you / By the strength of your hands and hardness of your fists. / Your cattle will be on the plains – Everyone in the land will have a place / And the exploiter will be driven out'.[69] The play pits the interests of capital against the working-class land workers, so that history is the consequences of a power struggle between the different interests of capital. Andy McChuckemup, a Glasgow property operator in the play, exploits not just the local people and corrupts local government officials, but commodifies 'Scottishness' in his vision of the future:

> right there at the top of the glen, beautiful vista – The Crammem Inn, High Rise Motorcroft – all finished in natural, washable, plastic granitette. Right next door, the 'Frying Scotsman' All Night Chipperama – with a wee ethnic bit, Fingal's Caff – serving seaweed-suppers-in-the-basket, and draught Drambuie. And to cater for the younger set, yous've got your Grouse-a-go-go.[70]

Texas Jim, an oil-merchant, claims Scottish ancestry yet is blithely indifferent to the natural and social consequences of his oil development plans: 'So leave your fishing, and leave your soil, / Come work for me, I want your oil. // Screw your landscape, screw your bays / I'll screw you in a hundred ways – //... I'll go home when I see fit /All I'll leave is a heap of shit // You poor dumb fools I'm rooking you / You'll find out in a year or two'.[71] The humour in this is also cartoon-like, and the readiness of these entrepreneurs to expose their shallow, tasteless plans is surely too reassuring, especially to those oppresssed by their real-life counterparts.

Herstories: Caryl Churchill and Timberlake Wertenbaker

The public space in which history occurs is not as neutral as some of these plays represent it. Class, race and gender all shape its possibilities. Many women playwrights, therefore, sought to use the insights gained from their active work in feminist politics to open out this space to women and other excluded groups. Deriving part of its impetus from the political model of black civil rights and the growth of 'New Left' politics, but also from the growing consolidation of the women's movement and its notion that 'the personal is political', women's drama increasingly interrogated orthodox and received representations of history and what was understood to be their implicit formation and preservation of masculine power. Whether among women playwrights such as Megan Terry, Tina Howe, or Myrna Lamb and the predominantly psychological approach in their work in the United States, or British playwrights like Caryl Churchill, Maureen Duffy, Pam Gems, Timberlake Wertenbaker or Louise Page, with their stronger concerns with class and its relation to gender,[72] their stress has been on disrupting the constitutive power of the 'male gaze', and subjecting the historical representation of women to critical scrutiny. Michelene Wandor, citing such plays as *Destiny, Romans in Britain* and Hare's *Slag* and *Teeth 'n Smiles*, argues that most of the celebrated plays by male authors in British theatre since 1968 represent women as passive and separated from the decision-making, history-producing, politically-active masculine sphere. The public realm is engendered by men whose epic-scale plays reduce the significance of the private sphere as a space for exploring the intimate relationships between individual characters:

> On the whole, men are presented as custodians of public issues and political ideas, but, in keeping with the general tendencies of the plays of this period, are no longer concerned with the nature of masculinity, male sexuality or personal identity. The men inhabit the worlds of ideas and organisation, the women the world of survival.[73]

Wandor concludes that this drama divorces the public and private apparently in the belief that 'political activism and personal life cannot go together, and must be ruthlessly separated';[74] hence the repeated images of women who are ignorant, diseased or appear threatening and intrusive.

Hare's women (like Peggy in *A Map of the World*), 'are essentially bystanders to the main events of history, powerless to influence them, and rarely responsible individuals'.[75] If male playwrights have reacted to the still-dominant Carlylean notion that history is singular, then feminist playwrights have sought to challenge the implicit masculinity of that conception of history.

The creation of a socialist feminist dynamic in drama has been a central preoccupation for Caryl Churchill. Since her first stage success with *Owners*, her plays have always tackled 'the under-side of history': the unspoken complexities of gender in history. Her historical drama is a technology of memory which self-reflexively focuses upon moments, actions and sites where opportunities for more inclusive and communicative models of citizenship and subjecthood were discussed, explored, pursued, probed and lived, before being derailed or re-routed. As her preface to *Light Shining in Buckinghamshire* makes clear about the brief spell of revolutionary belief in the time of the English Civil War, subsequent popular accounts of this period of English history have curtailed any recognition of libertarian potential and revolutionary ideology:

> The simple 'Cavaliers and Roundheads' history taught at school hides the complexity of the aims and conflicts of those to the left of Parliament. We are told of a step forward to today's democracy but not of a revolution that didn't happen; we are told of Charles and Cromwell but not of the thousands of men and women who tried to change their lives. Though nobody now expects Christ to make heaven on earth, their voices are surprisingly close to us.[76]

The history of the Civil War becomes the occasion for Caryl Churchill's investigation of the censorship of history and especially the suppression of ideologically disturbing events. Like Brenton's treatment of Winston Churchill, Caryl Churchill's depiction of the motives and actions of Cromwell and the Roundheads, demythologises the historical narratives of English democracy and freedom. In a manner reminiscent of Christopher Hill, the Civil War is represented less as an issue of monarchical power and more in terms of different discourses searching for political ascendancy. The war is an interweaving of competing discourses – Christianity, racial history, materialism, ethics, privilege, royalist and parliamentarian ideologies. In many respects, the representation of the war could be likened to the Volosinovian battle for control of signifiers. The conventional focus on the war as a triumph for British democracy (which the play knowingly presupposes in its audience), is slowly eroded by the play, as women, the Irish, the Levellers and the Diggers and the peasantry, are excluded from the power-base established in the name of parliamentary democracy. This is the story of the disillusionment of people who set out in high anticipation that the Civil War would usher in a new Utopia. There is a gradual shift in consciousness as the Parliamentarian army is shown to be wedded to ideologies of property, privileged hierarchical rights, authoritarianism and state power, completely betraying the hopes and ideals of those who signed up in its support.

Women are kept oppressed by the dominant patriarchy embedded in Christianity. When Hoskins speaks out in church to question the contradictory tenets of the church, we see how women are forced into silence, because the right to question authority rests exclusively with the male domain. The convenient debilitating belief in the legacy of original sin – Eve's sin visited upon us all[77] – is used by the patriarchal church to great effect against women in particular; even women complicitly acknowledge their own guilt: '"No, I'm wicked, all women are wicked, and I'm –" / "It's a man wrote the Bible"'.[78] As in *Vinegar Tom*, which Churchill wrote at the same time and which dealt with the cognate issues of the suppression of women in the Middle Ages by branding them as witches, the motive which drives women into such anxiety and depression appears to be the internalisation of a masculine neurosis about female sexuality. Churchill uses such historical material partly as a means to demonstrate how little the exclusionary mechanisms of patriarchy have changed over the centuries, as well as to employ the 'prefigurative' potential of debates staged in a simulated public sphere.

Light Shining in Buckinghamshire concludes with the disillusioned revolutionaries forced into isolated acts of individual protest, lonely exile and silence. It is precisely this internal exile and enforced silence which preoccupies Timberlake Wertenbaker's adaptation of the myth of Tereus, Procne and her sister Philomele in *The Love of the Nightingale* (1988). She works not with factual history but legend and myth, and treats the narratives of archetypal human actions in myth as if they took place in history. The male chorus is explicit about the status of myth:

> MALE CHORUS: What is a myth? The oblique image of an unwanted truth, reverberating through time.
> MALE CHORUS: And yet, the first, the Greek meaning of myth, is simply what is delivered by word of mouth, a myth is speech, public speech.
> MALE CHORUS: And myth also means the matter itself, the content of the speech.
> MALE CHORUS: We might ask, has the content become increasingly unacceptable and therefore the speech more indirect? How has the meaning of myth been transformed from public speech to an unlikely story? It also meant counsel, command. Now it is a remote tale.
> MALE CHORUS: Let that be, there is no content without its myth. Fathers and sons, rebellion, the state, every fold and twist of passion, we have

> uttered them all. This one, you will say, watching Philomele watch-
> ing Tereus watching Philomele, must be about men and women, yes,
> you think, a myth for our times, we understand.
> MALE CHORUS: You will be beside the myth. If you must think of
> anything, think of countries, silence, but we cannot rephrase it for
> you. If we could, why would we trouble to show you the myth?[79]

Myth is history which remains current. Myth is not regarded as a narrative of wild fancy and extravagant imagination; rather, the play seeks to
recover history as a narrative refracted through a myth which works in
parallel to contemporary society, a 'myth for our times'. The function of
myth in *The Love of the Nightingale* is further exemplified by the tragedy
of Theseus and Phaedra that is performed before King Pandion in
Athens, who seeks to 'catch a phrase' which will provide him with guidance to his actions in life. Like our versions of history, myth is treated as
a mirror in which we indirectly see our own selves, our prevailing
ideologies, and our dominant beliefs.

Unlike Eliot's *The Waste Land*, where the myth of Tereus and
Procne is interpreted as yet another example of the regenerative power
of metamorphosis when Philomele is turned into a nightingale,
Wertenbaker's treatment is an analysis of male brutality perpetrated upon
women's bodies – as the Male Chorus says, 'about men and women'.
The play explores women's history as a problem of censored language,
of speech and silence, of a discourse which is trying to break a
commandment of silence a thousand years old. Wertenbaker's play
might be described as 'anti-classical', seeking a position within classical
drama from which women can speak and resist the 'inexorable encase-
ment' within masculine history.

Philomele's barbarously enforced silence is indicative of the manner
in which women's access to language has been denied historically by
patriarchal power structures. This ideological marginalisation of women
has been figured frequently in images of exclusion, dispossession, dislocation, disconnection and displacement:

> PROCNE: Where have all the words gone?
> HERO: She sits alone, hour after hour, turns her head away and laments.
> IRIS: We don't know how to act, we don't know what to say.
> HERO: She turns from us in grief.
> JUNE: Boredom.
> ECHO: Homesick.
> HERO: It is difficult to come to a strange land.
> HELEN: You will always be a guest there, never call it your own, never
> rest in the kindness of history.
> ECHO: Your story intermingled with events, no. You will be outside.

IRIS: And if it is the land of your husband can you even say you have chosen it?

JUNE: She is not one of us.[80]

Since Procne and Philomele are taken to Thrace from their homeland of Athens, they always find themselves in exile, outside themselves, elsewhere, in literal, metaphorical and ontological senses. Having escaped the paternal home, the two women experience the fruits of their freedom. Philomele's silence, women's dispossession of language, and their sense that language slips from their grasp, is reiterated in Procne's question about the disappearance of words. In the same scene iv, she repeats her question:

PROCNE: Where have all the words gone?

ECHO: Gone, Procne, the words?

PROCNE: There were so many. Everything that was had a word and every word was something. None of these meanings half in the shade, unclear.

IRIS: We speak the same language, Procne.

procne: The words are the same, but point to different things. We aspire to clarity in sound, you like the silences in between.[81]

Language has become a series of obscurities for Procne, since signs appear to have become severed from their referents. Procne realises that whereas previously she felt herself to be part of a community in which reference was apparently unanimous for everybody, she now inhabits a world of signifiers in which reference is detached and divided for different people, and particularly different genders. Women appear to be condemned to silence.

Philomele's fate is an echoing image of women's future history figured in the Greeks' anachronistic prescience of contemporary urban racial unrest and paedophilic murder. This overlay of the past and the present offers a vicious circle of history in which male power imprisons minds and severs tongues, which binds society into more violence and barbarism. This vision of history is reinforced by the play's bleak final lines, when Itys, Procne's son, questions Philomele:

PHILOMELE: Do you understand why it was wrong of Tereus to cut out my tongue?

ITYS: It hurt.

PHILOMELE: Yes, but why was it wrong?

ITYS: (Bored) I don't know. Why was it wrong?

PHILOMELE: It was wrong because –

ITYS: What does wrong mean?

> PHILOMELE: It is what isn't right.
> ITYS: What is right?
>> (The Nightingale sings.)
>> Didn't you want me to ask questions?
>> (Fade.).[82]

Itys' disinterest in the ethics of violence and his lack of understanding about the cruelty perpetrated by his father, suggests that the cycle of violence will continue. A certain hopelessness in the situation is evident in the lack of response that Philomele gives to Itys' final two questions; it is as though she abandons trying to explain because Itys' level of ethical and moral understanding is so elementary and unsympathetic (earlier in the play, Itys declares that he wants to 'be brave. I want to be a great captain. Lead thousands into battle. Like Mars',[83] demonstrating that he has already imbibed the patriarchal ideology of violence as the path towards greatness), that Philomele's resort to silence is an admission of the futility of explanation, and a tacit acknowledgement that many more female tongues are yet to be cut out.

These feminist playwrights often have less explicit engagement with the overtly political themes of 'the matter of Britain' which concern their male counterparts. As against the local and contemporary historical particulars of so many of the male plays set in postwar Britain, feminist playwrights often appear to adopt a more symbolic and metaphorical approach. This is emphatically not to suggest that the feminist playwrights are ahistorical in their drama. On the contrary, their drama seems to suggest that the political and social reasons for our currently limited and restricted concepts of citizenship lie in perspectives which go back long before 1945. Theirs is not a short-term focus on what they perceive to be a long-term problem. Furthermore, these feminist plays also produce a more nuanced qualification to the confident masculine rejection of psychology and the will. Their drama implies an understanding of history that crucially depends upon the internalised psychology of human consciousness and its interaction with external social factors. As feminism has so convincingly argued, the possibility of social change does not rest solely upon an analytical grasp of the economic bases of a social organisation. The possibility of altering the paradigms of subjectivity within the public sphere depends upon an emotional as well as a cognitive grasp of those everyday minutiae of history excluded by the 'grander' concerns of public political figures and their organisations. Feminist drama has been actively concerned not only with the redemption of a British past hidden by the forces of right-wing reaction, but also with those groups on the Left who appeared blind to the way many of their attempts to create socially integrated public spheres, nevertheless structurally perpetuated the age-old exclusion of women.

African-American theatre: August Wilson

The staging of history in Britain during the twenty years from 1968 to 1988, focused principally on forging a more inclusive public sphere. Drama in the United States could not even assume that such a public sphere existed at all, and consequently sought to recover buried histories in order to challenge the prevailing ideology of civil society. As Toni Morrison has shown, African-Americans have much reason to try and recover the past. Exhuming buried pasts and making the 'invisible man' visible again, the playwright August Wilson has been engaged in writing a cycle of ten plays which explore the black historical experience in the twentieth century: 'I'm taking each decade and looking back at one of the most important questions that blacks confronted in that decade and writing a play about it ... Put them all together and you have a history.'[84] Wilson's investigations of history are closely associated with discovering one's self-identity, and they do this through another form of performance, song. As DeVries explains: 'by mining black American music, which Wilson sees as one of the few traditionally acceptable venues of black American culture, Wilson is able to reveal the cumulative history informing his protagonists: nearly all his characters are in search of their individual songs of identity'.[85]

Wilson's repertoire numbers several full-length plays and some smaller pieces. Of *Two Trains Running* (1988), *The Piano Lesson* (1987), *Joe Turner's Come and Gone* (1986), *Fences* (1986), *Ma Rainey's Black Bottom* (1984), the latter two are his most successful and plays to date. *Fences* deals with the experiences of a family in Pittsburgh in the 1950s, and the increasingly tense relationship that develops between Troy Maxson and his son. *Ma Rainey's Black Bottom* is set in the 1920s, within the context of the African-American jazz scene being gradually exploited by white culture and focuses on the human tensions in a small blues group while recording their music in a studio.

Fences explores the effects of racism upon Troy Maxson, a one-time player for the Negro Baseball League, but now a garbage collector, trying to hold together a family in difficult economic circumstances. The play, as its title suggests, is concerned with how and why barriers are erected – of social, psychological, political, racial, gender and historical natures. The fence becomes the symbolic demarcation of the family against the 'outside' world, meaning different things to different people: Rose sings about Christ protecting her by being 'a fence all around me every day'[86]; when Troy builds Rose a literal fence around their small garden, his friend Bono comments: 'Some people build fences to keep people out ... and other people build fences to keep people in. Rose wants to hold on to you all. She loves you'[87]; while for Troy, the perimeter fence to his property is meant to be a secure material foundation for his family, as well as a magical barrier against death: 'Alright ... Mr. Death. See now ... I'm gonna tell you what I'm gonna do. I'm gonna take and build me a fence around this yard. See? I'm gonna build me a fence around what belongs to me. And I want you to stay on the other side'.[88] Building the fence becomes a means of keeping the outside world from impinging on Troy, establishing the inner self as inviolate.

Rather than psychologising the conflict, the play argues that it is the material circumstances of the family within a white-dominated society that is the root cause of the tragic fragmentation of the family. Owing to Troy's bitterness about the racist treatment he received in the baseball leagues, he encourages his son Cory to get an education, to hold down his part-time job at the local supermarket and to go to college. However, Cory has been selected to play football for his school, and this sporting path sets him in emotional and physical conflict with his father, eventually causing Troy to cast Cory out of the house, putting his things 'on the other side of that fence'.[89] This pivotal Oedipal struggle is not presented as an inevitable playing out of a universal theme, but as a direct consequence of the social pressures of racism. Rose, Troy's wife, clearly sees that Cory does want to emulate and model himself on his father, but is constantly thwarted by his father's ingrained sense of how racial oppression can prevent career development in the conventional white manner. His father's desire to fence him in makes Cory feel so claustrophobic that he realises he has to achieve independence from the patriarchal power and force which has shaped and moulded his existence:

> The whole time I was growing up ... living in his house ... Papa was like a shadow that followed you everywhere. It weighed on you and sunk into your flesh. It would wrap around you and lay there until you couldn't tell which one was you anymore. That shadow digging into your flesh. Trying to crawl in. Trying to live through you. Everywhere I looked, Troy Maxson was staring back at me ... hiding under the bed ... in the closet. I'm just saying I've got to find a way to get rid of that shadow, Mama.[90]

This dual relationship between Troy and Cory may be a response to those father–son struggles that litter the plays of O'Neill, Miller and Pinter. Wilson shows that the roots of this tension in a black family are the outcome of the forms of racial violence Troy has experienced: his relationship with his own father and the violence that entailed make him feel the need to assert that he is 'boss' and must have a 'yessir' from

Cory. All these forms of violence and affirmations of personal authority can be seen as internalisations of the violence derived from the racial struggle. Troy's assertion – and desire to have affirmed – of his patri-archal authority, is partly an attempt to retrieve a sense of social dignity which is denied to him outside the family. The family inside the fence becomes the site where the deprivations of social existence in a racist society are worked out, and familial respect is forced as a substitute for social respect.

The play concludes with Uncle Gabe, Troy's brother (who has had a metal plate inserted in his head after a war wound), apparently a marginal figure up to this point, right at centre-stage. He attempts to open the gates of heaven, as he warns St Peter of the approach of Troy, and then, at the crucial moment, the stage directions indicate that the trumpet ironically doesn't work: blown three times in classic fashion, it emits no sound:

> GABRIEL: Hey, Rose. It's time. It's time to tell St Peter to open the gates. Troy, you ready? You ready, Troy. I'm gonna tell St Peter to open the gates. You get ready now.
> *(Gabriel, with great fanfare, braces himself to blow. The trumpet is without a mouthpiece. He puts the end of it into his. mouth and blows with great force, like a man who has been waiting some twenty-odd years for this single moment. No sound comes out of the trumpet. He braces himself and blows again with the same result. A third time he blows. There is a weight of impossible descrip-tion that falls away and leaves him bare and exposed to a frightful realization. It is a trauma that a sane and normal mind would be unable to withstand. He begins to dance. A slow, strange dance, eerie and life-giving. A dance of atavis-tic signature and ritual. LYONS attempts to embrace him. GABRIEL pushes LYONS away. He begins to howl in what is an attempt at speech. He finishes his dance and the gates of heaven stand open as wide as God's closet.)*
> That's the way to go!
> *(BLACKOUT.)*[91]

What is one to make of this scene, heavy with Christian symbolism, with Uncle Gabe (Gabriel) apparently crazy from shell-shock in a final act of bathos? It appears to suggest that Christianity cannot provide the goods. The dance and 'song' in the play gesture to a new identity lodged in another cultural heritage – tribal African roots. The etymology of 'atavistic' means 'beyond grandfather' and the stage directions' inter-pretation and commentary imply that these characters find a greater affinity with their ancestors beyond their parents.

The abandonment of the white Christian ideology and the inscrip-tion of the African traditions, sends Troy beyond the whole black history of slave culture belonging to his father and the southern plantation negroes, in search of an African cultural identity and liberation. An episode from *Ma Rainey's Black Bottom* provides a gloss on this ending. Wilson's interest in the importance of the African heritage and its contemporary relevance to and function in the struggle for black identity, surfaces in a conversation between the band members:

> TOLEDO: That's African.
> SLOW DRAG: What? What you talking about? What's African?
> LEVEE: I know he ain't talking about me. You don't see me running around in no jungle with no bone between my nose.
> TOLEDO: Levee, you worse than ignorant. You ignorant without a premise.
> *(Pauses).*
> Now, what I was saying is what Slow Drag was doing is African. That's what you call an African conceptualization. That's when you name the gods or call on the ancestors to achieve whatever your desires are.
> SLOW DRAG: Nigger, I ain't no African! I ain't doing no African nothing!
> TOLEDO: Naming all those things you and Cutler done together is like trying to solicit some reefer based on a bond of kinship. That's African. An ancestral retention. Only you forgot the name of the gods.[92]

Toledo's point is that their actions are rooted in African culture. Only by working through the social memory out of which one's cultural identity emerges can the gates be opened; only then is it possible to achieve any personal religious or spiritual revelation. The past is crucial to an epistemological knowledge of the present:

> I think it's largely a question of identity. Without knowing your past, you don't know your present – and you certainly can't plot your future. ... You go out and discover it for yourself.[93]

August Wilson's drama offers a useful perspective on the British debates about agitprop and its rejection of a psychological naturalism. Wilson's drama is a psychological theatre; and like much of the feminist drama, it would seem that a drama which takes up the previously silenced cultures must retain or rework psychology. Far from being critical of its ideological import, Wilson appears to need the ruminative space afforded by psychological drama to trace and plot the 'structures of feeling' which white organisations of emotion and consciousness have sought to implant in the African-American psyche. He suggests that the psyches of the various racial groups are different, and that the norms of white psychology are not always pertinent to African-American culture. This forces a suspension of judgement on a white audience, which is called upon to make an act of 'imaginative empathy' with characters who have been excluded from its social experience and cultural understanding, in order to understand some of their own white cultural limitations, and possibly also the systematic self-deceptions of whiteness. Such 'ideal role-taking', experience-by-proxy if you will, aims to enable its audiences to feel the necessity to transform social paradigms with desires, feelings, anxieties and happinesses disclosed or discredited by the surrogate experience of theatrical performance. These new textual memories are made possible by the simulated public sphere of the theatre where different histories and their pasts can be tested. The British drama of history without psychology succeeded at presenting alternative histories but its unintended exclusions of gendered, personal and racial experience left it unable to do this wholly effectively.

Notes

1 Adam Smith, quoted in Keith Joseph, *Stranded on the Middle Ground? Reflections on Circumstances and Policies* (London: Centre for Policy Studies, 1976), p. 55.

2 Kenneth Baker, (ed.), *The Faber Book of English History in Verse* (London: Faber, 1988).

3 Sir Keith Joseph, 'Why teach history in school?', *The Times Educational Supplement*, 17 February, 1984, p. 32. For more on this debate, consider Martin Walker, 'Tory historians find a heritage to nationalise', *Guardian*, 21 June 1983.

4 Margaret Thatcher, *The Downing Street Years* (London: HarperCollins, 1995), pp. 595–6.

5 *Parliamentary Debates (Hansard)*, Sixth Series, 173 (1989–90), May 21–June 8 (London: HMSO, 1990), pp. 323–4.

6 Christopher Hill, 'Lies about crimes', *Guardian*, 29 May 1989. For further discussion and contributions to this debate, see Carolyn Steedman, 'True romances', in R. Samuel (ed.), *Patriotism: The Making and Unmaking of British National Identity*, (London: Routledge, 1989) pp. 26–35; Robert Aldrich (ed.), *History in the National Curriculum* (London: Kogan Page, 1991); 'History, the nation and the schools', *History Workshop Journal*, 29 (Spring 1990), 92–133, 30 (Autumn 1990), 75–128.

7 V. N. Volosinov, *A Marxist Philosophy of Language* (1911; Cambridge, MA: Harvard University Press, 1984), pp. 23–4.

8 Ibid., p. 23.

9 Ibid.

10 Guy Debord, *Society of the Spectacle* (Detroit: Black and Red, 1983), p. 143.

11 Ibid., p. 134.

12 J. K. Galbraith, *The Culture of Contentment* (London: Sinclair-Stevenson, 1992).

13 Habermas's adaptation of the original ideas of G. H. Mead, suggests that 'Practical discourse can also be viewed as a communicative process *simultaneously* exhorting *all* participants to ideal role taking. Thus practical discourse transforms what Mead viewed as *individual, privately enacted* role taking into a *public* affair, practiced intersubjectively by all involved'. Jurgen Habermas, *Moral Consciousness and Communicative Action*, trans. Christian Lenhardt and Shierry Weber Nicholsen (Cambridge: Polity Press, 1990), p. 198.

14 Andy Lavender, 'Theatre in crisis', *New Theatre Quarterly*, 5/19 (1989), 210–17.

15 Ibid., p. 211.

16 Howard Brenton, interview in *Theatre Quarterly*, V, 7 (1975), 20. See also Howard Brenton's essay on the Situationists and their cultural and political influence on Howard Brenton, 'The spaceman among the tower blocks', *Hot Irons: Diaries, Essays, Journalism* (London: Nick Hern Books, 1995), pp. 38–43.

17 Howard Brenton, *Magnificence* (London: Methuen, 1973), p. 102.

18 Sadie Plant, *The Most Radical Gesture: The Situationist International in a Postmodern Age* (London: Routledge, 1992), p. 1. On Situationism in the UK see Greil Marcus, *Lipstick Traces* (London: Secker & Warburg, 1989).

19 Debord, *Society of the Spectacle*, p. 158.

20 Plant, *The Most Radical Gesture*, p. 29.

21 C. W. Bigsby, 'The politics of anxiety: contemporary socialist theatre in England', *Modern Drama*, XXIV, 4 (1981), 393–403.

22 Timberlake Wertenbaker, *The Grace of Mary Traverse* (London: Faber, 1985), p. 57.

23 Michelene Wandor, *Carry On, Understudies: Theatre and Sexual Politics*, 2nd edn (London: Routledge and Kegan Paul, 1986); and *Look Back in Gender* (London: Methuen, 1987).

24 D. Keith Peacock, *Radical Stages: Alternative History in Modern British Drama* (Westport: Greenwood Press, 1991), pp. 67–8.

25 John Bull, *New British Political Dramatists* (Basingstoke: Macmillan, 1984).

26 Plays of such determined aspiration might well include John McGrath and 7:84 (Scotland)'s production of *The Cheviot, the Stag and the Black, Black Oil* (1974); Trevor Griffiths' *The Party* (1974), *Occupations* (1972), and *Comedians* (1976); David Edgar's *Destiny* (1976) and *Maydays* (1983); Howard Brenton's *Magnificence* (1973), *The Churchill Play* (1974), *Weapons of Happiness* (1976), *The Romans in Britain* (1980); David Hare's *Knuckle* (1974), *Plenty* (1978), and *A Map of the World* (1982); Caryl Churchill's *Light Shining in Buckinghamshire* (1976), *Cloud Nine* (1979), *Top Girls* (1982) and *Serious Money* (1987); and Brenton and Hare's collaborations in *Brassneck* (1973) and *Pravda* (1985). In addition, one would need to take account of all those agitprop and fringe theatre productions by groups like Brighton Combination, Red Ladder, Belt and Braces Roadshow, Foco Novo, General Will, 7:84, Joint Stock Theatre Group, Welfare State, Hull Truck, Gay Sweatshop, Monstrous Regiment, and the Women's Theatre Group, many of whom were also intricately involved with the productions of the above writers.

27 Howard Brenton, interview in *Theatre Quarterly*, V, 7 (1975).

28 Howard Brenton, *Measure for Measure* (Sheffield: Sheffield Academic Press, 1989).

29 Paul Connerton, *How Societies Remember* (Cambridge: Cambridge University Press, 1989), p. 3.

30 David Hare, 'The play is in the air', *Writing Left-Handed* (London: Faber, 1991), p. 29.

31 Ibid., p. 34.

32 Ibid., p. 26.

33 Ibid., p. 32.

34 Peacock, *Radical Stages*, p. 16.

35 Alex Callinicos, *Theories and Narratives: Reflections on the Philosophy of History* (Cambridge: Polity Press, 1995), p. 210.

36 Brian Friel, *Making History* (London: Faber, 1989), pp. 8–9.

37 David Hare and Howard Brenton, *Brassneck* (London: Methuen, 1974), I, iv.

38 David Hare, *Knuckle* (1973), in *The History Plays* (London: Faber, 1984), p. 44.

39   Ibid., p. 55.
40   Howard Brenton, *The Churchill Play* (London: Methuen, 1974), p. 161.
41   Mike's speech contains information lifted straight out of Angus Calder's book,
     p. 210.
42   Howard Brenton, interview in *Theatre Quarterly*, V, 7 (1975), p. 20.
43   H. Zeifman, 'Making history: the plays of Howard Brenton', in J. Acheson (ed.),
     British and Irish Drama Since 1960 (Basingstoke: Macmillan, 1993), pp. 130–45.
44   Howard Brenton, interview in *Theatre Quarterly*, V, 7 (1975), p. 12.
45   Ibid., p. 8.
46   Brenton, *The Churchill Play*, p. 158.
47   Ibid., p. 165.
48   Ibid., p. 166.
49   Ibid.
50   Ibid.
51   Ibid.
52   Ibid., p. 167.
53   Ibid., p. 168.
54   Ibid., p. 169.
55   Ibid.
56   Ibid.
57   Ibid., pp. 169–70.
58   Bigsby, '*The politics of anxiety*', p. 397.
59   David Edgar, 'Ten years of political theatre, 1968–1978', in *The Second Time As
     Farce: Reflections on the Drama of Mean Times* (London: Lawrence and Wishart,
     1988), pp. 24–47, 28–9, 34.
60   John McGrath, 'The theory and practice of political theatre', *Theatre Quarterly*, 9,
     35 (1979), 43–54, 46. (This paper formed part of a conference at Cambridge at
     which David Edgar's paper 'Ten years of political theatre, 1968–1978' on the
     contemporary inefficacy of agitprop theatre was also delivered. They became the
     basis for a far-reaching debate in Britain about the respective values and defi-
     ciencies of socialist realist and agitprop theatres.)
61   D. Keith Peacock, 'Fact versus history: two attempts to change the audience's
     political perspective', *Theatre Studies*, 31/32 (1984–85/1985–86), pp. 15–31.
62   Ibid., p. 29.
63   John McGrath, 'Popular theatre and the changing perspective of the eighties',
     New Theatre Quarterly, I, 4 (1985), pp. 390–400, 392.
64   John McGrath, *The Cheviot, the Stag and the Black, Black Oil*, rev. edn (London:
     Methuen, 1981), p. 77.
65   Connerton, *How Societies Remember*, p. 50.
66   John McGrath, 'Celebration, spectacle, carnival', *The Bone Won't Break: On
     Theatre and Hope in Hard Times* (London: Methuen, 1990), pp. 153–4, 166.
67   Edgar, 'Festivals of the oppressed', *The Second Time as Farce*, p. 242.
68   Ibid., p. 245.
69   McGrath, *The Cheviot*, p. 74.
70   Ibid., p. 49.
71   Ibid., pp. 59 and 61.
72   See Helene Keyssar, *Feminist Theatre* (London: Methuen, 1984), p. xiii, for this
     loose distinction between the approaches of women playwrights in the United
     States and Britain.
73   Wandor, *Look Back*, p. 154.
74   Ibid., p. 162.

75 Wandor, *Carry On*, p. 156.

76 Caryl Churchill, Preface to *Light Shining in Buckinghamshire*, in *Churchill: Plays One* (London: Methuen, 1985), p. 183.

77 Ibid., p. 204.

78 Ibid., p. 236.

79 Timberlake Wertenbaker, *The Love of the Nightingale* (London: Faber, 1989), p. 19.

80 Ibid., Sc. iv, p. 6.

81 Ibid., Sc. iv, p. 7.

82 Ibid., Sc. xi, p. 49.

83 Ibid., Sc. xvii, p. 38.

84 Quoted by Hilary DeVries, 'The drama of August Wilson', *Dialogue*, 83 (January, 1989), 49–54; 49.

85 Ibid., p. 50.

86 Wilson, *Fences* (London: Penguin, 1988), p. 39.

87 Ibid., II, i, p. 79.

88 Ibid., II, ii, p. 95.

89 Ibid., II, iv, p. 107.

90 Ibid., II, v, pp. 114–15.

91 Ibid., II, v, pp. 118–19.

92 August Wilson, *Ma Rainey's Black Bottom* (London: Penguin, 1988), p. 146.

93 DeVries, *Dialogue*, p. 54.

CHAPTER 6

Poetry as memory: the autobiographical lyric in contemporary British and American poetry

Open almost any anthology of contemporary poetry and one will be struck by the sheer mass of detail from everyday life accumulated by the poems. A black lace fan decorated with wild roses, stripping cellophane off a cigarette packet acquired from a GI as a marker of gang membership, gargling with Vimto in 1964, a father shovelling snow, a leak in the lavatory roof – these are a tiny portion of the seemingly endless memories of everyday life in a recent British anthology, *The New Poetry* (1993) edited by Michael Hulse, David Kennedy, and David Morley.[1] A more canonical anthology of American poetry edited by Helen Vendler, *Contemporary American Poetry* (1985), despite the greater use of modernist techniques, easily yields a similar range of specific observations and intimate details of ordinary observation: lawn sprinklers; trading cards; a screen door; riding in the cab of a locomotive.[2] These details are not, however, simply the result of a poetics of heightened attention, a philosophy of the ordinary or a populist politics. Neither is this what Maurice Blanchot has in mind when he recalls the ancient connection between poetry and Moira: 'poetry is memory; this is the classical assertion ... the song itself is *mé-moire*, the space where the justice of memory holds sway'.[3] These poems are almost invariably explicit products of personal or autobiographical memory. Mark Strand asks 'where are the waters of childhood' and takes the reader to a boarded-up summerhouse he knew as a child that is now 'the kingdom of rot', and then re-enacts a boat trip so that he can look down into the sea and find a timeless moment, saying 'now is the time'.[4] The two final poems from the two youngest poets represented in the latest *Norton Anthology of Poetry* are memory poems. Li-Young Lee's poem 'Persimmons' opens with a single painful recollection of being slapped by a teacher for 'not knowing the difference / between *persimmon* and *precision*', and Cynthia Zarin recalls an anthill which kept rebuilding itself next to the house she lived in as a child.[5] Different as all these proliferating memories are, they usually display an aura of pastness, and are invested with the historical emotions of grief, longing and fear of loss, and above all a passionate desire to memorialise personal history in a public space. The poets appear to share Eavan Boland's belief, cited earlier, that 'if a poet does not tell the truth about time, his or her work will not survive it',[6] and believe that telling the truth about time means remembering the personal past and giving it a permanent, public record in poetry.

It is the personal, 'confessional', colloquial style of this poetry which is usually noticed rather than the prominence of memory. The dominant mode of contemporary poetry is normally described as the autobiographical poetry of voice, an artifice of expression that depends heavily on its implicit claim to authenticity. Personal experience backs up what is said, and is often also the subject-matter. This poetry has become so widely promulgated that it is now the dominant paradigm for contemporary poetry, a success usually attributed to ideologies of individuality, especially the belief that selfhood inheres in the voice. What has been less noted is the significance of the treatment of time and memory in the poetry, and what this tells us about the public desire for literary sites of shared regret and grief that has helped make this paradigm dominant. Its influence has been such that even avant-garde poetry, with little apparent interest in confessionalism, still devotes much of its inventive energy to rethinking the relations between poetic form, individual memory, history and temporality.

The significance of memory is especially evident in the more recent work selected for the new *Penguin Book of Poetry from Britain and Ireland Since 1945* (1998) edited by Simon Armitage and Robert Crawford, an anthology whose mapping of UK poetry is about as canonical as is possible today. Andrew Motion's poem 'The Letter' is a young woman's vivid recollection of seeing a German pilot shortly before he was killed. Only the intensity of the sharply observed and highly specific details enables a reader to respond to the narrator's opening gambit – 'If I remember right' – with credence in the speaker's sincerity and likely accuracy, although the ordinary reader will have no means of assessing them beyond what the poem provides. Helen Dunmore's poem 'Wild Strawberries' recalls for an unidentified interlocutor the taste of fruit gathered in the woods above Chepstow racecourse. It too checks on the rightness of the memory in a way that both excludes the reader's epistemological prowess – 'If you remember / we were in the woods' – and invites the reader to acquiesce in a vicarious recollection founded on her or his own personal memories cued by the triggering words and images. Sean O'Brien apostrophises an old overcoat which symbolises for him the northern proletariat, saying, 'be memory, be conscience, will and rage', and this speech act, like those of Motion and Dunmore, makes the poem itself into a costume of memory that the reader might try on. Memory permeates the objects in the anthology's poems so much that Michael

Hoffman is able to describe the skin of a woman with whom he had a passing liaison, as 'eidetic white'. Kathleen Jamie's poem 'Mr and Mrs Scotland are dead' interprets the interesting rubbish on the 'civic amenity landfill site' – postcards from Peebles, a John Bull puncture repair kit – as memorial traces of the lives of two stereotypical Scots, and then imagines a future in which others, other poets perhaps, go through her own leavings and try to recreate the world they project. Is such poetry merely evidence of a widespread hunger for nostalgia or has poetry become a cultural means of practising history through the mass observation of everyday life commemorated by these small lyric memorials? If so, what sort of history or social memory is this?

All these poems are written by 'professional' poets working within a range of different local poetic traditions which share certain basic assumptions about poetry, memory and history. Reading a recent poem written for a singular occasion by two young amateur poets which was widely printed in the newspapers will make clearer what these assumptions are and how they operate. The unusual combination of a local, untutored implementation of the paradigm with widespread media exposure makes exceptionally visible the collusion of autobiographical form and memorial practices that pervade this main form of contemporary poetry and provide a style as ready for imitation and appropriation as rap or house music.

In July 1998 a funeral was held for three young boys burned to death in an arson attack on their house during widespread protests against the banning of an Orange Order march at Drumcree in Northern Ireland. A poem entitled 'Little Lips' written by two teenage girls was read at the service, and extensively reprinted in the newspapers. From its opening line – 'I woke up this morning to hear the horror on the news' – through its denunciation of the 'evil' people who planned the attack, and its recollection of the boys themselves – 'Richard, Mark and Jason, in our memories you will stay. / I can still feel the cold, wet lips of when I kissed you and then you ran away' – to its elegiac conclusion – 'I miss you so much ... Rest in Peace' – it was a tearjerker.[7] Even the hardened television correspondents were visibly moved by it.

As a poem it is pretty rough-hewn, so what made it powerful enough to be read at the service, replayed on the television news and then reprinted in the newspapers the next day? Was its power to move readers due to anything more than its association with the tragedy? Why was it important that it was a poem and not a short letter or epitaph? Its lines vary awkwardly in length, the rhyme scheme is erratic, the vocabulary is stereotyped, and the rhythm judders at times, but none of this matters, of course. What mattered was that it was a recognisable poem of mourning which could express the grief of its authors and, more

importantly, provide an occasion for mass grief as well. To be successfully cathartic the poem needed to observe certain conventions and this
it did extremely well. To begin with, it was left pinned to the ruins of
the house, giving the text a very tangible physical context – the burned
out house where the boys died – and also demonstrating that this was a
spontaneous memorial act rather than mere literature or self-absorbed
cathartic expression. This was reinforced by the way in which it opened
the third stanza by saying 'father', giving itself the momentary form of
that most socially justified utterance, the prayer to God, while using a
word whose semantic and social range would enable it to be heard
metaphorically as a call to religious and perhaps even political leaders as
well. But it was also a poem with 'poem' written all over it. Despite its
joint authorship the writers stuck to the autobiographical convention of
contemporary verse and used the first person singular to make its expression of sorrow seem as genuine as possible. The rhyme, rhythm, stanzas
and poetic diction the poem uses are all conventional markers of the
poetic, and so although the awkwardness severely limits the literary
quality of the work as a poem, it both makes it more audibly poetic and
lends credibility to the poem's tacit claim to be an authentic outpouring
of sorrow. Finally, the poem contains its own instructions for use. It not
only recalls an actual encounter with the boys themselves, it uses this to
instruct its listeners and readers in the maintenance of social memory. If
the boys are kept 'in our memories' like they are in this poem, this will
help to ensure that the significance of their lives and their meaning in
history builds social memory on a proper foundation of individual acts of
remembrance.

Some elements of the Ballymoney poem have a long tradition.
Poems have always been offered as part of public rituals of mourning,
from royal funerals to intimate local ceremonies. Events like the
Lofthouse Colliery Disaster in 1973 can provoke outpourings of local
poetry by people who wish to express their grief and share consolation,
people who may not otherwise write poetry and certainly have no ambition to have careers as poets.[8] The Ballymoney poem also demonstrates
that the current dominant paradigm of poetry includes the belief that its
reliance on memory is intensified by the dialectic of trauma. Even two
inexperienced writers could quickly create an elegy from this paradigm
for a pressing occasion.

When the poet Gregory Orr was asked whether he agreed that 'one
becomes a lyric poet because of a deep and long-lasting hurt, some sort
of trauma', he replied that he did: 'The more I deal with it, the more I
come back to the feeling that lyric poetry at least has a source of hurt, in
the wound. What draws us to poetry is that: not the expression of the
wound, but a sense ultimately that the wound can be transformed, that

poetry is a healing process.'[9] Memory in such poems would be much more than nostalgia, regret or curious hindsight; memory would be a site of trauma and, therefore, also dangerous and likely to evoke the fear of the past we encountered in Chapter 1. Trauma is usually thought of as an individual, internal wound, but like other psychoanalytic concepts it is also transindividual and, can therefore, also be located within the reading process. This is what the poet Ann Lauterbach does in her unusually explicit discussion of poetry and memory. She believes that the tricky task of reconstructing memory after catastrophe might be managed by creating a poem which simulates the energy and structure of the remembered trauma but without its poison. She does this by giving a new interpretation to the idea that a good poem is a memorable one: 'Writing, I want to make a primary event, one that will cause memory in you'.[10] By calling it a 'primary event' she borrows associations from the dominant discourses of historical trauma, especially the language of repressed memories and the primary process that sustains the repression. Such a poem would be capable of having the same degree of psychic impact on the reader as a trauma, but paradoxically done to heal not harm. This would be a homeopathic poem, administering its aestheticised trauma to the readers in order to enable them to work through their own psychic damage, in a form that replicates the structure of historical catastrophe without its deadly violence, just as a homeopathic remedy borrows the structure of a poison without its power to kill, in order to stimulate the body's healing responses. It could be that the memorial form of the personal lyric somehow homeopathically simulates greater public, historical disasters which shape modern memory.

Lauterbach's idea that the poem should have sufficient force to 'cause memory' can be looked at in Orr's way as individualised reading therapy, but it could also be a strategy for thinking about public spheres as constituted not just by ongoing conversations and debates, but also by forceful memories. This suggests a fruitful connection with recent theories of the public sphere. According to Maria Pia Lara, 'force' is the measure of the public effectiveness of discourses because successful claims for recognition will need 'illocutionary force'. The philosopher J. L. Austin defined illocutionary acts as speech acts in which you do something by the very act of speaking, as Lara explains: illocution is the 'performance of an act *in* saying something as opposed to performance of an act *of* saying something'.[11] Austin invented the concept of 'illocutionary force' on the analogy of such idioms as the statement that a certain utterance 'had the force of a question'.[12] Lara argues that in practice this force capable of creating 'moral identities' is the outcome of 'performative narratives between social groups and civil society that simultaneously create and reconfigure the symbolic order'.[13] Feminists in the 1970s, for

example, managed to create narratives of identity that 'created media-
tions between particularistic and universalistic claims', especially between
their new textual representations of forms of the good life overlooked by
dominant dogmas of justice, and the claims made for this justice that it
encompassed everyone equally and impartially. Lara takes for granted
that it was narrative texts that effected these challenges to existing public
spheres. Lauterbach's speculation about poems of memory suggests that
they too might have the illocutionary force to help society develop new
self-understandings, especially if they employ the metamemory of
trauma.

A short poem on the *Titanic* by Michael Donaghy, entitled
'Reliquary', prompted by the extraordinary submarine photography of
the sea-bottom wreck, helps demonstrate what a poetics of trauma will
look like in the genre of personal lyrics. His poem implies that the major
historical traumas are too readily available as emotionally manipulable
intertexts. He juxtaposes a series of short, end-stopped sentences listing
familiar scenes, beginning with television images of the shipwreck,
whose 'fish-cold nurseries' then evoke a sequence of other images: toys
discovered at Pompeii; infant shoes found at Auschwitz; and images of
what is presumably a girl's murder as reported in the news. Abruptly he
recoils from the emotional demands of these historical traumas and thinks
of a cynical counter-example of journalistic manipulation, a photojour-
nalist taking a broken doll with him on assignment to use as a poignant
prop for photographs of a disaster.

Donaghy's poem clearly raises a question about whether poetry can
or should trade in the memories and sentiments of disaster, and their relation to the supposedly more reliable and more authentic memories of the
individual. It is an argument based on similar assumptions to those made
by Lauterbach and Orr. Personal memories of loss are likely to be the
best form in which tribute to the traumatic histories of the public past
should be paid. Many contemporary poets appear, at least unconsciously,
to share this belief. Donaghy's somewhat complacent equation of events
of the awful magnitude of the Holocaust with the relatively minor
sinking of an ocean liner should make us cautious about accepting its
implications, however, even if ideological constructions of social memory
give some justification for doing so.

The risks of splicing personal and historical trauma are very evident
in the early poetry of Sharon Olds. Her first two books offer a pungent,
painful autobiography of abuse, violence, hatred and lucky escape from a
dysfunctional family, and her subsequent struggle to avoid recreating her
brutal public attacks on her own family. Her father is a special object of
attack. She likens him to various hate figures of modern history, and in
'The Departure', even asks him directly: 'Did you weep like the Shah

when you left?'. Has he, she wonders, repressed all memory of the way he once tied her to a chair?[14] In 'That Year' she adds more accusations about these 'tyings by the wrist to the chair' to force food down his children's throats, comparing her father to a guard at Auschwitz. In this family romance she sees fathers everywhere, and even her sister becomes one of these reincarnations of modern evil. The account of her sister's night-time tormentings is not only shocking but a powerful reminder of the way that much of this kind of autobiographical, narrative poetry has a tabloid power to make public revelations from private experience:

> Hitler entered Paris the way my
> sister entered my room at night,
> sat astride me, squeezed me with her knees,
> held her thumbnails to the skin of my wrists and
> peed on me, knowing Mother would
> never believe my story.[15]

The parallel between Hitler and her sister creates bathos as much as evoking the remembered fear and terror, although it is also a knowing attempt to use psychoanalytic narratives, perhaps drawn from Melanie Klein as well as Freud, as justifications for the excess of these projections of intrafamilial violence on to modern history.

Without the Ballymoney poem, the story of the sectarian murder would have been much less affecting and might have had less social and political impact. It helped in a small way to constitute a temporary public sphere. What sort of public spheres do the literary poems of memory help constitute? Are they memorial public spheres in which regret, loss and grief about the past can be empathically piggybacked on to personal memories? This question can be easily misinterpreted by a literary analysis that tries to integrate the poem considered as a singular text, directly with a public culture that is obviously an extended, heterogeneous history of exchanges, interactions, languages and emotions. We need to recognise that poems, too, are not singular objects; they lead a less material, more 'spectral' existence. As Peter Middleton wrote in an essay on poetry readings: 'Instead of thinking of the poem as something that moves around being variously interpreted, read aloud, published in different forms and generally provoking distinct interpretations, we might be better to think of it all as a large heteroclite entity that mixes texts, people, performances, memories and other possible affines in a process that engages many people, perhaps only briefly, over a long period of time, whose outcomes are usually hard to see, and which has no clear boundaries, not the page, the reading, the critical study'.[16] Just as the Ballymoney poem followed a trajectory from literal attachment to its occasion, the burnt house upon which it was pinned, on to the ritual of a public reading at the funeral, and then to distribution in print for readers who wanted to share its information and sentiments, so the dominant mode of contemporary poetry also progresses through similar stages of participation in different public spheres. The poem usually presents itself as originating in a specific time and place, and speaks (rather than writes) with an individualised voice of the past as a place of intense personally experienced moments commonly haloed with regret. It is performed by the poet at public poetry readings, and also distributed through magazine and eventually book publication to readers who do not know the author personally or the occasion that apparently prompted the poem, yet are encouraged by the structure of the poem to identify with its emotional investments enough to enact their own memorial rituals in the reading of it. Like the Ballymoney poem, this poetry not only finds a passage through public culture, it helps form it. This is only one passage, however. Other modes of poetry, especially those of the so-called avant-garde, not only use different formal methods in the poetry itself, they also rework, in many different ways, the entire process of going public as well.

The remainder of this chapter traces possible answers to these questions about contemporary poetry and memory in a series of close readings of poems by British and American poets. Close reading is often suspected of a hidden agenda that will predetermine its outcomes despite its claims to be open to the promptings of the text. We believe that this is only likely to be true of an anti-theoretic stance. Close reading in the context of an explicitly conceptualised analysis is a recognition of the full scope of the cultural poetics at work when texts are located in public culture. The complexity of effect in poems is as significant a part of their contribution to argument as the conceptual niceties of deconstruction or psychoanalysis. Fiction criticism often seems to avoid any hint of the derided practical criticism, but only because it is able to use plot and character as a convenient shorthand for discussion. Poetry rarely has any such counterpart which commands wide acceptance (prosody and imagery having become regrettably neglected). We do recognise that close reading of poetry makes special demands on readers, not least because most discussions of modern poetry, like ours, have to limit citation for copyright reasons. We urge readers to go to the poems themselves and have tried, therefore, to make reference primarily to poems that are also published in readily available anthologies, although we hope that interested readers will find the original collections too. Close readings of individual poems also help us to look behind some of the current generalisations about movements and relations to dominant culture, and to register the dissonances and dissidence within what are often caricatured as monolithically organised movements. Philip Whalen wrote a wonderful essay on his own practice as a poet, in which he says that he really became a poet when he realised that 'poetry didn't belong to me, it wasn't my province; it was older and larger and more powerful than I, and it would exist beyond my life-span'.[17] We too would like to underscore the extensiveness of poetry's past, present and future, and its agonistic multiplicity as well as its commonalities. Jacques Derrida's plea for us all to acknowledge the spectres of once and future possibility, which he calls 'a *politics* of memory, of inheritance, and of generations' applies to the reading of poetry too, both because of its 'spectral' presence and because it too attempts to do justice to the world:

> No justice – let us not say no law and once again we are not speaking here of laws – seems possible or thinkable without the principle of some *responsibility*, beyond all living present, before the ghosts of those who are not yet born or who are already dead ... Without this *non-contemporaneity with itself of the living present*, without that which secretly unhinges it, without this responsibility and this respect for justice concerning those who *are not there*, of those who are no longer or who are not yet *present and living*, what sense would there be to ask the question 'where?' 'where tomorrow?' 'whither?'[18]

The poems that we have chosen could never be representative of the full diversity of recent poetry's treatment of memory and history. They do, however, represent certain widely acknowledged dominant tendencies within this diversity. Sarah Maguire and Jorie Graham belong to a wide spectrum of poets who are published by commercial publishers and receive the majority of the grants available for writing and touring from the main funding councils. Their work is usually accessible to a non-specialist reader, avoids both political and formalist extremes, and as we argue, relies heavily on narratives of personal identity (or avowedly fictional simulations of it). Robert Creeley and Lyn Hejinian represent two different generations of the American versions of the heterogeneous avant-gardes of the past fifty years and, therefore, offer both a contrast with the more mainstream poetics, and a comparison of the two most influential avant-garde practices in modern American poetry since the Second World War. Hejinian's work is presented here as the most recent and searching exploration of these issues, but it would be misleading to extend this position beyond the terms of our analysis. Other contemporary American poets, and other British poets such as Allen Fisher, Maggie O'Sullivan and J. H. Prynne, could equally stand alongside this discussion and provide contrasting insights into time and memory in contemporary poetry's historicisms. Discussion of them would undoubtedly complicate this account. Nevertheless, we believe that the poems we have chosen do reveal some of the most salient dilemmas and aporiae of poetry's recent treatment of history, time and memory, and also extend beyond their own generic contexts to the larger questions raised in this book.

Sarah Maguire: 'Spilt Milk'

'Spilt Milk' by the young British author, Sarah Maguire, was the title poem of her first collection and reprinted in Jo Shapcott and Matthew Sweeney's anthology, *Emergency Kit*, a popular Faber anthology of contemporary British and American poetry.[19] The book, *Spilt Milk*, establishes its poetic community with blurbs from Selima Hill, Bernard O'Donoghue and Michael Donaghy who praises it for making 'unsettlingly deep impressions on all five senses'[20] – shocking, but not too shocking. These are poems which look unmistakably like poems while remaining accessible; their idiom is informal and the vocabulary familiar. Structurally, they are mostly short, stanzaic, quietly metrical. Ruth Padel, in her 'masterclass' discussion of the poem 'Spilt Milk', finds a prosodic mimesis at work: the man's 'sharp *a* and *k*' are 'a contrast to all this liquid dactylic flow'.[21] Language is meant to appear to grow organically out of its narrative locations, and the poems make sure to locate each poem's narrator in specific places – the garden, the fireside, the bedroom, the beach – and in nations – Britain, Ireland, Poland, Tunisia – in the midst of specific actions – reading *Mansfield Park*, watching a friend peel an orange by the fire, holding a broken light bulb or a fragment of the Berlin Wall – and in public history marked by the texts of Clement of Alexandria, Maria Edgeworth, Goethe, Freud and Derrida. Love is remembered, mourned, celebrated. Skin, nipples, sweat, blood, colon, abscess, pores – the body remembers too. Even Freud, in a poem which imagines him writing home to his fianceé, talks of a corporeal memory: 'dissecting desires and memories unfleshed'.[22] Freud's voice merges with the author's because, although the tone is autobiographical 'offering an illusion of closeness to the reader and an intimate, even confessional tone ... the speaking subjects of the poems float free from autobiographical or biographical continuity', and 'boundary lines between memoir and fiction are blurred'. The reviewer also insists, in a manner that recalls the characterisation of episodic memory by cognitive psychologists, that her recognition of 'wider issues' works because she is 'observant of local detail' and never loses the 'primary sense of physical presence'.[23]

'The common style of our time', as the Pulitzer prize-winning poet Mary Oliver says in a handbook for aspiring poets, presents 'a definite sense of a *person*, a perfectly *knowable* person, behind the poem'.[24] 'Spilt Milk' works hard to put a personable, recognisable imitation of the author into the world projected by the poem. A recent British manual on writing poetry by Sweeney and John Hartley Williams in the 'Teach Yourself' series, offers the cliché that 'everyone has a story to tell', and reassures the novice who might still be struggling to find this inner narrative that inspiration may arrive at any moment: 'something bubbles up in your memory, or catches your attention as you're walking around or reading, or simply jumps into your head from nowhere'.[25] Of the four sources of inspiration – recollection, perception, intertexts and random inspiration – memory bubbles are likely to be the best method of telling the world your story. The memory bubble in 'Spilt Milk' shimmers with an absent lover, a hotel room and secret sex. Like 'Little Lips', it relies heavily on a reader's identification with loss, and uses the first person as a marker that its history and emotions are autobiographical in order to give the readily exchangeable affects of grief, longing and love as much authenticity as possible. It too signals its poetic vocation strongly, both in its form (three-line stanzas that almost make a sonnet but end with a single thirteenth line as if the experience is too painfully incomplete to inscribe in the closure of a fourteenth line), and its insistence on the narrator's authorial activity: 'I imagine'; 'I write'. Like the Ballymoney elegy, the poem is presented as if it were the written trace of a specific verbal act located precisely in spacetime and directed to an absent recipient, but there the similarities end. This is a letter to an absent lover rather than a prayer to the unseen 'Father', and the poem is openly unrepentant about what the church might consider sins, offering intimate details of the author's moral and sexual life. This confessionalism uses details of ordinary life to function like the awkwardness in the other poem as signs of its authenticity. These are signalled strongly as true memories, although since most readers are not in a position to assess the veracity of the events and feelings recounted in the poem they have to take these signs on trust, and there is nothing to say that the entire scenario is not a fiction, and the speaker simply an adopted persona. Some contemporary poets do use a persona, as Andrew Motion does in his poem about the Second World War mentioned earlier, but readers are shown the contours of the mask and persuaded that this is what authenticity would look like if this persona were to write a poem.

Bubbles are fragile things and memory bubbles are no exception. Detail on its own would not be enough to sustain the cinema of memory with its turbulent emotions, traumas and provings of identity. A sturdy temporal and spatial framework is needed to locate the dramaturgy of the poem, and this has to be provided by language and form as well as reference to actions and events. As Joan Retallack says: 'all poetry displays a set of instructions which when followed initiate the reader into a particular experience of linguistic space-time'.[26] 'Spilt Milk' does this well, making autobiography a dynamic temporal venture in which the poem will work as a transferable memorial, capable of travelling beyond its inaugurating occasion into public culture.

Maguire's treatment of time and the first person is the result of a long development of poetic technology that now provides the operating system for the contemporary personal lyric. The poem opens descriptively, setting the scene in a particular time and place, in a manner characteristic of the autobiographical lyric. Its tone is not unlike the warm friendly voiceover of a commercial persuading us of the value of some proffered commodity:

> Two soluble aspirins spore in this glass, their mycelia
> fruiting the water, which I twist into milkiness.
> The whole world seems to slide into the drain by my window.
>
> It has rained and rained since you left, the streets black
> and muscled with water.

Clear distinctions of temporal location between several different pasts are measured from the origin of a 'now' in which she takes the painkiller and reads about adulterous women. In one past 'you came into my mouth', in another an adulterer had her ears and nose removed, in another 'it has rained and rained', and at some moment in that extended rainy past her lover cashed the cheque she gave him. The present time from which these temporal excursions set out is announced by transitive verbs that emphasise the presentness of the speaker's actions: 'I twist'; 'I imagine'; 'I sit here'; 'I write'; 'I drain the glass'. These are not continuative verbs, like 'twisting', 'imagining' or 'writing', as one might expect if the aim were to show herself caught up in an unfolding, unfinished situation. By using the perfective aspect, the poem avoids having to refer to the internal temporal constituency of the situation. As a narratologist explains it, the text can then look 'synthetically "from the outside", seeing situations as unanalyzable wholes, with well-defined results, boundaries, or endpoints'.[27]

These present perfect verbs are key to the encoding of the poem's instructions to the reader to produce a double temporality. In one temporality, expectations of prose narrative are operative in so far as the poem is addressed to a general reader, and the present tense makes actions happen in a punctuated manner as the poem moves along, so that each action is complete and witnessable, finished as soon as named, as if it all happened in the past. Indeed, if the poem were put into the past tense the surface sense of the lines would be barely altered, except that the narrated events would appear to be leading somewhere, towards a narrative outcome and its correlative, the subsequent time of the narration when their teleology and full significance would become apparent. Whether narrated in past or present tense, a narration presupposes that there is a present time which is the future to the events recounted, and from where the narrator is able to say, 'Now that it is all over I can see the whole situation'. But the poem also reads as a present tense utterance, and in this mode its temporality is different. If we read the poem not as narrative but as present moment speech, then these present tense verbs take on a rich field of possibilities. When she says that everything seems to 'slide into the drain' outside her window, this could be a general observation that everything is metaphorically 'going down the drain', prompted by the noise of the rain-water outside in the conduits. The speaker's image of the lover cashing the cheque, which begins 'I imagine', can be heard not only as a specific act of imagination taking place there in the room with the aspirin, but as meaning that this is how she typically thinks of him. Each of these verbs is a crossroads of inter-pretation, subtly and emotionally polysemic for the reader who enters the field of identifications produced by the poem.

Behind the simple poetic interface is some careful linguistic programming to give authenticity to memory's sense of time. When one uses the present tense in actual speech it need not locate just what is referred to in the present. It can also refer to the past or future, as well as to what is common knowledge, repetition or to the timeless: 'The simple present is unmarked for time, indicating "the fact of process"'.[28] In writing, however, especially narrative prose, the relations are reversed, and the past perfect tense becomes unmarked. This is why most novels are narrated in the past tense; it gives maximum opportunity for the interrelation of reported events, reflections, general truths, anticipations and memories to create the density of a lived world of memory. Using the present tense in poetic first person narrative enables the poet to simu-late the novelistic effect within the aura of the authenticating utterance, and set up a productive ambiguity. This poem is, after all, retrospective. Even the aspirin swirled before it was written about, unless readers are intended to imagine some prodigious act of writing as the events unfolded. By having a first person voice presented as if it were actually speaking the poem to someone, the poem allows itself the opportunity to combine written narrative's world-projecting power with the sincerity of the knowable person's speech. The perfect present tense would be unmarked in such a direct utterance and, therefore, enable the speaker to handle the many dimensions of temporality that intermingle in the present with the fluency afforded by this linguistic convention. This unstable doubling of voice and narrative also depends on what seems perfectly natural in this poem, the use of hypotaxis, a continuous syntax of hierarchical clauses and sentences that follow one another both causally and logically.[29] It is unstable not least because in actual speech, time does enter as hesitations for thought, redirections following new trains of thought, and as deferrals of explicitness which recall or antici- pate an interlocutor. To create this illusion of direct speech various devices are needed, especially a continuity of syntax, which will prevent the entry of such unwanted subjectivity and its disruptive temporality that might creep into any disjunctions.

The linguistic event of the poem is timeless; it is a continuous verbal structure whose syntax and morticed sentences make it appear to arise from an instant of articulated thought and feeling. Its double struc- ture of narration and speech gives it a referential time that is also double, a past that still has presence. An event is simultaneously narrated as a specific completed action, and spoken of in a present moment utterance so that what happened can be rediscovered in a present that, if treated as a point on a linear continuum of time, would exclude the past as finished. The poem's double structure seems to be demonstrating that history can still be productively active in the present, but does so only by giving the speaker a curious position in relation to time and history which is figured by the timelessness of the poem. The poem's atemporal textuality gives it a position like that achieved at the end of history when everything becomes clear, a point beyond time and space from where the full signif- icance of events can finally be comprehended and redeemed.[30] Although this temporality is complex to analyse, it seems perfectly commonsensical and open to a contemporary readership, as the success of this mode shows. As Mary Oliver says: 'Very likely the mood that develops between you and such poems is one of confidence, even intimacy. You feel that the poems might have been written to you. They are not unlike letters you might have received from a good friend'.[31]

The how and when of reception must be discreetly concealed, however, as is evident in Mary Oliver's advice on lexical integrity to the novice poet. Her anti-postmodernist warning against intertextuality assumes that it is equated to textual memory in the way we discussed in Chapter 3. She tells the beginner that 'poetic diction is language in which all freshness is gone'; the stale, thick layering of past literary usage of such language bears the unavoidable scars of time. The ideal contempo- rary poem is internally ageless; nothing changes or decays within its bubble of presence. Nothing changes in the psyche of the rememberer who is presented as the entire source of the narration of 'Spilt Milk', even though aspirin dissolves and 'goods trains' come and go outside the hotel window.

Placing this poem against the amateur elegy for the terrible deaths of children during the Northern Irish struggles puts both poems under stress. The elegy looks unable to sustain itself beyond the moment of its need, and the love poem can look trivial in such company given the obvious contrast in the public importance of the two events. One reaction to poems like Maguire's might, therefore, be to ask why a reader should be interested in the ordinary experiences of a total stranger when events like Ballymoney seem so crucial to our social future. How important are these authenticating intimate details of an individual's everyday life for the strangers who are readers of contemporary poetry?

One answer would be that the autobiographical turn in contemporary poetry since the 1950s is just one aspect of an entire culture of vicarious autobiographical entertainment. Sidonie Smith and Julia Watson claim on the basis of the ubiquity of autobiographical discourses in contemporary American culture that the 'telling and consuming of autobiographical stories, this announcing, performing, composing of identity becomes a defining condition of postmodernity in America'.[32] Maguire's feminist meditation would be a version, admittedly a sophisticated one, of the mainstream preoccupation with trading first-person stories. Smith and Watson argue, in what sounds remarkably close to the advice of the poetry manuals, that the widespread consumption of these autobiographical narratives, images and expressions of affect, depends upon the acceptance of a myth that the individual story is 'singularly formative', and that 'the narrative lies there waiting to be spoken'.[33] Instead of recognising that these autobiographies draw on a cultural pool of identity paradigms whose explanatory status is already defined, and which are often a means of establishing some collective, dialogic identity, the myth is that each instance reveals an original identity. The television talk show, for example, is a site where 'social conflicts and crises are simultaneously depicted and managed through the construction of preferred explanations and rationales that help reproduce existing social arrangements'.[34] Yet if this were all that these narratives achieved, they would not have the power they do within popular culture. They also enable people to make small revisions, transformations and reflections on the conditions under which identity is produced in the contemporary world, so that they can negotiate their identities within hegemonic ideologies that suppress or hinder them. Personal lyrics could be described as similar to pieces of clothing and jewellery. Like Sean O'Brien's overcoat woven of memory, conscience, will and rage, they can be worn by readers who wish to project different identities.

Robert Creeley: "'I Keep to Myself Such Measures'"

Robert Creeley's poem frequently anthologised poem, "'I Keep to Myself Such Measures'" (1965), is an unusually explicit attempt to reason with the temporal predicament of the autobiographical lyric of which he is a brilliant exponent.[35] It typifies his distinctive use of a reflexive voice struggling to arrive at articulation in very short stanzas and vernacular idioms which avoid imposed metrics. As a result it reads as a 'pre-utterance' compared with the confidence of statement in Maguire's poem. We have chosen it because it meditates on exactly the theme we have just been puzzling over – the apparent need for unique, intimate details of the poet's life as proof of its validity as an authentic expression of the poet's identity, details which appear to give the poem body and weight. Without them a poem would appear likely to be swamped and sink into the anonymity of convention, or float off into abstract argument lacking the necessary authority of institutions and discourses to lend it context. Creeley takes the risk of enacting reflection on the conditions under which the continuity of identity is maintained, using a metaphorics and speech act typical of the genre of the memory poem, and thereby suggests that the demand for the weight of detail derives from the existential conditions of textual memory.

Robert Creeley has been one of the most influential of all avant-garde poets in postwar America as an editor, essayist, teacher and correspondent, as well as through the example of his own poetry, with a generous capacity for creating and sustaining large poetry networks even within a literary climate of suspicion about such work. Although he is now usually thought of as a 'New American Poet' (after the movement-forming anthology edited by Donald Allen, *The New American Poetry* (1960)), his influence extends beyond North America, and he has supported British and other poets as well. Both before and since Creeley wrote '"I Keep to Myself Such Measures"' in the early 1960s, it has been necessary to work hard to sustain poetry audiences. The poetry readership in America, and subsequently in Britain, underwent rapid changes beginning in the 1950s which intensified with the advent of the radical social and political movements of the 1960s. During this time the pattern of the circulation of poetry which we mentioned earlier became firmly established. Poetry readings gave the poetry a social space which could at least represent a potential public sphere, and also enabled the poets to train readers in the reception of the poem, showing them how to mean what was said in the poem. Cheap methods of printing made it possible to produce small magazines without the need for financial investment of the kind required by mainstream publishers, and often without the kind of official scrutiny that might restrain expression. Public readings, little magazines and small presses helped form communities of writers and readers, further complicating an already complex situation described with some justice by Vernon Shetley as a new rift in the audience for modernist writing. It was a division between those who accepted that the radical impulses of modernism could be perpetuated within the university culture which had now, after the war accepted the significance of poets like T. S. Eliot, Ezra Pound and W. B. Yeats (and the modernist prose of James Joyce and Samuel Beckett), and those who rejected that situation in favour of a community in which 'antibourgeois energies were channeled into bohemian life-styles and utopian politics'.[36] Creeley was a key figure in the formation of this anti-academic poetic community, one of the 'chief architects' according to Donald Allen (the others were Charles Olson and Allen Ginsberg).[37] Yet the rift was far from complete. Both sides shared 'a sense of the enormous consequences of the decision to write in "closed" or "open" forms', which Shetley interprets as an almost metaphysical belief in the significance of poetic form. The reason for this, as we shall see in the case of Creeley, Graham and Hejinian, is that form has been a signifier for the inscription of time and history in the poem, and almost all poets have shared a conviction that the only way to challenge dominant historical metanarratives was by finding another more authentic temporality.

'"I Keep to Myself Such Measures"' approaches the dilemma as if it were just a problem of dysfunctional personal memory, using the extended conceit of a comparison between the remembering of everyday life and the use of stone markers on a long journey (which might metaphorically be the journey of life) through unmapped territory. The entire poem appears at first sight to be one continuous argument made of connected sentences, broken by sometimes unexpected line breaks:

> I keep to myself such
> measures as I care for,
> daily the rocks
> accumulate position.
>
> There is nothing
> but what thinking makes
> it less tangible. The mind,
> fast as it goes, loses
>
> pace, puts in place of it
> like rocks simple markers,
> for a way only to
> hopefully come back to
>
> where it cannot. All
> forgets. My mind sinks.
> I hold in both hands such weight
> it is my only description.[38]

If this were a continuous statement of the kind we have already met in the autobiographical lyric, then it, too, would take place outside the temporal conditions it describes. At first it does seem to belong to this genre since it begins with the first person singular pronoun and a present tense verb. Reading on, however, the possibility that this could be a narrative drops away as it becomes evident that this is the unmarked present tense which refers to a habitual condition, because embedded within the lines is the idiom, 'I keep to myself', so that the first two lines mean that the speaker values privacy and neither imposes on others nor encourages unnecessary confessions and intimacies. Already, therefore, the autobiographical convention of the personal lyric has been inter-rupted. Personal lyrics don't keep their measures and intimacies to themselves. Does the speaker refuse to tell others what measures (and does measure here mean poetics, politics or ways of assessing space and time?) he cares for, or is he simply saying that he believes that only measures that are deeply embedded in experience are valid? Creeley's poem doesn't halt here though, and the next two lines retrospectively alter the import of the idiom, as more words and new syntax pile up, although these new words do not help clarify the meaning as much as might have been hoped, because the meanings that come into view compel further reassessments of the semantic field. This second half of the stanza refers to a repetitive state of affairs in a narrative mode that might be a useful clarifying image of what the poem means by its opening abstractions, except that when read more closely they raise new problems. Are these rocks markers, rocks that make him stumble, or rocks that obstruct? The final word 'position' seems an odd predicate for the verb 'accumulate'. How can objects collect 'position'? Does he mean that inner beliefs gradually give one a position (on the government, or taxes)?

Closely scrutinised language always produces ambiguities and inde-terminacies, and this is a poetry that exerts a strong pressure to ponder its words and their speaker. The short lines direct readers to give it this slowly moving attention, and Creeley reinforced the demand for this mode of reading by his characteristic public reading style. Line breaks sound like catches in the breath, the tone of the voice is laden with emotion that makes the words appear hard to enunciate, and the mean-ings struggled for. In silent reading, the asseverative force of small phrases and single words in such a voiced text also makes the first person speaker not only more visible, but more vulnerable to the language of its expression, as if the voice were struggling to articulate these words and might well slip into vagueness and inaccuracy in the face of such delay as language imposes.

The strange phrase 'all forgets' in the final stanza is typical of another strategy widely used by Creeley and his contemporaries (J. H. Prynne is a brilliant exponent), the use of the line break to sheer off the expected completion of a phrase, here probably 'all gone', and abut a word whose antecedents are then retroactively created out of words and lines which did not seem previously to be leading to this point. Here the word 'one' or 'everyone' hovers liminally across the line preceding 'forgets'. The use of personal pronouns with indeterminate antecedent references has also become a widely used device among the New American contemporaries. The 'it' in the final line can refer to the weight, but it can also refer to much else that has gone before, including the entire poem. In doing so, the last line further qualifies a reading of the previous line as a reference to a specific action and instant. This sequencing of words and line breaks moves the reading position from one meaning on to another which then replaces the first, making it impossible to return to the earlier position. The first line of the second stanza, for 'there is nothing', for example, sounds bleak on its own. Even with the second line it seems to imply that nothingness is a mental construction, and only when the third line arrives is the impact of the word 'nothing' suddenly muted by the completion of another idiom that turns out to be using the word synonymously with 'no single thing' or 'no exception'. What Creeley's subtle poem does, therefore, is to use these swerves away from idiomatic phrases and conventional sentence patterns, along with frequent line breaks and unexpectedly obtrusive gaps between sentences, as textual markers of time elapsing within a subject's consciousness. Time is made to appear to elapse as the poem proceeds.

This constant interruptive revising makes the poem extremely reflexive, and capable of a metapoetic relation to the genre from which it begins. The opening stanza could be a metacritique of the typical strategy of the genre we examined in the previous section, which tries to hold on to memories and yet give them to the reader at the same time. To achieve this effect, the poem needs readers who will recognise the cues to make these extrapolations. Some readers might have recalled that most influential of all books of memory poems, Robert Lowell's *Life Studies*, where he talks about his childhood home and says that 'there, the vast number of remembered *things* remains rocklike',[39] and taken Creeley, whom they would also have known disliked Lowell's poetry and its influence, to be deliberately challenging the logic of such metaphors of memory. They would surely have recognised that the word 'measures' had become a synonym for poetics in Creeley's circle, and read this opening statement as an enactment of the gesture of a poetics based on what can be most closely identified with the self, which turns out to be what can be 'kept', remembered, placed in the safe-keeping of an authentic personal lyric statement of one's care. 'Care' is also a cue for locating the poem within a philosophical discourse of poetics derived from Heidegger: 'care'; 'nothing'; and 'way' are all important concepts in

Heidegger's lexis. Care is the way in which Dasein (or the condition of being already in the world) relates to the world as concern and solicitude, but it is fundamentally temporal, concerned with potentiality and possibility. The use of these verbal echoes in Creeley's poem creates a puzzling paradox. Might not the use of these echoes of the philosophical discourse of authentic being actually render this poem's attempt at spontaneity and authenticity decidedly inauthentic? Isn't this just the latest version of the modernist poetics of Eliot and Pound, using explicit intertextuality to incorporate history as tradition, rather than demonstrating a new modernism of immersion in the immediacy of experience? Richard Jackson, in a Heideggerian reading of time in recent American poetry, notes the pauses for breath and the subtle use of line breaks in the poetry of Creeley, Denise Levertov and other New American poets, and interprets them as Heideggerian manifestations of the condition of language: 'These mark the hesitations, the doubts and re-beginnings, within language itself; the points which pace, time, measure out the temporality of words, distinguishing them from a continuous and therefore timeless sounding'.[40] This perceptive reading of form ignores the self-consciousness of the artifice and its anticipations of performance and reading. The time of self-interrupted subjectivity has been constructed by the use of the short line and untimely line break which function as signs of the stuttering, breathless voice of the author for a specific audience. The sounding that takes time belongs most strongly to the poetry reading rather than the text read silently. Jackson's Heideggerian reading tacitly assumes that this is a poetry with parallel ambitions to the philosopher, rather than a poetry that is working with a specifically constituted audience who will recognise the Heideggerian allusions as cues for a specific mode of reception.

An entire structure of reception worked hard to ensure that readers would be able to produce a specific social meaning from a poem like '"I Keep to Myself Such Measures"'. In this case the readership would feel that the poet was discovering the truths of Heidegger's existential vision in his own personal experience, and thereby both validating the philosophy and confirming the importance of this stance towards history and authority. The structure of reception worked to avoid certain other readings which we have not discussed, notably a reading of the poem as mocking with caustic irony (perhaps as Adorno might have done) the ponderous jargon of authenticity, in which case the poem's narrator would become a stupid, clownish figure who believes all this nonsense with comical results. An equally unwanted reading might result from almost ignoring the force of the line breaks to hear it as a solipsistic moan. These readings did not occur because textual memory was closely managed within the readership, as we shall see from both his own and others' writings about his poetry, and the creation of an interpretative community through key anthologies. This was not a one-way process at all. It was such poems as '"I Keep to Myself Such Measures"' that helped create the constituency of New American poets.

The poem's significance is first of all dependent on a small network of writers. In an interview with Linda Wagner, Creeley talks about his sense of readership and poetic fellowship. Most important of all was Charles Olson, with whom he had an extended correspondence about poetics, on which Olson drew for his influential essay 'Projective Verse', and the volume *Mayan Letters*. 'Olson was the first reader I had, the first man both sympathetic and articulate enough to give me a very clear sense of what the effect of my writing was, in a way that I could make use of it – his early senses of how I might make the line intimate to my own habits of speaking – that is, the groupings and whatnot that I was obviously involved with ... was of great release to me'.[41] Olson even reviewed Creeley's first major book of poems, *For Love*, praising it fulsomely, especially its handling of time and space: 'Or how time ... and space, which in him is as carefully drawn close, almost to a generalized symbiosis of himself and those he places in the forged landscape – time of course stays right on his own terms, by the governing term of his severe and exacting demand anyway, that it be this way or why have anything to do with it'.[42] Olson was not the only fellow poet with whom Creeley maintained very close contact. In a later essay he jokes about being able to look out of the window almost and see certain compatriots and forerunners: 'Williams, Pound, H.D., Stein, Zukofsky, Olson, Duncan, Levertov, Ginsberg, Dorn, Bunting, Wieners, McClure, Whalen, Snyder, Berrigan ... there's been a way of doing things which found company with others'.[43] The easy assumption of a perspective centred on the poet suggests another question. What do these poets outside the window see when they look inside? Edward Dorn saw 'a model of a social universe located with a high degree of resolution' in his review of *Pieces*, where he appears to be trying to defend Creeley against any suspicions of sentimentality, solipsism or triviality by making a rhetorical appeal to discourses of science, sociology and other large-scale concerns. Location was the key, and it meant a temporal process: 'the confrontations, within the organism of their emotional time, are the exactitude of the world insofar as it can be accurate.'[44] This praise was consonant with a key statement about poetics from Denise Levertov, another member of the immediate audience outside the window, in one of her most widely read essays, 'Some Notes on Organic Form' (1965). She ties the time of perception closely to the time of the syntax: 'The varying speed and gait of different strands of perception within an experience (I think of strands of

207

seaweed moving within a wave) result in counterpointed measures.'[45]

Even poets whom Creeley could not see had heard the message about the importance of temporality for any poetry with radical credentials. In a 1965 anthology which attempted to survey the entire literary scene and to acknowledge the divide between the New American poets and the academic modernists, called not surprisingly, *A Controversy of Poets*, one editor, Robert Kelly, readily endorsed the New American poetics without naming it. He repeatedly uses the buzz words 'rise' and 'arise': poetry has the power 'to sustain life by the creation of new forms, genuine new verbal structures arising out of our condition to sing to us of all times', poems in which 'the word, shaping itself through the breath or utterance of the poet, rises into form'. Such a poem can 'talk to us in our own speech, our own asymmetrical, nervous, alive, embattled, *present* hearing' as long as it pays complete attention to the 'powers of source energy ... arising' in the poet in the act of composition, and eschews the 'time-worn, pre-existent patterns' used by the academic poets.[46]

The construction of a readership with expectations of a particular temporal form is also evident in an anthology of poetry and prose which Creeley helped edit during the mid-1960s. Anthologies not only consolidate the public perception of a poetic movement, but they can provide interpretative frameworks for its reception. *The New Writing in the USA* (1967), composed with the assistance of Donald Allen, whose earlier anthology, *The New American Poetry* (1960), helped bring these poets to public attention and give them a sense of network, set out to do this. It presents the Beats, Olson and his immediate circle, the urban poets of San Francisco and New York, as poets associated with a way of reading time and memory in poetry. Although the anthology is not lacking in cultural politics, whether of race, homosexuality, national identity, ecological concerns or religion, these are not the issues that Creeley underlines as crucially defining in his introduction. There the emphasis falls on a specific relation to the past: New American writing is strongly modernist because it repudiates history. It breaks with tradition, and even more importantly, with the past as a determinant of present action and consciousness. 'What can be said is something itself particular – to senses of form, to the literal nature of living in a given place, to a world momently informed by what energies inhabit it'.[47] This represents worthwhile utterance as entirely originating in a moment, as the unfolding articulation that speaks through the writer, because only then is a revolutionary politics possible. Anything else is repetition. Recent literary theory claims that language speaks the subject; in Creeley's poetics the moment speaks the subject. He tells a literary history of rebellion against an older generation who assumed that poetic form from beyond the moment of the writing carried authority. The past as traditional form imposed itself to the degree that the generative moment of the 'immedi-ate' environment was thwarted. His own authorities are fellow poets. He cites Olson saying that the poet should try to write only about what is happening within the field of the poem during its conception and avoid all past thought's influence, the *pre*-conceptions 'from outside the poem'. He also cites William Burroughs saying that 'what is in front of his senses at the moment of writing' is all that matters. History is void; writers' life experience tells them that they can no longer assume that 'all presence is defined as a history of categorical orders'.[48] Even descriptive writing would fail the test because it would take place in a time outside and, therefore, caught up in pastness or futurity, the immersion of real expe-rience. This Heideggerian authenticity entails a prescription for action as taking place within the world. 'That undertaking most useful to writing as an art is, for me, the attempt to *sound* in the nature of the language those particulars of time and place of which one is the given instance, equally present'.[49] This is a writing which emulates the work of memory as it happens, yet it assumes that all pastness is outside oneself, that time happens elsewhere. Any intrusive self-consciousness would be an impo-sition from outside this time and place, a textual memory imposing its form on the pure perceptual transmission from event into language. The world is always present, and it is only the subject who risks bringing in too much pastness in the form of tradition. What is not considered is whether the past might inhere somehow in that 'social universe' or in the 'particulars of time and place'.

In this context, '"I Keep to Myself Such Measures"' would be read not as a complaint about a poor memory or as a mockery of the jargon of authenticity, but as further confirmation of a poetic with growing social purchase, and an alliance with all the new social movements based on a repudiation of existing hierarchies and authority. This exclusion of other possibilities is not in itself a criticism of the poem or its readership, and one might make the case that the ambition and risks of weighing down a minimal structure like this poem with such significance, require a trained audience to recognise the potential complexities at work. Yet this convergence of poem and readership is achieved by setting aside historicity, and this can be seen even in the way the poem and its critical discourses discourage attention to both the intertextual histories we considered earlier, and the social meaning of its own terms. Weight is the effect of gravity on mass and independent of subjectivity. Yet any recog-nition of weight occurs through a social system of measurement. The rocks that exhibit this weight are likewise formed by non-human processes originally but they are likely to have been shaped by historical forces, even if they are simply now part of a 'landscape' resulting from cultivation and human occupation. However abstract or minimalist the elements of the poem, they will reveal social memory in their mode of appearance to the observer. In a poem that Creeley wanted to include in the anthology, but was unable to, Robert Duncan's 'Apprehensions', Duncan cites a mystical text which says that 'time and space are distant mountains'. We might reverse this, and say that the mountains (or rocks) in any environment are modes of social time and space. A new readership might well read Creeley's poem in this manner.

Jorie Graham: 'What the End is For'

Jorie Graham, who began her poetic career as the New American Poetry was losing momentum at the beginning of the 1970s, also shares a sense that in the words of 'What the End is For', we are surrounded by 'useless / splinters of memory, the chips / of history'.[50] She, too, has been highly influential on her generation of poets, largely through her position at the Iowa Writers' Workshop, the most important creative writing course in American universities, which has produced many well-known, widely published American poets. She has also been widely praised for combining awareness of temporality with an attention to history. Reviewers often single out her attentiveness to temporality for praise: 'her poems repeatedly face the problem of capturing a moment and being faithful to its capture'.[51] They also emphasise the importance of authentic individual subjectivity as the jumping-off point for this lyric transcendence: 'she repeatedly begins with an ordinary moment ... which she then ramifies through the filter of her voice to conclude ecstatically'.[52] 'Graham's art is one of submission, bound to a Bergsonian raft in the flood of duration',[53] said another reviewer apparently carried away with these river-of-time metaphors. An earlier review places this flood firmly in the mainstream of contemporary poetry: 'Like all good poets, she illuminates moments, but she is like no-one else, neither in her rhythms, nor in her insistence on opening up, scrutinizing, and even reversing our experience of time and space within those moments'.[54] This amounts to a strong prescriptive stance similar to that we encountered among the New American poets: to be a good poet you must become an investigator of the inner structure of the moment. Graham takes a quasi-religious perspective on temporality that has some affinities with Levertov's interest in the numinous, and Duncan's mysticism, and for this reason, according to Charles Altieri, she rejects 'the banal secularity of the generation of (male) poets immediately preceding hers' as well as any 'traditional foundations for that transcendence'.[55]

She is, therefore, not a poet of the margins. As a teacher at Iowa, a poet anthologised in the *Norton Anthology of Poetry* and in Helen Vendler's anthology from which we quoted examples of personal memory, and as one of the most widely reviewed contemporary poets she is now a central figure. Indeed, Vendler comes close to choosing her as the poet of the millennium in a recent study of American poetry, on the grounds that Graham's work captures perfectly the historical imperatives of the end of the century, not least its refusal of millennarianism: 'The continuum of history – rather than the events that demarcate and thereby organize time – is her subject. The continuum resists being called the *fin* of anything.'[56] It does so, presumably, because it is 'open' rather than 'closed'. In this sense Graham is a poet of the *durée*, a poet of the emerging moment. Vendler compares Graham's poems in *Region of Unlikeness* (1991) to Don DeLillo's novel *Mao II*, in which she also detects a sense of the ending of a period of history because both share 'the conviction that one can speak authentically only of "lyric" personal experience ... and an equal conviction that one must speak also of incomprehensible mass events (in *Mao II*, the Moonie mass marriage) [which] struggle for dominance at this historical moment'.[57] Paul de Man, writing about Wordsworth's *Prelude*, argued that Romanticism tried to deny the temporal structure of being: 'The temptation exists, then, for the self to borrow, so to speak, the temporal stability that it lacks from nature, and to devise strategies by means of which nature is brought down to a human level while still escaping from "the unimaginable touch of time".'[58] Vendler echoes de Man in her praise of Graham's poem, 'The Phase of History', by saying that it resists the temptation to treat any history as a stable foundation. History is 'mere construction' and, therefore, 'nothing guarantees its future except the restless and unstillable flux of the human gaze, suicidal in its metaphysical uncertainty and in its constant determination to annihilate its own past'.[59] Vendler finds further evidence of Graham's refusal of inauthentic history in the concluding passage from Graham's poem 'History', where the poet expresses a longing to look up at the 'intended time, / punctual, / the millisecond I was bred to look up into ... the eyes of my own / fate not the world's'.[60]

It is not difficult to see why a poem like 'History' might encourage such judgements. This first person meditation on the difficulty of finding adequate images for what is almost unrepresentable – history and past-ness – is acutely conscious of the contrast between the linear time measured by the clock and a different phenomenological awareness of time that places both history and future firmly in the present. Three images derived from the same winter landscape provide the armature of the poem: a flock of birds; a frozen river; and the invisible presence of time imagined as a mysterious 'x' like an algebraic placeholder in an equation. Like Maguire's poem, it uses the doubled temporality of narration and voice, and like Creeley's poem it attempts to incorporate duration into the text itself, by using novelistic devices such as questions about what is happening, statements that time is passing and sentences without verbs which act as sequential mental snapshots of duration. Despite its tone of authentic, first-hand contemplation, it too is richly allusive for readers who share its intellectual context.

This context is much less specialised than the one we saw in Creeley's poem. 'History' begins with a vivid account of witnessing black storks landing in a tree in a style reminiscent of Annie Dillard in *Pilgrim at Tinker Creek*. As they land, it looks as if 'something that was whole cloth floating in a wide sky' were rumpling as it settled on the branches, recalling Dillard's vast flock of starlings who 'extended like a fluttering banner ..., bobbed and knitted up and down ... like a million shook rugs'.[61] Like Dillard, Graham takes such a sight to represent the rapidly changing and constantly surprising, moment by moment appearance of the world, which requires unremitting attention to be observable. Dillard believes that this attention has to be free of interfering self-consciousness, because self-consciousness is a hindrance to full recognition of the fountaining presence of phenomenological time. If she is watching a tree, once self-awareness rushes in:

> the tree vanishes, uprooted from the spot and flung out of sight as if it had never grown. And time, which had flowed down into the tree bearing new revelations like floating leaves at every moment, ceases. It dams, stills, stagnates.[62]

Graham's poem argues this too, in an allegorical mode that would have satisfied Paul de Man, who said that allegory 'always corresponds to the unveiling of an authentically temporal destiny'.[63] Poems in *The End of Beauty* constantly describe actions and events as moments of narrative, and this lends support for allegorical reading. Eve contemplating the apple on its branch in the Garden of Eden sees 'the passage along the arc of denouement once the plot has begun'.[64] The 'whole cloth' which the birds appeared to create in the sky is easily allegorised by the reader as the 'whole story', the past or history that would be fully known, and the breaking up of this pattern as the birds noisily land on a winter tree, is likened to the breaking up of the scene caused by the aesthetic eye: 'now getting sucked back down / into the watching eye'.

Abandoning the tree, the poem then takes another familiar image of time, the river, and considers the contrast of the frozen surface with the current below, as if it too might provide an experience and image of time. It spookily imagines that all the reflected images of passersby, the moments of the past, are still somewhere retained in its depths, as if the river were a form of material memory and the past were 'saved in there with all the other slaughtered bits'. This echo of Hegel's image of the 'slaughter-bench' of history jolts the narrator back to the chronological present and its demands, in a mode similar to Maguire. Now that the time is four o'clock in the afternoon, she must leave for an appointment. With the tree of phenomenological time 'above' her, and the river of time, history, frozen solid below her and unable to reflect the present, she is trapped in a now that is announced in the poem with a capital letter and a subsequent colon, as if the poem could then finally manifest this present. Yet what follows is textual memory, an intertextual reference to Virginia Woolf's *The Waves*. A 'creature, the x' is chained beside her, a re-appearance of the 'chained beast' which haunts Louis with its evocation of time monotonously passing without sufficient human meaning to save it from sheer menace: 'The bird flies; the flower dances; but I hear always the sullen thud of the waves; and the chained beast stamps on the beach'.[65] Graham imagines this beast as the counterpart to her still attentiveness to the present: 'Everything has its moment. / The x gnaws on its bone'. This is both an image of the violence of the past, and its continual attempt to make historical narratives, 'whole long stories which are its gentle gnawing'. Its chain is her own desire to have a perfect moment of revelation, that punctual transcendent moment when she would gaze into the eyes of her own destiny, rather than the world's, in a moment of supreme self-consciousness. Graham's poems are always aware of the force of error, and 'History' is typically aware that the desire 'to have looked up at the only / right time, the intended time, / punctual', may be an existential mistake. Yet its assumption that history is dangerous goes unexamined, a beast that needs chaining by the power of existential commitment to the present ('my own / fate not the world's').

As we saw earlier, the dominant mode of poetry today takes the use of autobiographical materials for granted as a source of authenticity and transmissible value. In a rare moment of self-reflection on the conditions of this practice, Graham said it helped her work with materials which resist imaginative transformation because they demand historical objectivity.

> I tried to use the kind of fact we think of as autobiographical as the texture against which I was testing my sense of what *knowing*, or *thinking*, or *feeling* is. In many ways, I used autobiographical fact in those poems as a kind of tuning fork by which to gauge the *sense of reality* in what I was saying. I'm not sure I would consider them "confessional" poems, or poems that are interested in using autobiographical detail to *explain* anything about how the speaker of the poem has ended up being who she is ... I was trying to find those places in my autobiography where the facts were unalterable (uninterpretable really) ... I did something in it that is difficult for me: I didn't change facts. There are certain details in it about my father's and mother's life for example, that I might have

altered slightly 'to protect the innocent', as it were, but I didn't (emphasis in original).[66]

The narrative of personal identity is incidental; these facts signify the irre-deemability of the past, or what is 'uninterpretable' about the past. The personal past resists allegorisation and, therefore, resists temporal stability. In her deconstruction of autobiography, *Landscape for a Good Woman*, the cultural historian Carolyn Steedman meditates on the earliest dream she can remember, in which she sees her mother wearing a 'New Look' dress. Her explanation of its significance helps explain what Graham is reaching for: 'That dream is the past that lies at the heart of my present: it is my interpretative device, the means by which I can tell a story'.[67] The uninter-pretable moments are markers of that for which history has not yet found a story. Interpretability really means a certain kind of reusability, a quality of information that could provide evidence for theories and histories that bring with them a social network of discourses. The uninterpretable, unal-terable facts of the past are meant to resist historicism and demonstrate that it may be reasonable to reject history.

One of Graham's best known poems, 'What the End is For', published in *The Norton Anthology of Poetry*, is constructed around such uninterpretable moments and the attempts to allegorise them. It registers the effects of the Cold War on American lives by counterpointing two narratives of past events; one a memory of watching B-52 bombers on the runway at Grand Forks, North Dakota, running their deafening engines in permanent readiness for take-off in case of a nuclear attack; and the other a poignant memory of her last conversation with a lover. The poem generates its energy from the juxtaposition of the two times. The earlier memory is supposedly recounted to this former lover (a struc-ture very similar to that used by Maguire); the boy who took her to see the planes is said to have been very like the lover, and in both memories twilight falls, gradually erasing the forms of the aeroplanes, and the planes of the man's face as he talks to the poet.

The poem works hard to ensure that readers believe it, as if concerned about possible scepticism. Readers expect historical accuracy, as the Norton anthology inadvertently proves when it wades in with an extremely gratuitous and patronising footnote, saying that the factual detail about the scale of America's Cold War alert is wrong: 'fewer than a squadron (fifteen planes) would actually run their engines at a time, for no more than about an hour'.[68] Interpretation has, after all, crept in. This footnote tells us much more about ruling assumptions of authenticity and verisimilitude than about either America's nuclear arms strategy or the poem; it tells us that valid poems are reliably accurate about the past. This also suggests that one reason why poets rely on personal, uncheck-able details is that 'facts' about public history are subject to constant correction and reinterpretation. Graham herself provides plenty of unchallengeable details about the past, about the light on the planes and her friend's behaviour, sufficient to establish the past's credentials for its appearance in her poem.

Facts also matter because the poem cross-cuts the narrative of modern American history with the personal past, implicitly making claims about the nature of history and the position of the individual. History is once again represented as memory recorded by an eye-witness to a perceptible event. Sensory experience – the noise of the engines, the helical barbed wire flaring in the sun, the ground on which they lie – these are the guarantees of a valid personal memory. Their slow absorption into the darkness of evening provides an allegory of the absorption of an event into the invisibility of the past. The second memory acts as an implicit commentary on the significance of the first, reinterpreting it with hindsight and inviting the reader to find enactments of the first scene's significance in the confined domestic tensions of the second. Deliberate verbal parallelism between the air force jargon for practice bombs or *shapes*, as reported by her guide to the bombers, and the description of herself and the lover in the darkening kitchen as 'shapes the shapelessness was taking back', adds an otherwise undisclosed explosiveness to this latter scene and hints at some deeper causal connection. Has America's Cold War paranoia so infected the population that this man is unable to brave the danger of intimacy and cross the room? It is an implication far more subtle than anything in the poetry of Sharon Olds, yet it works in a similar way.

The poem reserves explicitness for references to time. The fading light of the kitchen is likened to both 'useless / splinters of memory' and to 'chips / of history, hopes, laws handed down'. An academic reader will notice that one likely source of these associations between light and the past is Emerson's essay 'Self-Reliance', where he writes as if history were a constraint on the self trying to live creatively in the moment. After the famous epigram that 'a foolish consistency is the hobgoblin of little minds', he adds that a 'great soul ... may as well concern himself with his shadow on the wall'.[69] Instead of constantly looking over one's shoulder at the image of oneself created in the past, one should jettison 'this corpse of your memory', and reinvent oneself continually. Emerson even uses the imagery of light to make his point. The past is darkness, and although 'the soul is light; where it is, is day; where it was, is night'.[70] Graham's past also casts long shadows not easily dispelled by the present; the past remains a large threatening public history of Cold War weaponry threatening to destroy the ability to hear, talk and see the world.

'What the End is For' has a form that is easily recognisable as not belonging to the poetics of the New American poetry or its avant-garde successor, Language Poetry, although at times it comes close to the former (notably to Ron Loewinsohn's poem 'Against the Silences to Come' in Creeley and Allen's anthology in *The New Writing in the U.S.A.*). What are these recognisable formalist differences? There is little emphasis on the temporality and embodiment of the voice of the narrator; the narrator recounts events from a time that is unaffected by the act of articulation; sentences are built up as logical units rather than units of speech; the sentences connect up into both larger narrative and as syllogistic structures; and the narrative assumes that what it refers to exists in a spacetime separate from the articulation. Content also distinguishes it from the New American Poetry. Graham alludes to Greek myth (Orpheus and the Maenads), and she unobtrusively but densely packs the poem with symbolic connections that hark back to Robert Lowell, for example. Yet set aside these formalist issues and other affinities with both Creeley, and our final poet, Lyn Hejinian, become apparent, as we shall see.

Lyn Hejinian: 'Yet we insist that life is full of happy chance' from *My Life*

Ann Lauterbach believes poets can use the sentence as a valuable means of time-space expansion: 'Each sentence or line enlarges the present, makes it contain more than itself as it fills with tenacity, forbearance, gratitude, as I watch my curiosity track its string of words before it is ransacked by closure'.[71] Lyn Hejinian's poetry has found many original ways in which to investigate the ecstatic temporality of sentences and the openness that resists closure. She, too, has been an influential figure in her own context, the heterogeneous activities now widely known as Language Writing, which have been documented in Douglas Messerli's *From the Other Side of the Century*, and to some extent in Paul Hoover's *Postmodern American Poetry*. Language Writing or Poetry remains largely outside the main centres of literary influence, although some of its practitioners have begun to move into the academy (but not usually as teachers of writing), and their books now receive wider distribution (although they are still produced by smaller, non-commercial publishers). It is still too early to assess Hejinian's role in all this, although her editorship of *Poetics Journal* and publication of the *Tuumba* series of chapbooks contributed enormously to the formation of an extended community of writers and readers. *My Life* (1987) has become her best known work and is taught on some university courses in contemporary literature.

This long poem 'enlarges the present' by meditating on how time is inscribed in the sentences of an autobiographical writing. To start here with autobiography could seem misleading at first, because the book appears to demand a formalist approach to its 115-page sequence of 45 prose poems. Each section or poem has 45 sentences, her age when she composed this second edition of the work – an earlier version written when she was 37 and published by Burning Deck Press in 1980 had 37 poems of 37 sentences – and each section centres on memories of the year in the sequence (the 29th section corresponding to the author's 29th year), although they all move centrifugally outward into her entire life. The effect of the fixed number of sentences is to make it seem that the work could have carried on; what was chosen is only a part of what it might be possible to write. Numerological structure is not fore-grounded and only an informed or curious reader is likely to register this matrix of regularity, for the frontage of the poem is a series of meditative, nostalgic, autobiographical and anecdotal sentences that mostly do not properly connect with one another. In ordinary prose, successive sentences have implicit connectives hooking them together, which might range from a simple conjunction to words like 'although', 'nevertheless' or 'moreover'. The juxtaposition of sentences implies a relation between them that may be logical and signify inference, conse-quence, justification and so forth, or some form of temporal sequence, whether causality or mere succession. In this prose most sentences do not form such ordinary relations with one another, as we can see in this extract from 'Yet we insist that life is full of happy chance', which is section 29 (although the sections are not so numbered).

> The coffee drinkers answered ecstatically. If your dog stays out of the room, you get the fleas. In the lull, activity drops. I'm seldom in my dreams without my children. My daughter told me that at some time in school she had learned to think of a poet as a person seated on an iceberg and melting through it. It is a poetry of certainty. In the distance, down the street, the practising soprano belts the breeze. As for we who 'love to be astonished', money makes money, luck makes luck. Moves forward, drives on. Class background is not landscape – still here and there in 1969 I could feel the scope of collectivity. It was the present time for a little while, and not so new as we thought then, the present always after war. Ever since it has been hard for me to share my time. The yellow of that sad room was again the yellow of naps, where she waited, restless, faithless, for more days. They say that the alternative for the bourgeoisie was gullibility. Call it water and dogs. Reason looks for two, then arranges it from there.[72]

Gertrude Stein experimented with disjunctive prose in various modes, but almost always kept to a three-dimensional field of reference. The choppy, startling effects of *Blood on the Dining Room Floor*, her mock detective novel, for example, are achieved by rapidly shifting, often sentence by sentence, from external reference to internal reflection to textual self-reference. Metacommentary on the preceding text is usually especially disorienting to the reader, and creates eddies of unresolved attention. Hejinian's sentences leave what she calls a 'gap of meaning'[73] between themselves, because the 'distance' (another of her spatial metaphors) from one sentence to the next cannot be bridged easily by an inferred logical operator or by a narrative schema of succession, as most argument or fictional narrative does. 'Reason looks for two, then arranges it from there', but rarely finds two sequential sentences, and so the reader wobbles after each period, trying to figure out how to make the leap from one sentence to the next, and soon becomes conscious that this could be a reversible or commutative text with no forward arrow of time for reading. The imposed form appears to be the primary determinant of meaning, not the subject matter or even intrinsic qualities of its language, such as imagery or rhythm.

Most readers, however, once they are familiar with the form's demands, are likely to begin to assume that the subject-matter provides a partial mimetic justification for its transgressions of consecution. They will begin to explain its persistent intermittence as the effect of memory's flashbulb glimpses and torn fragments on anyone's attempts to glimpse their personal past. Paul Hoover, for example, introducing his selection of sections 1, 2, 7 and 29 in the Norton teaching anthology, describes the poem in terms that show why readers would find a realist explanation of the formal structure helpful: 'In *My Life*, Hejinian gradually creates a portrait of her own childhood, through a mosaic of discontinuous sentences and glimpses'.[74] Strictly speaking it is not a mosaic because it neither presents a complete picture nor is it constructed from single monochrome units (it is much more like an unstarted jigsaw), but Hoover's metaphor points up how readily a reader is likely to attempt to reassemble these fragments as if they were the tessellations of a large memory mosaic fractured by the passing of time and the transition from childhood confusions to adult understanding. The reader is likely to reason that the stream of consciousness is surely far from smooth-running once memory enters and breaks it up into an intermittent flow of recollections jumping back and forth across time, flicking between coherence, vagueness, passion, blankness and the cryptic. Isn't *My Life* a particularly realistic portrait of the helter-skelter rush of broken memories of one's past which any extended moment of reflection is likely to produce? The occasional pairing of consecutive sentences into a momentary argument or narrative seems to confirm this, as does the identification of several sentences some distance apart which appear to belong to the same narrative (as in the story of the airplane that triggered off a panic fear that an air raid was about to begin). A few sentences recur repeatedly throughout the entire sequence, like particularly explicit anamnesic leitmotifs hinting at solid episodic memories just beneath the surface.

The assumption that this is a meditation in and of memory gains force from pervasive rhetorics of temporality which are even more active than they are in John Ashbery's poetry. The time of this poem would seem at first to emerge from narrative retrospection, part of that process which Ricoeur describes as self-knowledge, the shaping of narratives of identity. From a present of composition, the past is narrated as memory prompts it. Considering just the readily available Norton selection we find chronology, age, history, duration and temporality invoked repeatedly. Here is memory, calendar and temporality – 'There was no proper Christmas after he died'; memories nested within one another – 'My daughter told me that at some time in school she had learned to think of a poet as a person seated on an iceberg and melting through it'; nostalgia – 'The windows were open and the morning air was, by the smell of lilac and some darker flowering shrub, filled with the brown and chirping trills of birds'; identity and change – 'I am a stranger to the little girl I was, and more – more strange'; internal time-consciousness – 'I picture an idea at the moment I come to it, our collision'; both chronicle history and a future that is now in the past – 'She came to babysit for us in those troubled years directly from the riots, and she said that she dreamed of the day when she would gun down everyone in the financial district'; calendrical time and *zeitgeist* time – 'Class background is not landscape – still here and there in 1969 I could feel the scope of collectivity'; the extended or 'specious' present (as William James, a pervasive influence on Hejinian, called it) – 'It was the present time for a little while ...'. Some sentences appear to be instructions on the linguistic spacetime of the poem: a sentence in the first section of the poem says that 'long time lines trail behind every idea, object, person, pet, vehicle, and event'. In the context of the first year of life this might mean that a young child has a confused sense of objects as everlasting, as constitutive of its existence and world and, therefore, without a beginning or distinctive present moment existence, but readers are more likely to treat it as a metapoetic comment on the practice of the entire work. Any moment we recall is entangled with past, present and future, and so an episodic memory is perhaps like embroidery. From the front it creates a neat, clear figure; from behind there is a tangle of loose threads and merging colours.

However persuasive this might be, there is a problem with using this one metapoetic sentence as a guide to reading the entire poem as a demonstration of memory through autobiography. It is not just that, as a New Critic might have observed, all the elements in a text are participant in the possibly paradoxical tension of meanings and emotions. The problem here is more radical. The poem's numerological formalism and refusal of consecution have withdrawn authority from any proposition that a single sentence might make. The metapoetic statement about time and memory in the poem has an authority as a single sentence which extends only from its opening capital to its closing full stop. It goes nowhere else. It does at least have this small authority; the structure is not a form of irony that calls assertions into question as some misreadings of Language Poetry have claimed. It is just that if we were to treat this one sentence about time lines as a general judgement of the poem as a whole, we would have to treat all the other sentences as similarly valid and possibly competing authorities on the meaning of the poem. The insistently metapoetic effect of all the sentences arises in fact from the very feature that renders them unable to rise to the level of the work as a whole, the isolation produced by the formalist attack on consecution.[75]

Ordinary Language philosophers developed an analytic technique with similarities to the 'New Sentence' as Ron Silliman christened the practice of Hejinian and other Bay Area writers.[76] The philosophers cite a sentence, and then ignore its pragmatic significance in order to treat it as an instance of some local limit of language. The sentence – 'But can one imagine a madman in love' – which reads like a response to a quotation of Shakespeare's line – 'the lunatic the lover and the poet are of imagination all compact' – can be read as an almost Wittgensteinian meditation on the difficulty of reconciling the deficient reasoning of madness with the enhanced psychic activities of love. It could be an instance of a particular kind of question, one which although addressed to another person, directs its interrogative force in both directions, reflexively to the speaker and directly to the listener. Sentences vary in the degree to which they solicit such attention, but they all have this potential. The sentence – 'Their random procedures make monuments to fate' – could be read metapoetically to suggest that the sequence of sentences form an aleatory avant-garde text whose use of randomness actually attests to the manifold of physical processes working according to laws and determinations that we call fate.

Metapoetry is so insistent that it no longer works in the quiet unnoticed manner of discreet instructions imagined by Ann Lauterbach. In 'Preliminaries consist of such eternity' (not in the Norton selection), the poem recounts a Russian's view of bourgeois poetry which resonates with the theme of this chapter: '"Do you know what middle-class people expect from poetry?" said Parshchikov later in Moscow, "a glimpse of eternity"'.[77] Other seeming kernel sentences from the Norton selection make similar critical comment on the desire for inalienable memories: 'Are we likely to find ourselves later pondering such suchness amid all the bourgeois memorabilia?'; 'I was in a room with the particulars of which a later nostalgia might be formed, an indulged childhood'. These are only the most prominent. Almost every sentence is an instruction but the effect is deconstructive rather than instructive. The spacing between sentences provides such a rich habitat for metadiscursivity that sentences which might have formed part of an autobiographical narrative are redirected, without quite losing their memorial gleam, into reflections on (or should we say from?) the temporality of identity, language and poetry. Another more sophisticated realist explanation then suggests itself. As Peter Osborne says of theories of time in a manner similar to Barbara Adam: 'All such totalizations abstract from the concrete multiplicity of differential times co-existing in the global "now" a single differential (however internally complex) through which to mark the times of the present'.[78] A linguistic structure of disjunctures could be read as exploring the contemporary condition of co-existent temporalities spread out in the geographical condition of postcolonialism, because 'times which are coeval co-exist chronologically in a way which is determined by the social dimension of their spatial relations, and is productive of further temporalities'. If we interpret 'social dimension of their spatial relations' in the possibly reductive form of a reader negotiating the distances between sentences, this could further justify the impression that this is a text which captures the complexity of our present times.

We need to be cautious about reading the work in such ways, because it maintains such a resolute distance between its internal references and the world. This is a textual metamemory more than a recognisably textual memory. Its principles emerge clearly in some of Hejinian's essays, which have functioned like Creeley's, to help train a readership. Discursive guides to the new writing have been a distinctive feature of Language Writing, to the degree that the movement actually gets its name from a journal, $L=A=N=G=U=A=G=E$, which only published theoretical prose about poetics. The movement has also promoted 'talks', or informal lectures by writers that have helped to foster discussion about poetics and its implications for practice. In her influential talk 'The rejection of closure' (1985), Hejinian calls detective novels nostalgic because they present a familiar, well-remembered world.[79] They achieve this by their inventorying of the ordinary furnishings of everyday life, just as autobiographical memories convince us of their veracity and sincerity by the use of incidental detail. 'Detail in detective novels is socializing', she says (we might recall Owen and Sassoon making friends over the detailed memories in *Regeneration*), therefore authenticating detail enables the law to be restored and mortality to be contained. The physical presence of local detail in Maguire's poetry, like the 'rocklike' things in Lowell's memory, are means of warding off the threat of losing one's way in the anarchic and mortal muddle of existence. Like Ralph Waldo Emerson, she believes that you should bury 'this corpse of your memory' because the actual world is not experienced like this at all; it is 'vast and overwhelming; each moment stands under an enormous vertical and horizontal pressure of information, potent with ambiguity, meaning-full, unfixed, and certainly incomplete'.[80] There is an avalanche of textual memories, not a lack of reminiscences or loss of trust in their veracity. It is significant that these are textual, because modern thinkers have also noted this insistence of the past's unmanageable traces, but described them in more material terms. Shaun Gallagher, for example, neatly summarises Maurice Merleau-Ponty's idea that the material world is a vast treasure house of the elapsed:

> The fact that intentionality always takes place in a place, the fact that consciousness is always situated, provides convenient storage for such pasts. These pasts, however, are not there in an objective fashion; they are not necessarily intentional objects of consciousness, retained or remembered in overt presence. Rather, they are there only insofar as they have a real, and often covert, effect on intentional consciousness – a trace effect that, in some instances, 'comes over' us, an effect that we have no option but to suffer or cope with. A place can do this. So can a song, a phrase, a practice. So can another person.[81]

Our individual practices of memory are necessary acts of attentive selection from this overwhelming, seemingly infinite accumulation of the past in our worlds.

Hejinian's essay imagines a distinctly textual memory at work. The intrusion of geometric metaphors for what are both the temporal connections of the present to past and future, and the immense space of contemporaneity (its actions, knowledges and individuals), derives from Roman Jakobson's argument that language has both horizontal and vertical axes of combination and substitution. What is overwhelming is not a shower of atoms of perception like those which Virginia Woolf vividly evoked as the starting point of experience, but an unending intertextuality. Like Woolf, she uses the image of the phenomenal swirl of immediacy to justify a specific kind of text, in this case the 'open text' that 'both acknowledges the vastness of the world and is formally differentiating', but by using metaphors that allude to linguistic phenomena to describe the primary process of perception, the argument circumvents discussion of subjectivity and memory, even though they remain assumed by its formalist logic.

The crux of her argument follows. Formal devices can help open a text so that it invites the reader to be an equal in its production of meaning, thereby resisting the 'commodification' at work in bourgeois memorabilia, and also rejecting 'by analogy, the authority implicit in

other (social, economic, cultural) hierarchies'.[82] Put more plainly, the
text is expected to impel the reader towards new political activisms by
'arrangement and rearrangement', a formalist device which can 'open' a
text by endlessly deferring the reader's arrival at meaning and, therefore,
enacting a process that cannot close. Phrases are repeated either exactly
or with slight alterations, always in new contexts which torque their
earlier meanings, and this opens the textual field out into the endlessly
emergent present: 'Since context is never the same and never stops, this
device says that meaning is always in flux, always in the process of
becoming created ... a perpetual beginning'.[83] The open text demonstrates the necessity of making distinctions within this vast textual
memory while recognising its sublimity. Reading this text will help
develop an ethically responsive self, especially by alerting it to its own
powers to make distinctions. Her odd attribution of speech to the
'device' is a rhetorical strategy similar to the statement that the open
text's anti-authoritarian stance towards the reader sets up an implicit
critique of other forms of authority. Not what is being said, but the
very demonstration that anti-authoritarianism is possible in the field of
textual memory, has the power, as she explained in her later essay,
'Reason', to start up communitarian political initiatives, by 'activating
relationships within [the] plurality' of contemporary social life.[84] We
should, therefore, be looking not for portraits of childhood, or representations of the decentred memory, or even for an *écriture* of
heterogeneous social time, in *My Life*, but thinking of it as a retraining
of the capacity to make such portraits, representations and writing.

This essay, 'Reason', offers her fullest retrospective account so far,
of how texts like *My Life* are intended. It is also informed by her more
recent work on *The Border Comedy*, *Oxota* and *Sight*, but it implies a more
general relevance to her entire body of work. At first, the essay might
seem to support the interpretation of her work as the result of inscribing
contemporary social time's diversity, because it contrasts two kinds of
historicism. One way of thinking the past is based on metaphor, as, for
example, in a description of the light in wintry Saint Petersburg as both
'wet', and 'like a summer San Francisco fog'.[85] Watery metaphor educes
a memory of damp weather previously experienced in America, to stand
for the present moment in Russia.

> Such comparisons, reaching out of the present situation to another,
> previously experienced, recollected one, may appear to constitute the
> 'making of a context' for the current context, but a context made in such
> a way is a transported one, acquired by way of metaphor. And such
> metaphors, cast in the form of similes and intended to smooth over
> differences, deny incipience, and to the degree that they succeed, they
> thereby forestall the acquisition of history.[86]

'Incipience' is an unusual word to use in this context, because although it means being in the state of beginning, it has not on the whole been used by philosophers for their descriptions of the present moment as a wellspring of emergence. By using it, she underlines the importance of recognising that the present is not wholly determined, that somehow it breaks with the past as much as it fulfils the promise of that past.

We have already seen a similar preoccupation with the unfolding present and its significance for memory in poets as different as Maguire and Creeley. The degree to which the wish that writing should not betray the ceaseless creativity of life in time is shared with poets who use very different formal techniques; and underlines its importance as a contemporary problematic and requires brief further investigation before we can resolve the question of why Hejinian works with memory in *My Life*. Jorie Graham, as we saw, has been repeatedly praised by critics for her 'attempts to be in the flow before demarcating it'.[87] The form of Graham's poetry is, however, very different from that of Hejinian. It retains narrative, is centred on a present moment set in relation to a later time of recollection, uses sentence connections to measure passing time, and is based on an opposition of self-consciousness and pure instantaneity. Hejinian argues her way round this opposition by rethinking what a moment is. 'It is the task of poetry to produce the phrase *this is happening*'[88] which will be a form of self-consciousness, 'the *experience* of our experience'. Notice that it produces neither a feeling of duration, nor a moment captured in words, but a verbally self-conscious awareness of duration. Because it is verbal it opens out into reason, that she once again uses as a term that can overcome the traditional opposition of world and representation. Reason is both the past as a cause (the reason why something has happened), and the past as a reason or teleology that will only be realised in the future when it retroactively organises the past. Reason creates a context of thought and history, or as she expresses it: 'context is a past with a future'.[89] This is what *My Life* is supposed to be doing, prompting the phrase 'this is happening', which in turn opens out into a temporality in which there is now a context that can be the matrix of a renewed history.

It is a highly abstract argument, not least because it derives from assumptions about history that the essay does not have space to develop, but a clue to them is the subtle reconfiguration she gives Hannah Arendt's theory of the creativity of human action. The first step is to reinterpret the persistent idea of the endlessly renewing moment of time in which we live, which has entangled so many poets, as Arendt's 'action':

Something which wasn't here before is here now; it appears and it appeared to us, and it is acknowledge [*sic*] by the sensation *this is happen-*

ing. And as such, as a moment of incipience, it constitutes, in a very particular and crucial sense, an *action* – since (to continue Hannah Arendt's argument) it is engaged in 'founding and preserving' something, which 'creates the condition for remembrance, that is, for history' and it therefore undertakes 'the task to provide and preserve the world for, to foresee and reckon with, the constant influx of newcomers who are born into the world as strangers.'[90]

In *The Human Condition* (a book which has had a large influence on avant-garde poets, notably Robin Blaser), Arendt tries to outline the bases of sociality without either reducing it entirely to the social means of production or attributing it to a determining tradition. Her innovation is to emphasise the importance of speech as an active process in the maintenance of social life. She first distinguishes three kinds of human activity: labour (the basic tasks of staying alive); work (the production of material culture and the employment that it takes); and action ('the capacity of beginning something anew' and close to more recent concepts of communicative interaction). Action is capable of bringing into the world what did not exist before (the 'unexpected', the 'infinitely improbable') as long as it is made manifest in language. This is the link that makes Arendt so attractive to writers. Hejinian takes Arendt to mean that action is the primary form of social memory, because Arendt says in her opening remarks, that action, 'in so far as it engages in founding and preserving political bodies, creates the condition for remembrance, that is, for history'. In her quotation from this passage, as we see, Hejinian omits the reference to institutions, which therefore extends the power of action, and makes all action, whatever it is, a potential engineer of social memory. The idea that all human action helps create social memory is persuasive if we think of action as action through language, because it then makes social memory into an aggregate of oral and written memory.

Arendt didn't think that all action was incipience, but rather that action was the real source of the creativity which Bergson mystifyingly attributed to time itself. Since action requires language, especially speech, to manifest itself, this will mean that some kinds of writing are better capable of creating a textual memory of the innovations of human action than others. Arendt herself assumes without argument that this primary textual method is narrative. Her concern is that readers might think that she was endorsing the view that people write their own lives: 'Although everybody started his life by inserting himself into the human world through action and speech, nobody is the author or producer of his own life story. In other words, the stories, the results of action and speech, reveal an agent, but this agent is not an author or producer.'[91] This has implications for writing. A literary text, however saturated with a distinctive style, personal confessions and unalterable facts of the author's life 'remains mute itself and escapes us if we try to interpret it as the mirror of a living person'.[92] This muteness takes us very close to the problem of *My Life*, which as we have seen, refuses to authorise its own memories and its models of individual and social memory. Clearly what Arendt meant was that patterns would run through the textual memory of a life, which the author could neither intend nor read, because they would only be discernible from a spatial and temporal location beyond that subjectivity. Is *My Life* attempting to speak of its own muteness, in what would be a paradoxical action if this muteness is a necessary condition of human action? Or is this muteness the silence of those 'political bodies'? The 'political bodies' omitted from Hejinian's summary of Arendt do the same work that the open text is supposed to do through its readers, and this is why she sees no need for further institutions. Action can operate at this level as well as at the public, institutional one. It is readers who belong to the readership constructed around Language Writing who will do the work of remembrance through their practice of incipience. They will speak the text's silence.

This recognition of the muteness of personal memory when placed in the public sphere is an advance on the assumption that sincere recollection will provide credentials of authenticity sufficient to gain a hearing for the autobiographical poem as it circulates in public culture. Coupled with a recognition of the phenomenology of time, this enables Hejinian's text to demonstrate the appearance of new temporalities that make it necessary to find new literary forms. Each of the poets we have discussed in detail attempts to find a form of textual memory capable of answering these demands. Hejinian's speculation is that if we treat the unfolding present as an unfolding *textual* time, then it might be possible to circumvent the dilemmas that, as we have seen, arise all too readily in contemporary poetry. Her own reading of her earlier work is that the textual enactment of the process of emergence will do more than this and also help maintain social memory. She is not alone in this. This was the ambition even of Sarah Maguire. A personal memory when published will contribute its small image to the picture of collective history. Hejinian imagines the process at a more fundamental level than simple contribution of a fragment of past to the building of history: her own text aims to empower its readers to take back the creativity of action and become its architects. Each time a new sentence comes along in *My Life*, incipience is supposed to be reinaugurated, and action initiated with the aim of founding and preserving 'something'. But what is this something? What is it that is founded and preserved in *My Life*? Not a traumatic, identity-forming memory, not a memorial heritage which affirms status, not an apodictic gesture towards the unrepresentable flux of time, not an epiphany which manages to suture phenomenological time and cosmic time, but as Hejinian says, the 'experience of experience', or the memory of memory. This practice of metamemory as if it were a language, therefore, achieves its impressive critique of the practices of the poetries represented here by Maguire, Graham and to some extent, Creeley, at the risk of muting the social memory which works through social bodies, political institutions and their representative readers. It is a price that many readers are obviously unwilling to meet because they go on preferring the confessional poetries that dominate the marketplace. What we have shown is that their dominance is not simply due to the culture of confession, however. These poems express a longing for personal and social memory to be rewoven into a history that is capable of an ecstatic temporality that will elude the linear temporality of the master narratives of the nation, and recognise the value of the individual. Hejinian's brilliant reconfiguration of memory writing in *My Life* actually depends on this existing exchange system that trades in memory and, despite its plans and insights, does not yet know how to start building those 'political bodies' that mediate between incipience and history. This is not the end of the story, however. Her more recent work, in *A Border Comedy*, *Oxota* and *Sight*, has added history and dialogue to her earlier more introspective concerns with results that remain to be explored by readers.

Contemporary poetry's provision of personal memories as the secular verbal equivalents of wayside shrines sets up an economy of personal memories in which some of these architects of retrospective emotion gain status from the authenticity, skill and traumatic force of their poetic memorials. This aesthetic exchange economy relies not just on an appeal to the reader to acknowledge the intimacy and sincerity of the confession, but also on the carefully constructed re-enactment of the past moment in an unfolding continuum. The time of the utterance, however, is zero. The speech act of the poem is projected from a verbal structure that is as timeless as any propositional prose. The utterance learns nothing, is affected by nothing, simply goes on in the way it began. Avant-garde writers have attempted to explore the reflexive possibilities of writing in order to give the text a time and, therefore, to investigate the conditions of memory. In doing so they have often resorted to ahistorical strategies that so heavily emphasise the moment's transformative powers that the residual traces of earlier intertexts and actions are taken for granted and not thematised. Creeley's brilliant introspective drama of memory and forgetting relies on a historicity that it cannot acknowledge. Graham attempts to borrow from both antecedent traditions, the memorial and the temporally authentic, and the result is a poetry that makes more of history while allowing both the narrative constructions of the time of narration and the time narrated, and the temporalising allegories of reading to emerge. She remains unable to halt the syntactic mimesis of temporal flow, however. Hejinian's radical formalism might have simply tipped the balance back in the other direction, except that the weight of the domestic and personal detail, and the constant self-interruption at both the cognitive and more importantly, the affective level (about which much more could be said), allows incipience to begin to bear the weight of at least the personal realisation of a social history. The conjunction of the four poems should have demonstrated just how much we need to read contemporary poetry as a cultural and social production. Only then can its practices of time and memory reveal the cathexes and labours they demand of us.

Notes

1 Eavan Boland, 'The black lace fan my mother gave to me'; Michael Donaghy, 'Shibboleth'; Carol Ann Duffy, 'The captain of the 1964 *Top of the Form* team'; David Hartnett, 'Two winters'; Michèle Roberts, 'Lacrimae return'; Michael Hulse, David Kennedy and David Morley (eds), *The New Poetry* (Newcastle Upon Tyne: Bloodaxe, 1993), pp. 48, 207, 228, 181, 152.

2 Helen Vendler, *The Faber Book of Contemporary American Poetry* (London: Faber and Faber, [1985] 1990).

3 Maurice Blanchot, *The Infinite Conversation*, trans. Susan Hanson (Minneapolis: University of Minnesota Press, 1993), p. 314.

4 Mark Strand, 'Where are the waters of childhood?', in Vendler, *The Faber Book of Contemporary American Poetry*, p. 325.

5 Li-Young Lee, 'Persimmons' and Cynthia Zarin, 'The Ant Hill', in Margaret Ferguson, Mary Jo Salter and Jon Stallworthy (eds), *The Norton Anthology of Poetry*, 4th edn (New York: W. W. Norton, 1996), pp. 1878, 1880.

6 Eavan Boland, *Object Lessons: The Life of the Woman and the Poet in Our Time* (Manchester: Carcanet, 1995), p. 153.

7 Andrea Ramsay and Amanda McAlonan, 'Little lips', *Guardian*, 15 July, 1998, 2.

8 See the discussion of the Lofthouse Colliery disaster poems in Roger de V. Renwick, *English Folk Poetry: Structure and Meaning* (London: Batsford, 1980).

9 Gregory Orr, 'Conversation at Brockport', *Richer Entanglements: Essays and Notes on Poetry and Poems* (Ann Arbor: University of Michigan Press, 1993), pp. 151–62, 152–3.

10 Ann Lauterbach, 'On memory', in James McCorkle (ed.), *Conversant Essays: Contemporary Poets on Poetry* (Detroit: Wayne State University Press, 1990), pp. 519–24, 524.

11 Maria Pia Lara, *Moral Textures: Feminist Narratives in the Public Sphere* (Cambridge: Polity Press, 1998), p. 99.

12 J. L. Austin, *How to Do Things with Words*, 2nd edn (Oxford: Oxford University Press, [1962] 1976), pp. 98–9 *passim*.

13 Lara, *Moral Textures*, p. 24.

14 Sharon Olds, 'The departure', *The Dead and the Living* (New York: Knopf, 1984), p. 36.

15 Olds, 'That Year', p. 44.

16 Peter Middleton, 'The contemporary poetry reading', in Charles Bernstein (ed.), *Close Listening: Poetry and the Performed Word* (New York: Oxford University Press, 1998), pp. 262–99, 294.

17 Philip Whalen, '"Goldberry is waiting"; or, P.W., his magic education as a poet', in Donald Allen and Warran Tallman, (eds), *Poetics of the New American Poetry* (New York: Grove Press, 1973), pp. 453–59, 456.

18 Jacques Derrida, *Specters of Marx: The State of the Debt, the Work of Mourning, and the New International*, trans. Peggy Kamuf (New York and London: Routledge, 1994), p. xix.

19 Sarah Maguire, 'Spilt milk', *Spilt Milk* (London: Secker & Warburg, 1991), p. 9; and in *Emergency Kit: Poems for Strange Times*, ed. Jo Shapcott and Matthew Sweeney (London: Faber and Faber, 1996), p. 75.

20 Cited on the back cover of *Spilt Milk*.

21 Ruth Padel, 'Sunday poem 17: Sarah Maguire', *Independent on Sunday*, 4 April, 1999.

22 Ibid., p. 41.

23 Tim Dooley, *Starter's Orders*, *Times Literary Supplement*, 10 May 1991, p. 23.

24 Mary Oliver, *A Poetry Handbook* (New York: Harcourt Brace, 1994), p. 79.

25 Matthew Sweeney and John Hartley Williams, *Writing Poetry and Getting Published* (London: Hodder Headline, 1997), pp. 75, 5.

26 Joan Retallack, 'Non-Euclidean narrative combustion (or, What the subtitles can't say)', in McCorkle, *Conversant Essays*, pp. 491–509, 499.

27 Benjamin Lee, *Talking Heads: Language, Metalanguage, and the Semiotics of Subjectivity* (Durham and London: Duke University Press, 1997), p. 285.

28 Ibid., p. 287.

29 For a discussion of the poetics of hypotaxis and parataxis see Bob Perelman, *The Marginalization of Poetry: Language Writing and Literary History* (Princeton: Princeton University Press, 1996), chapter 4.

30 See Peter Osborne's discussion of Walter Benjamin, in *The Politics of Time: Modernity and Avant-Garde* (London: Verso, 1995), pp. 133–59.

31 Oliver, *A Poetry Handbook*, p. 80.

32 Sidonie Smith and Julia Watson, (eds), *Getting a Life: Everyday Uses of Autobiography* (Minneapolis: University of Minnesota, 1996), p. 7.

33 Ibid., p. 90.

34 Janice Peck, 'The mediated talking cure: therapeutic framing of autobiography in TV talk shows', in Smith and Watson, *Getting a Life*, p. 139.

35 Robert Creeley, '"I Keep to Myself Such Measures"', *The Collected Poems of Robert Creeley 1945–1975* (Berkeley: University of California Press, 1982), p. 297; also in Paul Hoover (ed.), *Postmodern American Poetry* (New York: W. W. Norton, 1994), p. 150.

36 Vernon Shetley, *After the Death of Poetry: Poet and Audience in Contemporary America* (Durham: Duke University Press, 1993), p. 15.

37 Donald Allen, 'Writer as native: preface', in Donald Allen and Robert Creeley (eds), *The New Writing in the U.S.A.* (Harmondsworth: Penguin, 1967), pp. 9–11, 9.

38 Robert Creeley, *The Collected Poems of Robert Creeley 1945–1975* (Berkeley: University of California Press, 1982), p. 297.

39 Robert Lowell, '91 Revere Street', *Life Studies* (London: Faber and Faber, [1956] 1959), p. 21.

40 Richard Jackson, *The Dismantling of Time in Contemporary Poetry* (Tuscaloosa: University of Alabama Press, 1988), p. 196.

41 Robert Creeley, interview with Linda Wagner, in Robert Creeley, *Tales Out of*

School: Selected Interviews (Ann Arbor: University of Michigan Press, 1993), p. 67. Linda Wagner says that the interview was finished in 1965 in an earlier version of the interview published in Robert Creeley, Contexts of Poetry: Interviews 1961–1971 (Bolinas: Four Seasons Foundation, 1973), p. 71.

42 Charles Olson, 'Robert Creeley's For Love: Poems 1950–1960', in Additional Prose: A Bibliography on America, Proprioception and Other Notes and Essays (Bolinas: Four Seasons Foundation, 1974), pp. 47–9, 48.

43 Robert Creeley, 'Was that a real poem or did you just make it up yourself?', in The Collected Essays of Robert Creeley (Berkeley: University of California Press, 1989), pp. 571–8, 572.

44 Edward Dorn, 'Robert Creeley's Pieces', Views, ed. Donald Allen (San Francisco: Four Seasons Foundation, 1980), pp. 118–21, 121.

45 Denise Levertov, 'Some notes on organic form', New and Selected Essays (New York: New Directions, 1992), pp. 67–73, 71.

46 Robert Kelly, 'Postscript II', in Paris Leary and Robert Kelly, (eds), A Controversy of Poets: An Anthology of Contemporary American Poetry (Garden City, NY: Doubleday, 1965), p. 565.

47 Robert Creeley, 'Introduction to The New Writing in the U.S.A.', Collected Essays, pp. 89–96, 89.

48 Ibid., p. 94.

49 Ibid., p. 96.

50 Jorie Graham, The End of Beauty (New York: Ecco Press, 1987), p. 28.

51 John Redmond, 'Accidents of priority', in London Review of Books, 22 August 1996, pp. 25–6, 26.

52 David C. Ward, 'Breaking the cloud embrace', in PN Review, 24/2, no. 118, November/December 1997, p. 74.

53 John Peck, 'Two at the top: Jorie Graham and Susan Howe', Partisan Review, 3 (Summer 1997), pp. 497–503, 497.

54 Stephen Burt, review of 'The more she disappears', Times Literary Supplement, 17 July 1996, p. 26.

55 Charles Altieri, 'Eliot's impact on twentieth-century Anglo-American poetry', in A. David Moody (ed.), The Cambridge Companion to T. S. Eliot (Cambridge: Cambridge University Press, 1994), pp. 189–209, 204.

56 Helen Vendler, Soul Says: On Recent Poetry (Cambridge, MA: Harvard University Press, 1995), p. 244.

57 Ibid., p. 245.

58 Paul de Man, 'The rhetoric of temporality', in Blindness and Insight: Essays in the Rhetoric of Contemporary Criticism (London: Methuen, [1971] 1983), p. 197.

59 Vendler, Soul Says, p. 253.

60 Jorie Graham, 'History', The Dream of the Unified Field: Selected Poems 1974–1994 (Manchester: Carcanet Press, 1996), p. 147.

61 Annie Dillard, Pilgrim at Tinker Creek (London: Picador, 1988), p. 47.

62 Ibid., p. 80.

63 de Man, 'The rhetoric of temporality', p. 206.

64 Graham, The End of Beauty, p. 8.

65 Virginia Woolf, The Waves (London: Granada, [1931] 1977), p. 39.

66 Jorie Graham, 'Jorie Graham talks to M. Wynn Thomas (and others). Swansea, 31 March, 1995', Swansea Review, 16 (1996), pp. 9–15, 12.

67 Carolyn Steedman, Landscape for a Good Woman (London: Virago, 1985), p. 28.

68 Note on 'What the end is for', in Margaret Ferguson, Mary Jo Salter and Jon Stallworthy, (eds), The Norton Anthology of Poetry, p. 1849.

69 Ralph Waldo Emerson, *Essays and Lectures*, Joel Porte (ed.) (New York: Library of America, 1983), p. 265.

70 Ibid., p. 46.

71 Lauterbach, 'On memory', p. 521.

72 Lyn Hejinian, 'Yet we insist that life is full of happy chance', *My Life* (Los Angeles: Sun and Moon Press, 1987), pp. 74–5.

73 Lyn Hejinian, 'Reason', *Shark*, 1 (Spring 1998), pp. 33–44, 34.

74 Paul Hoover, *Postmodern American Poetry* (New York: W. W. Norton, 1994), p. 385.

75 Marjorie Perloff argues that 'Wittgenstein's stringent and severe interrogation of language has provided an opening for the replacement of the "autonomous", self-contained and self-expressive lyric with a more fluid poetic paradigm in the poetry of Hejinian and some of her contemporaries'. It seems likely to us that Ordinary Language philosophers have made readers who are at all familiar with contemporary discussions of the intersection of language and thought, *metadiscursive* readers. Marjorie Perloff, *Wittgenstein's Ladder: Poetic Language and the Strangeness of the Ordinary* (Chicago: University of Chicago Press, 1996), p. 22.

76 Ron Silliman, 'The new sentence', *The New Sentence* (New York: Roof Books, 1987), pp. 63–93.

77 Hejinian, *My Life*, p. 95.

78 Osborne, *The Politics of Time*, p. 28.

79 Lyn Hejinian, 'The rejection of closure', in Bob Perelman (ed.), *Writing/Talks* (Carbondale and Edwardsville: Southern Illinois University Press, 1985), pp. 270–91, 271.

80 Ibid., p. 271.

81 Shaun Gallagher, 'On the pre-noetic reality of time', in M. C. Dillon (ed.), *Ecart and Différance: Merleau-Pony and Derrida on Seeing and Writing* (Atlantic Highlands, NJ: Humanities Press, 1997), p. 145.

82 Hejinian, 'The rejection of closure', p. 272.

83 Ibid., p. 273.

84 Hejinian, 'Reason', p. 40.

85 Hejinian, *My Life*, p. 35.

86 Ibid.

87 Helen Vendler, *Soul Says*, p. 244.

88 Hejinian, *My Life*, p. 37.

89 Ibid., p. 39.

90 Hejinian, 'Reason', p. 36; Hannah Arendt, *The Human Condition* (Chicago: University of Chicago Press, 1958), pp. 8–9.

91 Arendt, *The Human Condition*, p. 184.

92 Ibid., p. 211.

CHAPTER 7

Histories of the future: American science fiction after the Second World War

From the radiating point of Siwenna, the forces of the Empire reached out cautiously into the black unknown of the Periphery. Giant ships passed the vast distances that separated the vagrant stars at the Galaxy's rim, and felt their way around the outermost edge of Foundation influence.

Worlds isolated in their new barbarism of two centuries felt the sensation once again of Imperial overlords upon their soil. Allegiance was sworn in the face of the massive artillery covering capital cities.

Garrisons were left; garrisons of men in Imperial uniform with the Spaceship-and-Sun insignia upon their shoulders. The old men took notice and remembered once again the forgotten tales of their grandfather's fathers of the times when the universe was big, and rich, and peaceful and that same Spaceship-and-Sun ruled all.

Isaac Asimov, *Foundation and Empire* (1952)

How can you tell the legend from the fact on these worlds that lie so many years away? – planets without names, called by their people simply The World, planets without history, where the past is the matter of myth, and a returning explorer finds his own doings of a few years back become the gestures of a god. Unreason darkens that gap of time bridged by our light-speed ships, and in the darkness uncertainty and disproportion grow like weeds.

In trying to tell the story of a man, an ordinary League scientist, who went to such a nameless half-known world not many years ago, one feels like an archeologist amidst millennial ruins, now struggling through choked tangles of leaf, flower, branch, and vine to the sudden bright geometry of a wheel or a polished cornerstone, and now entering some commonplace, sunlit doorway to find inside it the darkness, the impossible flicker of a flame, the glitter of a jewel, the half-glimpsed movement of a woman's arm.

Ursula K. LeGuin, 'Semley's Necklace' (1964)

Fal thought it must be very strange to live on a planet and have to look over a curve; so that, for example, you would see the top of a seaship appear over the horizon before the rest of it.

> She was suddenly aware that she was thinking about planets because of something Jase had just said. She turned round and looked earnestly at the dark grey machine, playing back her short-term memory to recall exactly what it had just said.
>
> 'This Mind went *underneath* the planet in hyperspace?' she said. 'Then warped inside?' ...
>
> 'What does this thing actually look like? I mean you never see them by themselves, they're always in something ... a ship or whatever. And how did it – what did it use to warp with?'
>
> 'Externally,' Jase said in its usual, calm, measured tones, 'it is an ellipsoid. Fields up, it looks like a very small ship. It's about ten metres long and two and a half in diameter. Internally it's made up of millions of components, but the most important ones are the thinking and memory parts of the Mind proper; those are what make it so heavy because they're so dense. ... Only the outer envelope is in real space, the rest – all the thinking parts, anyway – stay in hyperspace.
>
> Iain M. Banks, *Consider Phlebas* (1987)

These passages from well-known science fiction writers exemplify most readers' ideas of what constitutes the genre: spaceships; vast galactic empires; alien worlds; and intelligent machines, all set in a future when technology and social change have made their worlds possible. The past, the present and even the history between our time and the future are ruined, forgotten, and all that matters is a future whose vast resources of space and time are a main source of plots, while the temporal relations between the time of reading and the time of the narrative go unexamined. Futurity is big. Here the unimaginable distances and times of the universe that modern science has observed, calculated and theorised, are made scenes for action and subjectivity by realist narrative. Futurity is also big enough for the non-human, for the most alien forms of otherness, and for a technology as advanced as Banks's hyperspace Mind. This future is so capacious it even contains at least part of the past. Asimov's empire evokes the Third Reich, the Austro-Hungarian empire, perhaps even Rome. LeGuin makes her narrator sound like an archaeologist, and in Banks's narrative there are faint echoes of the traditional culture of seafaring, as well as the social relations between masters and servants. A famous science fiction novel like *Dune* (1965) is permeated with images from the medieval world despite its future setting. Although the future provides this space of seemingly infinite possibility, especially for rerunning the past, there are few explicit treatments of its significance by science fiction writers and critics. It is usually thought of as a neutral, spacious container for these narratives as if what mattered were the plots, cultures, technologies, aliens and moral dilemmas, not their temporal location. Yet this futurity is far from neutral, as we shall see. Science fiction's ideas, images and fantasies of the future are extremely revealing of our culture's relation to time, both past and future.

These passages could easily be read by an unsympathetic reader as examples of the badness of 'pulp' writing (with the possible exception of LeGuin). Why, such a reader might ask, should we take this writing seriously enough to be concerned with its ideas or even its fantasies about the future? There are quicker routes to a critique of ideology than unintelligent or confused escapist fantasy. This question has often troubled writers themselves. Philip K. Dick, the science fiction writer now best known as the author of the novel that became the quintessential postmodern film *Bladerunner*, went as far as to say that futurity was not a defining characteristic of science fiction. The cheap thrills sought by pulp writers in the future's vast playground of spacetime, undermine his confidence in any attempt to define the genre solely by its temporal setting. Science fiction, he writes, 'cannot be defined as "a story (or novel or play) set in the future", since there exists such a thing as space adventure, which is set in the future but is not sf ... also, there can be science fiction set in the present: the alternative world story or novel'.[1] This division of good (restrained in its temporal speculations) from bad (too futuristic) science fiction is unlikely to persuade the critical reader, both because bad writing can surely be set in the present or even alternative worlds (Keith Laumer's entertainments might be an example), and because this doesn't address the issue of literary quality. The resistant reader will want to know how a narrative lacking most of the hallmarks of the literary novel, with little character development, simplistic style or lack of rigour, can be taken seriously.

The answers to these questions from the sceptic is not to deny the significance of literary value and narrative intelligence for a critique of science fiction's use of futurity, but to recognise that these texts can have strengths different from those of the modernist or literary modern novel. The modernist text exalts authorial individuality, however impersonal or significant its intertexts, and the realist novel, as we saw in the case of historical fiction, is praised for the thoroughness with which it renders the forces at work on individuals and their worlds within its own borders. The novel's world is within itself, and poor writing will be treated as direct evidence of a failure of authorial imagination. Science fictional texts can also fail, but are likely to do so as much through a failure of textual memory as through the poor handling of the usual markers of literary value. Damien Broderick explains that 'the coding of each individual sf text depends importantly on access to an unusually concentrated "encyclopedia" – a mega-text of imaginary worlds, tropes, tools, lexicons, even grammatical innovations borrowed from other textualities'.[2] The collective activities of science fiction writers and readers have developed a set of images, narratives, concepts and terminologies that enable any one writer to construct a story whose power can be amplified by using these other elements, rather in the way that computer programmers are now able to incorporate ready-written routines from 'libraries' of already written code in their new programmes. Calling this an encyclopaedia draws attention to its textuality, but it is equally important to acknowledge that this 'mega-text' is a communicative and investigative process undergoing constant revision. Since its earliest days, science fiction has been a self-conscious formation of writers and readers active in magazines, local groups and fan conventions, whose collective endeavour is far more than simply a collective escapism. Individual works depend upon an intensive textual memory of the genre. Orson Scott Card claims, with only a little exaggeration, that:

> for many years, the appetite of science fiction readers far outstripped the production of science fiction writers and publishers. About 30,000 or 40,000 readers were so hungry for another sf novel that they'd buy anything, however bad it might be, as long as it had a rocket on the cover. As a result, while science fiction never sold very much, it did sell a certain guaranteed minimum.[3]

As a result, from the early 1940s until at least the late 1960s, the reading community for science fiction was both active and cohesive enough for the literary critic, T. S. Shippey, to argue persuasively that science fiction of this period was 'a "thinking machine" for the convenience of people largely without academic support or intellectual patronage'.[4] The intensely absorbed community of readers and writers was engaged in more than just a shared fantasy game, since it was also maintaining a collective research project on the effects of technological change on cultures and societies. Any literary critical methodology that isolates the text from its social history of production and reception will have problems with the collective and conventional character of science fiction of this period, because it 'foredooms to failure the search of isolated fictional pearls', as Shippey neatly explains away the absence of literary masterpieces of this period.

This almost communal authorship also generated important intertextual effects within the narratives themselves, as Richard Grossinger explains: 'In recalling science fiction plots there is a tendency toward stimulus generalization. The single books are forgotten, and all stories of our colonization of the planets and our movement into the galaxy and galaxies are remembered as a single tale'.[5] The result was a shared imaginary futurity which was a collective invention strong enough to transcend local differences from text to text and become a textual memory of the future. Its materials were both traditional literary archetypes and modern scientific knowledge, which is why major scientific developments could have a marked effect on the community. Brian Aldiss attributes the drop in sales of science fiction magazines in the late 1950s to the launch of Sputnik in 1957 and the consequent feeling among readers of science fiction that 'when space travel became reality, the dream was taken away from them'.[6] Science had suddenly run ahead of fantasy. The general acceptance of certain kinds of interstellar transport, the widely used concepts of hyperspace and androids, and the knowing use of earlier plots and devices, were revisionary co-operation as much as repetition. Writers and critics of the genre have often criticised otherwise accomplished writers because they either don't understand the mega-text or even those who use it knowingly but without adding to it in any interesting way. Science fiction shows that commercial literary forms of popular culture can generate new ideas and narratives even in the midst of much that is trite, ideologically determined and mere unreflective fantasy, if they sustain a collective intelligence that exceeds each single textual instance, because each story can represent an argument with existing states of thought in the genre as a whole.

Shippey and Broderick are keen to stress the intelligence and ideas at work in this collective project, rather than its flights of fantasy, in order to defend the genre against charges of bad writing and escapism. To investigate its treatment of the cultural politics of time we will, however, have to look not only at its conscious treatment of temporal logics but also at the spacetime trajectories of these flights, which can project both contemporary concerns and historical events into the future. In Clifford Simak's novel *Time and Again* (1951), for example, a novel set hundreds of years into the future, the protagonist Asher Sutton writes a book about 'destiny' which will become the liberation text for the enslaved androids of his time. This fantasy of a future Lincoln freeing the machines emulates a stretch of American history that remains deeply troubling. We need to ask what this temporal relocation of the history of slavery into the future tells us about current fantasies and beliefs about the past. Why should it be satisfying to readers to work through the affects and arguments about slavery in a putative future?

Discussion of two short stories, Larry Niven's 'There is a tide' and Ray Bradbury's 'The Third Expedition' will begin to answer these questions.[7] 'There is a tide' (1968), is a comic account of galactic beachcombers that shows that one answer is the fear of the past embodied in dinosaurs and revenants we discussed in Chapter 1. A race called the 'slavers' left behind a few extremely valuable traces of their culture which was otherwise destroyed – 'The Tnuctipon-Slaver war had wiped out most of the intelligent species of the galaxy, a billion and a half years ago'. Slavery is obviously very much a thing of the past in the spacetime of this narrative, unlike its readers' local historical reality of only a century earlier, as if one of the effects of science fictional representation were to multiply the time spans of historical events when transmuted into story. Traces of Slaver domination reappear occasionally, as they do in this story, when an extremely valuable 'stasis box' is spotted by the misanthropic, lone protagonist Louis Gridley Wu, as he navigates near an unknown planet ('something like Earth') in a remote, unexplored corner of the galaxy. Stasis boxes are rare and considered invaluable because they contain objects that were put into them for safe-keeping by the Slavers all that time ago, and may contain examples of lost technologies such as 'the secret of direct conversion of matter' or the ultimate weapon with which the slavers ended the war – 'and all its participants' (p. 212), as the narrative drily adds. So far the stasis boxes had not yielded much. We are told that weapons, tools, meat and a 'small tarsier-like sentient being, still alive' – which soon died of old age once released into history – have been found inside them, because 'no time passed inside a closed stasis-box'. Freud's observation that the unconscious has no time might encourage us to interpret the stasis box as a mnemonic trace of the historical trauma of slavery and war. The historical unconscious might contain knowledges of inestimable value; the difficulty is finding signs of them and then recovering them. Niven's story does not develop in the way we expect, however. Suddenly there is another, unknown alien spaceship competing for possession of the stasis box – a small silvery sphere – that might contain the ultimate weapon of destruction. In a comic reduction of the Cold War between the US and the Soviet Union, the man and the 'Trinoc', a grotesque distortion of human traits – he has thin legs and a beer barrel paunch – meet on a 'definite beer party beach' to decide who should have the stasis box by tossing the alien equivalent of a coin. It is a set-up. The alien has concealed from Wu that he has a crew ready to take off out of weapon range and seize the precious artefact; the plan goes into action and Wu is held at gunpoint by his captor. Things go suddenly wrong for these dishonest Trinocs when the stasis box turns out to be a tiny sphere made of compressed matter so dense that it has the gravitational force of a planet, and their approaching space ship is crumpled 'like tinsel paper in a strong man's fist' (p. 215).

Everything that we have learned about Slavers and stasis boxes is now irrelevant, except as an explanation of motive. The somewhat perfunctory comedy has constructed a series of symbolic narrative trans-formations; it therefore equates slavery, ultimate weapons, the past, the suspension of duration represented by the stasis box, the historical uncon-scious, and the irresistible attractive force of 'ten feet of nearly solid neutronium'. The supposed eliminator of time produces a series of formal effects which culminate in the discovery that it is a deadly eradicator of

all form, ending the quest to bring the past into the present with a spec-
tacularly destructive implosion. The gravitational force that destroys the
alien spaceship represents the power of the symbol of slavery, and more
generally the past, to eradicate all attempts to seize it, open it and let the
past it contains out into the present. It is a history which this fiction finds
sublime because it overwhelms all attempt at cognition and becomes an
object as hard to represent as the collapsed matter that starts the narrative going.

A somewhat untypical story of this period, Ray Bradbury's story
'The Third Expedition' (1951) (untypical in its literary pretensions),
suggests that the problem of the past is that it is both seductively attractive, calling for its repetition in a futural redemption of its losses, and
remains so dangerous that it can easily crush those who would treat its
promises as realisable. His story is unusual because its monitory allegory
concludes that futural relocation may not always be sufficient to contain
the threat of a destructive repetition of history. A spaceship from Earth
lands with sixteen men to explore the planet Mars and instead of an alien
landscape they find something utterly recognisable, a small American
town that might have been designed by Norman Rockwell. From the
start they are faced with the question of whether this is a simulacrum or
an actual American place. The captain looks out of the spaceship's glass
port at a geranium and says to his crew: 'Think of the thousands of years
it takes to evolve plants. Then tell me if it is logical that the Martians
should have: one, leaded-glass windows; two, cupolas; three, porch
swings; four, an instrument that looks like a piano and probably *is* a
piano' (p. 33). As the crew argue about what to do about this unexpected
apparition they admit that the 'good, quiet, green town' looks remarkably like their own home towns, not noticing the apparent logical
impossibility of such a shared place. The first of several theories to
account for it is proposed: the Martians are actually Americans who
discovered space travel before the First World War. Then the explorers
meet an inhabitant who insists that the town is 'Green Bluff, Illinois, on
the continent of America, surrounded by the Atlantic and Pacific
Oceans, on a place called the world, or, sometimes, the Earth'
(p. 38). Perhaps they should have noticed the possible pun in the town's
name, but instead they worry over the nature of the journey through
space and time that they have just made. Although they seemed to travel
only through space and the elapsed time of the journey, could they have
travelled back in time as well? Readers would have already been familiar
with the time-dilation paradoxes of Einstein's general theory of relativity,
which were widely discussed in the science fiction magazines and had
already been made the basis of many narratives. Einstein's theory doesn't
explain temporal regression, although it does give warrant for assuming

that unexpected temporal effects of space travel are possible.

The captain quickly rejects this explanation as they walk round the town looking for other inhabitants. Admiring its Victorian houses, he conjectures that this is a loving recreation of American pastoral created by survivors of earlier expeditions to Mars (none of whom has ever returned) trying to assuage some kind of 'psychotic' homesickness. This theory is blown away by the appearance of kin to all the crew, and none of the 'rocket men' questions the absurdity of the congregation of so many disparate kin in this one place. Even the captain, who meets his brother, is swept along by this desire to return to the past when he meets his parents and calls out like a child, 'Mom, dad!' as he reaches the steps of his old house. That night, lying in bed with his brother, the captain suddenly begins to rethink the events of the day, the theories about the town on Mars, and to wonder if there might not be another explanation. Perhaps the town is constructed by 'telepathy, hypnosis, memory, and imagination', using powerful childhood memories, by Martians who have constructed a trap. If the captain is right, the story has played an epistemological trick on the reader in parallel with this hallucinatory trap set by the aliens, by treating the sensory perceptions of the crew as if they were the same as the actuality. The captain's sudden disenchantment is followed immediately by his murder and the murders of all the other men by the inhabitants, but at this point the story does not completely ratify the captain's awful realisation by presenting the real Martians. The illusion ought to disappear, leaving the reader with a landscape of homophagous aliens, but instead the story's final paragraphs maintain the hallucinatory past and the band quite literally plays on, in the form of a brass band accompanying coffins and weeping kin to the cemetery. Only a hint of alien behind the mask peeks out, at moments when the face of the mayor, 'was sometimes looking like the mayor, sometimes looking like something else', but the horror is kept at bay, and at first reading the story's conclusion might appear to belong in a quite different type of narrative: 'the brass band, playing "Columbia, the Gem of the Ocean", marched and slammed back into town, and everyone took the day off'. We might have wandered into a story about the effects of the Second World War on small town America, except that if these figures are really Martian aliens, then presumably they took all the succeeding days off too, if taking the day off means no longer pretending to be a small town full of the childhood homes of the men from Earth. But why go on pretending once all the human explorers are dead? Only the reader cares about appearances now, and would surely like to see the unrepresentable made visible at last. It is the failure to do this that gives the story its great power.

This disquieting tale can be read as another narrative of the horror of the past with which we began this book – velociraptors hiding behind the clapboard waiting to consume the subject who tries to confront historical memory. Given that these Martians are themselves indigenous and the humans are aliens, the story could be taken to be expressing a guilty collective fear about the relation of European invaders to the North American indigenes projected out onto another planet, both to contain the unbearable horror of social memory, and to register the disturbances of ordinary time and space produced by this history. Like all such fables, its power derives from its multiple potential interpretations. The horror could also be explained in terms of the mass experience of immigration as aliens to America. History is potentially alien, just as America itself is, because American identity is always constructed and never given. All the Americans are aliens or recent descendants of aliens who emigrated to the New World, and aliens like them can keep on coming to the US from anywhere, move into its houses and then generate the appearance of real Americans using memory and imagination – and perhaps also those fantasy psychic powers that represent a degree of social control that would eliminate autonomy altogether: hypnosis and telepathy. The story might have been written to illustrate the trap that Adorno and Horkheimer, in *Dialectic of Enlightenment*, attribute to the Sirens: 'Even though the Sirens know all that has happened, they demand the future as the price of that knowledge, and the promise of the happy return is the deception with which the past ensnares the one who longs for it'.[8] Bradbury's Martians have recreated a past whose seductive power lies in the way it seems to promise that this time everyone will be united in one history capable of dispelling all alienness. The final paragraph's refusal to end the illusion that this is history we are witnessing, expects to elicit the American reader's own fantasies about the past. It entraps the reader in the plot, as if the hallucination were now drawing its material from the reader's own mind, just as it previously drew energy from the explorers, and doing this so effectively that the truly alien landscape is still not perceptible even though the protagonists are dead. Now it is the reader who is redeeming the past. But if the reader is now maintaining the illusion, isn't the reader like these murderous aliens, and also constructing the past out of memory and imagination, if not the hypnosis and telepathy of reading and intertextuality?

Although Niven's story is more typical of the genre, and the ontology of its spaceships, galactic travel, future civilisations and aliens seems stable, it too shares the sense that the future in science fiction is a space for fantasies of the past, both its terrors and the powerful wish to repossess it or redeem it. Both stories demonstrate that in science fiction, as Philip K. Dick said, 'the hardware is in the future, the scenery's in the future, but the situations are really from the past'.[9] They also show that narrative form is placed under strain by this displacement, making it necessary for interpretation to measure the fantasy distortions which result from the displacement of past into future.

In her recent study of national identity, *States of Fantasy* (1996), Jacqueline Rose argues that we should not think of fantasy as merely personal and, therefore, of limited interest to studies of social and political life. Instead, it might be helpful to replace the terms 'culture' and 'identity' with the more politically tangible 'states' and the more psychically complex 'fantasy', in order to trace these interrelations in the modern world. Fantasy is the binding agent of modern societies but also, she says, 'we should not forget, either, that fantasy's supreme characteristic is that of running ahead of itself ... something coerced and coercive, but also wild and unpredictable'.[10] Although her own analysis focuses on 'good' literature, this formulation could well be applied to science fiction's capability to act out contemporary fantasies of social power, justice and science in their full temporal and spatial extent, not least because of its collective practice. Wildness and the predictability of unpredictability are staples of the genre. Science fiction enables the fantasy that 'runs ahead of itself' to find a location in the future, and in doing so provides a space for narrative investigation and reflexive reading of this distantiation of fantasy. Critics of the badness of science fiction miss the degree to which these are cultural fantasies rather than authorial *accidie*, because as Rose argues, the assumption that 'fantasy is only a private matter is perhaps the supreme fantasy'.[11]

Although science fiction as a popular genre is usually traced back to the magazine editor Hugo Gernsback, and to particular antecedents like Jules Verne and H. G. Wells, as well as to a sporadic tradition of utopian fiction traceable back through Morris, Swift and More, its present-day character emerged after the Second World War. A shift to book publishing in the 1950s, a growing audience and a new confidence in the power of technology, co-existing with a fear for the future under the shadow of the atomic bomb, gave science fiction a renewed scope and emotional force. The roots of this can be seen in writing from the time of the Second World War, when the combination of temporal logic and wishful fantasy was especially closely tied to the tensions developing around the military appropriation of science, and the effects of secrecy on popular understanding of the future plans of the state. This is a good place to begin looking more closely at the implications of science fiction's colonisation of the future with problems from the past.

The future's relation to the present

There have been times this century when the present should have seemed too pressing for predictions about anything other than the immediate future to be relevant. In February 1943 Rommel's troops regrouped in Tunisia after a retreat from Egypt that had taken several months, and although Hitler's position in the Mediterranean was worsening, the outcome of the entire war was far from certain. Moreover, a new worry had surfaced among the allies: the Germans were believed to be developing an atomic bomb. Robert Oppenheimer, chosen to lead a secret project to develop a counter-weapon despite his former communist sympathies and consequent lack of security clearance, was travelling around America trying to persuade atomic physicists to join him in New Mexico, where they would have to live in an enclave surrounded by high barbed-wire fences, 'walled off where knowledge of their work was concerned not only from the world but even from each other'.[12] That same month, the latest issue of the London School of Economics journal *Economica* appeared from its temporary home in Cambridge with the second part of Friedrich von Hayek's essay 'Scientism and the study of society'.[13] Hayek is now best known as the right-wing guru of the free market, but he was then also interested in more high-altitude speculations about theories of social planning, and his theoretical argument in this essay could well seem at first sight irrelevant to the course of the war. Its opening sentence deplores the misuse of science by social theorists in a tone that sounds remarkably similar to Alan Sokal's recent denunciations, saying that the natural scientist sees the sociologists 'habitually commit all the mortal sins which he is most careful to avoid',[14] especially unjustifiable speculation about social action based on limited data. Despite the widespread belief that 'human history, which is the result of the interaction of innumerable human minds, must yet be subject to simple laws accessible to human minds'[15] an adequate 'science of society' does not exist, and cannot be based on analogies with scientific prediction based on natural laws. Such a science of history is not possible: 'The claim of these theories of history to be able to predict future developments was regarded as evidence of their pre-eminently scientific character'.[16] Hayek's reason for writing this at the height of the war then becomes clearer. Theories of history have helped create the ideological climate for the present war.

Just how this was supposed to happen he left unclear, but his associate Karl Popper was more explicit about this and the perils of futurology in an essay that began to appear the following year, the first version of his famous essay, 'The poverty of historicism'. Theorists of history may admit that the methodology of physics cannot be applied directly to societies, because historical change would render hopeless any such attempt to find laws indifferent to space and time, yet they still look for scientific laws that determine social practice, and so devise 'laws which *link up the different periods*' of the past in the hope of making 'large-scale forecasts' of the future.[17] 'Moral futurism' is, therefore, a treatment of the future that entails a manipulative, one might almost say, postmodern treatment of history. A misleading use of Darwinian theories of evolution for this fortune-telling only makes matters worse because the actual course of evolution is a singular, historical process. Popper draws the conservative conclusion that theories of history that purport to predict the future of social groups by scientific means not only fail to achieve their ends, their utopian social engineering justifies anti-libertarian regimes whose extremism has helped create the conditions for the world war.[18] 'Moral futurism' or 'moral modernism' is a dangerous misapplication of science that leads to anti-moral ends.[19] The Second World War has its roots in a war for the future encouraged by theorists who persuaded ideologues that society's future could be planned and fought for along objective, scientific lines. Futurism is dangerous.

The slow Allied advance against Hitler began to accelerate in July when the largest sea-borne invasion of the war began in Sicily, and slowly worked its way up through Italy. Oppenheimer was at last given security clearance, and General Groves supported his counter-intelligence aide, Colonel John Lansdale's, proposal that intelligence specialists join the expeditionary force with the aim of trying to find out more about just how far the Germans had proceeded with their supposed atomic bomb programme. So worried did they become that summer, that wild plans to bomb Heisenberg's laboratories in Berlin, or to target him specifically for assassination, were briefly touted.[20] In America, one of the less illustrious American 'pulp' magazines, *Fantastic Adventures*, presented a short speculative essay about war on the planet Venus.[21] Although this now sounds comically escapist at a time when war on Earth was so pressing that one of their regular contributors could no longer write his column because he had been posted to the naval yard in Florida, its context in a mixed genre magazine of war, fantasy and science fiction stories, with titles such as 'Caverns of time', 'Nazi, are you resting well?', and 'Other worlds', may have made it seem more reasonable at the time. War on Venus is allegedly inevitable since it is 'logical that civilization must have developed on this world almost along the same stage of development as ours', and the watery nature of the planet would have encouraged the evolution of two intelligent races, one humanoid and the other a race of sea-dwelling, amoeboid creatures, whose simultaneous territorial claims over scarce resources would lead to war. Most of the article describes incidents in the war between the brave humanoids in their boats and submarines, and the 'amoeba people' who 'fight "hand-to-hand" too, using their heavy, strong, octopus-like tentacles to strangle, and to drag helpless victims into the water, where the struggle becomes an unequal one in the favour of the amoeba'. An illustration on the back cover shows creatures that look like a pair of wings supporting one giant eye and hanging tentacles, holding deadly water guns. They hardly qualify as 'people', even 'amoeba people', but by the end of the essay a slippage has occurred, and it is hard to know whether this is really Venus or the site of the Mediterranean campaign when we read that 'submarine ships hold constant vigil'. Half a century later it is hard to see anything but the crudest displacement of the world war in such clumsiness. The concluding word – 'Yes, warfare on Venus is a grim business too' – is presumably supposed to reassure readers of the continuing importance of Venus and other science fictional worlds in their thoughts at this difficult moment in the war, when it still seemed possible that those earthly 'amoeboid people' in Germany and Japan might win the war. Weakly written as it is, the story is confident that it is doing more than simply affording temporary imaginative relief from the rigours of war. Its pulp author was part of a growing genre of writers who would share with their readers the belief that fictions of the future were of great relevance to the present. One of these was the writer Isaac Asimov, who began publishing his *Foundation* stories about the attempt to predict the course of future history and the consequences in 1942.

Philosophical argument about the claims of sociology to be a scientific theory of history, and whimsical speculations about inter-species conflict on another planet read like Adorno's 'torn halves' of modern culture. Although Hayek writes as if the future should be off limits to social theorists, and the pulp writers of science fiction spend most of their imaginative energy travelling there, both theorist and writers share the conviction that Western society projects futures of remarkable solidity from its progressive models of technology, science, politics and culture. Science fiction writers would probably have agreed with Hayek that 'the belief that human history, which is the result of the interaction of innumerable human minds, must yet be subject to simple laws accessible to human minds is now so widely held that few people are at all aware what an astonishing claim it really implies'.[22] For them, however, it was not so clear that misapprehensions of science were to blame for the belief that the future could be controlled, or that these possibilities should be so readily dismissed by theoretical argument. The politics of the future interested them, and they recognised that beliefs that the future could be comprehended were both a part of lived experience and deeply embedded in social and political practice. Even Popper could be excited by the 'progress of science' and sound momentarily the same note as the pulp journal, calling this future 'one of the greatest spiritual adventures that man has yet known'.[23] Most science fiction writers shared the sense of excitement at adventuring into the future with science, and many also shared his conviction that the study of futurist speculation could help us understand the ideological basis of the war, and so they would take the futurist fantasies of the collective imaginary, and the temporal logics of modernity, and shape them into narrative investigations of futurity. To do so they might have to report from a war on Venus, although in fully-fledged science fiction a protagonist with whom the reader can identify would get wet in the Venusian wars; and an argument that evolutionary theory predicts a parallel development of Venusian species would not be so vulnerable to direct logical or scientific refutation because its validity would depend largely upon its realisation as a 'thick description' of a world manifested in plot, action, and dialogue, and its textual memory of the future.

The convergence of philosophers and pulp writers occurs because modernity, especially the twentieth-century version, has been persistently concerned with what one thinker calls the 'colonisation of the future'.[24] Urban construction, technological development, financial markets, insurance and the legal system all attempt to secure the future for the present. Simon Critchley argues that deconstruction has shown that even modern 'democracy has a futural ... structure; it is always democracy to come'.[25] Science fiction emulates these strategies for appropriating the future, and in doing so, subjects them to the tests of extrapolative fantasy and analysis. Grossinger's 'colonization of the planets', which can mean anything from the terraforming of Venus to the growth of empires in the fictional galaxies of Asimov, LeGuin, Banks and Niven is endemic to science fiction. An example will show how this often works.

In Poul Anderson's story 'Turning point' (1963) – a thoughtful story about the discovery of a race of humanoids whose intelligence far outstrips that of existing human beings despite the pastoral simplicity of their lives – their discoverers are an advance party of a shadowy imperialism.[26] It is in part a redemptive fantasy in which a rerun of the encounter of Western society and indigenous peoples in America and the Pacific turns out differently than before; this time the achievements and potential of the native peoples are fully recognised and prized. There are darker sides to this, however. The story also covertly justifies that earlier colonisation of Western history by figuring these newly encountered, uncivilised peoples as a threat and, therefore, implying that those earlier encounters might have had some similar rationale driving their destructiveness.

In this gentler future all at first seems to go well. The mere act of contact sets in motion a rapid series of inventions in a culture that was previously static, whose hidden cognitive and cultural potential begins to emerge, much to the awe of the narrator, who sounds at first like a neutral guardian, an objective observer of events, until certain cues in the discourse of his report on the expedition give his ideology away: 'The star is catalogued AGC 4256836, a K2 dwarf in Cassiopeia. Our ship was making a standard preliminary survey of that region' (p. 67). Preliminary to what?, the reader might ask, receiving only hints about possible trade links and federal government control that can range from interdicts to genocide, if the debate between these explorers is a guide to their government's willingness to exterminate 'dangerous cultures'. This sea-going coastal culture poses a terrible threat to its discoverers only because its people possess an inherent intelligence far in excess of their discoverers, just waiting for a kickstart from outsiders. Now cultural development is accelerating fast, and once they have assimilated the new science and culture to which they are now being exposed, which they will obviously do with ease, they will be on the way to becoming 'superbeings'. This raises an ominous concern with race: 'the question is what race is going to dominate this arm of the galaxy?' (p. 77). Anderson's skilfully understated revelations about the imperialist principles of his heroes make their analysis of the dangers of future cultural confrontation sound like the rationalisations of all conquerors. If this newly discovered people is left alone, reason the explorers, the indigenes will constitute a force capable of making human beings feel completely inferior:

> how could they help but destroy our painfully built civilization? We'd scrap it ourselves, as the primitives of our old days had scrapped their own rich cultures in the overwhelming face of Western society. Our sons would laugh at our shoddy triumphs, go forth to join the high Jorillian adventure, and come back spirit-broken by failure, to build some feeble imitation of an alien way of life and fester in their hopelessness. (p. 77)

The explorers' solution is a version of the American melting pot – immediate complete assimilation into the immensities of galactic culture – a pot so large that the aliens will melt into it unnoticed and disperse their intelligence across the entire mixture of peoples before they can form an elite racial group with a distinctive technological culture equivalent to or greater than the existing one. The story works through the colonisation of America to arrive at a redemptive reinscription of history as a future – a potential remaining to be fulfilled in the present of the reader. These indigenes will be all right, their abilities will be recognised and the invaders will be justified in their destruction of the existing form of life they encountered. Most importantly, this pulp version of the eternal return reassuringly shows past and present continuing a colonising expansion of the future by the reader's assumed Western – perhaps just American – culture.

The development of science fiction since the 1920s has proceeded in parallel with modernism's qualitative change in cultural relations with the future. All societies have had to plan for the future, and some archaeologists argue that it was the emergence of art and language that made possible a social memory sufficiently durable to learn from history to manage the foresight necessary to shape the future with insights learned from the past. Anthony Giddens traces the beginnings of our futurism to the transition from hunting and gathering to agrarianism: 'The radical historicity associated with modernity depends upon modes of "insertion" into time and space unavailable to previous civilisations. "History", as the systematic appropriation of the past to help shape the future, received its first major stimulus with the early emergence of agrarian states, but the development of modern institutions gave it a fundamentally new impetus.'[27] Others give science a large role in these changes. Robert Heilbroner characterises the pre-scientific world as one in which the future was assumed to be certain to be similar to the past, because the same forces, outside human control, that created the past would continue into this future. 'There was therefore nothing to be expected of the world of social relations, of collective good and bad fortune, of the shape of things to come, other than what had been experienced before'.[28] Science, enlightenment and the growth of democracy awakened hopes for the future that no longer seemed utopian but achievable. Although, as he says, belief in progress is now tempered by anxiety and cynicism, it is still a pervasive cultural ideology. As we began writing this book, a new Microsoft programme, *Windows '95*, was launched with tremendous media hooha about whether or not this would be the 'future of computing', as if the operating system would somehow operate the future too. One speculative social thinker, Alvin Toffler, made his name by arguing that our society is now so engaged in incorporating the future to present-day policies and desires, that we needed to raise social awareness urgently by creating 'a heritage of the future ... a concentrated focus on the social and personal implications of the future, not merely on its technological characteristics'.[29] His practical proposal for helping develop the necessary ideas and practices to work constructively with the increasing futurity of everyday life was a somewhat utopian model of grassroots democracy, a new 'social future assembly' of representatives actively planning for the future, but he might have looked in a different place for the 'social future assembly' whose policy agenda would be the future, to the already existing cultural practice of science fiction. Its 'thinking machine' and spacetime for fantasy had already made a bid to be 'consultants on the future'.[30]

The traditional way to think of this role would be as utopian literature. In the short preface to a collection of science fiction short stories simply entitled, *All About the Future* (1955), the editor, Martin Greenberg, explained that this was the fifth anthology in a series, each of which was devoted to different major themes in science fiction. It is easy to see why the future had to wait; earlier volumes collected stories about prominent themes such as 'space travel, the history of mankind, life on other worlds and the history of the robot', all of which are evident in the excerpts with which we began.[31] It is not even clear that the future can be called a theme at all. Although he offers the succinct characterisation of science fiction as a novel combination of 'imagination with realism and logic', this is clearly too general to be adequate, so he reaches for the category of utopian fiction. The future is Utopia, a world into which writers and readers project 'dreams and hopes and aspirations' for a better future. There are, however, at least two reasons why this categorisation is misleading as a description of the future in science fiction, as Kim Stanley Robinson's novel *Pacific Edge* (1990) cleverly shows. The mainstream practice of the genre has been neither as utopian nor as idealistic as Greenberg appears to suggest; Robinson demonstrates this with the metafictional narrative of a writer who explicitly wants to create a fictional utopia to inspire his contemporaries to revolutionary action, a traditional justification for the utopian vision. As we begin reading *Pacific Edge*, none of this is evident, because it is one of those narratives which reads like a literary version of an optical illusion. We think we are reading a novel about a group of ecological progressives living a laid-back Californian life, about a hundred years from now, until near the end of the novel we realise that this is a mistake, and that the novel we have been reading is only a novel, a utopian fantasy about a world that does not exist, the invention of an author living in a totalitarian America terrified by AIDS, trying to justify writing this text during a time of worldwide environmental disasters, who has been rounded up and incarcerated in a concentration camp for suspected disease carriers, and only just managed to arrange his release. Eventually he offers this conclusion: 'if someday the whole world reaches utopia, then that dream California will become a precursor, a sign of things to come, and my childhood is redeemed.'[32]

The explicit fictionality of this futurist narrative of Californian Greens is a reminder that the utopian novel is located nowhere, and the persistence of personal and social problems in this world makes plain that happiness and social harmony are seemingly also unrepresentable. This is made very evident by the ending; its protagonist feels that he is 'the unhappiest person in the whole world' after he loses both the woman he loves and an environmental campaign he has organised, although he can still laugh at his own self-dramatising and self-pity. The mild irony of this closure – a would-be utopian novel turns out to remain stubbornly dystopian – is an acknowledgement of the widespread belief that utopian thought is too likely to be a dreamy distraction from the constraints of present-day social capacities, especially to hard-headed social thinkers. Even Greenberg, in his editorial essay, is keen to disclaim any optimistic idealisation characteristic of utopian fiction. His description suggests that he doesn't want his futural topos to be a non-location; he has chosen stories which look at 'the problems that may face us in the future'. Not only will the future not be idealised, it will be related temporally to the present, unlike a Utopia, since the same collective readership, the 'us', is imagined to continue from present to future. The future will be carefully tied to our present by the extrapolated chronology of a future history that prevents the science fictional narrative from floating away into pure fantasy that could never be realised. But Robinson doesn't entirely dismiss his writer-protagonist's ambition to write a Utopia either (and he has gone on to write a series of novels about the settlement and terraforming of Mars that explore the conditions for the creation of a just society in detail). Utopian visions can be a recognition that transformations of existing resources, ideas, technologies and even desires may be possible. Sometimes time does not move forward without disjunction. This is the basis of Seyla Benhabib's argument that utopias can offer a necessary 'politics of transfiguration' which 'emphasizes the emergence of qualitatively new needs, social relations, and modes of association, which burst open the utopian potential within the old'.[33] They are discontinuous with the forces, desires and identities at work in the present and, therefore, indicate not possibilities latent in present-day social arrangements, but transformations to which we might aspire. They cannot be simple extrapolations of the present. Robinson's complex narrative represents the complexity of science fiction's relation to the present and past; it is not just utopian – it retains the space for Benhabib's politics of transfiguration. The fictional author's dream of redeeming either the personal or the historical past, requires more than the utopian novel alone can achieve, because the futural relation with the present also signifies the constraints of possibility which need to be recognised.

What then is the logic of this futural topos if it is not primarily u-topic? When Philip Dick defines paradigmatic science fiction like that in the earlier examples, he avoids setting it in the future only by introducing a more generalised concept of extrapolation from the present. The world in a science fiction story 'is a society that does not in fact exist, but is predicated on our known society; that is, our known society acts as a jumping off point for it; the society advances out of our own in some way, perhaps orthogonally, as with the alternative world story or novel'. Dick himself was a brilliant practitioner of orthogonal fiction in novels like *The Man in the High Castle* (1962), but by far the greatest part of science fiction is not 'orthogonal', and simply jumps off into the future where what Dick calls its 'conceptual dislocation' can be plausibly and realistically narrated. The future is, therefore, a space in which both continuity and transfigurative discontinuity are imbricated. Only in the future can Asimov set a 'foundation' of scientists who use scientific methods to predict the course of history, or LeGuin show how mythic thinking might co-exist with advanced science, or Banks imagine a machine capable of sustaining an entire culture in space. When the writer Pamela Sargent explained that her move from science fiction into historical fiction should not surprise readers, because both genres have much in common, she cited Robinson as an explanation of the affinity of the genres. Robinson believes that historical extrapolation is the very basis of the genre:

> Science fiction is an historical literature. In fact this historicity defines the genre. The simplest way to say this is, 'Science fiction stories are set in the future.' Unpack this statement and we get something like the following: 'In every [science fiction] narrative, there is an explicit or implicit fictional *history* that connects the period depicted to our present moment.' The reader assumes that, starting from our present, a sequence of events will lead us to the 'present' described in the narrative.[34]

Some writers even proclaim themselves future historians. In his introduction to *Tales of Known Space*, Larry Niven proudly announces that his 'Known Space series now spans a thousand years of future history, with data on conditions up to a billion and a half years in the past' and reaches outward from 'a bubble sixty light-years across' of space controlled by humans.[35] Niven's mild irony suggests that he is not intending readers to take this too seriously (although he offers a 'timeline for Known space', a diagram of where all his writings can be placed in a long chronology), but even critics occasionally treat science fiction as part of the wider genre of historical fiction. David Cowart makes large claims for it as the most comprehensive form of historical fiction, the category 'that contains all the others' because it can address 'those broader events in the human aggregate that constitute history' and show how they will develop.

The reason why science fiction can be considered as an effective mode of historical fiction is evident in Michel de Certeau's optimistic claim that 'literature is the theoretic discourse of the historical process'; literature is 'the analogue of that for which for a long time mathematics has been for the exact sciences: a "logical" discourse of history, the "fiction" which allows it to be thought'.[36] A futurist narrative could be an investigation of the relations between past, present and future in contemporary history. From Cowart's point of view, freedom from the demands of historical accuracy paradoxically makes it possible for writers of science fiction (although his canon is limited to literary novelists who borrow the conventions of the genre for 'literary' fiction) to concentrate entirely on showing historical forces at work without the limitations imposed by expectation that the novelist will accede to the actual irregularities of history whose contingencies always exceed the analytic patterns of hindsight. This claim is itself an extrapolation from George Lukács's idea that historical fiction offers 'not the concentrated essence of some particular trend, but, on the contrary, the way in which the trend arises, dies away etc. ... the novel aims at showing the various facets of a social trend'.[37] Lukács's description is particularly apt for the world that Asimov presents in his *Foundation* trilogy, where the novelist's insight has been taken over by an elite of scientists.

Utopian fiction makes too radical a break with the present to be able to represent its temporal dilemmas, but Cowart's model of futurist fiction goes too far in the other direction. He argues that 'the future recapitulates the past or satirically mirrors the present'. It is significant that the examples of fictions of the future which qualify as historical fiction in Cowart's eyes, are almost all literary rather than generic: *A Clockwork Orange*, *The Handmaid's Tale*, *Riddley Walker*. Only Walter M. Miller's *A Canticle for Leibowitz* (1960) would ordinarily be considered mainstream science fiction. It is simply not the case that science fiction generally recapitulates or mirrors the past, even though it certainly reworks elements from it; it is the distortion, the fantasy or working through of this material, which is most significant.

Like the past, this textual futurity has a logic dependent on contemporary beliefs about space, time and history and is, therefore, a part of the literary textual memory. Hans-Georg Gadamer argued in his study of historical consciousness and hermeneutics, *Truth and Method*, that 'when our historical consciousness places itself within historical horizons, this does not entail passing into alien worlds unconnected in any way with our own, but together they constitute the one great horizon that moves from within and, beyond the frontiers of the present, embraces the historical depths of our self-consciousness'.[38] Gadamer's metaphor of 'alien worlds' is intended to describe past worlds that ought not to be alien to a fully developed historical consciousness. Its echo of the science fictional scene of many fantastic adventures suggests that the projection of alien worlds in a vastly amplified narrative space sanctioned by the authority of astronomy and physics, might partially result from difficulties of projecting that collective historical consciousness into the past. The Gorgon's head of the past might be more safely viewed in the mirror of the future, but the aim of the inversion could still remain similar to that proposed by Gadamer, to overcome the sense of isolation in the present: 'There is no more an isolated horizon of the present than there are historical horizons. Understanding, rather, is always the fusion of these horizons which we imagine to exist by themselves'.[39] Science fiction can be described as an attempt to understand history by first making the horizons visible by the science fictional device of exaggerated scale of time and space, taking the whole galaxy or universe for space, and long millennia for time, and then fusing the horizons by imaginatively traversing them in the varied symbolic forms of aliens, spaceships, time travel, androids and hyperspace. Science fiction did believe it was necessary to go into alien worlds, and strove hard to connect them to our own. Its necessary fictiveness is a front for explorations of how the past persists and decays, how it influences the present and how it might be transformed. Stories about the future are, therefore, indices of the ways in which contemporary culture lives in time and history, because they act out fantasies of transforming and sometimes redeeming the past, as well as hopes of sustaining present conditions. Location in the future works not just at the obvious diegetic level we saw in our examples, but as a torque on the entire narrative, on its reader-relations and processes of signification. We might paraphrase Iain Banks and say that only the outer envelope is in the real space of the future, and the rest – all the thinking parts, anyway – stay in the past of forgotten tales and millennial ruins. The challenge is to find them without losing sight of this futural translation's transfiguration of the past, and the desires which are projected through it.

Although science fiction strives hard to retain this connection between present and future, it creates a temporal logic that threatens what Hayek and Popper feared: a loss of freedom to a deterministic vision. Looking again at Poul Anderson's story we can begin to see how this might happen. Our discussion focused primarily on its extrapolation of our history of colonialism into a future where a redemptive fantasy about past genocide could work through some of the emotional and cognitive issues that still require public mourning and reparation. But this narrative is set in our future and is, therefore, the outcome of our world's actions and plans. This, the logic of the story implies, is our future we are reading about. Unfortunately this also forecloses on the future because the openness of futurity to the unexpected and unplanned is lost, and the paradoxical result is closure and consequent loss of the freedom that we ordinarily associate with the indeterminate domain of futurity. Yet the story does not read as an obvious closure of all unexpectedness; the explorers did not know what they would find when they landed on the planet, and nor do they ever know within the time-frame of the story what the outcome of their decisions about the Jorillians will be. Two visions of the future are in tension with one another, each having its roots in different modern ways of conceiving temporality. The very act of depicting this future world as our future threatens to destroy the freedom of the present (in which the reader is situated) to become anything else, while the unfolding action of the narrative retains a sense of the future as unrevealed potential in the adventures of its protagonists.

Governing the future: Isaac Asimov's *Foundation* Trilogy

At the same time that *Fantastic Adventures* was fighting wars on Venus, and Hayek was demanding that ideologues give back the future, a young physicist, Isaac Asimov, was writing the first of a series of stories which depicted a future society in which historical change is not only scientifically predicted, but secretly controlled by a powerful hidden elite of scientists. Begun in 1942 and finished in 1950, the *Foundation* series of novels explored the consequences of the discovery of a mathematical theory of history in a fantasy that, while obviously flattering to the scientists who felt that politicians had seized their inventions and exploited them for dangerous ends, also questioned both the temporality of science itself and the futurity of its chosen genre, science fiction.

The 'psychohistory' discovered by a mathematical genius called Hari Selden, enables an elite of experts to calculate the likelihood of future events to a very high degree of accuracy just by the statistical analysis of large numbers of people who are unaware their future is being assessed, and this makes it possible to manipulate the future. The ambiguities of this idea are deliberate. In one sense, no one has any less freedom than before, and all that the experts are doing is to work out the doings of the 'hidden hand' of society, the unintended consequences of a myriad actions. In another way, there is something dangerous about this knowledge which might give its possessors the power to control the path of history without the knowledge of those being governed. Such knowledge would run completely counter to the avowed principles of a democracy (although in the novel, Asimov is fairly unconcerned about the relative merits of different political systems), because it could be used to govern behind the back of the openly legitimate system of rule. These experts arrive at the conclusion that a 'foundation' of encyclopaedists settled on a planet at the margins of empire is the best way to safeguard knowledge against the collapse of this already decaying galactic empire, and ensure that instead of many millennia of barbarism, a better federation of worlds is created within at most a single millennium (even at this stage the novel could be read as a metafictional account of the establishment of Broderick's encyclopaedic mega-text of science fiction). Echoes of the Manhattan Project's isolation of some of the finest scientists of their time on the margins of America in New Mexico are easy to recognise. From the beginning of the novel, Asimov introduces the idea of a division between the intellectuals who will form this first foundation of encylopaedists, and a more shadowy 'second' foundation of scientists or 'psychohistorians' – successful clairvoyants who appear to have disproved Popper because they can predict and, therefore, shape the future, and have no ethical reservations about their intention to administer this experiment with history for centuries to come.

A number of science fiction authors besides Asimov, notably the influential editor of *Astounding Science Fiction*, John W. Campbell, knew at first-hand the grand historical syntheses of Arnold Toynbee and Oswald Spengler, but similar ideas and speculations about history and the prediction of mass social behaviour were widely popularised in the 1930s and 1940s.[40] This was one reason why Hayek and Popper believed it was so important to argue that 'it is impossible for us to predict the future course of history'.[41] It was imperative to persuade social theorists and politicians that attempts like Marx's or Hari Selden's to predict the future course of history are delusions; they have failed in the past and will continue to fail. Unfortunately such pseudo-scientists have 'misled scores of intelligent people into believing that historical prophecy is the scientific way of approaching social problems'[42] and still threaten to undermine the only desirable form of society, a society of individuals who are able to make decisions for themselves. Yet Selden's theory sounds plausible. It is a highly mathematical theory 'which deals with the reactions of human conglomerates to fixed social and economic stimuli', and only works for an extremely large population which needs to be 'unaware of psychohistoric analysis in order that its reactions be truly random'.[43] One clue to the narrative deceptions that create this plausibility, is Asimov's presentation of this calculus of futurity as the direct manifestation through symbols of historical events which need no further discursive interpretation. When Selden demonstrates the power of mathematics to predict the fate of a vast galactic empire to a novice on a pocket computer, he displays a series of equations which correspond to the current social order ('the known probability of Imperial assassination, vice-regal revolt, the contemporary recurrence of periods of economic depression, the declining rate of planetary explorations ...' (p. 381)), and shows that they can be extrapolated into the future to the point where he can point to a row of symbols and say that they represent the capital world in five hundred years time. This is a clever merger of two meanings of symbol. On the one hand, these symbols are like more condensed versions of the words of the narrative, but on the other, they represent mathematical laws which are independent of the governing conditions of narrative because they are timeless: imperial assassinations like gravitational forces, produce certain measurable effects which are always the same if the initial conditions are the same. Selden's psychohistory is a fantasy in which the two times of modern science – the timelessness of laws and the history of discovery – are magically merged into one. That the result should be the elimination of social freedom is highly significant.

Popper's more detailed explanation of his resistance to such theories reveals that he, too, values autonomy but locates it in the uncontrolled future history of science, which necessarily unfolds unpredictably into the future. History, according to Popper, is not therefore shaped simply by the unintended actions of all those individuals who can be treated as a statistical mass by the psychohistorians; history is shaped by 'the growth of human knowledge' based on science. A Selden plan of the 'future growth of our scientific knowledge' would be impossible because it would entail a paradox'.[44] Scientific knowledge and its accompanying technology would have to be able to conceptualise the future using only the methods of the present, and not the benefits of future scientific discoveries which will form the knowledge and technology that in turn shape future history. We shall see in a moment that this is not quite what happens in Asimov's novel, but first we shall look at an odd hybrid text, neither quite science nor quite fiction, yet combining some elements of both, where the extrapolation of the future is so complete that it demonstrates exactly what Popper fears. It also demonstrates why science fiction retains the utopian, transfigurative element of surprise.

The science fiction novelist Brian Stableford collaborated with David Langford, to write a future 'history of the world: AD 2000–3000', entitled *The Third Millennium*, as if written from the stance of a fourth millennium historian looking back across the achievements of the third millennium to our own time.[45] Although it is obviously fiction, it has no plot, characters or dramatised scenes, just a measured assessment of changes in technology, social planning and cultural aspirations, and none of the quasi-Hegelian spiritual autobiography of mankind that typifies one of its principal inspirations, Olaf Stapledon's founding science fiction text, *Last and First Men* (1930).[46] The main trace of this influence is their explicit reference to the key narrative resource, the backward gaze, which also opens Stapleford's future history:

> When people look back over the last thousand years (AD 2000–3000), the first reaction is always, 'What enormous changes!' ... In recalling these past times, we must remember that we are the heirs not only of our parents, grandparents and the many generations of our individual bloodlines, but of *all* the men and women who lived and died in those turbulent years. Nothing that has ever happened in the past is irrelevant ... We believe that if the people of the twentieth century could glimpse this record of what happened to the world they bequeathed to their descendants, they too could feel proud of it, despite its moments of tragedy. (p. 8)

The Third Millennium is based on the idea of the present as the matrix of the future: 'The achievements of the third millennium were built upon foundations laid by them, just as their own achievements were founded in those of earlier generations' (p. 8). Its authors apparently share

Selden's (and Alvin Toffler's) view that we do need to know how to predict the future and go so far as to say that the people of the twentieth century 'could not know the future, and their ignorance provided perfectly rational grounds for their fears' (p. 212). These writers see none of the dangers of prophecy diagnosed by Hayek and Popper. The book's willingness to treat the present as the matrix of the future becomes a beguiling fantasy of cultural immortality because all the developments of technology and politics turn out to be based on an extrapolation of existing knowledge: 'we have unearthed no fundamental laws for many centuries, and this suggests that we have uncovered every secret of the universe that human perception can reach' (p. 212). The text is a vindication of the idea that the future is a recapitulation of the past, a curious and implausible assumption of historical stasis which is directly related to their handling of innovation.

There are obvious difficulties for the writer who tries to imagine new fundamental laws of science, so this might be no more than a strategy for keeping the imaginative demands of the narrative under control, but if this is the reason it would make the text even less interesting than it is. One would hope that there were more compelling reasons for presenting the future as a fulfilment of the present than mere expediency. The real reason for the problem stems from the relation between this imagined future history and existing science fiction. All the scientific and social developments that form the fabric of the narrative are derived from the 'encyclopaedia' of science fictional hardware, software and sociological predictions, which is already extant in our time as if the future history were being programmed by a Foundation like Asimov's. For example, its discussion of the development of a ramjet starliner that uses the conversion of interstellar hydrogen into pure energy in the years 2486 to 2512, knowingly refers to science fiction, using a tone that pastiches science writing:

> The extravagant claims of Coris, Eggar, Mazidi and Rune in the academic synthetape *On the Amelioration Of Mass Ratio Restrictions For Autonomous Space Vehicles* (2492) were chaffed as 'science fiction'. By the beginning of the twenty-sixth century, though, a second-stage funnel was operating near Earth, a demonstration model whose far-reaching electromagnetic 'fingers' provided another unexpected mass-source by trawling in a proportion of the thousand-odd tons of micrometeors which fall to Earth each day. (p. 172)

Despite the pretence of ironic contempt for science fiction, the idea for this drive comes directly from the ideas of several science fiction writers, notably Larry Niven's carefully described 'ramjet' space ship.[47] So too does the entire history, but this is not the same sort of derivation on which the genre as a whole depends. This is an attempt to write an explicit version of Grossinger's 'single tale' which the science fiction reader constructs out of the many different narrative versions of the future and its furnishings – the genre's 'Mega-text'. Instead of adding another variant to it, this hybrid speculation's claim to be a history places it altogether outside the generic universe of science fiction's future, because its future trumps all the others. It doesn't take place in the common generic futurity that shades off at the undiscernable edges into many other intertexts, because its initial premiss excludes participation. This text maps the totality of the future, leaving no moment in its extrapolated millennium unknown. Instead of a metonymic relation to its futurity that leaves most of the world to come in the dark, this leaves no areas unaccounted for and open to inference – no space for alternative futures. Inadvertently, this makes evident how closely bound to our contemporary world's projections of the future its vision really is; by contrast, the science fiction story's realist illusion of unfolding events has a provisionality that ensures that it can take place in the space of the genre's encyclopaedic futurity.

Stableford and Langford's future not only loses out on the futurity effect of the genre's intertextuality, it also lacks something which almost all other science fiction novels have and need: unpredictability. Its own scope for surprise has been terminated by its unwitting acceptance of determinism in the guise of extrapolation. The central difficulty for science fiction narratives is the implicit determinism of Philip Dick's idea that the science fictional world advances out of our own. The very act of extrapolating this future world threatens to destroy the freedom of the present in which the reader is reading the future to become anything else. In the words of the philosopher John McCumber, the future's unknowability 'structures all our cognition', because – in Emmanuel Levinas's words – the 'future is what is not grasped, what befalls us and lays hold of us'.[48] By creating a historically plausible world of the future, science fiction simultaneously denies futurity to the actual world of the present. As so often, Wittgenstein outlines the logical error of our everyday thought with epigrammatic precision: 'When we think of the world's future, we always mean the destination it will reach if it keeps going in the direction we can see it going now; it does not occur to us that its path is not a straight line but a curve, constantly changing direction'.[49] As the world curves away from such daily futures, they accumulate into a largely unrecorded history of futurisms, an immaterial but highly significant part of our social history. Science fiction seems to be caught in a bind. It represents the primordiality of the future in the constitution of the modern self, yet misrepresents it at the same time because it must inevitably deny the future's difference from all expectation by attempting to represent it.

Asimov's *Foundation* trilogy builds its plot from this dilemma. Popper's blunt announcement that the prediction of future history is impossible might seem to undercut Asimov's narrative premise completely, and in one sense it does. Selden's plan works only because there is no major change in scientific knowledge throughout the known cosmos during the centuries of the plan, a pre-requisite we have already encountered in *The Third Millennium*, although at least Asimov has a plausible excuse for this lack of progress. The social regression that follows the break-up of the empire makes it hard to hang on to even the existing science and technology. Since a narrative which followed a predicted course century after century, in which the planner of the future is proved right again and again, would be dull plotting, Asimov introduces a random historical factor capable of upsetting the entire plan. A genetic mutant who can control minds is not someone who could have been anticipated, because the plan relies on predicting the movements of social wholes, not individuals, and certainly not someone born with the singular, and extra-human, power to treat other minds as if they were machines with a control mechanism that could be altered to create any emotion the mutant wished to induce. This Hitlerian figure called the 'Mule' quickly invalidates all the predictions, apparently derailing the entire plan as far as the Foundation is concerned, by rapidly creating an empire of his own, run by people whose emotional loyalty he completely controls. The future is once again 'ungraspable', a domain of novelty, but seemingly at great cost. Is the only alternative to the determinism of the future, this endless repetition of the past, a boundless will to dominance?

At this point Asimov introduces an unexplained twist in the plot; indeed, we could say he cheats. His plot difficulties, however, are very revealing of the tensions at work in science fiction between the time of science and the time of history. How is this new dictator to be defeated? First he introduces the 'Second' Foundation of psychohistorians who have been secretly monitoring history to make sure it stays on the path towards Utopia. Advanced psychohistorical mathematics has apparently brought with it the surprising benefit of telepathic control of other minds to its users, so fortunately the galaxy does have people capable of resisting the mutant after all. The Second Foundation is, therefore, actually staffed with 'Mules', except that these men and women are capable of fathering and mothering the future (unlike the sterile man whose nickname is the object of some commentary), and have an ethics of history which at least makes them respect the desire of the mass of the population to live as if they are free to choose their own future, even if they are not. In the eventual psychic shoot-out between the psychic leader of the Second Foundation and this mutant threat to future history, the Mule loses and his mind is altered so that he will continue to rule an empire for a few more years before his weak, mutant's body brings early death to a man who is no longer a totalitarian, expansionist ruler. The odd thing about this new development in the plot is that it ought to destroy the entire logic of Asimov's 'psychohistory', since this elite can now enforce social development rather than waiting for the material forces of history to do it for them. The mathematics of psychohistory are now theoretically redundant, and everything we have seen supports the idea that they will not be able to resist tinkering with the minds of other leaders and perhaps even ordinary citizens who unknowingly stand in the way of their thousand-year plan. Asimov tries to circumvent reader disquiet in the final section of the trilogy, by launching the idea that a few intellectuals in the First Foundation now suspect 'infiltration' by the Second Foundation, and are appalled by the loss of free will resulting from secret mental manipulation. Eventually the Second Foundation allow a few token volunteers to be sacrificed and the First Foundation believes that it has won a great victory, making it 'absolute master of the Galaxy. No further barrier stood between themselves and the Second Empire – the final fulfilment of Seldon's plan'.[50] There is a whiff of the anti-communist paranoia of the late 1940s when this was written, when the fear that a fifth column was readying America for Soviet takeover took hold, but the main allusion is to the secrecy that surrounded the Manhattan Project.

The leader of the Second Foundation, Preem Palver, who achieves victory over the Hitlerian Mule is disguised at one point as an ordinary farmer, almost certainly a knowing joke about the alias of one of the key Los Alamos scientists, Enrico Fermi, who was known as Henry Farmer. The Manhattan Project, in the words of one somewhat uncritical history, 'represents, in the opinion of most engineers, scientists and industrialists ... the greatest single achievement of organized human effort in history', but it was a curious effort, requiring the largest sphere of secrecy in American history by far.[51] Over a short space of time it drew into itself nearly 150,000 people organised to keep information from each other let alone others (the scientists at Los Alamos were not even able to visit relatives), spent around $2 billion and became as large as the entire automobile industry.[52] All this was aimed at destroying what had seemed to be the very foundations of the material universe, the atom. Metaphysics apart, the project created major anxieties about its destructive potential. One scientific observer of the Trinity test was still worried that Fermi's prediction that a chain reaction might torch the world could after all be correct: 'We saw the whole sky flash with unbelievable brightness in spite of the very dark glasses we wore ... I believe that for a moment I thought the explosion might set fire to the atmosphere and thus finish the earth, even though I knew this was not possible'.[53] Richard Rhodes cites a fourth-grader in Hiroshima who asked the key question that troubles Asimov's novels: 'Those scientists who invented [the bomb] what did they think would happen if they dropped it?'.[54] What did happen was that the project continued on into the years after the war as a supposed safeguard against the Soviet Union, while also maintaining American military superiority, and the atomic bomb also radically altered everyone's view of the future by making it possible that there would be none. Robert Oppenheimer expressed it well: 'atomic weapons are a peril that affects everyone in the world'[55] and at worst the atomic bomb would be a 'weapon of genocide'.[56]

The double nature of the Second Foundation in Asimov's novel, governors of the future and defenders of freedom, clearly owes much to contemporary ambivalence about what the secret organisation of atomic bomb scientists had created. The self-cancelling nature of the Foundation as far as the plot is concerned, points to a much wider problem with both science fiction and social uses of scientific time. The dual time we encountered earlier in Stephen Hawking's account of modern physics, confronted the timelessness of the laws of the material world discovered by science with the time of discovery. This we recall was also why Popper believed that predicting the future was impossible. Scientific discovery cannot be predicted without creating a paradox. Such prediction would negate what science is. Yet science as a social discourse of time and, therefore, the future is a discourse of determination, prediction and law-governed behaviour, and Asimov's psychohistory is a narrative symbol of this. This is why Asimov has to introduce something as non-scientific as mind control, something new and unpredicted, and yet keep quiet about its radical challenge to the premiss of psychohistory. What he has introduced is a form of free action oriented towards the future, which counters the determinism of the endlessly extrapolating future, and which is, ironically, the ordinary staple of most science fiction novels, where individuals take on the might of the entire futural universe. It is only because Asimov has set up the framework of a planned future that all action is in danger of lacking both surprise and innovation.

To see what is at stake here, we need to look at one of the fullest accounts of this second kind of futurity in Martin Heidegger's *Being and Time*. 'Dasein', Heidegger's name for the 'being' of human beings, is a being for whom its very existence is a matter of concern, and so it constantly projects itself into the future. 'Anticipation makes Dasein *authentically* futural', although this anticipation is not a failure to live in the moment, but a necessary reflexivity, a 'coming towards itself'.[57] This is because Dasein can only have a past, or 'having been' in so far as it is futural: 'The character of "having been" arises from the future, and in such a way that the future which "has been" (or better, which "is in the process of having been") releases from itself the Present'.[58] Hubert Dreyfuss summarises this idea by saying that Dasein 'is thus *already in*, *ahead of itself*, and *amidst*'.[59] The reason this language seems so obscure is that Heidegger does not want to treat time as a thing, a substance, a process or, indeed, any kind of entity at all. As John McCumber explains it, Heidegger is attempting to free metaphysics from a longstanding Western belief that can be traced back to Aristotle and beyond, that all real things are somehow forms of substance, or *ousia*, and manifested by their 'presence'. Therefore, Heidegger insists that time is fundamentally non-present, or what he calls an 'ecstasis', deriving his usage from the word's etymology, which means outside oneself: 'temporality is the primordial "outside-of-itself" in and for itself'.[60] It is not a series of 'nows', a linear continuum of presents reaching back into the past and forwards into the future as the idea of extrapolation would imply. Stephen Mulhall suggests that it helps to think of Heidegger's time as both objective and subjective: 'world-time is more objective than anything we might come across within the world because it is the ecsta-tico-horizontal condition for the possibility of coming across entities in the world. And it is subjective in the sense that the ontological roots of its worldliness lie in the human way of being'.[61] There are three different temporal 'ekstases', related to what we ordinarily call future, present and past, but the future is the primary one, because of Dasein's finitude, its mortal future and Heidegger goes so far as to say that 'the primary meaning of existentiality is the future'.[62] He is aware that time extends beyond the individual life, but this does not mean that time is funda-mentally a backdrop to a single human existence. Jacqueline Rose said that fantasy runs ahead of itself, and this is precisely the characteristic which Heidegger attributes to Dasein, which is also 'constantly ahead of itself'.

This is not a theory of representations of the future – Heidegger is concerned to understand authentic being, not the nature of time itself – let alone science fiction, but it is helpful for grasping the tensions inter-nal to fiction narratives of a future that is somehow connected to our own. Psychohistory represents the failure to imagine the future as anything but a realisation of the possibilities of the present, that result from the absence of free initiative, or what the British author of *The Day of the Triffids*, John Wyndham, thought of as mere 'adventure'. He dismissed it as no more than a regrettable commercial necessity, saying that science fiction and the adventure story were linked accidentally only by the commodification of the genre:

> The best definition of the science-fiction story that I know is Mr Edmund Crispin's: that it 'is one which presupposes a technology, or an

effect of technology, or a disturbance in the natural order, such as humanity, up to the time of writing, has not in actual fact experienced'. The disposition of something like ninety per cent of science-fiction to use this definition only in conjunction with the adventure-narrative form of story is primarily an accident of commercial exploitation.[63]

But adventure is much more than this. Adventure is a narrative device that situates a subject in an unfolding universe of unexpected challenges to be met by the creativeness of action; adventure is simply another name for the futuralism of Dasein. Adventure is a form of action and action, as Hannah Arendt argued, is what makes human society possible, because it is not only the capacity for innovation and the bringing about of the 'unexpected' – even sometimes the 'infinitely improbable' – it is also the foundation of social memory: 'action, in so far as it engages in founding and preserving political freedom, creates the condition for remembrance, that is, for history'.[64] Narrative adventure manifests individuality in its account of the corresponding sensations and self-consciousness of the protagonist, whose antagonists represent the impersonal forces of the scientifically comprehended universe. The sometimes the gigantic heroism of a few individuals fighting against the galactic empire is easy to ridicule in novels like those of Asimov and Banks, but its principle is simply that of a Dasein whose ecstatic temporality enables it 'to break into space',[65] and like so much else in science fiction, a giantism of signification in order to convey the experiential impact of the extension of space and time in modernity. Yet the critics of space adventure are also right. Pure adventure is also unsatisfactory.

Science fiction's critics too readily blur the distinction between adventure and the spatio-temporal giantism of the genre. The improbably galactic heroism of a few individuals fighting against some vast space empire is a symbolic intensification of the disturbing experience of the expansive spatio-temporal pressures of modernity projected out into this accommodatingly large canvas. We can see how this blend of action adventure and spacetime dimensions works in a likeable novel that would be open to criticism from a Wyndham. *Star Bridge* (1955) by Jack Williamson and James E. Gunn[66] (described by the science fiction critic, Peter Nicholls, in his reference guide to science fiction, as 'no more than a competent space opera'[67]), is the story of a man who helps overthrow an empire of planets that is literally held together by tunnels of energy along which ships can travel at faster-than-light speeds, typifies the importance of these strong individual centres of consciousness for the genre. At the same time, narrative allows the reader to experience events as they unfold so that, although a story takes place in the future, at any point in the narrative the immediate future is usually unknown unless there has been some strategic narrative foreshadowing. Its effects depend on the continual disruption and restoration of equilibrium over time, organised by a process whose specific articulation and discursive resources are organised into genres.[68] The Western shows a discursive order articulated in terms of the law which is broken and then re-established by physical violence organised according to recognised codes. Melodrama shows the effect of heterosexual desire on such a social order. Wyndham's argument that classical science fiction is marked by the introduction of an anomaly – alien invasion, for example – into an ordered world can be reformulated: an ordered linear temporality of past, present and future – typified by scientific progress – is disrupted, and then restored on what is usually a wider scale.

Star Bridge opens like a Western with a rider on a buckskin pony nearing complete exhaustion, setting up the individual consciousness in a familiar mode. Suddenly, a shift of temporal frames within the diegetic field of the story confronts the reader with evidence of an initially inexplicable alien element: 'The rider was motionless, but his hard, gray eyes were busy. They swept the hot, cloudless blue sky. No tell-tale shimmer disclosed the presence of an Eron cruiser' (p. 8). The Western reasserts itself as the rider pushes on, but his destination is Sunport not Laredo, and his weapon is a 'unitron pistol' not a gun. These initial clues, easily spotted by an experienced reader of the genre, set up a tension between two possible times: the nineteenth-century frontier; and some so far unidentified future in which Eron cruisers, Sunport and unitron pistols are all explicable parts of the material culture. Only by the end of the novel will they and the other mysteries about this world be resolved, and in resolving them, a relation to the past will be established. In between times, plenty of thematic speculation and adventures in time and history will further increase the suspense and its staccato resolutions, and this will all be registered as an individual's experience. A particularly glaring example of the way this suturing of adventuring consciousness and the theoretical frameworks at the limit of what is plausible, occurs when Horn travels in a space suit but without a ship through one of the energy bridges. As he travels through the tube his thoughts are impressively metaphysical: 'He willed his mind to feel. At the end of eternity, he gave up ... Eternity. The Tube was timeless, too. Every instant was eternity' [ellipses in original] (p. 87). They are also, for knowing readers, intertextual. The phrase 'the end of eternity' was the title of a novel by Isaac Asimov published in book form that same year. The adventuring consciousness makes it possible to register the confrontation with the farthest limits of the laws of physics in narrative terms.

One reason that it is possible to find an analogy between self-appointed heroism and Dasein, may be that there is a certain degree of solipsistic arrogance about the way in which Dasein itself is conceived as a being for whom its being is an issue. What, we might ask, about *other* beings – are they not an issue also for it in a fundamental way, and if so, doesn't this alter what is meant by the future? One early criticism of Heidegger's account of time and the future made just this point. Levinas argued in a series of lectures given in 1946 and 1947, that the problem with Heidegger's analysis of time is that it treats temporality as entirely internal to the individual subject, and so obscures the social character of time. Because both the Other and time are 'ungraspable and unknowable', temporality really emerges not from a Dasein living in splendidly authentic isolation, but from its necessary relation to the Other. He concludes, therefore, that 'the other is the future'.[69] Unfortunately, he does not offer much in the way of elaboration of this arresting idea, although we can speculate that he would have said something along the lines of what Jean Luc-Nancy says about the community: if the other is the future, then the future is the condition for the sustaining and recreation of community and emancipatory politics – 'Existence, as the ontological condition of finite being, is time outside itself, the opening of a space of time in time, which is also the space of the "we", the space of community, which is open and "founded" by nothing other than this spacing of time'.[70] By making the future a world subject to the unexpectedness of adventure within a narrative that depends upon a community of readers whose relations to their own world are deviated through the text's backward gaze at their world, the past's generativity of new possibilities of community is restored.

The peculiar idea of a history of events that have been already preceded by their reception, which constitutes the backward gaze, makes this possible. Most of its fictions are written as if some narrator in the future has taken the trouble to remember the ancestors (perhaps in a grand act of filial piety) and talk back to us in our earlier, more primitive, ancestral era, offering histories of what has not yet occurred in our world. The future looks back at us and tries to reconstruct who we are from the few traces available. It has a spaciousness our time can never have, because it is the sum of our possibilities as well as actualities, and its purposes are free of the narrative trammels of arriving at the actualities of our time. But all this speaks of a terrible lack. Our time has something that the future can never have, the adventurous uncertainty that allows hope, planning, expectation and futurity or freedom. This future lacks a future and has only a past, which is why it can be so readily imagined telling its story to the past we are.

Asimov's novel, *The End of Eternity*, brilliantly captures these paradoxes. It explores the premise that an elite group of temporal scientists might decide to act as guardians of mankind's future and in doing so, inadvertently take upon themselves the power to destroy and create worlds by the use of time travel. An elite organisation of time travellers (their name, 'Eternals', shows how much they represent a secularisation of powers once assumed the sole province of gods) have mapped out future human history for about seventy thousand centuries, and used their time travel technology to carefully mould human culture, by making decisive interventions ('Reality Changes') which redirect the course of events into desirable channels. Changes can be drastic – people may disappear from one change to another, and the lives of others may be substantially altered. To do this work they have set up bases outside time in a location they call 'Eternity', and from there they intervene in human affairs in small ways that will have often massive consequences for the course of human history. They recruit their scientists from the world of ordinary time, in a manner which owes a lot to the recruitment practices of the large corporations of the early 1950s. Throughout the early 1950s the large aircraft and electronics corporations – Lockheed, Boeing, Douglas, Hughes, RCA and Bell – were all recruiting engineers with promises that they would join elite teams of scientists. One could become a 'Boeing man' or join Pratt & Whitney who announced that 'an aircraft engine powered by nuclear energy will, in the not-too-distant future, be a reality' and said that 'the development of such an engine offers a challenge to men in all branches of science'.[71] The inaccuracy of this seductive prophecy is a reminder of just how much the future was manipulated by the great corporations who treated it as their business to project and shape the future.

We share the consciousness of one Eternal, Andrew Harlan, as he enters a moment in the 2456th century which has been closely observed in advance, wearing a 'wrist-borne field generator so that he was surrounded by an aura of physiotime' (p. 59) and by moving a container from one shelf to another creates such far-reaching consequences in the future of this moment, that a camera image of the landing field for spaceships in the 2481st century suddenly looks quite different: 'a change had ... blasted the space-port'. To the inhabitants of history no subjective alteration will be noticed, and they will imagine that one rusty spaceship was all that ever stood there. As the story unfolds it becomes clear that these authors of human history are trying to apply general ethical principles to the shaping of history, trying especially hard to prevent wars and slave societies developing, even if at the cost of innovation and expansion. Asimov manages to give his idealistic secret rulers and their technology considerable plausibility by keeping silent about some aspects of the organisation (we are never told where the stations for each century are physically located), and using judicious pseudo-scientific explanations, like the idea that interventions into the universe of temporal change are felt for only a limited number of centuries before they gradually die away, as if future history has an in-built inertia that resists runaway change. Eternity is in a condition of static time and so represents a particularly effective narrative image of the ideal of scientific invariance that has been integral to both the natural and social sciences. The constant 'Reality Changes' correspond to the history of scientific facts: scientific method constantly revises its models and theories over time so that the reality of the timeless will also change even if it does not contain the capacity for the temporal change-ability of history within itself. Eternity is an institution based on time travel for reasons that are made clear by Greenhouse's summary of why modern institutions depend on temporal discourses: 'institutional attempts to mobilize the relationship between time and eternity or (to put it in modern secular terms) history and principle involve basic cultural connections among the state, law, sovereignty, the individual, textuality and the sacred'.[72] By writing about time and eternity, and not history and principle, Asimov is able to hint at the underlying theology of time at work in this state appropriation of science. These scientist-guardians of the ethics of history have arrogated all social agency to themselves, making the state synonymous with theological eternity and, therefore, their ethical idealism undermines itself: they deny freedom of action to the people on whose behalf they work with time. It is in the light of this that we should hear Harlan's final damning judgement on Eternity as 'a sink of deepening psychoses, writhing pit of abnormal motivation, a mass of desperate lives torn brutally out of context' (pp. 188–9) (almost certainly a judgement on the effects of the bomb on the community of scientists at Los Alamos).

Eternity is the result of a time loop set up by a man the Eternals sent into the past in the first place, and this provides the opportunity to over-throw its power by turning its own methods against it. Harlan and his lover from the far future, Noys Lambent, who has been sent back secretly from the future to destroy Eternity's empire, are returned to the America of our era, that familiar ground zero of the past, to inaugurate the loop, but once they are there she persuades him to pull the plug on Eternity. Instead of transmitting the time-machine technology to this world of irreversible time, they end up living there permanently, and abandon time travel, in order to create a new reality in which Eternity itself does not exist. At this point the plot could have halted, but a further interference in history proves too tempting to resist. His lover then proposes to initiate a further historical change by sending a letter to Italy to encourage a physicist to 'begin experimenting with the neutronic bombardment of uranium' (p. 187), which she says will accelerate the development of the atomic bomb a millennium earlier than had happened in Harlan's world. This in turn will almost certainly lead to 'a galactic empire', although somewhat alarmingly she admits that there is a risk of the Earth ending up as a radioactive hulk that even her skills as a person from the far future cannot eliminate. This complex involution of time schema and loops means that our reality as readers turns out to be the end point, the future, of Eternity, and not, as we have assumed for most of the story, the 'primitive history' of its past. Our world is 'the end of eternity' where atomic energy, even the atomic bomb and the Cold War, are transformed into the first stages of a cosmic colonisation of the future by our culture. In this novel the 'future' really does turn out to lie in our past, and the perils of the Cold War are redeemed as the necessary preliminaries for a great imperialist future of free action.

This final reductive temporal equation of atomic energy and a fortunate future of galactic colonisation makes evident how powerful was the popular belief that science controlled the future. It also emphasises why this might attract fantasies of redemption. Asimov's novel would have been read against changing perceptions of the significance, value and legitimacy of the Manhattan Project by readers, who like the Eternals, might have wanted to alter the meaning of this history as its consequences emerged progressively over time. The suspension of moral responsibility by the Eternals in favour of scientific objectivity and an unanalysed appeal to vague ideals of human betterment copies the affectless functionalism of some government publications on nuclear history. Their lack of any ethics of history is shocking. In the *United States Department of Defense Report on The Effects of Nuclear Weapons,* for example, whose preface explains that it will help plan American defence against future attack, there are abundant photographs of Hiroshima and Nagasaki presented with captions such as: 'Figure 5.89b Multistory reinforced-concrete frame building showing the failure of columns and girders (0.36 mile from ground zero at Nagasaki)'.[73] No people appear in the photographs; the images are presented as if they were merely useful evidence gained by neutral experiments to measure nuclear bomb damage in order to assess the vulnerability of American architecture against possible future attack. Readers becoming aware of this abnegation of any ethics of history might be looking for consolatory fictions like Asimov's. Perhaps the atomic settlement of the Cold War had ensured a long-term perpetuation of our culture. Noys's claim that the letter to Fermi will be the last 'Minimum Necessary Change' of reality, supposedly leaves us in a world where scientific discovery goes on without any interfering prophetic manipulation, and the autonomy of science represents the possibility of living in a temporality that is not controlled by the past as Popper claims. The 'Reality Change' instigated by her letter could, however, be interpreted in a more sinister way. Is it not a reminder that this entire new future and its atomic physics of time and space has been determined by a shadowy force from the far future, creating some other even more extensive time loop, and hiding even more successfully the extent of the control over people's autonomy?

Gary Saul Morson's study of Russian fiction and its attempts to find narrative strategies to convey the ordinary experience of 'open temporality', or the sense that the future is not fully determined, offers a means of resisting the Medusan stare of the backward gaze of Stableford and Langford, and understanding further why the well-intentioned meddling of Asimov's time-travellers erases freedom.[74] Morson suggests that one means of avoiding 'chronocentrism' or the Whig approach to history, would be to imagine alternative histories, and engage in dialogue with them about our values: 'If some contingent historical event had turned out differently, if some invention we take for granted had not yet been made, what might the world look like now?'.[75] In particular, he says we might try and imagine how the future would see us. If, he asks, 'our successors should forgo chronocentrism and engage in open-ended dialogue with us, what might we learn about ourselves from this experience?'.[76] Eternity never does this; only the mysterious figure from the far future enters into such a conversation with a sense of 'open temporality' to maintain the freedom of the present in relation to the future – represented by her willingness to set a new world in motion and then let it develop. This is what was missing in Stableford and Langford. In most science fiction, including Asimov's, the colonising extrapolation of the present is also the opportunity to present an alternative history as action, and it is this, coupled with the stance of backward-looking dialogue, that offers an open temporality. This is an unstable combination, and one reason why the genre lends itself to narratives of grand attempts to control history and time, like Asimov's *Foundation* trilogy and *The End of Eternity* or *Star Bridge*.

The backward gaze is the work of a redemptive imagination. At best it is not, to use Seyla Benhabib's words for utopian thinking, 'a mere beyond' but the 'negation of the existent in the name of a future that bursts open the possibilities of the present'.[77] At its worst, as Peter Osborne describes some Hegelian thought, it denies the loss of the past altogether: 'the speculative projection of the future, as the basis for a totalized knowledge of past and present through which that future might be reached, acts as a form of redemption that obliterates those historical events which are not gathered up by its totalizing gaze, while denying the moment of absolute otherness inherent in its temporal distance from those which are recalled'.[78] The future becomes an image of the possibility of redemption to frame the various attempts to comprehend the recent past, especially the way 'scientific progress' colludes with wartime atrocities, social planning, imperialism and cultural change. It explores the desire to find ways of living scientific time, which seems at once to promise utopian transformations previously the prerogative of progressive social movements, and to deny the possibility of subjective time altogether, by denying the historicality of the unique sensuous particularity of things in favour of their invariant, law-predicted qualities. Narrative adventure enables it to show the possibility of historical redemption as an endless struggle between subjectivity and the detemporalising effects of social uses of scientific methodology.

Notes

1 Philip K. Dick, 'Preface', *Beyond Lies the Wub. Vol. I. The Collected Stories of Philip K. Dick* (London: HarperCollins, [1987] 1995), p. 9.

2 Damien Broderick, *Reading by Starlight: Postmodern Science Fiction* (London and New York: Routledge, 1995), p. xiii.

3 Orson Scott Card, *How to Write Science Fiction and Fantasy* (Cincinnati, OH: Writers Digest Books, 1990), pp. 5, 14.

4 T. S. Shippey 'The cold war in science fiction, 1940-1960', in Patrick Parrinder (ed.), *Science Fiction: A Critical Guide* (London: Longman, 1979), p. 108.

5 Richard Grossinger, 'A review of science fiction', *Io*, 6 (summer 1969), 4–30, 13.

6 Brian W. Aldiss, *Billion Year Spree: The History of Science Fiction* (London: Weidenfeld and Nicolson, 1973), p. 245.

7 Larry Niven, 'There is a tide', *Tales From Known Space* (London: Macdonald, 1992). Ray Bradbury, 'The Third Expedition', *Martian Chronicles* (London: Flamingo, 1995).

8 T. W. Adorno and Max Horkheimer, *Dialectic of Enlightenment*, trans. John Cumming (London: Verso, 1986), p. 53.

9 Philip K. Dick, from an interview, *Second Variety. The Collected Stories of Philip K. Dick,* Vol. II. (London: HarperCollins, [1989] 1996), p. 13.

10 Jacqueline Rose, *States of Fantasy* (Oxford: Clarendon Press, 1996), pp. 14–15.

11 Ibid., p. 79.

12 Richard Rhodes, *The Making of the Atomic Bomb* (New York: Simon and Schuster, [1986] 1988), pp. 454–5.

13 F. A. von Hayek, 'Scientism and the study of society, Part II', *Economica*, New Series, vol. x, no. 37 (1943), pp. 34–63.

14 Ibid., p. 34.

15 Ibid., p. 58.

16 Ibid., p. 59.

17 Karl Popper, 'The poverty of historicism II: a criticism of historicist methods', *Economica*, New Series, vol. xi, no. 43 (1944), p. 99.

18 Ibid., p. 132.

19 Ibid., p. 103.

20 Thomas Powers, *Heisenberg's War: The Secret History of the German Bomb* (Harmondsworth: Penguin, [1993] 1994), pp. 250-7.

21 Morris J. Steele, 'Warriors of other worlds', *Fantastic Adventures*, vol. 5, no. 7 (July 1943), 208. *Fantastic Adventures* was published by William B. Ziff and B. G. Davis (Ziff-Davis), and at the time of this issue was edited by Raymond A. Palmer. It ran between 1939 and 1953. Time is a strong preoccupation. The cover

of this issue announces a short novel, 'Caverns of time', by a new writer, Carlos McCune. A substantial biography of the author tells the story of a young man studying chemistry and then medicine, forced by the depression to work in the oil fields and mines, and later as a bank messenger, while he works his way slowly through university. The story takes a hero very like its author back through time to the world of the three musketeers, where he builds an airplane and generally uses his twentieth-century know-how to good advantage before returning to the modern world via a mysterious cavern that acts as a time machine. The effect of the combination of extended biography and novel, especially given the recognisable elements from the author's own experience of geology, is to invite the reader to read the narrative of time travel into the past as a fantasy appropriate to this experience.

22 Hayek, 'Scientism and the study of society', p. 36.

23 Popper, 'The poverty of historicism', p. 119.

24 See Barbara Adam, *Time and Social Theory* (Cambridge: Polity Press, 1990), pp. 138–9.

25 Simon Critchley, *The Ethics of Deconstruction: Derrida and Levinas* (Oxford: Blackwell, 1992), p. 212.

26 Poul Anderson, 'Turning point', *Time and Stars* (London: Panther, [1964] 1966).

27 Anthony Giddens, *The Consequences of Modernity* (Cambridge: Polity Press, 1990), p. 21.

28 Robert Heilbroner, *Visions of the Future: The Distant Past, Yesterday, Today, Tomorrow* (New York: The New York Public Library and Oxford University Press, 1995), p. 112.

29 Alvin Toffler, *Future Shock* (London: Bodley Head, 1970), p. 375.

30 Ibid., pp. 423–4.

31 Martin Greenberg (ed.), *All About the Future* (New York: Gnome Press, 1955), p. 8.

32 Kim Stanley Robinson, *Pacific Edge* (New York: Tom Doherty Associates, 1990), p. 300.

33 Seyla Benhabib, *Critique, Norm, and Utopia: A Study of the Foundations of Critical Theory* (New York: Columbia University Press, 1986), p. 13.

34 Pamela Sargent, 'The historical novelist and history', *Para. Doxa*, vol. 1, no. 3 (1995), 363–74, 372.

35 Larry Niven, *Tales of Known Space* (London: Futura, [1975] 1992), p. xi.

36 Michel de Certeau, *Heterologies: Discourse on the Other*, trans. Brian Massumi (Minneapolis: University of Minnesota Press, 1986), p. 18.

37 George Lukács, *The Historical Novel*, trans. Hannah and Stanley Mitchell (London: Merlin Press, 1962), p. 140.

38 Hans-Georg Gadamer, *Truth and Method* (1965; London: Sheed and Ward, 1979), p. 271.

39 Ibid., p. 273.

40 An account of the interest in a historicist theory of social entropy in stories written for *Astounding Science Fiction* by Campbell, Robert Heinlein and A. E. Van Vogt, can be found in Albert I. Berger, 'Theories of history and social order in *Astounding Science Fiction*, 1934–1955', *Science Fiction Studies*, vol. 15 (1988), 12–33.

41 Karl R. Popper, *The Poverty of Historicism* (London: Routledge and Kegan Paul, [1957] 1960), p. ix.

42 Ibid., p. 82.

43 Isaac Asimov, *Foundation* (London: Panther, [1951] 1960), p. 16.

44 Popper, *The Poverty of Historicism*, pp. ix–x.

45 Brian Stableford and David Langford, *The Third Millennium: A History of the World AD 2000–3000* (London: Sidgwick and Jackson, 1985).

46 Olaf Stapledon, *Last and First Men: A Story of the Near and Far Future* (London: Methuen, [1930] 1934). The novel begins: 'This book has two authors, one contemporary with its readers, the other an inhabitant of an age which they would call the distant future. The brain that conceives and writes these sentences lives in the time of Einstein. Yet I, the true inspirer of this book, I who have begotten it upon that brain, I who influence that primitive being's conception, inhabit an age which, for Einstein, lies in the very remote future' (p. 1). Stapledon had trained as a philosopher, and there are many echoes of German Idealism in the novel.

47 See, for example, Larry Niven, *A World Out of Time* (London: Futura, [1976] 1977). In this novel the technology is called variously a 'Bussard ramjet' and a 'ramship'.

48 Emmanuel Levinas, *Time and the Other*, trans. Richard A. Cohen (Pittsburg: Duquesne University Press, 1987), p. 77.

49 Ludwig Wittgenstein, *Culture and Value*, ed. G. H. von Wright, in collaboration with Heikki Nyman; trans. Peter Winch, amended 2nd edn (Oxford: Basil Blackwell, 1980), p. 3e.

50 Isaac Asimov, *Second Foundation* (London: Panther, [1953] 1964), p. 182.

51 Stephane Groueff, *Manhattan Project: The Untold Story of the Making of the Atomic Bomb* (London: Collins, 1967), p. 5.

52 See, for example, John Newhouse, *The Nuclear Age: From Hiroshima to Star Wars* (London: Michael Joseph, 1989).

53 Emilio Segré, cited in Rhodes, *The Making of the Atomic Bomb*, p. 673.

54 Rhodes, *The Making of the Atomic Bomb*, p. 734.

55 Ibid., p. 762.

56 Powers, *Heisenberg's War*, p. 467.

57 Martin Heidegger, *Being and Time* (Oxford: Basil Blackwell, 1962), p. 373.

58 Ibid., p. 374.

59 Hubert L. Dreyfus, *Being-in-the-World: A Commentary on Heidegger's 'Being and Time', Division I* (Cambridge, MA: MIT Press, 1991), p. 244.

60 Heidegger, *Being and Time*, p. 377.

61 Stephen Mulhall, *Heidegger and Being and Time* (London: Routledge, 1996), pp. 188–9.

62 Heidegger, *Being and Time*, p. 376.

63 John Wyndham, *The Seeds of Time* (Harmondsworth: Penguin, 1959), p. 7.

64 Hannah Arendt, *The Human Condition* (Chicago: University of Chicago Press, 1958), pp. 8, 178.

65 Heidegger, *Being and Time*, p. 421.

66 Jack Williamson and James E. Gunn, *Star Bridge* (New York: Ace, 1955).

67 Peter Nicholls, 'Jack Williamson', *The Encyclopedia of Science Fiction* (1979; London: Granada, 1981), p. 657.

68 This summary is based largely on Steven Neale, *Genre* (London: BFI, 1980).

69 Emmanuel Levinas, *Time and the Other*, trans. Richard A. Cohen (Pittsburg: Duquesne University Press, 1987), p. 77.

70 Jean Luc-Nancy, 'Finite history', in David Carroll (ed.), *The States of 'Theory': History, Art, and Critical Discourse* (Stanford: Stanford University Press, 1990), pp. 149–74, 168.

71 Advertisement in *Scientific American*, vol. 186, no. 6 (June 1952), p. 63.

72 Carol Greenhouse, *A Moment's Notice* (Ithaca: Cornell University Press, 1996), p. 182.

73 Samuel Glasstone (ed.), *The Effects of Nuclear Weapons*, rev. edn (Washington DC: United States Atomic Energy Commission, 1962), p. 241.

74 Gary Saul Morson, *Narrative and Freedom: The Shadows of Time* (New Haven: Yale University Press, 1994), p. 47 *passim*.

75 Ibid., p. 281.

76 Ibid., p. 282.

77 Seyla Benhabib, *Critique, Norm and Utopia: A Study of the Foundations of Critical Theory* (New York: Columbia University Press, 1986), p. 353.

78 Peter Osborne, *The Politics of Time: Modernity and Avant-Garde* (London: Verso, 1995), p. 43.

CHAPTER 8

Fictional cities and urban spaces: contemporary fiction and representations of the city

> A whole history remains to be written about *spaces* – which would at the same time be the history of *powers* (both these terms in the plural) – from the great strategies of geopolitics to the little tactics of the habitat. (emphasis in original)
>
> Michel Foucault, *The Eye of Power*.[1]

The confrontation between power and littleness is nowhere more apparent than in New York. When you walk down Fifth Avenue in New York, one of the most imposing skyscrapers which confronts you is the Trump Tower, a stunning monument to the visual consumption that so commands contemporary urban 'landscape'. Its interplay between nature and artifice is a knowing commentary on the very idea of landscape: the trees reflected innumerably in all the glass panes at the different staged levels above the street, are complemented inside by a waterfall which dominates the main atrium, as people sit drinking coffee in an artificial Mediterranean environment. Trump Tower stages corporate social control of nature as a symbolic expression of the power of capital and in so doing, makes unusually visible (not least to the person walking by) the way modern cities are formed by their massive concentrations of material resources and financial wealth. What is not visible is its relation to history, and least of all the history of space.

Since Foucault wrote his invitation to historicise space, many historians and theorists have researched the history, politics and social memory of space, and some have been inspired or provoked by his compelling investigations into the history of judicial punishment, sexuality, power and discourse. But certain aspects of his work have turned out to present obstacles to this very goal of writing a history of space. The problem is evident in the way he used Jeremy Bentham's extraordinary plan for a new model prison, the 'Panopticon', as a prescient figure for the government of populations outside the prison system by the new nation-states of the West. The Panopticon enables the warders to see the inmates who cannot tell whether they are being observed or not, and this, according to Foucault, is supposed 'to induce in the inmate a state

of conscious and permanent visibility that assures the automatic functioning of power'.[2] Foucault's description of this as an 'architectural
apparatus' invites an obvious question about urban structures like Trump
Tower. Is such a skyscraper a form of Panopticon? Although Foucault
himself avoids literalising his interpretative exemplum, his theorising of
power and regulation relies heavily on images and metaphors belonging
to the built environment of urban modernity, with significant consequences for subsequent attempts to understand the social reality of the
city. He uses the Panopticon as both analogy and metaphor for an entire,
complex regulatory system employed by modern nation states, because
he believes the basic mechanism is 'indefinitely generalizable'.[3] This
panoptic mode of power has replaced or transformed earlier methods,
'linking them together, extending them and above all making it possible
to bring the effects of power to the most minute and distant elements' in
what is an 'infinitesimal distribution of power relations'.[4] Although
Foucault does not spell this out, this is also a theory and history of space,
because he is envisaging the massive extension of control over space, as
his images of linking and distribution imply. Since these are precisely the
terms used in contemporary discussions of urbanism and globalism to
discuss the growth of communications, material production and the
myriad services ranging from sewers to information technology on which
urban environments depend, Foucault's metaphorics of power as surveillance can appear to describe a condition of total control of the urban
world. Trump Tower rules the street. In his later work on sexuality, this
metaphorics becomes even more powerful:

> Here, too, my main concern will be to locate the forms of power, the
> channels it takes, and the discourses it permeates in order to reach the
> most tenuous and individual modes of behaviour, the paths that give it
> access to the rare or scarcely perceivable forms of desire, how it pene-
> trates and controls everyday pleasure – all this entailing effects that may
> be those of refusal, blockage, and invalidation, but also incitement and
> intensification: in short, the 'polymorphous techniques of power'.[5]

There is nothing short about this sentence as a whole though; its mimetic
enactment of the long reach of power subtly reinforces his overall claim
that even the most violent resistance is no more than a controlled explosion. Despite his supposedly radical revalorisation of power as 'a
normalizing rather than repressive force', its extension all the way from
the towers of power to the smallest habitats means that it is potentially
more dominating than ever.[6] 'Norm, knowledge, life, meaning, the disciplines, and regulations' are all implicated in late modern sexuality,
leaving little obvious space for escape.[7]

   Henri Lefebvre's study of the material history of modern urban
space, *The Production of Space* (1974), had already taken Foucault to task

for his constant use of spatial metaphors in his critiques of subjectivity and epistemology, especially in *The Archeology of Knowledge*. Lefebvre suspects him of using the term to give his work a materialist basis, and dismisses it as failing to link the conceptual analysis and the 'space of people who deal with material things'.[8] Foucault's later work may well have been attempting to respond to such criticisms when it investigated specific structures like the Panopticon and focused on the dealings with material space, but Foucault remained committed to the idea of a history of space, rather than a history in space, as Lefebvre demanded, and other later social theorists and historians would offer, as we shall see. The other difficulty Foucault placed in the way of the study of urban space, was his vision of total dominance. Michel de Certeau asked the obvious question in his characteristically mildly ironic tone: 'If it is true that the grid of "discipline" is everywhere becoming clearer and more extensive, it is all the more urgent to discover how an entire society resists being reduced to it'.[9] What is needed is an investigation not just of the practices by which power reaches every nook and cranny of the urban world, but also of the 'innumerable practices by means of which users reappropriate the space organized by techniques of sociocultural production'.[10] Maybe even walking past the Trump Tower might turn out to be a small means of eluding its control over the paths of desire.

Western culture has repressed the spatial dimensions of history and memory with the discourse of linear time (and even such revisions as Bergson's theory of duration have perpetuated this spatial amnesia). It has been able to do this because, as Lefebvre says: 'Time is distinguishable but not separable from space. ... Space and time thus appear and manifest themselves as different yet unseverable'.[11] He argues that even radical thought has lacked an adequate awareness of spatial history. Hegel temporalised knowledge by arguing the significance of history and historicity for conceptual thought, and thereafter Marx reinforced the importance of socio-economic time over space. 'Nothing and no-one can avoid *trial by space*', not even history: 'Historical formations flow into world-wide space much like rivers debouching into the ocean'.[12] Many recent geographers concur. Space has a history as much as time according to theorists like Edward Soja, Doreen Massey and Torsten Hagerstrand (who has developed a theory of spacetime paths with his colleagues[13]). 'The city is a device for measuring time', according to Don DeLillo's novel *Mao II* (1992), as if its spatial structures were elapsed units of time.[14] In *The Infernal Desire Machines of Doctor Hoffman* (1972), Doctor Hoffman's machinations with desire exert a pressure on the fabric of urban presence which symbolises the aspirations of the novel, as he besieges a whole set of assumptions and paradigms connecting the city to history, time, empirical rationality, certainty and foundational thinking:

> Consider the nature of the city. It is a vast repository of time, the discarded times of all men and women who have lived, worked, dreamed and died in the streets which grow like a wilfully organic thing, unfurl like the petals of a mired rose and yet lack evanescence so entirely that they preserve the past in haphazard layers, so this alley is old while the avenue which runs beside it is newly built but nevertheless has been built over the deep-down, dead-in-the-ground relics of the older, perhaps the original, huddle of alleys which germinated the entire quarter. Doctor Hoffman's gigantic set of generators sent out a series of seismic vibrations which made great cracks in the hitherto immutable surface of the time and space equation we had informally formulated in order to realise our city and, out of these cracks, well – nobody knew what would come next.[15]

Any 'recovery' of space and especially of repressed spatial consciousness will, therefore, also make possible the 'recovery' of alternative and repressed histories.

How can this recovery of space be done? Recent theorists offer two main ways of approaching the question. The first is to consider the post-modern condition itself. Joan Didion's novel *Play It As It Lays* (1970) offers a poignant image of this: 'For miles before she reached the Thriftimart she could see the big red T, a forty-foot cutout letter which seemed peculiarly illuminated against the harsh unclouded light of the afternoon sky'.[16] The poignancy of the image lies in its naive redundancy; as the postmodern architect Robert Venturi makes clear in *Learning From Las Vegas* (1972), the economy of signs has so permeated our world that the environment is all sign. Scott Lash and John Urry provide a wide-ranging summary of recent debates about the economy of the sign in their *Economies of Signs and Space* (1994). Their discussion of the significance of the development of an increasingly 'individuated and symbol-saturated' urban world, suggests how contemporary urban fiction might be going about the recovery of social space and its history. They link the growing importance of signs and information to Manuel Castells's argument that 'information is in most cases embodied or objectified reflexivity'.[17] Thomas Pynchon imagines this urban landscape at the end of *The Crying of Lot 49* (1966), where Oedipa Maas feels she is 'walking among matrices of a great digital computer, the zeroes and ones twinned above, hanging like balanced mobiles right and left, ahead, thick, maybe endless.'[18] Translated into the terms of our study, we could say that this circulating information is a form of social memory. Whereas Castells treats information as forming part of the goods and services of a consumer culture, Lash and Urry believe that this artificially divides information from material culture. All goods and services are now, as they express it, 'information-soaked' and, therefore, all the commodities in circulation are effectively readable as information as well as serving other purposes. A Trump Tower, a guidebook to New York, a taxi-ride or a Paul Auster novel, are all 'information-soaked'. These examples are also to varying degrees exemplary of another complementary feature of contemporary urban sites, their dependence on cultural capital. Lash and Urry propose, therefore, that instead of treating the city as information, we should think in terms of symbol: 'All information is so to speak carried in symbols, yet the notion of information captures only a tiny part of the multi-dimensionality of symbol. Information is too one-sidedly cognitive. The symbol also contains moral, affective, aesthetic, narrative and meaning dimensions'.[19] Literary history suggests that the concept of symbol may not be the best way of representing this merging of imagination, emotion and reason, but it does point both to the expansive capabilities of the novel (where the moral, affective, aesthetic, and narrative are dimensions of the text's meaning), and the need for a postmodern transformation of the constraints of traditional narrative.

Where does this information embed itself in space? Lash and Urry talk as if space were still just a neutral background for all this frenetic hermeneutics elicited by the circulation of reflexive cultural capital and materialised social memory. But space itself is part of this process; it too carries the multi-dimensionality of symbol. The difference between the 'real city' and the city of the imagination, the representational city, is increasingly falling away: as Jane Jacobs states, 'the boundary between social reality and representations of that reality have collapsed'.[20] Michel de Certeau and others, have suggested that we should use the term 'place' to describe spaces that are as much parts of the social imaginary as people and ideas. Places are loci of memory; reference points of narratives, propositions and emotions; signs of the passing of time and the histories that mark it. They can almost elude public culture altogether: 'Places are fragmentary and inward-turning histories, pasts that others are not allowed to read, accumulated times that can be unfolded but like stories held in reserve, remaining in an enigmatic state, symbolizations encysted in the pain or pleasure of the body'.[21] As the sociologist James Donald has forcefully written:

> the city designates the space produced by the interaction of historically and geographically specific institutions, social relations of production and reproduction, practices of government, forms and media of communication, and so forth. By calling this diversity 'the city', we ascribe to it a coherence or integrity. The city, then, is above all a representation. But what sort of representation? By analogy with the now familiar idea that the nation provides us with an 'imagined community', I would argue that the city constitutes an imagined environment. What is involved in that imagining – the discourses, symbols, metaphors and fantasies through which we ascribe meaning to the modern experience of urban living –

is as important a topic for the social sciences as the material determinants of the physical environment.[22]

Cities are 'storied cities',[23] and as a character in Don DeLillo's *Mao II* puts it, 'cities age and stain in the mind like Roman walls' (p. 39). Contemporary fiction shows that some of these histories can be turned outward, and the new culture of information and cultural capital which makes the material environment a towering social memory, creates a productive tension between the older forms of place and the new productions of information-soaked urbanism.

The novel has a special relationship with the city, because it offers a 'structure of feeling' adequate to our experiences of abstract space. This discourse of 'feeling', of personal response, of subjective mood in relation to city experience, is part of the transformative power of fictional representations, because it structures our spatial awareness through a concretisation of our everyday spatial consciousness. Reacting to modernist representations of the city, and the modernist constructions of the city – which stressed its rational formations, its rigid structures, its reflections of social control in the urban structures – post-Second World War fictional representations of the city like DeLillo's or Paul Auster's or Thomas Pynchon's (New York, Los Angeles and London have all inspired the latter), have sought out new ways of articulating urban space, and of situating subjectivity in relation to that urban space. Representational concepts have become lived forms that govern our grasp of urban space. Fiction is able to mobilise emergent metaphors and rhetorical forms which have not yet become established enough to register on sociological screens. Indeed, some recent social studies of urban space acknowledge this by using autobiographical and narrative representations of urban space in order to support their analyses. John Lechte, for example, in a description very similar to the strategies of the Situationists, finds explanatory powers in a description of a personal visit to the Arche de la Defense, and to the Parc de la Villette in Paris.[24] Physically walking through and experiencing the city and its structures appears closely tied to the analytical impulse: the physical experience and the cultural analysis are inseparable.

Fictional representations of the city can sometimes even reach into those spaces that other representations cannot reach. This is particularly evident in Jay McInerney's novel, *Brightness Falls* (1992), where the narrative gaze plunges beneath the towering façades to unearth a geology of capital:

> After nearly collapsing in bankruptcy during the seventies, their adoptive city had experienced a gold rush of sorts; prospecting with computers and telephones, financial miners had discovered fat veins of money

coursing beneath the cliffs and canyons of the southern tip of Manhattan. As geologic and meteorological forces conspire to deposit diamonds at the tip of one continent and to expose gold at the edge of another, so a variety of manmade conditions intersected more or less at the beginning of the new decade to create a newly rich class based in New York, with a radical new scale of financial well-being. The electronic buzz of fast money hummed beneath the wired streets, affecting all the inhabitants, making some of them crazy with lust and ambition, others angrily impoverished, and making the comfortable majority feel poorer.[25]

Brightness Falls, like McInerney's earlier novel *Bright Lights, Big City*, explores the economic, social and cultural edifices of the 'yuppie' explosion in the 1980s. In a city where most belong but none is an uncontested owner, McInerney exposes the social contradictions and disintegrated individualism of New York, where peoples' aspirations are literally embedded in the spires of Wall Street. The urban unconscious is structured like the city, and its inhabitants develop specific consciousnesses within it, attuned to the minutest social alterations, the smallest vicissitudes of quotidian spaces and the slight shifts in structured environments.

If, following Kevin Lynch's suggestion, one ought to think of the city as a syntax, then the space of the city, like that of the text, appears constantly in motion, never still enough to encompass, and too filled with 'other' spaces to be informatively described or cognitively grasped.[26] Urban space is not simply a Cartesian set of co-ordinates for the natural container of everyday life, but something far more constitutive of the discourse and action that comprise that life. Italo Calvino's *Invisible Cities* (1974) wittily demonstrates how cities resist totalisation at every turn; postmodern cities are always messier and more diverse than the orderly images of realist narratives. City and narrative text construct labyrinthine twists and turns in their attempts to hold onto their representation of each other's elusive ontology. Wittgenstein uses the maze-like complexity of the city as a metaphor of language's historically sedimented density: 'Our language can be seen as an ancient city: a maze of little streets and squares, of old and new houses, and of houses with additions from various periods; and this surrounded by a multitude of new boroughs with straight regular streets and uniform houses.'[27] The city can be read as a text not least because the city is in the text. Always a site of conflict, ideologically as well as out on the streets, the city is a site where representation conflicts with itself, because the city is 'always *aporetic*, a "crisis-object" which destabilizes our certainty about the real.'[28] Any attempt at 'cognitive mapping' on the lines proposed by Fredric Jameson, must also attend to those 'nooks and crannies' in our spatial practices that are so clearly elucidated and uncovered in the work of Lefebvre and Michel de Certeau (and as so often, the highly suggestive anticipations of this in the work of Walter Benjamin).

Feminist cultural theorists have also brought out the implications of rethinking space for the treatment of the body, and this too has implications for contemporary urban fiction. Kristin Ross reminds us in *The Emergence of Social Space* (1988), her study of the way Parisian space was organised, demarcated and controlled during the mid-nineteenth century, that 'while words like "historical" and "political" convey a dynamic of intentionality, vitality, and human motivation, "spatial", on the other hand, connotes stasis, neutrality, and passivity'.[29] She also finds a clear hierarchy of gender associations at work in the priority accorded to temporality here. Doreen Massey develops similar ideas in her study of late twentieth-century urbanism, *Space, Place and Gender* (1994). Spaces are not forms of passive, static Being, because when they are experienced as place and locality they 'are about the intersection of social activities and social relations and, crucially, activities and relations which are necessarily, by definition, dynamic, changing. There is no stable moment, in the sense of stasis, if we *define* our world, or our localities, *ab initio* in terms of change'.[30] The association of place and identity is reactionary because it mistakenly assumes that identity is only associated with place; 'individuals' identities are not aligned with *either* place *or* class; they are probably constructed out of both, as well as a complex of other things, most especially "race" and "gender"'.[31] Neither place nor identity has to be monolithic and homogeneous. Just as a place can have multiple significances, so one subject can manifest different identities, and the momentary dominance of one will be the result of social negotiation and conflict: 'The past is no more authentic than the present; there will be no one reading of it. And "traditions" are frequently invented or, if they are not, the question of which traditions will predominate can not be answered in advance. *It is people, not places in themselves, which are reactionary or progressive'*.[32] Places are sites in which history can be negotiated. Fictions of the city are, therefore, ordered spatially as well as temporally, although as Hana Wirth-Nesher argues, city space in fiction has often been marginalised by critical discussions that miss the spatial dimensions of narrative, and focus instead solely on an unlocated psychology of the characters or atopic themes and plots.[33] Such neglect means that the embeddedness of the person in spatial environments and their histories, which forms an active part of many contemporary fictions, remains under-explored.

The metaphor of the city has frequently been used as the structure of narrative. Yet similarly, narrative structures have been implicated in imagining the city: anti-urban myths like the unnatural city, sin city and the city as a threat; and pro-urban models like the civilised city, the 'soft city', the free city and the radical city. The city challenges an ordered and coherent narrative, yet it also represents a space or matrix of confluence where the status of textuality is constantly being articulated and tested. The city is both the site of authority and social control, and the place where the evasion of authority can become most self-aware, which is why so much of the best recent fiction gravitates towards representatives of urban space and cities. The city is the magnet of the postmodern narrative, arranging the iron filings of the fragmented cities into a pattern, albeit an often enchanted or unrecognisable pattern. Fiction is able to represent those sites/spaces of the everyday which escape the purview of social control. Like the alleyways, backstreets, nooks and crannies and the 'heterotopias' of the city, so fiction has within itself similar investigations and spaces. It re-cements the fragmented experiences of everyday life, but not in any straightforward transcendental way; it need not elide the complexities and contradictions of social memory and the signs, images and narratives that dominant ideologies have attempted to shred from textual memory.

Recent fiction's deliberate foregrounding of the discourses of the interrelation of the sensual and the analytic, of private memory and public representation, of personal 'lived' experience and 'official' public constructions, parallels this 'new geography', by showing how spatial constructions are created and used as markers of human memory and of social values in a world of rapid flux and change. This chapter will enter the complex discursive matrix of urban space – sociological, architectural, geographical, philosophical – in contemporary fictional cities, focusing principally on Thomas Pynchon's *The Crying of Lot 49* (1966), Paul Auster's *The New York Trilogy* (1987) and William Gibson's *Neuromancer* (1984). These novelists typify the ambitions of many contemporary writers whose depiction of urban space in the postmodern metropolis is conceived of as part of an attempt to rescue the city from the rationalising and totalising forces of modernity. There are spaces and actions which the city protects, wraps around itself, hides from anyone who is not an engaged subject, a participant in this particular action, or a walker in that particular neighbourhood.

Architects of theoretical and social space

In *Civilization and Its Discontents* (1930), Freud calls on an ancient city as an analogue by which to chart the convolutions of the human psyche. He summons up the profusely layered past of Rome:

> Now let us, by a flight of imagination, suppose that Rome is not a human habitation but a psychical entity with a similarly long and copious past – an entity, that is to say, in which nothing that has once come into existence will have passed away and all the earlier phases of development

continue to exist alongside the latest one.[34]

Freud conceives of the geography of human growth as a temporal depository of stratum upon stratum. He might also have invoked Venice, the archetype of the city of historical involutions, whose complex economic and social strata (ranging from the palaces to the Jewish ghetto), and amphibious intimacy with the ocean trade routes have made it an icon of the city's power over the imagination.

In Winterson's mock-historical novel, *The Passion*, her two main protagonists argue about the usefulness of maps to negotiate early nineteenth-century Venice. Villanelle responds to Henri's request for a map to negotiate the labyrinthine twists and turns of the city by saying: 'It won't help. This is a living city. Things change'.[35] The social space of the city is created by the journeys that people make, and, as such, is not represented on any map: 'The cities of the interior do not lie on any map' (p. 114). Any secure cognitive knowledge of the city is completely unrealisable and rebutted, as each journey creates a new route:

> This city enfolds upon itself. Canals hide other canals, alley-ways cross and criss-cross so that you will not know which is which until you have lived here all your life. Even when you have mastered the squares and you can pass from the Rialto to the Ghetto and out to the lagoon with confidence, there will still be places you can never find ... be prepared to go another way, to do something not planned if that is where the streets lead you. (p. 113)

As a labyrinthine space, it becomes a subjective space, a city constructed by its inhabitants and their pedestrian trajectories. The volatile city of Venice refuses the totalising effects of mapping. J. B. Harley, a cartographer urging the necessity of deconstructing the textuality of maps, has recently argued that 'All maps employ the common devices of rhetoric such as invocations of authority'.[36] In her earlier novel, *Sexing the Cherry*, Winterson is even more sceptical:

> A map can tell me how to find a place I have not seen but have often imagined. When I get there, following the map faithfully, the place is not the place of my imagination. Maps, growing ever more real, are much less true.[37]

Although maps purport to accurately represent places, they actually produce ideological spaces, and in so doing ignore human experiences of spaces. Maps have invisible spaces within them, unspoken and unwritten places: 'every mapped-out journey contains another journey hidden in its lines ...' (p. 23). Harley makes a similar observation: 'where is the space-time of human experience in such anonymized maps?'.[38] Harley is particularly concerned with the way in which traditional and scientific cartography is predisposed to lose its hold on the lived world. Maintaining that cartography is ineluctably a form of power, Harley persuasively argues that maps are motivated by an impulse to synthesise alterity in their desire to contain and represent its lived experience with abstract notions of space. Henri's prior experience of space has been derived from the military campaigns of the French emperor who initiated Haussmann's rationalisation of Parisian space; it is a rational, fixed dimension that can be mapped, located and occupied: 'Where Bonaparte goes, straight roads follow, buildings are rationalised, street signs may change to celebrate a battle but they are always clearly marked'.[39] Winterson's Venice represents a promise of possibility lying untapped in the history of space, which has been displaced from the contemporary world.

What if Freud had invoked Los Angeles instead of Rome, or Winterson had set her arguments about maps there? Los Angeles works sideways, rhizomically, rather than by stratum, and time is stretched, not layered; displaced not stratified. Could this city project a new paradigm of subjectivity? Contrary to the Freudian model of subjects as repositories of layered (un)consciousnesses, as Fredric Jameson has described in his essay 'Postmodernism, or the cultural logic of late capitalism', one would have a subject which is all surface rather than depth, where subjectivity is displaced not stored. Now the bewildered schizophrenic is the paradigm subject in which

> the subject has lost its capacity actively to extend its pro-tensions and re-tensions across the temporal manifold and to organise its past and future into coherent experience ... the breakdown of temporality suddenly releases the present time from all the activities and intentionalities that might focus it and make it a space of praxis; thereby isolated, that present suddenly engulfs the subject with indescribable vividness, a materiality of perception properly overwhelming ...'.[40]

Jameson finds this new subjectivity highly plausible and makes Los Angeles paradigmatic of late capitalism's new logic of spatiality. He asserts that 'space is for us an existential and cultural dominant', having described postmodernism's dependence on a 'supplement of spatiality' that results from its depletion of history and consequent exaggeration of the present.[41] Michel Foucault argues that the twentieth century has brought about a correction to the nineteenth-century obsession with temporality, which occluded any critical sensibility of the spatiality of social life.[42] As we have seen recent years have witnessed far-reaching calls for the spatialisation of critical consciousness. The politics of place, the cultural function of geography and the importance of space is contested, asserted and marked out in diverse ways not only in the work of Henri Lefebvre, Michel Foucault, David Harvey, Edward Soja,

Doreen Massey, Fredric Jameson and Michel de Certeau, but also Derek Gregory, Pierre Bourdieu, Gaston Bachelard and others. In addition, discussions of the nature and utilisation of space in 'postmodern' architecture by such architects as the Krier brothers, Aldo Rossi, Peter Eisenman and Bernard Tschumi (and the latter's joint architectural projects and writings on spatial frameworks with Jacques Derrida), as well as the 'semiotics of environment' in the work of Robert Venturi and Charles Jencks, have contributed to this debate on the social consciousness of space. Furthermore, there have been a wealth of socio-economic-cultural studies on postmodern urban space, among which Mike Davis's analysis of Los Angeles in *City of Quartz*, Dayan Sudjic's analysis of the development of postmodern urban sprawls in *100 Mile City*, and Sharon Zukin's analyses of the commodifying function of capital upon cities and inner-city gentrification in *Landscapes of Power*, are exemplary.

Where Jameson exhorts 'Always historicise!', Henri Lefebvre adds 'Always spatialise!', because he believes that such an injunction mistakenly assumes that the temporalisation of history is sufficient. His conception of space as something that is 'felt' as much as 'known' or analysed, leads to the emergence of two sorts of space. One is the empirical rational space perceived as a void to be filled up. The other is what might be termed 'representational space', a space that is charged with emotional and mythical meanings, community symbolism and historical significances: 'This is the dominated – and hence passively experienced – space which the imagination seeks to change and appropriate. It overlays physical space, making symbolic use of its objects'.[43] Such existential space does not have an autonomous, objectively separate existence from subjects and objects; space is *produced* by the material forms of production. A similar intuition animates Mary Scott's amusing story, 'Whose was the corkscrew?' in the collection *Sex and the City*. A couple go out to 'Shopping City', a vast mall where they hope to complete their day's consumerism by purchasing a cooker, but fail to agree on which model and lapse into a terrible fight when they return home. At its climax they are suddenly reconciled by drunkenness, exhaustion and lust, but as they copulate, all the commodities in their house take on the violent and divisive energies of the city and we are told that things become so bad among these objects, that 'a hoard of plastic carriers, kept to hold the shopping of the future, rustled with ominous aggression' and 'one Austin Reed bag rallied those which could easily be identified with its cause and led a foray of Lacoste and Paul Smith against representatives of Laura Ashley and Monsoon'.[44] The city is 'a space of differences', a social space of possibilities and prohibitions experienced by people in their everyday lives which contrasts with the abstract space laid down by the actions of the state, science and the economic institutions of capital. The reproduction of the social relations of capitalism is, therefore, accomplished as a constant struggle between these different modes of reproducing space.

Lefebvre blames the occlusion of space in cultural theory on several causes, especially the dominance of Bergsonism: 'the erasure of focus on space has to do with an historicism and economism prevalent at a certain time, which separated time and space – Bergsonian philosophy where space was a "movement of matter against the spirit".'[45] If temporality absorbs the discourse of agency entirely, then space remains invisible, and open to exploitation. This is why Edward Soja argues that 'demystifying and politicizing the spatiality of social life is the critical nexus of contemporary retheorization'.[46] He argues that the recent spatial turn in postmodernism elicits a new sense of social subjectivity and ontology because it restores 'the existential link between spatiality and human agency: *Being, consciousness, and action are necessarily and contingently spatial*, existing not simply "in" space but "of" space as well. To be alive intrinsically and inescapably involves participation in the social production of space, shaping and being shaped by a constantly evolving spatiality'.[47] Saul Bellow captures this evolving, historical space in his images of a Chicago regressing back into the past of its meat trade as night falls:

> The stockyards are gone, Chicago is no longer slaughter-city, but the old smells revive in the night heat. Miles of railroad siding along the streets once were filled with red cattle cars, the animals waiting to enter the yards lowing and reeking. The old stink still haunts the place. It returns at times, suspiring from the vacated soil, to remind us all that Chicago had once led the world in butcher-technology and that billions of animals had died here. And that night the windows were open wide and the familiar depressing multilayered stink of meat, tallow, blood-meal, pulverized bones, hides, soap, smoked slabs, and burnt hair came back. Old Chicago breathed again through leaves and screens.[48]

Chicago's past history of slaughtering cattle is the living ghost behind the city's personification as an animal breathing, panting and spraying water to cool itself off in the heat of the night. The historical layering of the city space is prised open by the dormant smells excited by the heat, as the novel reaches for a certain kind of spatiality to explore the effects of the past on the present.

The spatial turn makes it possible to recognise the practice of space and therefore history, just as Marx's theory of the fetishism of the commodity revealed the reification at work in capitalist exchange relations.[49] The instrumental rationalisation, standardisation and uniformity of space that occurred in the architecture and town planning of concepts like Le Corbusier's cities and Mies van der Rohe's office towers, for example, had the dialectical twist of a total annihilation of space – it had the effect of transforming space into a uniform, homogeneous arena.

When the couple in Mary Scott's story give way to their erotic desires and stop threatening to separate and take all their possessions with them, the objects that define their space become surrealistically agitated, as if they had been trying to control the body and its desires in order to sustain the production of capitalist space and material culture. This connection between body and space is why the body always serves as the point of departure and destination in Lefebvre's analysis of the lived experience of space: 'Space – *my* space – is not the context of which I constitute the "textuality": instead, it is first of all *my body*, and then it is my body's counterpart or "other", its mirror-image or shadow: it is the shifting intersection between that which touches, penetrates, threatens or benefits my body on the one hand, and all other bodies on the other. Then we are concerned, once again, with gaps and tensions, contacts and separations'.[50] This suppression of the body's lived spatial experience and its sensual perceptions, debilitates and mystifies human knowledge, as well as perpetuating (politically useful) ideological illusions. Restoration of the practico-sensory realm of physical space could subvert the conventionally gendered spaces of modern life, rehabilitate 'underground, lateral, labyrinthine – even uterine or feminine – realities. An uprising of the body, in short, against the signs of non-body'.[51] Grenouille in Patrick Süskind's *Perfume*, for example, develops perfect mastery of his spatial environment through his olfactory powers: 'At the age of six he had completely grasped his surroundings olfactorily. There was not an object in Madame Gaillard's house, no place along the northern reaches of the rue de Charonne, no person, no stone, tree, bush or picket fence, no spot be it ever so small, that he did not know by smell, could not recognize by holding its uniqeness firmly in his memory.'[52] This olfactory revelation of space helps him become aware of the 'conflicts at work within it, conflicts which foster the explosion of abstract space and the production of a space that is *other*'.[53] In this constant enactment of a Logos–Eros debate – where rationality is persistently challenged by the eroticisation of lived experience – Lefebvre is interested in those spatial activities and productions of space which appear to be 'counter-spaces', spaces which escape or defy the violence of abstract logic. Leisure is one such space, that can bridge divisions, reveal vulnerable social breaking-points, and act as the 'epitome of contradictory space'.[54] Another contradictory space which is criss-crossed with conflicts, is urbanness: 'On the one hand, it makes it possible in some degree to deflect class struggles ... On the other hand, the city and its periphery tend to become the area of kinds of action that can no longer be confined to the traditional locations of the factory or office floor. The city and the urban sphere are thus the setting of struggle; they are also, however, the stakes of that struggle'.[55] Such contested urban spaces occur in Thomas Pynchon's description of the sewers in New York in *V* (1975), or in the churches in Peter Ackroyd's *Hawksmoor* (1985), spaces which are 'counter-spaces', which defy the violence of abstract urban logic. Such writing opens space – mentally and physically – where previous simulation, repression and convention have converged to predetermine being. Thus, fictional representations of urban space have the potential to make the locus of everyday life and its lived experiences – its homogenisation and differentiation, its separation and unification, its division and cementation – all critical to the politics of space.

Some designers of contemporary urban social space, like the architects Bernard Tschumi and Peter Eisenman, share these convictions, and give them a tangible form through the interaction of their discourses and buildings which points us to the production of urban fictional spaces for history. In his book *Questions of Space* (1994), the 'deconstructive' architect Tschumi argues that an increased awareness of the 'thickness' of space can also raise our consciousness of the effects of time and history, about which he is persistently concerned. The recent end-of-history debate must not be allowed to overshadow the insights of the new geography and architecture:

> 4.1. Does the Hegelian end of history mean the end of space as a product of history?
> 4.2 On the other hand, if history does not end, and historical time is the Marxist time of revolution, does space lose its primary role?[56]

He analyses architecture in terms of the erotic and violent implications that it has for the spatial organisation of bodies: '*The pleasure of space*: ... Approximately: it is a form of experience – the "presence of absence"; exhilarating differences between the plane and the cavern, between the street and your living room; symmetries and dissymmetries emphasizing the spatial properties of my body; right and left, up and down. Taken to its extreme, the pleasure of space leans toward the poetics of the unconscious, to the edge of madness'.[57] He has a strong sense of the interactions between bodies and the built environment which has its counterparts in fiction: 'First, there is the violence that all individuals inflict on spaces by their very presence, by their intrusion into the controlled order of architecture. ... Bodies carve all sorts of new and unexpected spaces, through fluid or erratic motions ... Each architectural space implies (and desires) the intruding presence that will inhabit it'.[58] Then there is the violence performed by architectural spaces on bodies – for example, by narrow corridors on large crowds – a violence

287

which has generally been ignored by architecture's aesthetic imperative that it 'should be pleasing to the eye, as well as comfortable to the body'.[59] He seeks to use this characteristic of urban space as a form of political resistance and subversion, and rather than the society shaping the city, he wishes 'the city itself [to] act upon society'.[60] His Parc de la Villette in Paris always stresses the self-reflexive spatial organisation of consciousness, in the belief that being aware of one's position and location are contemporary imperatives. Jacques Derrida has described this deconstructionist architecture as a *'socius* of dissociation':

> These *folies* destabilize meaning, the meaning of meaning, the signifying ensemble of this powerful architectonics. ... By pushing 'architecture towards its limits', a place will be made for 'pleasure'; ... the structure of the grid and of each cube – for these points are cubes – leaves opportunities for chance, formal invention, combinatory transforma-tion, wandering. ... Architect-weaver. He plots grids, twining the threads of a chain, his writing holds out a net. A weave always weaves in several directions, several meanings, and beyond meaning. ... An architecture of heterogeneity, interruption, non-coincidence ... aimed at a spacing and a *socius* of dissociation.[61]

Here is architecture revelling in absences and presences, in which space becomes the pleasurable invention for the walking, perusing subject liberating the multiplicity of spaces. Peter Eisenman is also concerned with overcoming the occluding effects of a history based on linear time for the event of social space: 'The tradition of history in fact covers up potential types which evolve today ... not in what we see in history but what we have not seen in history'.[62] His answer has been to build in a form which self-consciously 'lays bare' the organisation of space and the shaping of social movement. Architecture is now read as an infinite text of superpositions. Structured (or better, 'de-structured') by trans-figuration, displacement and trace through the material *deconstruction* of space, Eisenman's buildings, like his House No. VI or his Fin D'Out Hous, flagrantly open the door to interrogations of the conventional assumptions about what constitutes shelter, foundations, boundaries, constructions – indeed, the whole relationship between self-identity and the specificity of the space(s) one inhabits. Like Tschumi, he chal-lenges the boundaries between the inside and the outside, as well as those oppositions which have traditionally structured architecture – figure and ground, ornament and structure, aestheticism and function-alism – in a manner which shadows the representation of subjectivity in fictions of the city. With subjects now conceived of as fragmented, dispersed and tactically resisting spatial oppression, there is no completely rational space – space is 'now-here' and 'no-where', like the city of Bellona in Samuel R. Delaney's *Dhalgren* (1975), or Berlin in

Thomas Pynchon's *Gravity's Rainbow* (1973) – with the result that their disruptive spatial logics refigure and reconceive entrenched relations between bodies and spatial experiences.[63]

Thomas Pynchon's urban imaginary in '*The Crying of Lot 49*'

The city is at the core of modern and postmodern consciousness, persistently forcing humans to face up to the ontological nature of their being in (post)modernity. Being is a critical issue for the subject in the city, because self-consciousness emerges from the interaction with others mediated by city space. Paul Auster's protagonist in *Moon Palace*, Marco Fogg, is continually compelled to reflect upon his self-identity and the way in which different city environments construct and organise the human subject, because of the degree to which the city works its way deep into his subjectivity:

> In the streets, everything is bodies and commotion, and like it or not, you cannot enter them without adhering to a rigid protocol of behaviour. To walk among the crowd means never going faster than anyone else, never lagging behind your neighbor, never doing anything to disrupt the flow of human traffic. If you play by the rules of this game, people tend to ignore you. There is a particular glaze that comes over the eyes of New Yorkers when they walk through the streets, a natural and perhaps necessary form of indifference to others. [... In the park] I felt that I was blending into the environment, that even to a practiced eye I could have passed for one of the picnickers or strollers around me. The streets did not allow for such delusions. Whenever I walked out among the crowds, I was quickly shamed into an awareness of myself. I felt like a speck, a vagabond, a pox of failure on the skin of mankind. Each day, I became a little dirtier than I had been the day before, a little more ragged and confused, a little more different from everyone else. In the park, I did not have to carry around this burden of self-consciousness. It gave me a threshold, a boundary, a way to distinguish between the inside and the outside. If the streets forced me to see myself as others saw me, the park gave me a chance to return to my inner life, to hold on to myself purely in terms of what was happening inside me. It is possible to survive without a roof over your head, I discovered, but you cannot live without establishing an equilibrium between the inner and outer. The park did that for me.[64]

Everyday city life is thoroughly ritualised, patterned and structured according to 'a rigid protocol of behaviour', rules which are embedded in the fabric of the urban unconsciousness. Although these structures try to work directly on Fogg's unconscious and especially its corporeal memory, their frictional passage provokes resistances to the elimination of even the illusion of autonomous self-identity. Fogg articulates this awakening consciousness in terms of the park, a space apparently constructed for innerness to flourish along with the flowers and trees within its protective boundaries. By playing with the traditional opposition between nature and culture, Auster suggests that this comforting inwardness belongs to nature, but the text ironises the protagonist's relief at rediscovering an inner sense of self in the park with the subtext that this is a culturally managed nature. The park itself is under the control of the same powers manifested in the Trump Towers of the city.

One way the city creates the conditions for urban consciousness is, therefore, through its structuring of space. The most basic of these structures is the relation between centre and periphery, and this provides much of the framework for the articulations of urban consciousness. Modern cities like New York place such delineated spaces, especially any confidence in their fixity, under constant pressure:

> Years before, he'd moved to New York believing himself to be penetrating to the center of the world, and all of the time he lived there the illusion of the center held: the sense of there always being a door behind which further mysteries were available, a ballroom at the top of the sky from which the irresistible music wafted, a secret power source from which the mad energy of the metropolis emanated. But Los Angeles had no discernible center and was also without edges and corners.[65]

The decentred urbanism of Los Angeles, makes it, in a popular quip, 'seventy-two suburbs in search of city'. Sprawl is a familiar refrain in novelistic treatments of the city. Here is Robert Parker's Boston-based detective Spencer in Los Angeles, displaying the popular East-coast prejudice about the Californian lifestyle:

> I didn't know any place like it for sprawl, for the apparently idiosyncratic mix of homes and businesses and shopping malls. There was no center, no fixed point for taking bearings. It ambled and sprawled and disarrayed all over the peculiar landscape – garish and fascinating and imprecise and silly, smelling richly of bougainvillea and engine emissions, full of trees and grass and flowers and neon and pretense. And off to the northeast, beyond the Hollywood Hills, above the smog, and far from Disneyland were the mountains with snow on their peaks.[66]

The snow-clad mountains shimmering in the distance emphasise the remoteness of nature in such a counterfeit environment, levelling the distinctions between flowers, artificial signs and abstract human qualities – 'flowers and neon and pretense'. This lack of spatial hierarchies is persistently read as a sign of the loss of history, because the excess of surface means 'there was no past or future – only an eternal dizzying present'.[67]

Lack of spatial definition creates a paradoxical result, apparently compelling those who try to find adequate textual representations of the city to locate a new centrality in time rather than space. The eternal present of this cluttered diffusion of urban fragments along the Pacific coastal sun-belt called Los Angeles, has become a crucial 'spatial metaphor' because we think that the extended present moment of the city actually shows us the future – a paradigm of the microtechnocracy to which all western consumer societies are inexorably tending. A city which constantly reinvents and decentralises itself, it has produced a narrative of shifting landscapes of the global economy: it forces new modes of thought to be created as if invented to do just this. As Josh Cohen says of its extraordinary opaque surfaces that so bewilder various fictional protagonists, 'Los Angeles' visuality is remarkable in functioning not only as a feature of, but as an actual constitutive force in its developmental logic. Hollywood, Disneyland, 'revivalist' and 'fantastical' architectural styles, the futuristic skyscrapers of Downtown, and the widespread deployment of electronic surveillance converge to form a showcase for the globalist logic of postmodernity whose organising principle is the simulation of reality'.[68] Persistently characterised as a 'city of absence' – Alison Lurie's The Nowhere City (1965), or James Ellroy's The Big Nowhere (1988) – this absence of spatial definition creates a vast screen for projections of urban futures. Mike Davis brilliantly describes Los Angeles as a futuristic megalopolis, in which the gross political inequalities and countless varieties of self-interest in the city make for a continually destabilised community.[69]

This disappearance of history is the result of the way time is lived as much as the lack of a built heritage. Auster's account of space and subjectivity in New York, was quite literally, a pedestrian one, and could not be reiterated for many other modern cities where much faster forms of transportation choreograph interaction with urbanism. Dolores Hayden describes the modern American city in a way which reveals the importance of its circulation of people: 'A few tall buildings downtown tower over parking lots and garages. Perhaps there will be a park and some apartment houses. Then a tangle of porno shops, discount stores, fast food places and gas stations will lead to freeway ramps, and the freeway will connect miles and miles of similar, large single family houses on landscaped lots with shopping malls, industrial parks and the occasional school or church'.[70] Of all the 'apparatuses of circulation', as Laura Rice calls the transport, communications, and services that connect the buildings and people, it is the road that still has the greatest impact on city life.[71] Writers whose cultural narratives range across the landscapes of Los Angeles, converge on the belief that 'freedom of movement is the prime symbolic attribute of the Angel City'.[72] Speed thinks in Joan Didion's novel Play It As It Lays (1970):

> Once she was on the freeway and had manoeuvred her way into the
> fast lane she turned on the radio at high volume and she drove. She
> drove the San Diego to the Harbor, the Harbor up to the Hollywood,
> the Hollywood to the Golden State, the Santa Monica, the Santa Ana,
> the Pasadena, the Ventura. She drove it as a riverman runs a river,
> every day more attuned to its currents, its deceptions, and just as a
> riverman feels the pull of the rapids in the lull between sleeping and
> waking ...[73]

Like listening to the hum of money in Manhattan, driving the famous
names of southern California freeways becomes a sensuous activity, one
which defines and preoccupies one's finer sensitivities and emotional
responses. Driving becomes part of the plot for Bret Easton Ellis, because
it is one of the main ways in which Los Angeles' spatial environment
forces one to define and orientate oneself. Iterating the names of the
freeways is more mantra than route planning, opening the mind to the
sublime space:

> After leaving Blair I drive down Wilshire and then onto Santa Monica
> and then I drive onto Sunset and take Beverly Glen to Mulholland, and
> the Mulholland to Sepulveda and then Sepulveda to Ventura and then I
> drive through Sherman Oaks to Encino and then into Tarzana and then
> Woodland Hills.[74]

Narrative has lost almost all historicity as its temporal perspective is
spatialised into an arrangement of districts rather than events whose
temporality is measured against a location. The wide open spaces and
freeways spread out across the city in *Less Than Zero* (1985), are the
home of anomie and teenage *ennui*, suggesting that these fragmented
cultural identities result from the struggle to cope with the fractured existence produced by a dispersed contemporary urban space.

Fictions of the built environment deal with the affect of living in
these fast, atopic, urban spaces. By offering us imaginative (re)construc-
tions of our experiential negotiations of city spaces, novels intensify and
concentrate those acts of discovery and fabrication that are endemic to
our control and organisation of city life and exert a crucial structural
influence on our epistemological understanding of urban space. The
fractal spacetimes of New York and Los Angeles encompass cultural,
social, political, intellectual and sexual practices which are of particular
symbolic importance as dominant paradigms for these discursive
constructions of urban space. They become materialisations of cultural
memory and the symbolic elements for articulating the consciousness of
their occupants, who compose them into narratives of their own, like the
drivers naming stations of the daily commuting ritual. To an extent that
no other social space can begin to emulate, these cities of late modernity

even introject the novels about themselves into their urban unconscious. Much recent fiction is itself an urban space. At times this urban fiction works through the material memory of the city, allowing discussions, explorations and negotiations with repressed urban space. Although cities like New York and Los Angeles are very real, Sharon Zukin has argued that in their different ways 'they are built on the power of dreamscape, collective fantasy and façade. This landscape is explicitly produced for visual consumption. Moreover, they are *self-consciously* produced'.[75]

The novel of the city can also be thought of as an allegory of the practice of a necessary art of urbanism. Jonathan Raban calls this the 'soft' city:

> Cities, unlike villages and small towns, are plastic by nature. We mould them in our images: they, in their turn, shape us by the resistance they offer when we try to impose a personal form on them. In this sense, it seems to me that living in a city is an art, and we need to describe the particular relation between man and material that exists in the continual creative play of urban living. The city as we might imagine it, the soft city of illusion, myth, aspiration, nightmare, is as real, maybe more real, than the hard city one can locate in maps and statistics, in monographs on urban sociology and demography and architecture.[76]

This soft city is Oedipa Maas's landscape. The soft city may be 'imaginary' but as Oedipa finds out, this brings its own problems. 'San Narciso had no boundaries',[77] and this means that the material and imaginary cities constantly merge into one another. In *Less Than Zero*, Ellis describes how Los Angeles seems only to exist in the imaginary constructions of its speeding inhabitants:

> There was a song I heard when I was in Los Angeles by a local group. The song was called 'Los Angeles' and the words and images were so harsh and bitter that the song would reverberate in my mind for days. The images, I later found out, were personal and no one I knew shared them. The images I had were of people being driven mad by living in the city. Images of parents who were so hungry and unfulfilled that they ate their own children. Images of people, teenagers my own age, looking up from the asphalt and being blinded by the sun. These images stayed with me even after I left the city. Images so violent and malicious they seemed to be my only point of reference for a long time afterwards. After I left.[78]

The 'discursive' city and the 'real' city cannot exist without the other. For Oedipa this means that she cannot tell whether there 'was some Tristero beyond the appearance of the legacy America, or there was just America',[79] but she needs this paranoiac history of panoptic postal services as much as Ellis's protagonist needs the song of a cannibalistic city.

Raban's soft city is a place where there is a dynamic and symbiotic relationship between mapping urban spaces and mapping subjectivities.

When Oedipa looks down from a high vantage point on the anonymous suburban housing of the placeless city, she sees the machinery for communication: 'she thought of the time she'd opened a transistor radio to replace a battery and seen her first printed circuit. The ordered swirl of houses and streets, from this high angle, sprang at her now with the same unexpected, astonishing clarity as the circuit card had'.[80] Down with the bottom feeders she finds a different world. 'For an hour she prowled among the sunless, concrete underpinnings of the freeway, finding drunks, bums, pedestrians, pederasts, hookers, walking psychotic, no secret mailbox'.[81] The world under the freeway is the negation of the freedom and speed driven by the characters in the novels by Didion and Ellis. When Manuell Castells describes his 'informational city' as the 'disarticulation of place-based societies', in which 'the fundamental fact is that social meaning evaporates from places, and therefore from society, and becomes diluted and diffused in the reconstructed logic of a space of flows whose profile, origin, and ultimate purposes are unknown',[82] he could well be describing Oedipa's experience of the Tristero information system as a patterned meaning which always escapes and eludes her comprehension or definitive description. Gradually, Oedipa realises that her search for the Tristero information system leads her into spatial limbo, where things are no longer defined by their physical boundaries:

> But she'd lost her bearings. She turned pivoting on one stacked heel, could find no mountains either. As if there could be no barriers between herself and the rest of the land. San Narciso at that moment lost (the loss pure, instant, spherical, the sound of a stainless orchestral chime held among the stars and struck lightly), gave up its residue of uniqueness for her; became a name again, was assumed back into the American community of crust and mantle. ... San Narciso was a name; an incident among our climatic records of dreams and what dreams became among our accumulated daylight, a moment's squall-line or tornado's touch-down among the higher, more continental solemnities – storm-systems of group suffering and need, prevailing winds of affluence. There was the true continuity, San Narciso had no boundaries. No one knew yet how to draw them.[83]

Oedipa's sense of the city is no longer one of discrete boundaried spaces, and her established concepts of urban community, culture and space are disrupted, opened up to a new network of flows which form the nation state.

The most important insight in Raban's picture of the soft city is the degree of play it affords. Mike Fallopian's Peter Pinguid Society finds one of Brian McHale's 'dark areas' of history and creates the possibility of an earlier nineteenth-century confrontation between America and Russia. The possible naval encounter left Pinguid so demoralised that 'he and most of his crew settled near L.A.; and for most of the rest of his life he did little more than acquire wealth',[84] thereby founding the megalopolis in which Fallopian and Maas now live. It is at this point, just after the account of the history which this group of eccentric amateur historians try to sustain (reminders of *Titanic* enthusiasts perhaps), that Oedipa first encounters the Tristero underground mail system for which she later searches by the freeway pillars. She is not a fully converted 'city softie': she is resistant to the idea that the Tristero might be a necessary fiction for life in this city and wants a foundational epistemology.

The alternative mail system is more than just a consoling fiction, however. It is also an example of what de Certeau calls a 'tactic', a way of negotiating hegemonic powers within the 'practices of everyday life' such as eating, walking, shopping, etc. His project in *The Practice of Everyday Life* is to argue that while societies operate by culturally inscribed and deployed sets of rules, participants regularly resist these by aberrant ruses which undermine these explicit structures. De Certeau explores how these practices enable people to establish their own niches within the dominated space of a society: 'the goal is ... to bring to light the clandestine forms taken by the dispersed, tactical, and make-shift creativity of groups or individuals already caught in the nets of "discipline". Pushed to their ideal limits, these procedures compose the network of an antidiscipline'.[85] In the very heart of strongholds of economic power, de Certeau identifies a whole series of practices and arts of invention, combination, re-use and appropriation. One such practice which becomes something of a metaphor for de Certeau's interest in diversionary spatial activities, occurs in France, and is called 'la perruque' or 'the wigging':

> '*La perruque*' is the worker's own work disguised as work for his employer [like] a secretary's writing a love letter on 'company time' or ... a cabinetmaker's 'borrowing' a lathe to make a piece of furniture for his living room. ... *la perruque* actually diverts time (not goods, since he uses only scraps) from the factory for work that is free, creative, and precisely not directed toward profit. In the very place where the machine he must serve reigns supreme, he cunningly takes pleasure in finding a way to create gratuitous products whose sole purpose is to signify his own capabilities through his *work* and to confirm his solidarity with other workers or his family through *spending* his time in this way. ... *la perruque* re-introduces 'popular' techniques of other times and other places into the industrial space (that is, into the Present order).[86]

Analogous practices of 'making do' or 'ripping off' like *la perruque* occur in all walks of everyday life, tricking the actual order of things by styles of exchange that are insinuated into the mechanisms of social systems.

The W.A.S.T.E. system in Thomas Pynchon's *The Crying of Lot 49* is one such similar insurgent practice. In trying to unravel the legacy of her recently deceased lover, Pierce Inverarity, Oedipa Maas travels around his one-time investments in order to gather the necessary information. Visiting the Yoyodyne factory, Oedipa first comes across a picture of a posthorn in the toilet. Afterwards, her friend Fallopian explains how a secret delivery system has been inserted into the inter-office delivery system of the Yoyodyne corporation:

> 'We use Yoyodyne's inter-office delivery. On the sly. But it's hard to find carriers, we have a big turnover. They're run on a tight schedule, and they get nervous. Security people over at the plant know something's up. They keep a sharp eye out.' . . .
> 'How extensive is this?' asked Metzger.
> 'Only inside our San Narciso chapter. They've set up pilot projects similar to this in the Washington and I think Dallas chapters. But we're the only one in California so far.'[87]

As a secret and mysterious underground postal system, Oedipa learns that W.A.S.T.E. is an acronym for 'We Await Silent Tristero's Empire'. Pretty soon, Oedipa Maas is seeing post horns all over San Narciso, the symbols of W.A.S.T.E.'s omnipresence. All manner of alternative systems appear to be grafted onto mechanisms of authority: alternative lines in plays; official US postage stamps with small flaws; and histories of the Tristero system manifest themselves all over the place. The W.A.S.T.E. system gradually dominates Oedipa's consciousness: 'Last night, she might have wondered what undergrounds apart from the couple she knew of communicated by WASTE system. By sunrise she could legitimately ask what undergrounds didn't'.[88] Unable to determine whether she is on the track of a grand hoax or whether she has rumbled a massive, hidden, parasitic communication network, Oedipa's path veers uneasily through what seems to her the vital links in the chain of meaning of the Tristero. W.A.S.T.E. produces a parody of the US postal system, but it is presented as a metaphor of a less cluttered, less institutionalised, freer method of communication – an open, flowing rhetorical space. In her hermeneutic impasse, the W.A.S.T.E. system appears as both truth and illusion, fact and ruse. And de Certeau might well have been writing of W.A.S.T.E. when he describes *la perruque*, or its equivalent, as grafting itself onto the space of systemic activity, like a parasite which insinuates itself into the life-systems of another organism. De Certeau likens such systems and 'producers' to people who

> trace 'indeterminate trajectories' that are apparently meaningless, since they do not cohere with the constructed, written, and prefabricated space through which they move. They are sentences that remain unpredictable

within the space ordered by the organizing techniques of systems. Although they use as their *material* the *vocabularies* of established languages (those of television, newspapers, the supermarket or city planning), although they remain within the framework of prescribed *syntaxes* (the temporal modes of schedules, paradigmatic organisations of places, etc.), these 'traverses' remain heterogeneous to the systems they infiltrate and in which they sketch out the guileful ruses of *different* interest and desires.[89]

Using the discourse of insurgency, de Certeau is fascinated with those practices which formulate a resistant activity. He develops a crucial distinction between strategies and tactics. A strategy is defined as 'the calculation (or manipulation) of power relationships that becomes possible as soon as a subject with will and power (a business, an army, a city, a scientific institution) can be isolated. It postulates a *place* that can be delimited as its *own* and serve as a base ... every "strategic" rationalisation seeks first of all to distinguish its "own" place, that is, the place of its own power and will, from an "environment"'.[90] An art of the strong, strategic activity seeks to master time by the institution of an autonomous place, as well as to control space by panoptic practices.

A tactic, on the other hand,

is a calculated action determined by the absence of proper locus. No delimitation of an exteriority, then, provides it with the condition necessary for autonomy. The space of a tactic is the sphere of the other. Thus it must play on and with a terrain imposed on it and organized by the law of a foreign power. It does not have the means to keep to itself, at a distance, in a position of withdrawal, foresight, and self-collection ... It operates in isolated actions, blow by blow.[91]

As an art of the weak, like *la perruque*, tactical activity lacks its own place, relying on mobility, trickery and precise interventions in time. In short, 'strategies pin their hopes on the resistance that the *establishment of a place* offers to the erosion of time; tactics on a clever *utilization of time*, of the opportunities it presents and also of the play that it introduces into the foundations of power'.[92]

Paul Auster's '*The New York Trilogy*'

The New York Trilogy (particularly in its stories 'City of glass' and 'The locked room'), explores the manner in which urban space is occupied, inhabited and experienced both phenomenologically and emotionally, by individuals and communities.[93] It is a spatial cartography that explores the way in which human subjects are at the mercy of various structures and forms of power that traverse the body and the world, break it down, shape it and rearrange it – yet always fail to wholly conquer it. David

Harvey's account of Michel de Certeau's ideas captures exactly the vector of Auster's novel. De Certeau opposes Foucault's oppressive belief that modern society produces the 'technological system of a coherent and totalizing space', arguing that this is constantly dispersed by a '"pedestrian rhetoric" of trajectories that have "a mythical structure" understood as "a story jerry-built out of elements taken from common sayings, an allusive and fragmentary story whose gaps mesh with the social practices it symbolises".'[94] Auster similarly excavates those surreptitious forms created by the marginal, dispersed, tactical and makeshift creativity of groups or individuals already caught in the nets of 'discipline'. His novel shows that 'spaces' are more easily liberated than Foucault imagines, because the invention of new spaces also challenges the domination of space by the existing hierarchies of power. Within the despotic social and political climate of the city, as political resistors have continually shown during the twentieth century, the most radical and expansive political gesture against the totalitarian attempt to dominate spatiality is the challenge provided by the creative and imaginative space of the human body. Quinn, Blue and other characters are always negotiating various locales in the city, continuously working to make sense of and articulate both place and event; they are active, space-producing bricoleurs.

The novel might have been called 'walking New York', and this is not just some post-automobile eco-politics, but an argument about the city itself. We saw earlier that Roland Barthes likened intertextuality to a walk, which showed the agency of reading but also obscured the temporal relations at work in reading. De Certeau also takes the line that walking is a figure for interpretative agency, in this case of city-dwellers. He argues that the city is constituted by the 'raw material' of 'walkers, *Wandersmänner*, whose bodies follow the cursives and strokes of an urban "text" they write without reading'.[95] Many passages in Auster's novel are given over to the patterns traced through the city by Quinn's walks. How do these walks enact city and history?

Pre-eminently, walking enacts sequence and the consolations of movement as a means of preserving identity: 'One step and then another step and then another: that is the golden rule'.[96] This is only the initial value of the walk, however. Just as de Certeau's spatial tactics are built on the fundamental experience of walking through a city, gauging the topographical and emotional by traversing the landscape on foot, so Quinn derives his intimate knowledge of the city from his perambulatory experiences. Gradually Quinn's journeys assume an epistemological importance, walking being analogous to travelling from one thought to another. This is an idea upon which Auster expands in *The Invention of Solitude*:

just as one step will inevitably lead one to the next step, so it is that one thought inevitably follows from the previous thought ... and in this way, if we were to try to make an image of this process in our minds, a network of paths begins to be drawn, as in the image of the human bloodstream (heart, arteries, veins, capillaries), or as in the image of a map (of city streets, for example, preferably a large city, or even of roads, as in the gas station maps of roads that stretch, bisect, and meander across a continent), so that what we are really doing when we walk through the city is thinking, and thinking in such a way that our thoughts compose a journey, and this journey is no more or less than the steps we have taken.[97]

Journeys are equivalent to mental movements, and walking becomes an actualisation of cognition itself. In his poem 'White spaces' in *Ground Work*, Auster seeks 'To think of motion not merely as a function of the body but as an extension of the mind'.[98] Words shape and extend mental and physical spaces. Auster's sensitivity to the social experience of space by specific bodies, finds its expression as the spaces of the city, Quinn's mind and the textuality fuse together.

McInerney's protagonist in *Brightness Falls* liked New York because it was a definite place. Perhaps he never walked anywhere. Quinn's walking gradually dislocates him, giving him the Los Angeles experience of atopia in New York. It also re-enacts the Situationist *dérive*, that was supposed to help recreate the history in the city. Ivan Chtcheglov in his 'Formulary for a new urbanism', laments the collapse of imagination and narrative in urban existence, which cuts us off from the ghosts of history that lurk around every corner in the city: 'Everyone wavers between the emotionally still-alive past and the already dead future'.[99] As a remedy, he and his associates proposed a kind of performance art which would create a 'new vision of time and space' through its 'continuous dérive'.[100] Quinn is also a practitioner of this politics of aimless, attentive peripatetics:

New York was an inexhaustible space, a labyrinth of endless steps, and no matter how far he walked, no matter how well he came to know its neighbourhoods and streets, it always left him with the feeling of being lost. Each time he took a walk, he felt as though he were leaving himself behind, and by giving himself to a seeing eye, he was able to escape the obligation to think, and this, more than anything else, brought him a measure of peace, a salutary emptiness within. The world was outside of him, around him, before him, and the speed with which it kept changing made it impossible for him to dwell on any one thing for very long. Motion was of the essence, the act of putting one foot in front of the other and allowing himself to follow the drift of his own body. By wandering aimlessly, all places became equal and it no longer mattered where he was. On his best walks, he was able to feel that he was nowhere. And this, finally, was all he ever asked of things: to be nowhere. New York was the nowhere he had built around himself, and he realized that he had no intention of ever leaving it.[101]

The lexicon in this passage – wandering, chance, drift, labyrinth – evokes the critique of 'the society of the spectacle' and urban incandescence by the French Situationists. As a critique of the commodification of experience and the boredom induced by contemporary city life, the capacity to engage with the city rather than passively consume it, is what is lacking: 'Certain *shifting angles*, certain *receding* perspectives, allow us to glimpse original conceptions of space, but this vision remains fragmentary. It must be sought in the magical locales of fairy tales and surrealist writings: castles, endless walls, little forgotten bars, mammoth caverns, casino mirrors'.[102] In order to combat the 'mental disease [which] has swept the planet: banalization'[103] and the safe security into which passive subjects in 'the society of the spectacle' settle, the 'dérive' (literally 'drift'), is the Situationists' notion of a constantly changing landscape that perpetually disorientates the subject, and thereby forces social and experiential engagement with one's geography and spatial environment. This drifting, which refuses the organisation of the capitalist environment by wandering randomly through the urban landscape, is an attempt to redefine and reanimate the city. *The Situationist International*, No. 1, June 1958, defined 'dérive' as 'A mode of experimental behaviour linked to the conditions of urban society: a technique of transient passage through varied ambiances. Also used to designate a specific period of continuous dériving'.[104] Guy Debord, the principal theorist of this group, gives 'Two accounts of the dérive', in which he describes two long walks 'structured' by chance encounters and events, which constitute a mode of exploring 'the specific effects of the geographical environment, consciously organized or not, on the emotions and behaviour of individual', which the Situationists called 'psychogeography'.[105] Debord argued in 'Unitary urbanism at the end of the 1950s', that 'unitary urbanism' 'opposes the passive spectacle, the principle of our culture ... UU envisages the urban environment as the terrain of a game in which one participates'.[106] He continues: 'Unitary urbanism is opposed to the temporal fixation of cities. It leads to the advocacy of a permanent transformation, an accelerated movement of the abandonment and reconstruction of the city in temporal and at times spatial terms'.[107] The 'dérive', drifting down city streets, combined with assemblage – or what the Situationists called 'détournement', the rearrangement of what already exists – are the components for their vision of a new city. Hence, the 'dérive' can be construed as a mode of 'critical walking', in which subjectivity is constantly being scrutinised as a construction of the urban environment, and through which game element there is a corresponding expansion of subjects' 'dream life' and imagination.

In Auster's novel, this possibility exists in tension with the power of this special traverse of the city to negate the past and exit from time altogether. Walking can generate a state of 'emptiness', inner harmony, peace, escape and nothingness, and placelessness is crucial to his central characters' repeated general desire of attaining some form of purity of consciousness. Walking is not only a means of escaping from one's sense of self – achieving an oblivion of being in a massive metropolis – but also a revelling in space. Space swallows up Quinn. Approaching the weightlessness and aimless floating of astronauts in space, the real beauty of New York for Quinn lies in its endless variety of spatial experiences. Later in 'The locked room', the protagonist notes that: 'In general, lives seem to veer abruptly from one thing to another, to jostle and bump, to squirm. A person heads in one direction, turns sharply in mid-course, stalls, drifts, starts up again. Nothing is ever known, and inevitably we come to a place quite different from the one we set out for'.[108]

In this state of suspended time, in which Quinn follows the elaborate movements of Stillman through Manhattan, walking and signification gradually merge. Quinn becomes engaged in what are, to use de Certeau's word, 'illegible' improvisations which produce alternative spaces, and 'a *marginal*, or metaphorical, city thus slips into the clear text of the planned and readable city'.[109] The spaces carved out by Stillman's walks are associated with language in a literal way, since 'he had created letters by the movement of his steps, but they had not been written down'.[110] Just as walking and writing are conjoined for Stillman senior, so for his son moving and speaking are performed simultaneously: 'I forget how to make the words come out of my mouth. Then it is hard for me to move' (p. 21). Described as a 'map' (p. 70), Stillman senior's trajectories around the Upper West Side imitate letters of the alphabet, as writing and walking coalesce: space becomes an area for signification in a literal – letteral – manner. Stillman's lived experience in space and his conception of space are one and the same: to use Henri Lefebvre's terms, Stillman's representational space and his representations of space are the same. Walking becomes an inscription of letters in space; and yet, 'Stillman had not left his message anywhere ... There is no result, no trace to mark what you have done ... the pictures did not exist – not in the streets where they had been drawn, but in Quinn's red notebook' (p. 71). Auster's echo of Derrida's 'trace' to describe the ghostly non-presence of the letters, evident only in the lived and perceived experience of the body's spatial movement, is characteristic of the way the novel superimposes Paris on New York. Quinn is horrified that this evidence exists because he realises that his abstraction from Stillman's spatial movement is an imposition of significance due to his search for clues to an intentional pattern, perhaps even a plot, in Stillman's activities. The origin of signification is always in doubt: does it derive from the (objective) recognition of another's consciousness; or is it merely the subject's imposition of his own consciousness? Quinn's (and the reader's) dilemma arises because, despite what his walks have taught him about controlling space, he finds that inner and outer and, therefore, present and past, become far less distinct than he had imagined.

Quinn's uncertainty about the source of signification is intimately tied to the novel's representation of space. Hence, the shifting site of signification is linked to the novel's constantly shifting space, as it perpetually reconstructs the dimensions and points of motivation in the narrative. As Quinn puts it at one point, 'Everything becomes essence; the centre of the book shifts with each event that propels it forward. The centre, then, is everywhere, and no circumference can be drawn until the book has come to its end' (p. 8). The topography of the story is particularly important, as the reader is frequently alerted to street names and the directions taken by Quinn, Blue and other protagonists. Significantly, just before Quinn takes to living in the alleyway, there is a long meticulously detailed description of a walk around Manhattan, and the observations of the city life he makes in his red notebook. These observations are mostly of the marginalised people of New York: 'the tramps, the down-and-outs, the shopping-bag ladies, the drifters and drunks. They range from the merely destitute to the wretchedly broken' (p. 108). These people live a liminal existence, carving their space out of the 'official' space of the city, inhabiting oblivious niches within an urban indifference: 'Even though they seem to be there, they cannot be counted as present' (p. 109). Quinn is particularly struck by those social outcasts who appear mad, whose mental space appears to be completely divided from their physical space. Yet Quinn finally notes that his own identity and location are differentiated as well: 'Baudelaire: Il me semble que je serais toujours bien là où je ne suis pas. In other words: It seems to me that I will always be happy in the place where I am not. Or, more bluntly: Wherever I am not is the place where I am myself. Or else, taking the bull by the horns: Anywhere out of the world' (p. 110). Reminiscent of Lacan's phrase 'I think where I am not and I am not where I think' (and hence of the impossibility of the ego's self-possession in Cartesian terms), the separation of the spaces of consciousness and being, of thought and existence, clearly reiterates Quinn's desire to transcend the physical world. Following the Situationists' exploration of the effects of urban space on modern consciousness, and Tschumi's claims that architecture's disrupting potential excites human desires, Quinn's experience of the dislocation of identity is crucial to his desire for happiness.

'The city of glass' finishes with Quinn locked in a room, isolated and fed by an anonymous hand, disoriented as he spends his final days writing in his red notebook. The Beckettian absurdity of this conclusion, gradually losing self-consciousness and self-identity in a placeless place, epitomises the contemporary aim to elude the boundaries of a defined milieu. Quinn's existence within the locked room appears to replay the isolation and language experiment that Stillman senior purportedly played out on his son, Peter, and the other historical cases of attempting to determine the origins of language through the social isolation of children cited earlier in the story. Quinn manages to cast off concern for his physical life, and, locked in a dark space, his existence is measured by and completely identified with the writing space left in the red notebook:

> the case ... had been a bridge to another place in his life, and now that he had crossed it, its meaning had been lost. Quinn no longer took any interest in himself. ... He felt that his words had been severed from him, that now they were part of the world at large, as real and specific as a stone, or a lake, or a flower. ... He wondered if he had it in him to write without a pen, if he could learn to speak instead, filling the darkness with his voice, speaking the words into the air, into the walls, into the city, even if the light never came back again.
>
> The last sentence of the red notebook reads: 'What will happen when there are no more pages in the red notebook?' (pp. 130–1)

Space, language and life are completely interlinked, and one without the other appears to be absolutely impossible. Running out of writing space in the notebook intimates death. Quinn recognises while he is in the alleyway that he is falling (p. 117), and reaching the end of the notebook is also reaching the end of his fall.

The New York Trilogy shows the existential consequences of Lefebvre's theory of the dialectical interaction between the space of representation and represented space. We need, however, to recognise certain limitations on its capacity to fully represent the city of New York. Peter Brooker points out that the city of today is no longer mainly white, and that this has far-reaching cultural consequences. He cautions that novels like *The New York Trilogy* tell only part of the story of the city:

> What this fiction tells us, therefore, in recording and imagining the lives of the city, will be about its own condition; about the changing social position and consciousness of white in relation to subordinated or emergent groups. The sign of the 'postmodern', therefore, ... is the modern in crisis, a moment when its invisible norms become evident, and perhaps impossible, in a more deeply self-conscious way than a postmodern concern with form alone normally suggests.[111]

Nevertheless, if the demarcation of a specific space as a location, or place, is crucial to the establishment of social order then, as Quinn and other characters in the trilogy gradually discover, to challenge what that place might be, is to make a fundamental challenge to the social order that perpetuates even this racial hierarchy itself.

Simulation city

What we're selling is freedom. We offer you in technology what religion and revolution had promised but never delivered. Freedom from the physical body. Freedom from race and gender, from nationality and personality, from place and time.

So states the new corporate vice-president for Digicom, Meredith Johnson, a character played by Demi Moore in the film *Disclosure* (Warner Bros, 1994). The huge advertising campaign and public furore concerning the film's ostensible representation of the politics of male sexual harassment, obscured the film's focus on information and power, particularly the corporeal and mental 'liberations' promised by the new technology of virtual reality. One crucial scene in the film has Michael Douglas utilising virtual reality to enter a massive gothic corridor to find electronic video information which will save him from anticipated black-mail. As a consequence, his utilisation of this technological power enables him to protect his economic and patriarchal integrity against the encroachment of the newly powerful woman.

Disclosure, as well as a number of other films of the past two decades, including *Tron* (1982), *The Lawnmower Man* (1992), *Johnny Mnemonic* (1996) and *The Matrix* (1999), have been part of a gradual growth in interest in the new potentials of interactive computer tech-nologies in the popular imagination. Cyberspace: this formulation of a new kind of space owes much to its creation and popularisation by William Gibson in his novel *Neuromancer* (1984), the first of his 'cyber-punk' trilogy.[112] Variously known as the Net, the Web, or the Matrix, cyberspace promises, as Meredith Johnson suggests, a removal of one's objective associations with identity and immerses one in pure conscious-ness. In *Neuromancer*, one is introduced to it as the working medium of Case, an 'ex-console cowboy', who 'jacked into a custom cyberspace deck that projected his disembodied consciousness into the consensual hallucination that was the matrix'.[113] Scott Bukatman, in his excellent discussion of Gibson's 'metroscape' as a phenomenal elaboration of elec-tronic milieux, has argued that 'cyberspace certainly hyperbolizes the space of the city, projecting the metroscape into an exaggerated repre-sentation that accentuates its bodiless vertigo'.[114] Indeed, if Auster's city space of New York appears to be one massive, chaotic sprawl, then it is completely overwhelmed by BAMA – 'the Sprawl, the Boston–Atlanta Metropolitan Axis'.[115] William Gibson's futuristic representation of the technological megalopolis that subsumes and envelops the eastern seaboard of the United States, is repeatedly described in video–computer metaphors. The Sprawl is first represented as a light map of the frequency of data exchange:

> Manhattan and Atlanta burn solid white. Then they start to pulse, the rate of traffic threatening to overload your simulation. Your map is about to go nova. Cool it down. Up your scale. Each pixel a million megabytes. At a hundred million megabytes per second, you begin to make out certain blocks in midtown Manhattan, outlines of hundred-year-old industrial parks ringing the old core of Atlanta ... (p. 57)

Other city spaces, like the Ninsei enclave within Chiba City, are represented in a similar discourse:

> the ones nearest the port, beneath the quartz-halogen floods that lit the docks all night like vast stages; where you couldn't see the lights of Tokyo for the glare of the television sky, not even the towering holo-gram logo of the Fuji Electric company, and Tokyo Bay was a black expanse where gulls wheeled above drifting shoals of white styrofoam. Behind the port lay the city, factory domes dominated by the vast cubes of corporate arcologies. Port and city were divided by a narrow border-land of older streets, an area with no official name. Night City, with Ninsei its heart. (p. 13)

Later, Night City is described as 'a deranged experiment in social Darwinism, designed by a bored researcher who kept one thumb on the fast-forward button' (p. 14); and when a description of the design on a printed silk scarf is given, 'The pattern might have represented microcir-cuits, or a city map' (p. 17). In one narcotic-induced vision, Case fuses the experiences of urban space, drug hallucinations and cyberspace:

> Because, in some weird and very approximate way, it was like a run in the matrix. Get just wasted enough, find yourself in some desperate but strangely arbitrary kind of trouble, and it was possible to see Ninsei as a field of data, the way the matrix had once reminded him of proteins linking to distinguish cell specialities. Then you could throw yourself into a highspeed drift and skid, totally engaged but set apart from it all, and all around you the dance of biz, information interacting, data made flesh in the mazes of the black market ... (p. 26)

Time and again, the discourses of urban space and video–computer technology are interwoven. Thus, just as cities find their analogies in computer terminology, so symbiotically Case's experience of moving through the cubes of data within cyberspace is frequently represented in the discourse of urban space. In cyberspace, databanks become skyscrapers, information becomes glowing patterns of cosmopolitan neon signs and the circuits like maps of cities:

> Cyberspace. A consensual hallucination experienced daily by billions of legitimate operators, in every nation, by children being taught mathematical concepts ... A graphic representation of data abstracted from the banks of every computer in the human system. Unthinkable complexity. Lines of light ranged in the nonspace of the mind, clusters and constellations of data. Like city lights, receding ... (p. 67)

When Case uses the Kuang program in cyberspace in the attempt to crack the Tessier–Ashpool 'ice', the environment is described in terms which metaphorically evoke urban space: '... Kuang twisted and banked above the horizonless fields of the Tessier–Ashpool cores, an endless neon cityscape ... The Kuang program dived past the gleaming spires of a dozen identical towers of data, each one a blue neon replica of the Manhattan skyscraper' (p. 302). The analogies of the cyberspace environment and urban space continue: 'city of data' (p. 303); 'city of the cores' (p. 303); 'hapless suburbs of the city that was the mind of Tessier–Ashpool SA' (p. 304); 'the blue towers' and 'the ornate sunburst spires' (p. 309); and finally, echoing the earlier pattern of the silk scarf: 'But all of this receding, as the cityscape recedes: city as Chiba, as the ranked data of Tessier-Ashpool SA, as the roads and crossroads scribed on the face of a microchip, the sweat-stained pattern on a folded, knotted scarf ... (p. 310). Gibson's futurist vision of global information networks as urban space is close to Paul Virilio's. Virilio contends that advanced technologies disorientate the subject by effectively erasing traditional spatio-temporal categories, so that 'the greatest geo-physical expanse contracts ... everything is always already there, offered to view in the immediacy of an instantaneous transmission'. Physical properties are erased by *'speed time'*, and form instead *'an electronic shadow zone'*.[116] Oedipa's paranoid vision is realised. The city becomes a giant computer in which people are its electrons, and consequently, subjects are trapped and seduced into a belief in the pure and transparent consumption of energy.

Gibson's cityscapes owe much to the *noir* urban environments of American 'hardboiled' detective fiction, but also to other fictional urban representations; like the liminal space of the City of Interzone in William Burroughs's *The Naked Lunch*, where narcotics, gambling, social rejects, human detritus and ever-present threats of violence are the staple of existence in 'A place where the unknown past and the emergent future meet in vibrating soundless hum ...';[117] to the liminal city spaces in Pynchon's fiction, like Berlin in *Gravity's Rainbow*, which is a living inversion of itself, 'the city as outward and visible sign of inward and spiritual illness or health', and where 'everything's been turned inside out ... Inside is outside. ... All Berlin spends the daylight trying to make believe it isn't';[118] and to the cities of science fiction novels like Arthur C. Clarke's *City of Stars*, and Samuel R. Delaney's *Dhalgren*, in which a city called Bellona has suffered a disaster so cataclysmic that the very space–time continuum has been rent, producing an ominously oppressive city space of disintegrated individualism: 'Very few suspect the existence of this city. It is as if not only the media but the laws of perspective themselves have redesigned knowledge and perception to pass it by. Rumour says there is practically no power here. Neither television cameras nor on-the-spot broadcasts function: that such a catastrophe as this should be opaque, and therefore dull, to the electric nation! It is a city of inner discordances and retinal distortions'.[119]

Gibson's dystopian, dislocating urban environment, also explores the very way in which narratives spatialise history. Its treatment of the various marginalised spaces, like the 'borderland' of Night City, which acts as a loosely controlled experimental space for the technological corporations, can also be read as a metafictional account of the workings of narrative itself: 'There were countless theories explaining why Chiba City tolerated the Ninsei enclave, but Case ... saw a certain sense in the notion that burgeoning technologies require outlaw zones, that Night City wasn't there for its inhabitants, but as a deliberately unsupervised playground for technology itself'.[120] Ninsei acts as a space that defuses the threats posed by the illegal hustling of computer technology to the stranglehold of techno-corporate power. 'Power, in Case's world, meant corporate power. The zaibatsus, the multinationals that shaped the course of human history, had transcended old barriers' (p. 242). The liminal zone of Ninsei allows for criminal activity and niches of technological creativity, without threatening the delicate stability of the multinational powers. This, too, is likely to be the fate of the novel itself. What does have transformative energy is the interaction between people and place, especially through the sexualisation of space. In this hybrid zone where the economy is intimately charged with sexuality, people are 'all swarming the street in an intricate dance of desire and commerce' (p. 19). The dance is the place, and it would not be possible without the intricacies of desire.

As reality gradually falters before the advent of hyper-reality, so Gibson envisages a cityspace that is constantly fluctuating, continually under negotiation, always decentralised and structured by altering simulations. In a persuasive constellation of ideas from fractal geometry, the sci-fi novelist Samuel Delaney, the phenomenology of Merleau-Ponty and Brian McHale's analysis of science fiction and postmodernism, Bukatman observes how this persistent mutation of space and circulation of information, entails a collapse in the demarcations of public and private space, creating a new spatial experience for bodies. Like Castells's description of the 'informational city', we are witnessing 'the historical emergence of the space of flows, superseding the meaning of the space of places',[121] where the ease of information circulation facilitated by technological developments has precipitated a crisis in the anthropological experience and representational spaces of the city. One of Lefebvre's metaphors for the representation of urban space is drawn from hydromechanics, a model of flows which exemplifies urban space as a site of interpenetration and interference.[122] Caught in this conflicting wave of information, Bukatman argues that cyberspace is a 'paraspace', and through the mechanism of the computer, it becomes possible to have a mental space independent of a physical body. Frequently described as an infinity of light, 'bright lattices of light unfolding across the colorless void', the 'bodiless exultation of the cyberspace'[123] enables a complete physical transcendence. The analogy of narcotic hallucination for the experience of moving through cyberspace, reinforces this state of drug-like heightened consciousness. When at his most proficient agility within cyberspace using the Kuang Program Mark Eleven, Case experiences a moment of complete physical and spiritual harmony: 'Beyond ego, beyond personality, beyond awareness, he moved. Kuang moving with him, evading his attackers with an ancient dance, Hideo's dance, grace of the mind-body interface granted him, in that second by the clarity and singleness of his wish to die' (p. 309). Reminiscent of Quinn's ability to use walking in urban space as a means to achieve physical transcendence in *City of Glass*, Case's 'city of glass' inside the computer allows for complete spiritual harmony. Yet, although cyberspace appears to be a tangible, demarcated, produced space, paradoxically, its infinity has a certain absence: '... an infinite blue space ranged with color-coded spheres strung on a tight grid of pale blue neon. In the nonspace of the matrix, the interior of a given data construct possessed unlimited subjective dimension ... limitless gulfs of nothingness' (p. 81), or 'the infinite neuroelectronic void of the matrix' (p. 139). If, as Bukatman argues, *Neuromancer* symptomatically installs cyberspace as 'the characteristic space of a new era' which compensates for the loss of the public sphere by addressing 'the overwhelming need to reconstitute a phenomenal being' in a world of dislocation and estrangement,[124] then it does so at the expense of time and history. Gibson's representation of cyberspace suggests an escape from the temporal by its ecstatic revelation in a spatial experience that is free from the historical dimensions of material existence, as humanity achieves a utopian ontology of cybernetic being. Contrary to the long-standing arguments concerning historical self-consciousness as the royal road to freedom, cyberspace establishes spatial experience as the ultimate source of human liberation. Yet this temporal freedom and liberation is illusory: escaping from history is not that easy. For one thing, this mind–machine coupling appears to be a particularly masculine fantasy, and talk of its liberatory potential is frequently tempered by fears of the new technologies' militaristic and inhuman capabilities.[125] For another, cybernetic existences appear to be banally bound to time both as representation and through the 'real time' needed for the computer to work, especially when the machine does not have sufficient 'memory'.

Words about the city suggest a correlation between text and history, text with human negotiation with the city – a correlation that is constantly cancelled, effaced and over-inscribed in the volatile, changing space of the city. One inscription of the city is constantly substituted by another, which may supplement or cancel the first inscription. Just as streetnames, billboards, signs and posters are constantly overlayered, distorted and edited by graffiti and spray-can amendments, so whatever is marked in and by the city incites a negation, a cross-marking, a rewording. Hence, fiction, with its peculiarly suited labile and fluid narrative forms and strategies, is in a constant state of catch-and-play with its representations of the city, now shaping it, now losing it, now being deluded by it. There is a search for new ways and forms of narrative which will be appropriate to the new stories historians would like to tell. In the current debate about the extent to which history is about narratives or about events, about whether historians ought to tell stories or to analyse events, the fictional history of everyday life's negotiation with urban space might be instructive. Here is a form that gives a narrative structure without the exclusion of events. The point is not that only fiction can represent urban space, but that fictional representations of urban space open up all the questions of organisation and control on which spatial and temporal representations are made. The fascination of recent fiction with the urban spaces of the city and the implication that history ought to be supplemented by these fictional representations, suggests not only that history is incomplete without attention to spatiality, but also that historians' mastery of the city and its past is necessarily partial.

Each attempt to isolate and concentrate on the city, finds that the imagery of the city leaks time, tensions, absences, borders. In the permanent exasperation of the dilution of immediacy through its extension, the city's imagery instead invests representation with texture, intricacy, multiplicity, so that the great avenues of the city hold an immense flux of trajectories, a vivid generation of visual life. 'The truest city is the most private, and autobiography is the kind of writing which is least likely to muddy the city with the small untruths of seeming to know and deduce much more about its life than is really possible'.[126] The spatial is where the subject's relation to the totality is constituted. Hence, the increasing attention to and description of cities in the form of narratives of walking through the city.

Notes

1 Michel Foucault, *The Eye of Power*, in *Power/Knowledge: Selected Interviews and Other Writings, 1972–1977*, ed. and trans. Colin Gordon (Brighton: Harvester Press, 1980), p. 149.

2 Michel Foucault, *Discipline and Punish: The Birth of the Prison*, trans. Alan Sheridan (Harmondsworth: Penguin, [1975] 1991), p. 201.

3 Ibid., p. 216.

4 Ibid.

5 Michel Foucault, *The History of Sexuality: Vol. I. An Introduction*, trans. Robert Hurley (Harmondsworth: Penguin, [1976] 1981), p. 11.

6 Lois McNay, *Foucault: A Critical Introduction* (Cambridge: Polity Press, 1994), p. 95.

7 Foucault, *The History of Sexuality*, p. 148.

8 Henri Lefebvre, *The Production of Space*, trans. Donald Nicholson-Smith (1974; Oxford: Blackwell, 1991), p. 3.

9 Michel de Certeau, *The Practice of Everyday Life*, trans. Steven Rendall (Berkeley: University of California Press, 1985), p. xiv.

10 Ibid.

11 Lefebvre, *The Production of Space*, p. 175.

12 Ibid., p. 416.

13 See Torsten Hagerstrand *et al.*, 'What about people in regional science?', *Papers of the Regional Science Association*, 24 (1970), 7–21. See also Nigel Thrift's discussion of spacetime in 'Inhuman geographies: landscapes of speed, light and power', in *Spatial Formations* (London: Sage, 1996), pp. 256–310.

14 Don DeLillo, *Mao II* (London: Vintage, 1992), p. 27.

15 Angela Carter, *The Infernal Desire Machines of Doctor Hoffman* (London: Penguin, 1972) p. 17.

16 Joan Didion, *Play It As It Lays* (New York: Pocket Books, 1970), p. 76.

17 Scott Lash and John Urry, *Economies of Signs and Space* (London: Sage, 1994), pp. 221–2.

18 Thomas Pynchon, *The Crying of Lot 49* (London: Picador, [1966] 1979), p. 125.

19 Lash and Urry, *Economies of Signs and Space*, p. 222.

20 Jane Jacobs, cited in Anthony King, 'Introduction: cities, texts and paradigms', in Anthony King (ed.), *Re-Presenting the City* (Basingstoke: Macmillan, 1995), p. 3.

21 De Certeau, *The Practice of Everyday Life*, p. 108.

22 James Donald, 'Metropolis: the city as text', in R. Bocock and K. Thompson, (eds), *Social and Cultural Forms of Modernity* (Cambridge: Polity Press, 1992), pp. 417–61, 427.

23 See M. L. Ross, *Storied Cities: Literary Imaginings of Florence, Venice and Rome* (Westport, CT: Greenwood Press, 1994).

24 John Lechte, '(Not) Belonging in postmodern space', in Sophie Watson and Katherine Gibson (eds), *Postmodern Cities and Spaces* (Oxford: Blackwell, 1995), pp. 99–111.

25 Jay McInerney, *Brightness Falls* (London: Penguin, 1993), p. 8.

26 Kevin Lynch, *The Image of the City* (Cambridge, MA: MIT Press, 1960). See also

Peter F. Smith, *The Syntax of Cities* (London: Hutchinson, 1977).

27 Ludwig Wittgenstein, *Philosophical Investigations* (Oxford: Basil Blackwell, 1958), p. 18: 'Our language can be seen as an ancient city: a maze of little streets and squares, of old and new houses, and of houses with additions from various periods; and this surrounded by a multitude of new boroughs with straight regular streets and uniform houses.'

28 Rob Shields, 'A guide to urban representation and what to do about it: alternative traditions of urban theory', in King (ed.), *Re-Presenting the City*, p. 227.

29 Kristin Ross, *The Emergence of Social Space* (Basingstoke: Macmillan, 1988), p. 8.

30 Doreen Massey, 'The political place of locality studies', *Space, Place and Gender* (Oxford: Polity Press, 1994), p. 136.

31 Ibid., p. 137.

32 Ibid., p. 141.

33 Hana Wirth-Nesher, *City Codes: Reading the Modern Urban Novel* (Cambridge: Cambridge University Press, 1996), p. 3.

34 Sigmund Freud, *Civilization and Its Discontents* (New York and London: Norton, 1930), p. 17.

35 Jeanette Winterson, *The Passion* (London: Penguin, 1988), p. 113.

36 J. B. Harley, 'Deconstructing the map', *Cartographica*, 28, 2 (1989), 11.

37 Jeanette Winterson, *Sexing the Cherry* (London: Vintage, 1990), p. 81.

38 Harley, 'Deconstructing the map', p. 14.

39 Winterson, *The Passion*, p. 112.

40 Fredric Jameson, *Postmodernism, or, The Cultural Logic of Late Capitalism* (London: Verso, 1991), pp. 25–7.

41 Ibid., p. 365.

42 Michel Foucault, 'Of other spaces', *Diacritics* (Spring 1986), 22–7; and 'The eye of power'.

43 Lefebvre, *The Production of Space*, p. 39.

44 Mary Scott, 'Whose was the corkscrew?', in Marsha Rowe (ed.), *Sex and the City* (London: Serpent's Tail, 1989), p. 146.

45 Edward Soja, interview with Lefebvre, *Environment and Planning D: Society and Space*, 5, 1 (1987), 33.

46 Edward Soja, 'Regions in context', *Environment and Planning D: Society and Space*, 3, 2 (1985), 178. See also Edward Soja, in John Paul Jones, Wolfgang Natter and Theodor Schatzki (eds), *Postmodern Contentions: Epochs, Politics, Space* (New York: Guilford Press, 1993).

47 Soja, 'Regions in context', p. 177.

48 Saul Bellow, *Humboldt's Gift* (New York: Viking Press, 1975), pp. 114–15.

49 Soja, 'Regions in context', pp. 177–8.

50 Lefebvre, *The Production of Space*, p. 184.

51 Ibid., pp. 200–1.

52 Patrick Süskind, *Perfume*, trans. James Woods (Harmondsworth: Penguin, 1986), p. 27.

53 Lefebvre, *The Production of Space*, p. 391.

54 Ibid., p. 385.

55 Ibid., p. 387.

56 Bernard Tschumi, 'Questions of space', in *Architecture and Disjunction* (Cambridge, MA: MIT Press, 1998), p. 61.

57 Bernard Tschumi 'The pleasure of architecture', *Architecture and Disjunction*, p. 84.

58 Bernard Tschumi, 'Bodies violating spaces', *Architecture and Disjunction*, p. 123.

59 Ibid., p. 125.

60 Ibid., p. 5.

61 Jacques Derrida, 'Point de folie-maintenant architecture', *AA Files* 12 (Summer, 1986), pp. 65–75.

62 Peter Eisenman, in *Reconstruction and Deconstruction*, ed. A. C. Papadakis (London: Academy Editions, 1988), p. 13.

63 See Jane M. Jacobs, *The Edge of Empire: Postcolonialism and the City* (London: Routledge, 1996) and Homi Bhabha, *The Location of Culture* (London: Routledge, 1994), who both discuss the liminality and hybridity of urban space in the context of post-colonialism, with its structural and systemic absences and presences.

64 Paul Auster, *Moon Palace* (London: Faber, 1989), pp. 57–8.

65 McInerney, *Brightness Falls*, p. 389.

66 Robert Parker, *A Savage Place* (New York: Dell, 1981), p. 143.

67 Alison Lurie, *The Nowhere City* (Harmondsworth and New York: Penguin, [1965] 1977), p. 309.

68 Josh Cohen, *Spectacular Allegories: Postmodern American Writing and the Politics of Seeing* (London: Pluto Press, 1998), pp.115–16.

69 Mike Davis, *City of Quartz: Excavating the Future in Los Angeles* (New York: Vintage, 1992).

70 Dolores Hayden, 'Capitalism, socialism, and the built environment', in Stephen Rosskamm Shalom (ed.), *Socialist Visions* (Boston: South End Press, 1983), pp. 59–81, 59, cited in Laura Rice, 'Trafficking in philosophy: lines of force in the city-text', in Mary Ann Caws (ed.), *City Images: Perspectives from Literature, Philosophy, and Film* (New York: Gordon & Breach, 1991), pp. 221–39; 236–7.

71 Rice, 'Trafficking in philosophy', p. 237.

72 Reyner Banham, *Los Angeles: The Architecture of Four Ecologies* (London: Pelican, 1973), p. 36.

73 Didion, *Play It As It Lays*, pp. 13–14.

74 Bret Easton Ellis, *Less Than Zero* (London: Picador, 1985), p. 61.

75 Sharon Zukin, *Landscapes of Power: From Detroit to Disney World* (Berkeley: University of California Press, 1991), p. 219.

76 Jonathan Raban, *Soft City* (London: HarperCollins, 1974), p. 10.

77 Pynchon, *The Crying of Lot 49*, p. 123.

78 Ellis, *Less Than Zero*, pp. 207–8.

79 Pynchon, *The Crying of Lot 49*, p. 126.

80 Ibid., p. 80.

81 Ibid., p. 89.

82 Manuell Castells, *The Informational City* (Oxford: Basil Blackwell: 1989), p. 349.

83 Pynchon, *The Crying of Lot 49*, pp. 122–3.

84 Ibid., p. 34.

85 De Certeau, *The Practice of Everyday Life*, pp. xiv–xv.

86 Ibid., pp. 25–6.

87 Pynchon, *The Crying of Lot 49*, p. 35.

88 Ibid., p. 86.

89 De Certeau, *The Practice of Everyday Life*, p. 34.

90 Ibid., pp. 35–6.

91 Ibid., pp. 36–7.

92 Ibid., pp. 38–9.

93 For further discussion of Paul Auster's fictional treatment of urban space, see Tim Woods, '"Looking for signs in the air": urban space and the postmodern in *In The Country of Last Things*', in Dennis Barone (ed.), *Beyond the Red Notebook:*

Essays on Paul Auster (Philadelphia: University of Pennsylvania Press, 1995), pp. 107–28.

94 David Harvey, *The Condition of Postmodernity* (Oxford: Blackwell, 1989), p. 214.

95 De Certeau, *The Practice of Everyday Life*, p. 124.

96 Paul Auster, *The New York Trilogy* (London: Faber, 1987), p. 24.

97 Paul Auster, *The Invention of Solitude* (London: Faber, 1988), p. 122.

98 Paul Auster, *Ground Work: Selected Poems and Essays, 1970–1979* (London: Faber, 1990), p. 82.

99 Ivan Chtcheglov, 'Formulary for a new urbanism' (October, 1953), in I. Blazwick (ed.), *An endless adventure ... an endless passion ... an endless banquet: A Situationist Scrapbook* (London: ICA and Verso, 1989), pp. 24–5.

100 Ibid., p. 25.

101 Auster, *The New York Trilogy*, pp. 3–4.

102 Chtcheglov, 'Formulary for a new urbanism', p. 24.

103 Ibid.

104 Blazwick, *An Endless Adventure*, p. 22.

105 Guy Debord, 'Two accounts of the dérive', in Elizabeth Sussman (ed.), *On the Passage of a few people through a rather brief moment in time: The Situationist International, 1957–1972* (Cambridge, MA and London: MIT Press, 1989), pp. 135–9.

106 Guy Debord, 'Unitary urbanism at the end of the 1950s', *The Situationist International*, pp., 143–7.

107 Ibid., p. 144.

108 Auster, *The New York Trilogy*, p. 251.

109 De Certeau, *The Practice of Everyday Life*, p. 93.

110 Auster, *The New York Trilogy*, p. 71.

111 Peter Brooker, *New York Fictions: Modernity, Postmodernism, The New Modern* (London: Longman, 1996), p. 136.

112 However, as Philip Hayward and Rebecca Coyle point out, treating Gibson as the 'father' of cyberspace ignores the fact that there were many earlier and contemporaneous scientific developments unknown to Gibson at the time of writing his novel, especially the work of computer scientist Ivan Sutherland based at the Massachusetts Institute of Technology, who was a key contributor to cyberspace systems development. See Rebecca Coyle, 'The genesis of virtual reality', pp. 148–65, and Philip Hayward, 'Situating cyberspace: the popularisation of virtual reality', pp. 180–204, in Philip Hayward and Tana Wollen, (eds), *Future Visions: New Technologies of the Screen* (London: The British Film Institute, 1993).

113 William Gibson, *Neuromancer* (London: Grafton, 1986), p. 12.

114 Scott Bukatman, *Terminal Identity: The Virtual Subject in Postmodern Science Fiction* (Durham, NC: Duke University Press, 1993), p. 150.

115 Gibson, *Neuromancer*, p. 57.

116 Paul Virilio, 'The over-exposed city', *in Rethinking Architecture: A Reader in Cultural Theory*, ed. N. Leach (New York and London: Routledge, 1997), p. 385.

117 William Burroughs, *The Naked Lunch* (London: Paladin, [1959] 1986), p. 93.

118 Thomas Pynchon, *Gravity's Rainbow* (London: Picador, 1975), pp. 372–3.

119 Samuel R. Delaney, *Dhalgren* (London: Grafton, [1975] 1992), pp. 15–16.

120 Gibson, *Neuromancer*, p. 19.

121 Bukatman, *Terminal Identity*, p. 348.

122 Lefebvre, *The Production of Space*, p. 87.

123 Gibson, *Neuromancer*, pp. 11–12.

124 Bukatman, *Terminal Identity*, p. 156.

125 See Donna Haraway, 'A manifesto for cyborgs: science, technology and socialist feminism in the 1980s', *Socialist Review*, 80 (1985), and Sally Pryor and Jill Scott, 'Virtual reality: beyond Cartesian space', in Philip Hayward and Tana Wollen (eds), *Future Visions: New Technologies of the Screen*, pp. 160–79.
126 Raban, *Soft City*, p. 242.

Index